This book makes a comprehensive reassessment of the relationship between Enlightenment and religion in England. Recently, the debate about an 'English' Enlightenment has centred on the role of religion, especially the relationship between the established Anglican Church and the Dissenting confessions. It has long been accepted that liberal Rational Dissenters developed an Enlightenment agenda, but most literature on this topic is quite out of date. These interdisciplinary essays provide a fresh analysis of Rational Dissent within English Enlightenment culture. Equally, they contribute to the current debate over eighteenth-century religion and its social, political and intellectual meaning, focusing on the Irish and Scottish contributions to English Dissent. Its wide perspective and new research make *Enlightenment and Religion* an important and original contribution to eighteenth-century studies.

IDEAS IN CONTEXT

ENLIGHTENMENT AND RELIGION

IDEAS IN CONTEXT

Edited by QUENTIN SKINNER (*General Editor*)
LORRAINE DASTON, WOLF LEPENIES and J.B. SCHNEEWIND

The books in this series will discuss the emergence of intellectual traditions and of related new disciplines. The procedures, aims and vocabularies that were generated will be set in the context of the alternatives available within the contemporary frameworks of ideas and institutions. Through detailed studies of the evolution of such traditions, and their modification by different audiences, it is hoped that a new picture will form of the development of ideas in their concrete contexts. By this means, artificial distinctions between the history of philosophy, of the various sciences, of society and politics, and of literature may be seen to dissolve.

The series is published with the support of the Exxon Foundation.

A list of books in the series will be found at the end of the volume.

ENLIGHTENMENT AND RELIGION

Rational Dissent in eighteenth-century Britain

EDITED BY

KNUD HAAKONSSEN

Professor of Philosophy, Boston University

CAMBRIDGE
UNIVERSITY PRESS

CAMBRIDGE UNIVERSITY PRESS
Cambridge, New York, Melbourne, Madrid, Cape Town, Singapore, São Paulo

Cambridge University Press
The Edinburgh Building, Cambridge CB2 2RU, UK

Published in the United States of America by Cambridge University Press, New York

www.cambridge.org
Information on this title: www.cambridge.org/9780521560603

First published 1996
This digitally printed first paperback version 2006

A catalogue record for this publication is available from the British Library

Library of Congress Cataloguing in Publication data

Enlightenment and religion: rational dissent in eighteenth-century
Britain/edited by Knud Haakonssen.
p.   cm. – (Ideas in context : 41)
Includes index.
ISBN 0 521 56060 8 (hardcover)
1. Dissenters, Religious – Great Britain – History – 18th century.
2. Rationalists – Great Britain – History – 18th century.
3. Enlightenment – Great Britain.   4. Great Britain – Intellectual
life – 18th century.   5. Great Britain – Church history – 18th century.
I. Haakonssen, Knud, 1947–   . II. Series.
BX5203.2.E55   1996
941.07 – dc20   95-31226 CIP

ISBN-13 978-0-521-56060-3 hardback
ISBN-10 0-521-56060-8 hardback

ISBN-13 978-0-521-02987-2 paperback
ISBN-10 0-521-02987-2 paperback

Contents

Contributors

MARTIN FITZPATRICK is a Senior Lecturer in History at the University of Wales, Aberystwyth. He is editor and co-founder of *Enlightenment and Dissent* and is the author of numerous articles relating to the world of Rational Dissent. He has edited the early political writings of William Godwin, the first of seven volumes of *Political and Philosophical Writings of William Godwin*. He is currently working on a short study of the Enlightenment.

JOHN GASCOIGNE is a Senior Lecturer in the School of History at the University of New South Wales. He is the author of *Cambridge in the Age of the Enlightenment: Science, Religion, and Politics from the Restoration to the French Revolution* (Cambridge University Press, 1989) and of *Joseph Banks and the English Enlightenment. Useful Knowledge and Polite Culture* (Cambridge University Press, 1994). He is at present completing *Science in the Service of Empire. Joseph Banks, the British State and the Uses of Science in the Age of Revolution.*

KNUD HAAKONSSEN is Professor of Philosophy at Boston University. His books include *The Science of a Legislator: The Natural Jurisprudence of David Hume and Adam Smith* (Cambridge University Press, 1981), *Natural Law and Moral Philosophy: From Grotius to the Scottish Enlightenment* (Cambridge University Press, 1995) and, as editor, *Traditions of Liberalism* (CIS, 1988), Thomas Reid, *Practical Ethics* (Princeton University Press, 1990), (with M. Lacey) *A Culture of Rights* (Cambridge University Press, 1991), David Hume, *Political Essays* (Cambridge University Press, 1994). He is currently editing the *Cambridge History of Eighteenth-Century Philosophy.*

IAIN McCALMAN is Professor and Director of the Humanities Research Centre, Australian National University. His books include *Radical Underworld: Prophets, Revolutionaries and Pornographers in London,*

1795–1838 (Cambridge University Press, 1988) and, as editor, *Horrors of Slavery. The Life and Writings of Robert Wedderburn* (Edinburgh University Press, 1991). He is currently editing *The Age of Romanticism and Revolution: An Oxford Companion to British Culture, 1776–1832*.

WILFRID PREST is Professor of History in the University of Adelaide. His books include *The Inns of Court under Elizabeth I and the Early Stuarts 1590–1640* (Longman, 1972), *The Rise of the Barristers: A Social History of the English Bar 1590–1640* (Clarendon Press, 1986; rev. edn., 1991) and, as editor, *Lawyers in Early Modern Europe and America* (Croom Helm, 1981), *The Professions in Early Modern England* (Croom Helm, 1987), and *The Diary of Sir Richard Hutton 1614–1639 and Related Documents* (Selden Society, 1991). He is now completing *Albion Ascendant: England 1660–1815* (Short Oxford History of the Modern World).

ALAN SAUNDERS is a Producer in the Science Unit of the Australian Broadcasting Corporation's Radio National. He has been a Frances A. Yates Research Fellow at the Warburg Institute, University of London, and he wrote a doctoral dissertation on Joseph Priestley in the Institute of Advanced Studies at the Australian National University. He is the author of *A is for Apple* (Reed Books Australia, 1995), a collection of essays about food, and he is currently working on a history of British food culture in the eighteenth century.

JOHN SEED teaches history at Roehampton Institute in London, and from 1982–95 he was Review Editor of *Social History*. He has published essays and articles on eighteenth- and nineteenth-century British history including *The Culture of Capital* (ed. with Janet Wolff, Manchester University Press, 1988), and on twentieth-century politics, including *Cultural Revolution* (ed. with Bart Moore-Gilbert, Routledge, 1992), and on twentieth-century poetry, including studies of Basil Bunting and George Oppen.

M.A. STEWART is Professor of the History of Philosophy at Lancaster University. He is General Editor of the Clarendon Edition of the Works of John Locke. He has edited *Selected Philosophical Papers of Robert Boyle* (Manchester University Press, 1979), *Law, Morality and Rights* (Kluwer, 1983), *Studies in the Philosophy of the Scottish Enlightenment* (Clarendon Press, 1990), and co-edited *Hume and Hume's Connexions* (Edinburgh University Press, 1994). In 1994 he delivered the Robert Allen Memorial Lecture to the Presbyterian Historical Society of

Ireland, and in 1995 the Gifford Lectures on ' "New Light" and Enlightenment' at the University of Aberdeen.

ALAN TAPPER is Lecturer and Head of the Department of Philosophy at Edith Cowan University in Perth, Western Australia. He is the author of *The Family in the Welfare State* (Allen and Unwin, Sydney, 1990).

A.M.C. WATERMAN is a Fellow of St John's College, Winnipeg, and Professor of Economics and Director of the Institute for the Humanities in the University of Manitoba. He studies the relation between political economy and Christian theology in the construction of normative social theory. His *Revolution, Economics and Religion 1798–1833* (Cambridge University Press, 1991) was awarded the Forkosch Prize for intellectual history in 1992. He recently co-edited (with H.G. Brennan) *Economics and Religion. Are They Distinct?* (Kluwer, 1994).

R.K. WEBB is Professor of History, emeritus, at the University of Maryland, Baltimore County. His books include *The British Working-Class Reader, 1790–1848* (Allen and Unwin, 1955); *Harriet Martineau, a Radical Victorian* (Heinemann, 1960); and *Modern England: From the Eighteenth Century to the Present* (Harper Collins, 1980). He is completing three studies of English Unitarianism – of the ministry, of the Necessarian tradition, and a general history of the denomination.

DAVID WYKES is Research Lecturer in History at the University of Leicester. He has published on late seventeenth- and early eighteenth-century dissent, and late eighteenth- and early nineteenth-century Unitarianism, particularly dissenting academies. He is currently working on a new edition of the 1669 Conventicle Returns for the Church of England Record Society.

Acknowledgements

On behalf of all the contributors to this volume I warmly thank Elizabeth Y. Short for her superb copy-editing and Norma Chin for her expert computer work.

Knud Haakonssen
Canberra, December 1994

CHAPTER I

Enlightened Dissent: an introduction

Knud Haakonssen

A quarter of a century ago Peter Gay presented the Enlightenment as 'the rise of modern paganism'.[1] Gay's magisterial study was in many respects the apogee of a tradition in scholarship according to which the Enlightenment was anti-Christian, anti-Church and at the point of sliding into irreligion and proto-atheism. On this interpretation, the Enlightenment was further seen as socially and institutionally reformist in a way that begged to be made political and, eventually, revolutionary. Enlightenment was a time-bomb set for 1789, and it was set in France.

In recent years scholars have called into question most aspects of this way of understanding the Enlightenment. For one thing the Enlightenment has proliferated both nationally and socially. Instead of seeing it as an aspect of French cultural imperialism, we have come to consider the Enlightenment in national contexts from Aberdeen to Athens, from St Petersburg to Philadelphia.[2] At the same time, we have been urged to see it as not only a movement in the history of ideas, instigated by an intellectual élite, but also as a social process involving wide groups of local and national communities. Study of the Enlightenment has thus been intimately connected with methodological debates about the relationship between the history of ideas and intellectual history – the former conceived as analysis of the intellectual content of ideas formulated in the past, the latter considered as the social or contextual study of the intellects who proposed ideas in the past.[3] Methodology has again been

---

[1] Peter Gay, The Enlightenment: An Interpretation, 2 vols. (London, 1967), vol. 1: The Rise of Modern Paganism.

[2] See for example Roy Porter and Mikulas Teich, eds., The Enlightenment in National Context (Cambridge, 1981); Siegfried Jüttner and Jochen Schlobach, eds., Europäische Aufklärung(en). Einheit und nationale Vielheit, Studien zum 18. Jahrhundert, 14 (Hamburg, 1992).

[3] For programmatic statements of the idea of a social, as opposed to philosophical, history of the Enlightenment, see Robert Darnton, 'In Search of the Enlightenment', Journal of Modern History, 43 (1971), 113–32. Concerning the distinction between history of ideas and intellectual history, see the Introduction to K. Haakonssen, Natural Law and Moral Philosophy: From Grotius to the Scottish Enlightenment (Cambridge, 1995).

intertwined with pathology, namely the deconstruction of modernity viewed as 'the Enlightenment project'.[4]

The many Enlightenments that have resulted from these endeavours are beyond easy summary, and this is in any case not the place to attempt it. The important point in the present context is that the question of an English Enlightenment has been opened up for interesting discussion. Not least in this discussion is a scrutiny of the political colour and religious temperature of the Enlightenment. The present volume is a contribution to this scrutiny.

A fruitful point of departure is J.G.A. Pocock's complex notion of a conservative Enlightenment in England.[5] The central suggestion in this interpretation is that the Enlightenment was first and foremost a movement to preserve civilised society against any resurgence of religious enthusiasm and superstition, that is to say, of evangelical Protestantism and Counter-Reformation Catholicism. Europe had only just escaped the barbarism of religious wars, especially civil wars, and the task of enlightened minds was to preserve modern society from the confessional backwoodsmen of all creeds. The weapons in this struggle were 'sceptical' philosophy, sound theology, polite letters, science, and economic betterment: modern philosophy's systematic exploration of the deficiencies of the human mind inevitably suggested limits to its ability to re-fashion authority and social order; politico-religious contention was made safe for society by being subjected to the requirements of polite literature; science was dissociated from subversive spiritualism by being required to account only for the causal coherence of the providential order; and the means of securing the safety of modern society were, domestically, the discipline of the division of labour and, externally, trade. Conservation and modernisation were thus one and the same thing, namely the Enlightenment.

Enlightenment thus understood was evidently approximated in many parts of Europe; indeed I would suggest that it constituted the

---

[4] See for example Robert Wokler's discussion, 'Projecting the Enlightenment', in John Horton and Susan Mendus, eds., *After MacIntyre: Critical Perspectives on the Work of Alasdair MacIntyre* (Cambridge, 1994), pp. 108–26.

[5] Here I draw particularly upon the following works by J.G.A. Pocock, 'Post-Puritan England and the Problem of the Enlightenment', in Perez Zagorin, ed., *Culture and Politics. From Puritanism to the Enlightenment* (Berkeley, CA, 1980), pp. 91–111; 'Clergy and Commerce. The Conservative Enlightenment in England', in R. Ajello, ed., *L'Età dei Lumi: Studi storici sul settecento europeo in onore de Franco Venturi* (Naples, 1985), pp. 524–62; *Virtue, Commerce, and History: Essays on Political Thought and History, Chiefly in the Eighteenth Century* (Cambridge, 1985); 'Conservative Enlightenment and Democratic Revolutions: The American and French Cases in British Perspective', *Government and Opposition*, 24 (1989), 81–105; 'History and Sovereignty: The Historiographical Response to Europeanization in Two British Cultures', *Journal of British Studies*, 31 (1992), 358–89.

mainstream of the Enlightenment. The point pressed by Pocock, however, is that the conservative modernity he portrays was so peculiarly forceful in England as to set her apart from the rest of Europe. He even questions whether one can speak of an English Enlightenment in the same sense as that of the French, Germans or Scots. The reason seems to be the English – eventually British – constitution. The outcome of the English religious wars, and especially of the Glorious Revolution, was the sovereignty of the King-in-Parliament and the Anglican Church-state. The former turned ruling into a political process in which public opinion was so significant that it drew in educated minds as opinion-makers and -seekers and diverted them from becoming a secluded and potentially oppositional élite of philosophes. At the same time enlightened conservatism was obviously attractive to a large section of the Church, whose establishment as part of the English state was premised on the need for a bulwark against any resurgence of enthusiasm. There was thus a significant unity of purpose between Church and Enlightenment – Pocock even talks of the Enlightenment as 'clerical' – and the former learnt amazingly quickly to tolerate the 'sceptical' excesses of the latter. In short, the peculiarity of England was that the strong modernising drive that we identify with the Enlightenment was integral to the preservation of the establishment in state and Church.

Although Pocock has not had occasion to spell this out at any length, he seems to imply that in most parts of the European continent, and especially in France, the constitution of state and Church prevented such ready absorption of Enlightenment ideas. The ambiguity of the relationship between *ancien régime* and Enlightenment made the latter itself ambivalent, and its – often exaggerated – potential as an oppositional force was only brought out by a political culture unable to utilise schemes of reform to secure existing social and political institutions. It was this situation in France that allowed radical and eventually revolutionary ideas to take over – or overtake – Enlightenment on the Continent. In England, by contrast, the French Revolution soon came to be seen by many as a revolt *against* Enlightenment values and, in Burke's analysis, as a relapse into the barbarism of religious enthusiasm.[6]

---

[6] For Pocock's understanding of Burke, see 'The Political Economy of Burke's Analysis of the French Revolution', in his *Virtue, Commerce, and History*, pp. 193–212; 'Introduction', in Edmund Burke, *Reflections on the Revolution in France*, ed. J.G.A. Pocock (Indianapolis, IN, 1987), pp. vii–lvi; and 'Edmund Burke and the Redefinition of Enthusiasm: The Context as Counter-revolution', in *The French Revolution and the Creation of Modern Political Culture*, vol. III: *The Transformation of Political Culture 1789–1848*, eds. François Furet and Mona Ozouf (Oxford, 1989), pp. 19–43.

Although England was dominated by a conservative clerical Enlightenment, this was not the only form of Enlightenment in Britain. Scotland found herself complexly situated between continental and English traditions, and her attempts to respond in enlightened ways have attracted great scholarly efforts in recent years.[7] Similarly in England itself some of those who were excluded from full membership of the Anglican Church-state because of their dissent from its central articles of faith were clearly modern men of the Enlightenment. The question is whether their Enlightenment had more in common with the conservative one from whose clerical establishment they dissented or with the radical one that eventually emerged on the Continent. This question is the subject of the following studies.

It is tempting to see enlightened Dissent as a Trojan horse full of continental-style *philosophes* ready to burst upon the English *ancien régime*. As Pocock says,

> There was an Enlightenment of and by the increasingly rationalist sects, as well as an Enlightenment directed against the enthusiasm of the sects . . . If we were to present the Anglo-American crisis of the 1770s in Franco Venturi's terminology, as part of the *crisi e caduta dell'antico regime*, we should have to do so by saying that the Dissenting Enlightenment rose against the conservative Enlightenment, and particularly against the latter's aristocratic and clerical components (which did not cease to be enlightened in their own way).[8]

This rising became complete with the reaction to the French Revolution of Price, Priestley, Paine and Godwin, who all came from Dissenting backgrounds.[9]

The problem with this picture, as Pocock of course is well aware, is that it is too neat to capture the complexity of enlightened Dissent as a whole. The purpose of this volume is to present and analyse this complexity, which begins with the very label for the subject studied. Properly speaking 'Rational Dissent' meant the rejection of Calvinism and the denial of the necessity of spiritual regeneration.[10] Indeed, the label was – and is – often taken to be more or less synonymous with

---

[7] See the Bibliography in Richard B. Sher, *Church and University in the Scottish Enlightenment: The Moderate Literati of Edinburgh*, (Princeton, NJ, 1985), pp. 329–76; and the Introduction to Haakonssen, *Natural Law and Moral Philosophy* (fn. 3).

[8] Pocock, 'Conservative Enlightenment', pp. 97–8. Pocock's reference is Franco Venturi, *Settecento Riformatore*, IV (1): *La Caduta dell' Antico Regime; i grandi stati dell'Occidente* (Turin, 1984).

[9] See Gregory Claeys, *Thomas Paine. Social and Political Thought* (Boston, 1989); Mark Philp, *Godwin's Political Justice* (Ithaca, NY, 1986).

[10] See Alan Saunders, Chapter 10 of this volume.

intellectual Unitarianism. The problem with these definitions is that they exclude a large number of English Dissenters who found it eminently possible to adopt an Enlightenment agenda very similar to that of the mainstream clerical modernism of the establishment without committing themselves to quite so stark a choice between inspiration and reason as their guide to the Word. After editing the following essays, I prefer to use 'Enlightened Dissent' for this wider and much less well-defined group, but I have to agree that 'Rational Dissent' is commonly accepted in this sense too.

The opening essay by Robert Webb (Chapter 2) explains some of the necessary conditions for the emergence of such a phenomenon as Enlightened Dissent. Most important, perhaps, was a broadly based rational religion characterised by a determination to combine reason and faith and by a will to tolerate different ways of doing so. It was a spirit generous enough to appeal not only to a wide latitudinarian spectrum of the Established Church and, by the middle of the eighteenth century, to most Presbyterians, but also to many Congregationalists and Baptists, as Webb points out, even much later in the heyday of evangelicalism. Rational religion was, in other words, a *modus vivendi* in the broad field between High-Church Anglicanism, orthodox or evangelical Dissent and deism.[11]

The important point is that this common religious denominator was only made possible by the divisions it tried to straddle. Deep disputes in Christology and ecclesiology had divided English Protestantism over the question whether it was, or could be, an ecclesiastic polity. Yet England manifestly was a Christian Protestant polity and there was a need across a wide spectrum of denominations for some theological justification of this historical *fait accompli*. In accounting for the need, Webb's essay becomes an historical overview of the emergence of Enlightened Dissent.

In purely theoretical terms, views of state and Church may be divided into four broad categories: those that see both as divinely instituted (often as one body); those according to which both are conventional, 'man-made' arrangements; and those for which either state or Church is of divine, and the other is of human, making. In the first category, we find the basis for the dominant form of ecclesiastical politics in Britain. This was the notion which high, and not so high, Anglicans shared with

---

[11] See also Isabel Rivers, *Reason, Grace and Sentiment: A Study of the Language of Religion and Ethics in England, 1660–1780*, vol. 1: *Whichcote to Wesley* (Cambridge, 1991). For a wider intellectual context, see Peter Harrison, *'Religion' and the Religions in the English Enlightenment* (Cambridge, 1991).

Roman Catholicism, that Church and state are two aspects of the same historical body. On this view humanity, considered as a Church, is heir to the disciples' faith in Christ, hope for themselves and charity to each other. Considered as a state, humanity is organised to do duty to God's temporal vicegerents on earth and to themselves and each other in their respective stations in life. This standpoint is analysed in Anthony Waterman's essay (Chapter 8) and shown to be the central target for Rational Dissent.

Diametrically opposed is the idea that both state and Church are purely conventional bodies created through compacts of individuals for mutual convenience. On such a view, the state is a civil institution for the protection of all private organisations, and Churches are among the latter. This idea had its origins in the fundamental evangelical rejection of intermediaries, especially 'authoritative' intermediaries, between God's word and individual consciences. The primacy and privacy of conscience was the core of such religion, which was not, of course, exclusive to Dissent. It always had Low-Church representatives in the established Church. But one of the most important developments in this view took place, in the main, within Dissent. This was a gradual change from concern to protect the intimacy of the individual with his Maker, to concern for the privacy of conscience, whatever the latter was conscientious about. This was at the heart of the transformation from Old, orthodox Dissent to Enlightened and Rational Dissent, and it is a recurring theme in the following essays, reaching a concentrated discussion in Alan Saunders's analysis of the epitome of this development, Priestley's reception of the key Dissenting idea of candour (see Chapter 10).

A third and very wide category of Protestants would see the Church as, in some sense, of divine origin and the state as a conventional human institution. At least in its general form, this view facilitated a *rapprochement* between many elements of Enlightened Dissent and Whig latitudinarian Anglicanism. Of fundamental importance here was Bishop Hoadly's writing and preaching early in the century – sketched by M.A. Stewart as part of his complex story (Chapter 3) – while the full cultural, political and social impact of this alliance was felt only after mid-century, as explained at length by John Seed (Chapter 6) and John Gascoigne (Chapter 9).

The logical fourth possibility – the Church as a convention and political society as a divine institution – is at first sight implausible, yet in a sense it is most important to the following studies in complexity. For there was a significant strand in eighteenth-century British thought according to which sociability was the essence of the divine dispensation for human nature, while the mere *forms* of worshipping this dispensation simply swelled the ranks of *adiaphora*, things theologically indifferent. This is, in broad terms, the standpoint adopted by the mainstream of the Scottish Enlightenment, as initiated by Francis Hutcheson and George Turnbull.[12] According to these thinkers, man's natural sociability, or benevolence, demanded for its proper flourishing that the individual fulfil a set of duties and protect a number of rights. The means to this were contractual arrangements of civil and political society, but the goal was the realisation of the natural moral community to which humanity was providentially disposed. Depending on the emphasis required in particular situations, this line of thought could thus appear individualistic-contractarian in its conception of social life or as a holistic and teleological naturalism. Furthermore, the sociability ascribed to humanity could be stressed variously as a natural disposition or tendency and as a power of judgement about our action (in God's image) to promote the happiness of moral creation. Indeed, the latter could, with infinite nuances, shade into an ideal of rational piety that became one of the long-lasting legacies of Enlightened Dissent, as shown in Robert Webb's second essay (Chapter 12).

This flexible Scottish 'moderatism' was of utmost importance to the development of Enlightened Dissent in England, as we see from the close personal and institutional links studied in the essays by Stewart (Chapter 3), Martin Fitzpatrick (Chapter 4) and David Wykes (Chapter 5).[13] Yet relations were exceedingly complex. For one thing, the philosophical core of Hutcheson's and Turnbull's ideas was to a large extent formulated in the context of one of the early encounters between Church and Dissent after 1689. In Ireland, high Anglicanism, evangelical Dissent and Scots Calvinism met head-on in the 1690s yet, by the 1720s, the Irish stage had seen notable formulations of latitudinarianism and Enlightened Dissent, as well as Hutcheson's most important work. For both historical and doctrinal reasons, therefore, it is of great importance to include this Irish seed-time in our study of Enlightened Dissent, as Stewart's essay shows.

The complexity and ambiguity of the connection between Dissenters and Scots are compounded by the fact that so many on both sides felt

---

[12] See Haakonssen, *Natural Law and Moral Philosophy* (fn. 3) ch. 2.
[13] See also Peter Jones, 'The Polite Academy and the Presbyterians, 1720–1770', in John Dwyer, Roger A. Mason and Alexander Murdoch, eds., *New Perspectives on the Politics and Culture of Early Modern Scotland* (Edinburgh, 1982), pp. 156–78.

able to make some form of compromise between evangelical enthusiasm and Hutchesonian benevolism.[14] Consequently, it remained uncertain to what extent they would see society as a contractual association of individual spirits or as a moral collective for the exercise of virtue. The tendency of Dissenters to opt for the former and to seek political freedom to participate in governance, and of Scots Moderates to trust moral education to civic virtue in the service of the common good, often needed the forceful intrusion of momentous political events to be sharply crystallised. The American and French Revolutions were, of course, the events to do this, and we see these issues laid out in Fitzpatrick's analysis of the correspondence of the Dissenting banker Samuel Kenrick and the Scots minister James Wodrow (see Chapter 4).

The complexity went much further. Richard Price presented Rational Dissent's most forceful case for a vigorous participatory politics, as Fitzpatrick also reminds us. But Price did so on the basis of an – ultimately Neoplatonic – idea of the human mind as inherently active and sociable, and both the philosophy and the associated politics had more than a little in common with the foremost of Scottish Common-Sense thinkers, Thomas Reid.[15] The most notable other leader of Rational Dissent, Joseph Priestley, adopted a materialist and associationist philosophy and used it as the premise for a forceful individualistic ideal of political liberty, which Alan Tapper presents in Chapter 11. At the centre of Priestley's political thought was the sharpest articulation of the apolitical side of Dissenting ideals, namely that both moral and material economy could best be pursued with only minimal interference by government.[16]

Irrespective of philosophical differences, Dissenters in practice pursued the participatory ideal through practical political and social involvement for its realisation.[17] This was, in many ways, forced upon

---

[14] See Ned C. Landsman, 'Presbyterians and Provincial Society: The Evangelical Enlightenment in the West of Scotland, 1740–1775', in John Dwyer and Richard B. Sher, eds., *Sociability and Society in Eighteenth-Century Scotland* (Edinburgh, 1993), pp. 194–209.

[15] See Henri Laboucheix, *Richard Price as Moral Philosopher and Political Theorist*, trans. S. and D. Raphael (Oxford, 1982), pp. 73–4. For Price, see *Political Writings*, ed. D.O. Thomas (Cambridge, 1991). For Reid's politics, see 'Some thoughts on the utopian system', in his *Practical Ethics. Being Lectures and Manuscripts on Natural Religion, Self-Government, Natural Jurisprudence, and the Law of Nations*, ed. K. Haakonssen (Princeton, NJ, 1990), pp. 277–99.

[16] Priestley's central political ideas are now accessible in *Political Writings*, ed. Peter N. Miller (Cambridge, 1993). Important discussions of the relationship between Priestley's theology and politics include Mark Philp, 'Rational Religion and Political Radicalism', *Enlightenment and Dissent*, 4 (1985), 35–46, and Martin Fitzpatrick, 'Heretical religion and Radical Political Ideas in Late Eighteenth-Century England', in Eckhart Hellmuth, ed., *The Transformation of Political Culture: England and Germany in the Late Eighteenth Century* (Oxford, 1990), pp. 339–74.

[17] Cf. the work of James Bradley mentioned below.

them by the circumstances in which they had been placed by the law in the wake of the settlement in 1689. This legal framework for Dissent and the response to it by Dissenters through legal practice and jurisprudential thought is analysed by Wilfrid Prest in Chapter 7.

While Enlightened Dissent's not insignificant legal contribution has been little discussed, the question of its more general socio-economic and political impact has been the subject of controversy. In the much-discussed '*ancien régime* thesis' of Jonathan Clark a direct theoretical link is asserted between religious heterodoxy and political radicalism, an argument that is interestingly revised and developed in Waterman's essay (Chapter 8). At the same time Clark suggests that the Rational Dissenters who presented this politico-religious heterodoxy constituted a small intellectual élite of marginal men.[18] By contrast, James Bradley has maintained that while Dissenters were indeed politically influential, it was Dissent over a wide front that led to political activism and radicalism, that the role of Price, Priestley and their associates has been exaggerated, and that in regard to politics it is of little use to discriminate between the various Dissenting denominations.[19] In a wide-ranging survey of the issues raised by these and many more scholars, John Seed (Chapter 6) argues that in its heyday from the end of the 1770s to the end of the 1790s, Rational Dissent was a significant force in English public life which cannot be considered marginal. Its very success in integrating with the established order, however, led to deep ambiguities. On the one hand, it muted democratic, let alone more egalitarian, tendencies and made sure that Rational Dissent on the whole was very much part of the conservative Enlightenment indicated above. On the other hand, the fact that the legal and political basis for the Rational Dissenters' success was so tenuous tended in the opposite direction, namely towards a search for radical reform. The picture is further complicated by the fact that it is often difficult to fathom the extent to which apparent radicalism is simply dressed-up anti-authoritarianism resulting from Dissent's traditional anti-clericalism, a point stressed in Robert Hole's recent work.[20]

---

[18] Jonathan Clark, *English Society 1688–1832: Ideology, Social Structure and Political Practice During the Ancien Regime* (Cambridge, 1985), ch. 5. Cf. also Clark, *Revolution and Rebellion: State and Society in England in the Seventeenth and Eighteenth Centuries* (Cambridge, 1986), ch. 6.

[19] James E. Bradley, *Religion, Revolution and English Radicalism: Non-Conformity in Eighteenth-Century Politics and Society* (Cambridge, 1990). Cf. Bradley, *Popular Politics and the American Revolution in England: Petitions, the Crown and Public Opinion* (Macon, GA, 1986).

[20] Robert Hole, *Pulpits, Politics and Public Order in England, 1760–1832* (Cambridge, 1989). Concerning anti-clericalism and its political implications, see also J.A.I. Champion, *The Pillars of Priestcraft Shaken: The Church of England and Its Enemies, 1660–1730* (Cambridge, 1992).

Institutionalised Dissent began with the great ejection in 1662 of ministers, university dons and schoolteachers who refused to accept the Book of Common Prayer, and the ministry and education remained the defining factors in Dissent. The rationalising of parts of Dissent must therefore in large measure be understood as the rationalising of the clerical training. This is a recurrent theme in several of the following essays, but David Wykes provides a concentrated assessment. In a major revision of the now-dated standard literature,[21] Wykes concludes that, significant though they were, the colleges linked with Rational Dissent proper have been overrated in their significance both for Rational Dissent and for education in general. At the same time, however, he adds much evidence to the point made in several contexts in these studies, that the dividing lines between Orthodox, Enlightened and narrowly Rational Dissent were often extremely blurred. Dissenting colleges were decisive in spreading this broader and vaguer rational or intellectual approach to religion, which remained a coherent style well into the nineteenth century, as Robert Webb shows in a close analysis of the central ideal of rational piety (Chapter 12).

Generally speaking, we may say that the rational religion which was the basis for a broad spectrum of Enlightened Dissent shared with orthodox Dissent some belief in original sin and with radical Rational Dissent some trust in the powers of humanity to alleviate the effects of such sin through individual self-betterment and piety fostered by rational social and institutional arrangements. Variations on these themes sustained a wide field of ambivalent Dissent that was open to many different influences. Much work has been done on the rise of evangelicalism and its transformation of Dissent,[22] but there has been relatively little investigation of the extent to which Dissenters managed to combine evangelical piety with Enlightenment ways, such as the acceptance of scientific progress and the pursuit of politeness. Recently, however, David Bebbington has stressed the importance of the issue and Robert Webb's essay on rational piety (Chapter 12) mounts a spirited campaign on it.[23]

For the Rational Dissenters who rejected original sin, self-betterment and piety were no longer a compensatory mission but a fulfilment of

---

[21] See references in notes 3 and 4 to Wykes's essay (Chapter 5).

[22] See for, example, Deryck W. Lovegrove, *Established Church, Sectarian People: Itinerancy and the Transformation of English Dissent, 1780–1830* (Cambridge, 1988).

[23] See David W. Bebbington, *Evangelicalism in Modern Britain: A History from the 1730s to the 1980s* (London, 1989), ch. 2. Cf. also the fine discussions in John Hedley Brooke, *Science and Religion: Some Historical Perspectives* (Cambridge, 1991), esp. of Priestley, pp. 177–81.

God's promise for the future. For Dissenters of this turn of mind, the idea of the natural or original goodness of human nature was understood in strictly individualistic terms and, consequently, was always associated with individual freedom and suspicion of institutions and authority. At the same time the forward-looking character of this type of Dissent easily slid from progressivism to millenarianism. This is to be seen in many Rational Dissenters, but the towering figure is Joseph Priestley.[24] As Iain McCalman shows (Chapter 13), it was through him that Rational Dissent was closely linked to the popular millenarianism and enthusiasm of a radical London underworld well into the nineteenth century.

And so a circle is closed. It was the evangelical fervour of an earlier age that had emboldened the individual spirit to pursue truth for itself and thus tempted it to seek rational criteria for its progress; but when the progress of reason was projected to its completion, it could only be sustained through enthusiasm. Just as the religious mind was tempted into Enlightenment, so the enlightened mind exceeded itself and the excess was religious.

[24] Cf. Jack Fruchtman, Jr., *The Apocalyptic Politics of Richard Price and Joseph Priestley: A Study in Late Eighteenth-Century English Republican Millennialism*, trans. American Philosophical Society, 73, (4) (Philadelphia, PA, 1983).

CHAPTER 2

The emergence of Rational Dissent

R.K. Webb

In the eighteenth and early nineteenth centuries, those Protestants who worshipped apart from the Church of England were generally known, and knew themselves, as Dissenters. If one seeks a precise beginning for the long dominance of Dissent as the name of choice, it can be found on St Bartholomew's Day, 24 August 1662, when, as a result of the Act of Uniformity of the previous April, more than nine hundred clergymen, dons and schoolmasters in England and Wales were ejected from their posts for their conscientious refusal to give entire and unfeigned assent to everything contained in the Book of Common Prayer and to abjure the Solemn League and Covenant, as Parliament required; with earlier departures between 1660 and 1662, they brought the total of the ejected to slightly more than the two thousand of Dissenting legend. But that date may import too much exactness, for the roots of Dissent as both tendency and practice run back to the very beginning of Protestant England, if not before. The heretical ideas of the late-mediæval Lollards were reinforced by continental anabaptism in the earliest stages of the English Reformation, pulling in a radical direction at the time that others among the King's subjects were rising in defence of the Catholic faith. Certainly, dissidents presented a significant problem for those charged with implementing the Elizabethan settlement in the 1560s.

The Church of England, Catholic but not Roman and distinguished by as few departures from Roman belief and practice as were needed to warrant its Protestant autonomy, was, in its first decades, a political

Much of the work on which this chapter is based was done during a year's residence in the School of Historical Studies of the Institute for Advanced Study in Princeton. I am most grateful to my colleagues there and to the library of the Princeton Theological Seminary for making possible that productive and stimulating stay. The librarians and staff of Manchester College Oxford and Mr John Creasey, librarian of Dr Williams's Library, were, as always, helpful beyond measure in tracking down and copying material. In addition, I would like to thank Professors R.W. Davis and Barbara Shapiro, Dr Martin Fitzpatrick and Dr D.L. Wykes for their helpful reading of earlier versions.

creation in search of religious definition. Because contemporary conviction held that religion and citizenship should be coterminous, laws passed in Elizabeth's reign required that all the Queen's subjects conform to the Church without regard to differences in inclination, experience and belief; those who would not do so became liable to penalties that could be severe indeed, especially for Catholics. But mere outward, prudential observance did not fully satisfy the old Christian ideal of unity, especially as dissident groups gathered in secret conventicles; so the leaders of the Church tried to reduce its heterogeneity to the order so dear to its supreme governor, Elizabeth. The Queen may not have wanted to let windows into men's souls, but she preferred uniform facades, with no allowances for either historic uses or the requirements of the life within.

To some Englishmen, this expectation ranged from troubling to intolerable. In externals alone, many felt it essential to root out any reminders of the hated popery that had reduced the kingdom to subjection, murdered saintly men in the reign of Mary, and called the salvation of Protestants into question.[1] Roused first with respect to clerical vestments, the wrath of the purifiers (soon branded with the indistinct but distinctly hostile name of Puritans) was extended to time-hallowed practices incorporated in the conservative version of the Book of Common Prayer issued in 1559, such as bowing at the name of Jesus and the use of the ring in marriage. Some sought to change the administration of the Church by bishops to something closer to what was taken to be biblical prescription or primitive Christian practice. Still, what united these factions within the Church was greater than the liturgical or structural questions that divided them.

First among these unifying factors was the struggle against Roman Catholicism, made more pressing after Elizabeth's formal excommunication in 1570 by successive attempts on her throne and life, by the formidable threat of the Armada mounted from Spain in 1588, and by the Gunpowder Plot of Guy Fawkes and his fellow conspirators in 1605. Religious questions thus took on powerful patriotic overtones. A second unifying element was the Church of England itself: Puritans wanted to alter its practices, Presbyterians to govern it differently, but there was general agreement that a national Church was essential. It not only testified to unity and seemly order but had come to be seen as the carrier of

---

[1] The summary of grounds for anti-Catholicism twenty years earlier, given by Robin Clifton, 'Fear of Popery', in Conrad Russell, ed., *The Origins of the English Civil War* (London, 1973), pp. 144–67, still applies to the Restoration period.

national tradition, as the ecclesiastical embodiment of the English people parallel to the Crown in Parliament on the political side. A third force making for unity was Calvinism, the most recent of the great theological systems, which came in varying degrees to prevail within the Church, helped on especially by those Marian exiles who had taken refuge in the godly, Reformed city of Geneva and some of whom rose to the episcopal bench on their return.

By the 1580s, however, a new, subversive notion had appeared. Linked to older radical religious impulses and despairing of the Church's will to reform itself, separatists rejected the idea of a hierarchical Church, relying instead on autonomous congregations which could better control the admission of members and exercise a firmer discipline over them. Most open separatists were driven abroad, especially to the Low Countries and in time to America, but, in the early seventeenth century, a small number of English Christians withdrew to worship in defiance of the laws as 'gathered churches', little democracies, among the earliest of which the anabaptist influence continued to work. During the upheavals and civil wars between 1640 and 1660 there was an amazing efflorescence of religious enthusiasms, the most long-lasting and at the time most threatening of which was the Society of Friends, the Quakers, led by the charismatic, literally disturbing George Fox.[2] Remembering that in those same years the monarchy, the Church and the traditional structures of English society were brought down, it was easy for those who welcomed the Restoration of 1660 but feared for its permanence to see the sectarianism of the preceding generation as a likely future source of trouble.

The Act of Uniformity of 1662, which defined the Restoration religious settlement, was one of several statutes aimed at increasing national security and, incidentally, at giving new reality to the disciplinary aspirations of archbishops from Whitgift to Laud: the Corporation Act of 1661 laid down as a condition of membership in municipal governing bodies that communion be taken in the Established Church; the Conventicle Act of 1664, renewed with severer penalties in 1670, limited to a tiny number those outside immediate family members who could gather for religious services other than in an Anglican church; and the Five Mile Act of 1665 struck at the Dissenting pulpit by forbidding ejected

---

[2] The variety of competing views and organisations is splendidly conveyed in Michael Watts, *The Dissenters: From the Reformation to the French Revolution* (Oxford, 1978), as also is the marked divergence of scholarly interpretation of the origins and interrelations of different religious groupings and their mercurial naming. The early part of this chapter is much indebted to Watts's work.

ministers from coming within five miles of any parish in which they had served or of any city, corporate town, or parliamentary borough.

Beyond legislation, a number of alternatives presented themselves. For more than twenty years the authorities attempted to drive out Dissent through persecution, a policy doomed by the patchiness of its enforcement and by ultimate futility, though at times the harassment was intense and the threat of it continued, as reality or perception, for decades. Eventually the choice of policy came down to comprehension or toleration, between modifying liturgy and discipline in certain particulars so as to allow reincorporation of some moderate Dissenters or leaving most Dissenters free to worship as they would. The option of toleration won out in the Revolution Settlement of 1689, subject to some prudential, and demeaning, regulation and to continuing civil inequality entailed by religious difference. Dissent was thus confirmed as a reality in English life. It was the religion (or religions) of a small minority – in the early eighteenth century around 6 per cent of the population of England and Wales, rather unevenly distributed – and many observers, Dissenters and Anglicans alike, soon came to think it might eventually wither and die, until the great evangelical revival of the mid-eighteenth century dramatically reversed that expectation.[3]

The Dissent with which this volume is concerned was to be found in a sector of what came to be known as Old Dissent, the three denominations of Presbyterians, Independents (or Congregationalists) and Baptists, thus distinguished from the New, largely Methodist, Dissent that came into being in the eighteenth century. The Quakers, so central in the early decades of Dissenting history and the principal targets of persecution in the reign of Charles II, moved swiftly after 1689 to establish certain peculiar privileges, such as the right to affirm instead of swearing oaths, but during the eighteenth century they gradually abandoned their turbulent ways for quietism and a strictness with respect to language, dress and marriage that separated them from other Dissenters and, with a tendency to splinter, assured a long decline not reversed until the 'Quaker Renaissance' of the early twentieth century.

To understand the evolution of Rational Dissent within the body of the three denominations, we must go back to examine certain aspects of the seventeenth-century religious outlook, mostly within the Church of

---

[3] Watts, *Dissenters*, pp. 267–89, offers a careful calculation of early eighteenth-century numbers. The question of relative decline later in the century remains open.

England. Inevitably, the Church encompassed a wide range of religious tempers and inclinations, related to competing theological and ecclesiological systems as well as to differing personal needs and experiences. As always, the humble inhabitants of a predominantly rural England could hold reverently to a simple faith, put a Christian gloss on superstition, be caught up in a novel religious excitement, or betray the sullenness of those dragooned into observance by custom or the expectation of superiors; occasionally, impressively, a person of real religious genius might appear among them. Their betters, in country and town alike, ranged from the truly devout to the conventional, thoughtless, and even sceptical. But among those who took religion seriously and thought about it with equal seriousness, the seventeenth century posed a new order of challenges, from atheism or scepticism or degrees of heterodoxy, that most believers found as threatening as Roman Catholicism.

Socinianism – a label long used, justifiably or not, to condemn those suspected of straying from orthodoxy – was the most prominent of these affronts to traditional Catholic faith. Disputes over the central doctrine of the Trinity – the three persons of Father, Son and Holy Ghost united in one God – had preoccupied the first centuries of the Christian era and had resurfaced in the early sixteenth century, most prominently in the bold anti-Trinitarian views of Michael Servetus, a Spaniard eventually put to death in Calvinist Geneva. The term Socinian was derived later in the century from the Latinised name of Lelio Sozzini and his nephew Fausto, whose advocacy caused a scandal in Italy. From Italy, the movement spread across Europe, east as far as Hungary, where an active Unitarian church exists today, and west to the Low Countries, the great bastion of religious toleration.

Continental Socinian writings were well known to many of the more advanced religious thinkers in England, and a lonely missionary effort in the 1640s resulted in the imprisonment of Paul Best, who had been exposed to Socinianism while travelling in Poland and the Germanies. But it was not necessary to import heretical ideas. A far more common and potent source was individual study of the Bible, from which John Biddle, a graduate of Oxford and a Gloucester schoolmaster, derived the doubts about the Trinity that caused him to be repeatedly imprisoned or banished by different authorities from 1644 until his death in prison in 1662. In one interval of liberty, Biddle gathered a few converts in London, the most important of them being the wealthy merchant and philanthropist, Thomas Firmin. Secured by his immense reputation for saintliness against the penalties visited by the horrified governors of England on his less famous contemporaries, Firmin and an associate, Stephen Nye, rector of a small Hertfordshire parish, kept the Church in an uproar through their publications for more than a quarter of a century; authoritative Churchmen defending the Trinity fell out among themselves (or over themselves), even running the risk of other heresies, in their zeal to root out this alarming doctrine, until the 'Unitarian controversy' fell away in the 1690s, following Firmin's death.[4] But Socinianism, or Unitarianism as it later came to be known, repeatedly came to the surface and was to become one gauge of Rational Dissent, though not a necessary one.

Traditionalists in the early seventeenth century were also alarmed by a theological restiveness that undermined the Calvinism that remained the dominant system in the Church as well as among the Presbyterians and in the gathered churches. The principal tenet of Calvinism – the belief that salvation was limited to an elect determined by God's sovereign will from the beginning of creation – has served historically as a powerful stimulus to holiness of life and to bearing witness in the world, but it could also entail profound personal suffering and raise doubts about the beneficence of a deity who might be seen as arbitrary, even cruel, hence the many seventeenth-century efforts to mitigate the harshness of the doctrine.

That salvation was available to all was the central belief of the General Baptists who formed the first gathered churches in 1612 but, as Arminianism, so-called from the name of a Dutch theologian of that persuasion, it began to permeate the Church of England and by the 1620s had acquired a few outspoken representatives on the episcopal bench. In the person of William Laud, the reforming Bishop of London who became Archbishop of Canterbury in 1633, theological Arminianism was joined to the old Elizabethan commitment to discipline in a peculiarly narrow form. Enforced as national policy, the combination contributed to the Civil War in the 1640s and led to Laud's deposition, imprisonment and execution. But Arminianism could be construed more broadly than the Laudians had done, or were to do in the 1660s.

Throughout the era of the Reformation, there persisted a moderate, less embattled strain in European thought, concerned to maintain continuity in institutions and ideas and to seek reconciliation and peace.

---

[4] H.J. McLachlan, *Socinianism in Seventeenth-Century England* (London, 1951).

With it were associated some of the greatest names in the history of the European intellect, from Erasmus to Grotius, who, with their followers, were regularly denounced by sterner partisans for undermining the fortresses of creeds and for opening the way to scepticism or worse. In sixteenth-century England, such moderate men had seized on the idea, associated with Erasmus, that a distinction could be made between those things that were fundamental to Christian belief, on which everyone should agree, and those that were indifferent, where disagreement was to be expected and could be tolerated. At the end of the century, this moderate and conservative position received canonical statement in Richard Hooker's immensely influential *Laws of Ecclesiastical Polity*.

Within this moderate tradition in the seventeenth century was to be found a renewed commitment to rationalism. Reason, that God-given quality seen to separate men from beasts, had been called in as an aid to belief and faith at least from the thirteenth century, when the reintegration of Aristotle into western thought was accomplished. The later Middle Ages saw an immense elaboration of logical analysis which contributed by its very subtlety and complexity to the sense that 'scholasticism', the wisdom of the schools, ran counter to the true religious spirit, and so in the Reformation era there was a reaction against the abuses of reasoning. But rationalism maintained its strength among the moderates, who, by the middle of the seventeenth century, were finding more and more reasons for their confidence. The excesses of the sects during the Interregnum, and the conviction among some that God spoke directly to individuals, brought a reaction against an ungoverned religiosity that was coming to be known as 'enthusiasm', while the threat of atheism and scepticism seemed to demand the use of every weapon – and reason was thought the most impressive of them – to strengthen the Christian faith.

The seventeenth century was also an age in which the immense displacements brought about by the scientific revolution had to be coped with. The great herald of science early in the century, Sir Francis Bacon, maintained that the collection of facts and systematic experiment would, in the fullness of time, through the exercise of inductive reasoning, bring about a genuine understanding of nature; but Bacon relegated religion to a separate realm of faith, neither supporting nor aided by scientific activity. Baconian ideals were still in evidence in the early 1660s, when the new Royal Society became the principal forum for the collection and promotion of scientific knowledge.[5] But the bulk of both religious and

---

[5] Michael Hunter, *Science and Society in Restoration England* (Cambridge, 1981), ch. 1.

scientific opinion in the last half of the century held otherwise, believing that the central religious questions could in fact be resolved, at least to moral certainty, by the study of nature and by the study of history, as it was set out in the Bible, both activities that commanded the exercise of rational analysis and generalisation.

This confidence was strengthened by the temporary disrepute into which mathematical proof – recognised everywhere as a superior means of carrying conviction in scientific matters – had been brought by the philosopher Thomas Hobbes, whose proclaimed intention of applying the methods of geometry to moral subjects had ended, as contemporaries understood it, in an immoral glorification of tyrannical power and in atheism. Thus began the great age, lasting for at least two centuries, of natural religion, of the mutual reinforcement of science and revelation. Everywhere in the world and in the heavens were evidences of God's designing intelligence – omnipotent, ingenious, beneficent – working with exquisite skill to ensure the domination and the happiness of man. On the basis of those evidences, scientists and other scholars not only could prove the existence of God but could establish the laws by which he governed his creation. The famous chemist Robert Boyle was, for his own time, the most impressive of the representatives of this close linking of science and faith, but, for the succeeding century, it was the surpassing accomplishment of Sir Isaac Newton that was turned to again and again to demonstrate the grandeur of nature, the power and beneficence of its Creator, and the elegance of natural law. In much the same way, John Locke, in his *Essay Concerning Human Understanding* (1690), was seen as the discoverer of the laws of mind, which promised a view of man and society far more fruitful than the ambitions of Hobbes and without his evil consequences. Moreover, two other works by Locke, *A Letter Concerning Toleration* (1689) and *The Reasonableness of Christianity* (1695), became of the first importance in the emergence of liberal religion.

The implementation of the seventeenth-century rationalist programme was complex. It had preoccupied small groups of men like that gathered around Lucius Cary, second Viscount Falkland, for a few years from the middle 1630s to his death in battle on the royalist side in 1643. The openness of Falkland and his friends to every current of thought, at the risk of raising doubts about their orthodoxy, was carried impressively into wider spheres: by Edward Hyde, Earl of Clarendon, a splendid historian of his times as well as an uneasy adviser to both Charles I and Charles II, whose service to each ended in exile; by Gilbert Sheldon, Archbishop of Canterbury from 1663 to 1677; and by William

Chillingworth, who, after a brief dalliance with Roman Catholicism in the late 1620s, returned to a moderate course, also falling victim to the war in 1643. It was at Falkland's estate at Great Tew, near Oxford, that Chillingworth tested and wrote *The Religion of Protestants*, a famous controversial work that affirmed the impossibility of agreement on all matters of religious faith and the central importance of bringing reason to bear. It was, perhaps, Chillingworth's most enduring legacy to insist that the Bible, itself a subject for rational investigation and reflection, was the defining and uniting element of Protestantism.

A similar, though less immediately influential cluster was to be found among a small number of university teachers and preachers at Cambridge, most of whom shared a common origin in the Puritan foundation of Emmanuel College and who rediscovered the Platonic tradition as it had been mediated through the Neoplatonic school of the late classical period and the rediscovered Platonism of the Italian Renaissance. Though the Cambridge Platonists had more than their share of pedantry and sometimes descended to extremes of intellectual eccentricity, their intense spirit of devotion, sometimes verging on mysticism, and their emphasis on morality as the great public end of religion were to speak impressively to the theologians and historians who have rediscovered them over the past century or so. Like their predecessors at Great Tew, the Cambridge Platonists rejected the notion that there was a single truth to which men must adhere or be made to adhere. The very essence of reason made differing understandings, differing paths to the truth, inevitable, and so they were tolerant to a degree that characterised few of their compatriots and contemporaries.[6]

Critics of the Cambridge Platonists had stigmatised them as 'latitude-men', a term soon transmuted into 'latitudinarians' and affixed to the moderate and liberal party that was to play such an important part in English religion over the next century. Buoyed up by scientific confidence, the latitudinarians took up the adaptation of the Puritan 'plain style' advocated by Bishop John Wilkins, who, from a position that drew on both Puritanism and Anglicanism, was the centre of another influential circle, and turned their preaching to irenic and pleasing ends.

---

[6] On the Falkland connection, Hugh Trevor-Roper, 'The Great Tew Circle', in his *Catholics, Anglicans and Puritans: Seventeenth-Century Essays* (Chicago, 1988), pp. 166–230. The key works in the rediscovery of the Cambridge Platonists are John Tulloch, *Rational Theology and Christian Philosophy in the Seventeenth Century* (London, 1874); W.R. Inge, *The Platonic Tradition in English Religious Thought* (London, 1917); Frederick J. Powicke, *The Cambridge Platonists: A Study* (London, 1926, repr. 1971); and Ernst Cassirer, *The Platonic Renaissance in England*, trans. J.P. Pettegrove (from the German edn., Leipzig, 1932) (Edinburgh and Austin, TX., 1953).

Political circumstances gave these liberal Anglicans a strong position on the bench of bishops in the early eighteenth century, although even there they were a minority and were even more outnumbered (if not out-gunned) among the ordinary clergy. Still, they gave eloquent voice to a religious position that may have been overemphasised subsequently but that cannot be discounted.[7]

By the end of the seventeenth century, however, rationalism, particularly in association with the mechanical views of the universe that evolving science had made commonplace, had reached an extreme in the alarming threat of deism, the belief of a small number of advanced intellects that God created and then (in effect) abandoned the world to work according to the laws he had laid down; those laws, evident in nature, were sufficient to guarantee morality, and no recourse was needed to Revelation or, by implication, to an authoritative Church.[8] This subversive doctrine spawned a half-century of intense controversy, but the more moderate conclusions of the latitudinarians survived relatively intact to give a characteristic identity to eighteenth-century Anglicanism, in its upper, more visible sectors, and to provide inspiration and allies for the Rational Dissenters.

During the time in the middle of the seventeenth century when the Church of England was proscribed, an extensive range of accommodation was to be found, despite the fierce competition of theologies and sects. Loyal Churchmen accepted clerical posts under the new regime, and, amid the ferment of ideas, Oliver Cromwell himself argued for a limited toleration.[9] At the Restoration, until a hostile Cavalier Parliament

---

[7] For a succinct account of the emergence of latitudinarianism, John Gascoigne, *Cambridge in the Age of the Enlightenment: Science, Religion and Politics from the Restoration to the French Revolution* (Cambridge, 1989), chs. 2–3. On the broader intellectual situation, Barbara J. Shapiro, *John Wilkins, 1614–1672: An Intellectual Biography* (Berkeley and Los Angeles, 1969), and *Probability and Certainty in Seventeenth-Century England: A Study of the Relationships between Natural Science, Religion, History, Law and Literature* (Princeton, NJ, 1983). For a splendid survey of what is impossibly compressed here, John Hedley Brooke, *Science and Religion: Some Historical Perspectives* (Cambridge, 1991), with an extensive bibliography. John Spurr has admirably laid out the difficulties in seventeenth-century terminology in '"Latitudinarianism" and the Restoration Church', *Historical Journal*, 31 (1988), 61–82. Richard Kroll, Richard Ashcraft and Perez Zagorin, eds., *Philosophy, Science and Religion in England, 1640–1700* (Cambridge, 1992), and W.M. Spellman, *The latitudinarians and the Church of England, 1660–1700* (Athens, GA, 1993), appeared too late to be taken into account in writing this chapter.

[8] The literature on deism is vast, but for an authoritative recent study, see Robert E. Sullivan, *John Toland and the Deist Controversy: A Study in Adaptations* (Cambridge, MA, 1982).

[9] For a review of the controversy about toleration in the Interregnum and of the ambiguous role of the Independents, the sect to which Cromwell belonged, see Avihu Zakai, 'Religious Toleration and Its Enemies: The Independent Divines and the Issue of Toleration during the English Civil War', *Albion*, 21 (1989), 1–33.

with long memories took action to prevent the recurrence of the troubles, some broader settlement seemed a lively possibility. The Declaration of Breda, issued by Charles II on the eve of his return to England, spoke to the claims of tender consciences, and the Savoy Conference of 1661 was intended (though perhaps doomed) as a forum for negotiating a degree of comprehension. Men raised as Puritans or identified with them accepted preferment in the Church, and many of the men ejected in 1662 would have stayed within the fold had that seemed possible: they took their decisive stands on many differing points, though none aroused such strong feelings among so many of those who went into the wilderness as the requirement that ministers ordained during the Interregnum would have to be reordained to remain within the Church. No better or more anguished example of such torn loyalties can be found than Richard Baxter, who was offered and declined a bishopric and who, despite persecution and extreme personal suffering, never abandoned the middle position of 'meer Catholic', concerned to reconcile men of good will. The spirit of tolerance may have been eclipsed by those who fought from entrenched doctrinal positions, but it was not extinguished. In that uneasy atmosphere the devotion to reason continued to grow.

The storms over Socinianism and deism at first left most of the new Dissenters untouched: mostly loyal to Calvinism, they certainly disapproved of heterodoxy, but they were preoccupied with survival, and once that question was settled, they had to establish their churches as workable entities, fend off intermittent challenges to their security and cope with increasing difficulties rooted in their internal differences.[10] The brief periods of respite arising from royal declarations of indulgence in 1672 and 1687–8 led to the foundation of a number of congregations, some of which remain to the present day; this activity grew apace after 1689. To be sure, the Toleration Act was itself no more than an indulgence, a decision not to impose criminal penalties under laws that, as Blackstone was later to point out to the great distress of Joseph Priestley, remained legally in force. Not infrequently, chapels erected in the immediate post-1689 decades, when little seemed certain, were hidden away in the countryside or in the back streets of towns, and trust deeds sometimes contained provision for dispersal of funds should 'the toleration' be revoked. Only after 1715 did a new Dissenting confidence show itself in architecture.

---

[10] For a revealing account of the manoeuvres of one Presbyterian congregation, Tothill Street, Westminster, and its minister, see R.A. Beddard, 'Vincent Alsop and the Emancipation of Restoration Dissent', *Journal of Ecclesiastical History*, 24 (1973), 161–84.

Official pronouncements in the Church of England declared toleration to be a permanent feature of the constitution in Church and state, but that was not a position that came easily to many elements in the Church. Some of the warmer spirits among the Nonjurors – those Churchmen who had refused to abandon the oaths they had sworn to King James II – lashed out at Dissenting sects as nurseries of sedition, and most High Churchmen who remained within the fold felt more or less the same way. Clergymen who had to cope with the unsettling effects of Dissent in their parishes were also likely to take a jaundiced view of it. When this tense situation was complicated by the bitterly partisan political warfare in the reign of Queen Anne, Dissenters were easy targets. The High Church move to restore Convocation, the Church's legislative body, was successful in 1701, and thereafter, until Convocation was put back on the constitutional shelf in 1717, the Church was kept in turmoil by the feuding in the Convocation of Canterbury between the clergy of the lower house and the upper house, made up of the more politic bishops. The government's move to impeach the High-Church firebrand Henry Sacheverell in 1709–10 resulted in riots that left a number of Dissenting chapels in ashes, as was to happen again in the Coronation Riots of 1714 and in the disorder let loose by the Jacobite invasion in 1715.[11]

Two legislative initiatives aimed at Dissent seemed even more alarming. After many years of agitation on the question, an Act of 1711 forbade the common practice in which Dissenters took communion in an Anglican church as a *pro forma* qualification for municipal office, a violation of the spirit, if not the letter, of the Corporation Act of 1661. Until the Occasional Conformity Act was repealed in 1718, there was standing encouragement to ambitious Dissenters to abandon their sectarian loyalty for conformity rather than risk a very heavy fine. The Schism Act of 1714 forbade Dissenters from keeping schools; aimed in particular at the Dissenting academies that catered to young men excluded from the universities, it would, if enforced (as it was in some instances), have drawn laymen away and undercut the training of a Dissenting ministry. Because the Queen died on the day the Act was to take effect, it remained a largely dead letter and was also repealed in 1718, under a Whig Government with some obligations to its Dissenting supporters. But these Acts, with others, suggested in what direction a chill wind might blow.

---

[11] Paul Kléber Monod, *Jacobitism and the English People, 1688–1788* (Cambridge, 1989), ch. 6, esp. pp. 173–94, and ch. 7, which deal with Jacobite protest between 1715 and 1780.

The efforts of Dissenters to advance their constitutional position got nowhere, but they were successful in preventing erosion of the limited concessions already made. Building on ministerial collaboration in presenting addresses to the Queen early in Anne's reign and on the subsequent creation of a formal organisation of the London ministry, a lay committee, which came to be known as the Dissenting Deputies, emerged early in the reign of George II; it did valuable work as a watchdog and as a reconciler within the ranks of Dissent, and early in the nineteenth century the Deputies mounted a campaign, successful in 1828, for the repeal of the Test and Corporation Acts. This marked, it has been said, the end of 'the Anglican constitution', as Catholic Emancipation the next year marked the end of 'the Protestant constitution',[12] though some disabilities in such matters as marriage, church rates, and university entrance remained, as did the long-persisting social discrimination. Moreover, Dissenting unity was broken, as resurgent evangelical Congregationalists and Baptists attempted to recover endowments and buildings that had descended to the English Unitarians from their Presbyterian forbears and then challenged Unitarian leadership of Dissent as a whole.[13]

That split had been foreshadowed almost as soon as toleration was granted. While the Quakers, who counted the largest number of victims during the persecution of the Restoration era, had appeared to turn suffering to advantage in reinforcing their cohesion and their witness, the effect of persecution on the Presbyterians was devastating. While they had never gone as far as the Scots in setting up a hierarchy of Presbyterian institutions, neither had they contemplated a purely congregational polity, like that of their fellow Dissenters, offering, rather, the alternative of a reformed Church. As often happens, the middle position was the most exposed. But with the eclipse of Presbyterian hopes for comprehension and a reform of the national Church, Presbyterians were forced increasingly into a congregational mould.

They retained the advantages, however, of being not only the largest of the Dissenting sects, but the wealthiest, best educated, and most prominent socially and politically. Thus Dissenting leadership devolved

---

[12] G.F.A. Best, 'The Constitutional Revolution, 1828–32', *Theology*, 62 (1959), 226–34. Compare J.C.D. Clark, *English Society, 1688–1832* (Cambridge, 1985), pp. 393–420. The early history of Dissenting self-protection, with the more striking accomplishment of the Quakers, is set out in N.C. Hunt, *Two Early Political Associations: The Quakers and the Dissenting Deputies in the Age of Walpole* (Oxford, 1961). On the campaign against the Test and Corporation Acts, Richard W. Davis, *Dissent in Politics, 1780–1830: The Political Life of William Smith, M.P.* (London, 1971).

[13] See K.R.M. Short, 'London's General Body of Protestant Ministers: Its Disruption in 1836', *Journal of Ecclesiastical History*, 24 (1973), 377–93.

naturally on them and, for a time, on their successors, the Unitarians, while their emphasis on a learned ministry reinforced their tendency to be less rigorous in their churchmanship than those Dissenters in tightly self-policed congregations and to be more open to new currents of thought. These potential sources of division were largely masked for the better part of a century.

During the time of troubles after 1662, the regional groupings of ministers that had emerged in some parts of the country during the 1650s continued a shadowy existence, encouraging each other, raising funds, resolving differences, and after 1689 this impulse to collaborate had freer rein. Ministers in the West Country were planning a non-denominational association and a common fund early in 1690. A year later the Exeter Assembly came into existence, with some continuity from an earlier county association in the 1650s, and other such organisations of greater or less longevity appeared elsewhere in the country. But the most revealing of these efforts, because it involved the most dramatic failure, was in London. There, in March 1691, more than eighty ministers gathered to submerge the names of Presbyterian and Independent in the 'United Brethren', an initiative quickly hailed as the 'Happy Union'. It proved in the event to be neither. Almost at once, the Presbyterians took offence at what two centuries later would be known as a revival, in Northamptonshire. When the London Presbyterians summoned the offending minister, Richard Davis, to explain himself, his fellow Congregationalists at once sensed a revival of the synodical inquisition that had threatened their independence forty years earlier. Moreover, Presbyterians were alarmed by the implication of Antinomianism in the republished works of Tobias Crisp, an earlier seventeenth-century Independent. Just before he died in 1691, Richard Baxter launched an attack on Crisp's position, and the cause was subsequently taken up by Daniel Williams, minister of a prominent London Presbyterian congregation. Williams alive was a better target than Crisp dead, and his book, *Gospel-Truth Stated*, published in 1692, led to a pamphlet war in which Williams was accused of falling into the vice of Arminianism. Congregationalists began to withdraw from the United Brethren, and by 1695 the rupture was all but complete.[14]

---

[14] These developments are admirably traced in Alexander Gordon, *Freedom after Ejection: A Review (1690–1692) of Presbyterian and Congregationalist Nonconformity in England and Wales* (Manchester, 1917) and are conveniently summarised in Watts, *Dissenters* (fn. 2), pp. 289–97. See also G.F. Nuttall, 'Assembly and Association in Dissent, 1689–1831', in G.J. Cuming and Derek Baker, eds., *Councils and Assemblies* (Studies in Church History, 7) (Cambridge, 1971), pp. 189–202; Allan Brockett, *Nonconformity in Exeter, 1650–1875* (Manchester, 1962), pp. 64–73; and Roger Thomas, *Daniel Williams, 'Presbyterian Bishop'*, Friends of Dr Williams's Library, 16th Lecture (London, 1964).

The inroads of rational thought on Dissent became more apparent with the publication in 1712 of *The Scripture-Doctrine of the Trinity* by the eminent Anglican divine, Samuel Clarke, who set out to gather every text in the Bible that might touch on the Trinity. Clarke's collation of 1,251 texts and his fifty-five propositions demonstrated that full divinity belongs only to God the Father; the Son, while divine and having existence prior to his taking human form, is none the less dependent on the Father for that existence and for the power he exercises by delegation. Clarke thus became the fountainhead of what the eighteenth century understood as Arianism, so called after Arius, the fourth-century theologian over whom St Athanasius triumphed at the Council of Nicaea in AD 325. To the orthodox, of course, the drama of Calvary and of the Last Judgement lost grandeur and meaning if the god who died on the Cross was a secondary, derivative deity – 'denying the Lord that bought them', as one orthodox minister was to put it, for the worship of a mere creature.[15] In time, for others more radical, that devalued Christ came to appear as lacking in the full human qualities that might give special significance to his mission and so Arianism gave way to Unitarianism, but it survived in real influence for the greater part of a century.

Quite as important as the impetus Clarke gave to the complex and perhaps excessively refined reinterpretation of the theological question of divine substance was the manner in which he argued. He rested his case on biblical authority, true, with some assistance from theological commentary, but he approached his sources with greater confidence in the infallibility of human reason than in the weight of either the Bible or Church tradition. He was cautious and temperate without losing conviction and recognised that others might disagree or go part but not all of the way with him; thus, in proposition 10: 'When the Word, *God*, is mentioned in Scripture, with any High *Epithet*, *Title*, or *Attribute* annex'd to it; it generally, (I think, *always*) means the *Person* of *the Father*.' And when he set out to reconcile the language of the Prayer Book and other Anglican formularies with his interpretation of Scripture, he summoned an immense array of authoritative testimony from his fellow Anglicans against the so-called Athanasian Creed, rejecting its anathemas against those outside the Church as products of political embroilment at the time of its late composition. Clarke refused to follow his friend, the Cambridge mathematician William Whiston, into extreme Arianism;

---

[15] Henry Atkins of Exeter on 15 May 1717, quoted in Brockett, *Nonconformity in Exeter*, p. 80.

but Whiston lost his chair, and Clarke kept his living as rector of St James's, Westminster, where he survived until 1729, an intimate at Court and the focus of a circle of like-minded, free-thinking divines. He did not, however, get the bishopric which all agreed his early promise had made likely.[16]

Clarke's book was to have a long influence on Dissenting thought, in some instances confirming conclusions arrived at by independent study of the Bible, in others as the immediate means of striking scales from searching eyes. The most significant instance, however, took place soon after publication, in Exeter, where Arian ideas were being enthusiastically canvassed by some of the students at the academy there. One of them, Hubert Stogdon, was so struck by Clarke's book that he spoke openly about his views, thus raising doubts about the orthodoxy of three of the four ministers who shared responsibility for the three Presbyterian congregations in the town. When the matter seemed likely to come before the Exeter Assembly, the ministers attempted to defuse the situation by attesting to Stogdon's excellent qualities, while remaining silent about his ideas, so enabling him to be ordained to a congregation in Somerset, outside the Assembly's purview. But the threatened orthodox were not appeased, and when the three ministers were told to declare themselves on the subject of the Trinity, they divided, one eventually coming down on the orthodox side, another, Joseph Hallett, protesting against any test of belief, and the third, James Peirce, finally declaring himself a believer in the subordination of Christ. As was the custom, the matter was referred to the ministers in London, who considered it in a general assembly at Salters' Hall early in 1719. The crucial vote came on a motion to accompany advices to Exeter with a declaration of belief in the Trinity. Those in favour of sending the declaration, the subscribers, gained fifty-three votes against the nonsubscribers' fifty-seven. Historians suggest that had the vote been directly on the question of the Trinity rather than about sending a declaration, it would have gone the other way. What motivated the majority was the conviction that human formulations should not be imposed on Scripture: as the Master of the Rolls pithily summarised the situation, 'The Bible carried it by four'. But in Exeter, Peirce and Hallett were locked out by the trustees of James's Chapel and other chapels closed their pulpits to them, though eventually James's Chapel moved on in the heterodox path, and its successor after

---

[16] J.P. Ferguson, *An Eighteenth Century Heretic, Dr. Samuel Clarke* (Kineton, NY, 1976) is pedestrian, but it sets out the context and controversies in which Clarke's book must be placed.

1760, George's Meeting, was one of the most distinguished Unitarian congregations in the country.[17]

The divisions of the 1690s and in 1719 bring to light the persistence of two divergent tendencies thrown together in Dissent and surviving, at least down to mid-century, in easy (or uneasy) accommodation. There was often only one Dissenting chapel in a small or medium-sized town that had to cater to all views. When Job Orton, who had been a pupil and then a tutor at Philip Doddridge's academy in Northampton, was called to the High Street congregation in his native Shrewsbury, the small Independent congregation, its pulpit vacant, simply joined with the larger Presbyterian chapel. Some time later, Orton wrote: 'We never heed the distinction between Presbyterian & Independent in these parts of the kingdom, & it is idle & insignificant everywhere. But where there are two meetings in some towns these names are kept up for distinction's sake; & if they mean anything independent with the vulgar signifies calvinistical'.[18]

But even in larger places there could be a certain amount of give and take. At Leeds, the Presbyterians at Mill Hill and the Congregationalists at Call Lane had a long history of co-operation, but Mill Hill gradually found its way into heterodoxy. William Pendlebury, the son of an ejected minister, served there from 1705 to 1729, holding to a strictly Calvinistic and Trinitarian position. His successor, Joseph Cappe, the father of one of the most influential of Unitarians later in the century, had more relaxed views; and in 1748, he was succeeded by the openly heretical Thomas Walker.

Some of Walker's congregation began to leave for Call Lane, but trouble was eventually to arise there as well. One Call Lane member, a master clothier named Joseph Ryder, recorded in his diary his distress when he went to hear Walker preach: 'To hear the doctrines which our pious forefathers suffered for, but not only so, such doctrines as the Scriptures, in my apprehension of things, appear clearly to hold forth – in a manner confuted – it gives me great concern.' By 1758, however, the Meeting for Religious Conversation at Call Lane was also embroiled in argument about the imputed righteousness of Christ and about the Trinity, and when a friend rebuked Ryder for not speaking up, he

---

[17] This is an extremely compressed account of a highly complex series of manoeuvres, which are well laid out in Brockett, *Nonconformity in Exeter* (fn. 14), and in Roger Thomas, 'The Non-Subscription Controversy amongst Dissenters in 1719: The Salters' Hall Debate', *Journal of Ecclesiastical History*, 4 (1953), 162–86.

[18] Walter Wilson biographical collection, Dr Williams's Library.

confided to his diary that he should perhaps have been more forward, 'but I consider if one is not duly furnished with convincing arguments, I rather choose to say little than to make ill words on questions such as the greatest divines cannot bring down to our reason, being above reason'. Ryder also expressed puzzlement and even fear about the inroads of Baptists and Methodists: 'Sects and parties we have now in great numbers, and every-one perhaps think themselves to be right. What may be the issue of all is known only to God.'[19] The ministerial progression at Mill Hill and, no doubt, the confusion and distress at Call Lane were duplicated elsewhere; so was the departure of more conservative souls for Congregationalist chapels, as Arianism gradually gave way to open Unitarianism.

The ambiguities that shot through Dissent become evident in consider-ing one of the greatest figures in Dissenting history, Philip Doddridge, minister at Northampton and principal of the academy there from 1729 to his early death in 1751. It has been amply established that Doddridge belongs in a tradition descending from Richard Baxter, that passionate, idiosyncratic Puritan and Churchman of the late seventeenth century. 'The poor Church of Christ,' Baxter wrote, 'the sober, sound religious part, are like Christ that was crucified between two malefactors: the profane and formal persecutors on one hand, and the fanatic dividing sectary on the other, have in all ages been grinding the spiritual seed as the corn is ground between the millstones . . .' Surely, the greater good lay in preserving the Church and in saving men's souls, not 'that they should . . . tear the garment of Christ all to pieces rather than it should want their lace'. Bound in so many ways to his century, Baxter was a splendid exemplar of the broader tradition of moderation that we have seen as the principal source of the religious uses of reason.

Doddridge was Baxter's heir, in a happier time (though one not without its trials), when his irenic spirit could work amid almost universal admiration to warm and deepen the intellectual currents of an age proud of its enlightenment.[20] But while rational religion seemed to have

---

[19] The forty-one volumes of the Ryder diaries, in the John Rylands University Library of Manchester, are conveniently excerpted in Herbert McLachlan, *Essays and Addresses* (Manchester, 1950), pp. 20–38.

[20] On Baxter and Doddridge, see Alexander Gordon, *Heads of English Unitarian History* (London, 1985), pp. 56–101, and 'Philip Doddridge and the Catholicity of the Old Dissent', in his *Addresses Biographical and Historical* (London, 1927), pp. 185–237; Geoffrey Nuttall, *Richard Baxter and Philip Doddridge: A Study in a Tradition*, Friends of Dr Williams's Library, 5th Lecture (London, 1951), and the volume of essays edited by Nuttall, *Philip Doddridge (1702–51): His Contribution to English Religion* (London, 1951).

triumphed over its old enemies in the eighteenth century, almost from the moment of that victory new voices arose to deny, in puzzling and disturbing ways, what the rationalists had won: evangelicalism was on the march. To place Doddridge within this transition requires a somewhat closer reading of his work than has been needed thus far in this introduction, but so much attention has been paid to his place in the history of Dissent and especially in the emergence of evangelicalism that his importance in the history of Rational Dissent has been largely overshadowed.

Like Baxter before him, Doddridge was a great preacher who also taught, wrote and did good works. He headed an academy and even helped raise troops when the Jacobite rising of 1745 threatened. He gave sage advice on the composition and delivery of sermons, urging his students to emphasise the practical subjects their listeners wanted and to avoid metaphysical topics that were either agreed or too controversial and abstruse for gospel preaching. He underlined the importance of instructing and catechising the young, writing sermons specifically for children and even instructional verse, and stressed the importance of knowing and visiting all the members of the congregation, in sickness and in health. But to most contemporaries, as to most scholars since, Doddridge's central contribution was as the author of a supremely important work of devotion.

Here, too, he belongs in the Baxterian tradition. Baxter wrote *The Saints' Everlasting Rest* (1650) when he had withdrawn from active life in the momentary expectation of death. The glorious intensity of its prose is directed at two ends: to impress upon the reader the horror, less of eternal torment (though that is there) than of the loss that comes from failure to seize God's offer of salvation through his son; and to set out the ways by which that favour may be gained and held. Baxter returned again and again to the theme of conversion, mustering his argument now in the numbered paragraphs or alternating propositions, questions and objections of logical exposition, now in the white heat of a direct appeal to conscience, always buttressed by extensive citations of the unchallengeable Bible.

In *The Rise and Progress of Religion in the Soul* (1745), Doddridge's purpose was the same – to show the way to salvation – but the differences are instructive. Doddridge sees the plight of the careless sinner not in Baxter's cosmic setting but in a more personal, intimate way, no less compelling for being less awesome and lending itself better to the systematic, or, to use a contemporary word full of significance, methodical, tracing of the steps by which the turning can be accomplished and

secured. The chapters lay out the stages of the process, again with constant reference to the Bible, again with the certainty that few will take
advantage of the offer. But Doddridge's scheme is more of this world,
somehow more manageable, certainly more social.

One can imagine Baxter's language sounding ringingly and com-
pellingly from the pulpit or being read with electric effect in private;
despite his injunction (in *A Call to the Unconverted*, 1657) to read his book
over and over again in families and to ignorant neighbours to win their
souls, surely few ordinary men or women could have found the tones or
the eloquence to match the words to the visions. Doddridge, too, is
moving, but differently so: his title page describes his addresses as 'suited
to persons of every character and circumstance', and he apologizes in
his preface to those of 'more elegant taste and refined education' for the
plainness of speech he has adopted to make his message available to the
lowest of his readers. This is truly the language of the family circle as
well as of the reader in his closet, and the prayers that end each chapter,
enforcing the lessons therein, almost demand to be read aloud and are
the more effective for (as Doddridge would have put it) their condescen-
sion. But there is in his approach a suggestion that has not, perhaps, been
sufficiently considered.

The conventional view is well put by A.T.S. James.[21] For him,
Doddridge was 'by head and shoulders the greatest' of those who were
calling England back from 'a period of dead-weight in religion . . . the
very hey-day of self-complacency' between 1700 and 1750. To be sure,
James continues, Doddridge was aware of the dangers that lay in enthusiasm and excessive emotion, which he feared 'as much as he feared the
sand dunes of the philosophers'. But 'the great thing was that this
change of course did bring religion to men's hearths and doorsteps, to
the man in his shop and the peasant in the field; it was not a matter
chiefly for professional debate'. Doddridge may have lacked the
awesome intensity of John Bunyan and the literary imagination of
William Law, 'but his men are those he sees Sunday by Sunday in his

---

[21] A.T.S. James, 'Philip Doddridge: His Influence on Personal Religion', in *ibid.*, pp. 32–45. For an
elegant and perceptive portrait that explores the Northampton roots of a broad evangelical
sensibility on which Doddridge drew and to which he was a key contributor, see Alan Everitt,
'Springs of Sensibility: Philip Doddridge of Northampton and the Evangelical Tradition', in his
Landscape and Community in England (London, 1985), pp. 209–45. In what follows, I am drawing on
the memoir by Job Orton, published in 1766 and reprinted in the first volume of Doddridge's
Works (London, 1802), and on Andrew Kippis's biography, which draws heavily on Orton but
supplements it, in the *Biographica Britannica* (1791), reprinted as a preface to Doddridge's *The Family
Expositor* (Charlestown, MA, 1807), to which fns. 25–7 refer.

pews, or passes in the streets of Northampton', men and women he summoned to a personal religion 'built up on the Word of God and on prayer, and cared for in the Christian fellowship'.

It is important, however, to view *The Rise and Progress of Religion in the Soul* in a broader context. In Job Orton's memoir of Doddridge that book figures far less importantly in the catalogue. Its frequent republication is noted, as is the warmth of its reception; indeed, says Orton, 'perhaps there is no practical book better calculated for general usefulness'. But he reminds us of the manner of its writing. The book and its format – addresses on a wide range of subjects, each followed by 'a devout meditation or prayer' – were planned by Isaac Watts, who, aware of his own failing health, turned the project over to the younger man. Doddridge was reluctant, given his other commitments, but his admiration for Watts was so great and Watts's desire so strong that he could not refuse; Watts revised as much of it as he could. To point out this collaboration is not to diminish the book's historical importance or the intensity of Doddridge's convictions, but it does introduce a warning about taking it as the one true key to Doddridge's religious position.

Andrew Kippis names Baxter, John Tillotson and Charles Howe as Doddridge's models in practical divinity.[22] Certainly, his manner of structuring sermons is indebted to Tillotson, even in *Christ's Invitation to Thirsty Souls*, a sermon published in 1749 but written twenty years earlier, which Doddridge considered to be unequalled by any other he had preached, though he thought it 'destitute of almost every charm that might recommend it to a modern taste . . .'[23] Or, we might add, today's taste: even A.T.S. James noted how, in *The Rise and Progress*, Doddridge's words 'pour from him, and his long sentences often tumble over one another',[24] and the dense texture of scriptural citation makes the *Invitation* nearly unreadable, though it might have carried conviction in the hearing. Presumably these faults grew worse as Doddridge resorted increasingly in later life to extempore preaching – not out of conviction but for lack of time – though, again, Kippis argues that his attention to 'exact and careful' preparation in the early sermons so admired and

[22] On Howe's influence, see Nuttall, *Philip Doddridge*, ch. 7, and Everitt, 'Springs of Sensibility', p. 219.

[23] Alexander Gordon (*DNB*) points out that 'the mathematical form of his lectures (in philosophy and divinity), with the neat array of definitions, propositions, and corollaries' was taken from his predecessor at the academy at Kibworth, John Jennings, but, as has been often noted, Jennings lectured in Latin, while Doddridge was one of the first of the tutors to lecture in English. See also Roger Thomas, 'Philip Doddridge and Liberalism in Religion', in Nuttall, *Philip Doddridge* (fn. 20).

[24] James, 'Philip Doddridge', (fn. 21), p. 36.

imitated by his pupils resulted in 'a habit of delivering his sentiments usually with judgment, and always with ease and freedom of language'.[25]

Everyone is agreed on the openness that Doddridge exemplified, his lack of dogmatism in the Calvinism he espoused, and his profound tolerance for differing points of view, an openness that led to criticism from the more strictly orthodox. But Doddridge was also taken to task by great admirers, confident that they could trust in his candour. Thus Nathaniel Neal, a London attorney and close friend, welcomed the serious spirit of *The Rise and Progress*, but objected that it was more suitable to those of Calvinist views than to those who held to different principles, while its rules and prescriptions were impracticable for many busy people who were not the less pious for that: 'What is fit to be done by some persons, and in some special circumstances, may not be expected from the greater number of Christians; and care should be taken, that the heights of piety, to which some devout souls have soared, do not become matter of discouragement to young Christians, or those of an ordinary rank.' William Warburton, the noted defender of establishment, was candid on another count. Writing with respect to *Christ's Invitation to Thirsty Souls*, he argued that such weak and well-meaning rhapsodies

may do well enough with the people; but it is the learned that claim you. And though the intermixing with works of this cast *sober* books of devotion of your own composing, becomes your character, and is indeed your duty, yet your charity and love of goodness suffer you to let yourself down in the opinion of those you most value, and whose high opinion you have fairly gained by works of learning and reasoning inferior to none.[26]

Kippis, who had been Doddridge's pupil at Kibworth, prior to his settlement at Northampton, said that the sermons from that period pleased most of Doddridge's pupils more than the later, more Calvinist ones.[27] This remark and the concern that Doddridge clearly felt about

---

[25] Kippis, *Biographica Britannica* (fn. 21), p. xiv.   [26] *Ibid.*, pp. lviii–lx, lxvii.

[27] *Ibid.*, p. xv. It is worth noting that Doddridge's instruction to his pupils went far beyond his lectures, sermons and personal example. Orton (Doddridge, *Works*, vol. 1, p. 70) recalled his emphasis on pastoral responsibility: 'To qualify them for that part of their work, he not only gave them the best directions, but often took them with him, if the circumstances of the case and the family rendered it proper, when he went to baptise children, to visit persons under awakenings of conscience, religious impressions or spiritual distress; or those that were sick and dying; that they might see his manner of conversing and praying with them, and have their hearts improved by such affecting scenes. With the same view he introduced them to the acquaintance of some serious persons of his congregation. He thought a knowledge of their hidden worth and acquaintance with religion, and hearing their observations concerning the temper, character and labours of deceased ministers, would improve the minds of his pupils, and increase their esteem for the populace in general.'

his responsibility for, and his pupils' awareness of, the differences among the learned and ordinary, the reserved and the ingenuous parts of a Dissenting congregation, emphasise the bifurcated, tension-filled nature of his accomplishment.

Two works of controversy are particularly relevant here. One was Doddridge's response in 1742 to the younger Henry Dodwell, whose *Christianity Not Founded on Argument* was a deist tract masquerading as a work of faith. Doddridge, one of many drawn into the controversy, refutes Dodwell's contentions point for point, with particular attention to the importance of bringing up children in the right way, but very early in his argument he praises reason: 'Can any one indeed seriously think, that the noblest of our powers was intended only to the lowest and meanest purposes; to serve the little offices of mortal life, and not to be consulted in the greatest of concerns, those of immortality?'[28] The reconciliation and mutual reinforcement of faith and reason were the keystones in Doddridge's system of education and divinity, and if the kind of devotion of which Nathaniel Neal took so dim a view came to feature more prominently in Doddridge's later life, perhaps that is a phenomenon rather to be explained biographically and by an analysis of the congregations at Kibworth and Northampton than merely to be taken at face value as the true gauge of his importance. The second controversial work to be considered was another reply, this time to Strickland Gough, a young Dissenting minister who was soon to conform and who had published an explanation for the presumed decline in the Dissenting movement. Doddridge's *Free Thoughts on the Most Probable Means of Reviving the Dissenting Interest* (1730) inspires a wonderfully artful sentence from Michael Watts: 'Just as Gough's pamphlet foreshadows the eventual decline of Presbyterianism, so does that of Doddridge indicate the reason for the ultimate success of eighteenth-century Congregationalism.'[29] Watts is, I think, addressing the contrast between Gough's call for greater politeness, more attention to learning and closer approximation to the Church of England, and Doddridge's emphasis on practical religion, to which the vaunted spirit of liberty on which Dissenters prided themselves had to give way.

To be sure, Doddridge insisted that the strength of Dissent lay in that range of ordinary people distinguished by the seriousness of their religion and not at all by education, opportunity for study, refinement or

---

[28] *An Answer to a late Pamphlet, intitled, Christianity not founded on Argument...*, *Works*, vol. 1, pp. 467–590; the quotation is on p. 473.   [29] Watts, *Dissenters* (fn. 2), p. 384.

taste. Neglect them and they will become indifferent and irregular, go elsewhere or choose new ministers; show contempt for them, and we 'shall have the great pleasure of being entertained with the echo of our own voices, and the delicacy of our discourses, in empty places, or amidst a little circle of friends, till, perhaps, like some of our brethren, we are starved into a good opinion of conformity', and the cause will sink in ruin. Only in London might it be possible to divide Dissenting congregations into those catering to the 'bigotted and the generous'; elsewhere it would mean the death of even very large congregations. Certainly, as a pastor, he could not see himself abandoning nine-tenths of his flock. 'He who would be generally agreeable to dissenters, must be an evangelical, an experimental, a plain and affectionate preacher',[30] though a clever man might add a prudent measure of grace and beauty not only without damage but with genuine enhancement.

So far, Michael Watts's case for Doddridge as the prophet of nine-teenth-century Dissenting orthodoxy might seem established, but there is more to be said. Doddridge agreed with Gough that ministers must be masters of the classical languages and of English and accomplished in oratory; they must have 'genteel and complaisant behaviour' to make them acceptable to the superior ranks and even to the populace. But though Doddridge disclaimed 'clandestine and hypocritical methods' by which liberty was preached to undermine it, he saw a clandestine purpose in preaching an evangelical, experimental (i.e., experiential) faith. If bigotry follows from religious experience, then it must be seen as a fortress to be taken by sap, not storm, with the sapper's tools of elo-quence and style, to hold educated hearers while making the gospel message plain to the humbler members of the congregation:

When these exact people hear us preaching in a truly spiritual and experimental strain, and at the same time, in such a rational and graceful manner, as may set our discourses above contempt, and make them agreeable to the younger and politer part of our auditory, as well as to others; they will quickly see, that it is not for their own interest, or that of their children, to drive us away with a rigourous severity . . . And when they find, that they are handsomely treated by us, that no direct attack is made upon their darling notions; but that the great concerns of practical religion, as dear to them as to any people upon earth, are plainly and faithfully pursued by us . . . they will contract a tender, growing affection for us: And thus their bigotry will gradually wear away, till perhaps they come at last joyfully to embrace those more generous notions, from which they would at first have started back with horror.[31]

---

[30] *Free Thoughts*, pp. 213–19. [31] *Ibid.*, pp. 218–19.

With a prudent eye for congregational majorities and for the numbers that gave Dissent its standing in the nation, Doddridge offered a message of hope that the skilful minister might command all of his flock and, in time, by subtly calculated preaching, educate them. The language of we/they in that passage and the transparently superior stance plainly identify Doddridge with the liberal sentiments, the rationality and the piety of his heterodox students and of those who thought with them. No wonder that Warburton thought the anonymous pamphlet to be a work of genius and that, when he learned who its author was, could continue to claim Doddridge as, to borrow a Thatcherism, 'one of us'.

In Doddridge, then, there was a real, if increasingly unequal struggle between his Calvinism, moderate though it was, and his rationality, and between his rationality and his piety. But he had no doubt that rationality and piety could be, had to be, combined; a confidence shared by two or three generations of religious rationalists who continued to express their admiration for him, even as they found themselves driven to theological positions he would have found unacceptable.

After Doddridge's death in 1751, his academy was moved to Daventry, where the first student to enrol was Joseph Priestley, a young Yorkshireman of Calvinist stock. In the candid discussions at that institution, where all theological points of view were canvassed, Priestley became an Arian and then, after he had himself become an innovative teacher at Warrington Academy, he moved on in 1768 to Unitarianism, inspired by a work written more than thirty years before, but only just then published, by the great Dissenting scholar Nathaniel Lardner. In the heat of that new conviction, Priestley published a series of brilliant polemics intended to convert not only Arians, but Calvinists, Methodists, Anglicans and sceptics to his newly won theological position, and to persuade them as well to the philosophical necessarianism he had drawn from David Hartley. To a remarkable degree he was successful, at least in the 1780s, and at the same time, insisting on the grounds of principled Dissent, he moved more and more into the political radicalism that eventually led to his sufferings as a result of the Birmingham Riots of 1791 and to his exile to America three years later. But the high place that Priestley occupies in the history of the Unitarianism that supplanted a numerically weakened English Presbyterianism cannot be taken to exhaust rational religion or even Rational Dissent.

Later in this volume, John Seed quite rightly points to the distinctiveness of the Presbyterians within eighteenth-century Dissent and to the social impressiveness of those congregations identified with Rational Dissent (see Chapter 6). Though they had lost almost all their adherents among the aristocracy and gentry by the early eighteenth century, the Presbyterians were recruited from increasingly wealthy and imposing mercantile and professional levels in society. Far from the artisans and shopkeepers who appear to have made up the largest part of the Independents and Baptists, the Presbyterians and Rational Dissenters moved with increasing ease in respectable and even political society; indeed, Seed argues, far from being natural or even latent radicals, many of them were involved with the intimate workings of that society and even in its corruption. Yet he also notes their respect for their intellectual leaders and their firm adherence to certain theological positions as signs of a social cohesion that could become in its own way oppositional at least from the 1780s.[32] That evolving solidarity existed antiphonally with the similar solidarity evinced among a broader range of Christians with central obligations to, one might say, faith in reason.

Unitarianism was not the inevitable accompaniment to or result of Rational Dissent. To be sure, Anglicans, Congregationalists and Baptists who deserted their communions have played significant parts in the evolution of Unitarianism throughout its history as a denomination. After his departure from the Church following the failure to abolish subscription in 1772, Theophilus Lindsey founded the first openly Unitarian chapel in the country in 1774 – Unitarians were specifically excluded from the benefits of the Toleration Act until 1813 – and was succeeded in the pulpit by another renegade Anglican, John Disney; the Essex Street congregation numbered some highly impressive supporters, including the Duke of Grafton, former Prime Minister and Chancellor of Cambridge, who had recently avowed his heterodoxy. The Church of England provided other Unitarian recruits in the eighteenth century – the radical Cambridge Anglicans William Frend and Gilbert Wakefield were regarded, with some justice, as eccentric specimens – and fairly steadily thereafter, but the Church also served in about the same degree as a haven for disaffected Unitarians who, however, rarely forsook their rational beliefs in the transition.

Thomas Belsham, an Independent, dramatically resigned the principalship of Daventry Academy in 1789 and became the most important Unitarian theologian in the generation following Priestley's death in

---

[32] See Chapter 6 below and J. Seed, 'Gentlemen Dissenters: The Social and Political Meanings of Rational Dissent in the 1770s and 1780s', *Historical Journal*, 28 (1985), 299–325.

1804. The missionary and organisational work of the Unitarians early in the new century owed a vast debt to former Baptists, Robert Aspland, Richard Wright and Thomas Southwood Smith, the last an important theologian as well; while among the General Baptists, distinguished from the Particular Baptists since the early seventeenth century by an essentially Arminian position, the 'Old Connexion', which survived the departure of the 'New Connexion' in an evangelical schism in 1770, gradually merged with the Unitarians. But even in the heyday of evangelicalism, some Congregationalists and Baptists remained faithful to the middle way of tolerance and rationality, among them the great preachers Robert Robinson and Robert Hall and the celebrated essayist John Foster.[33] Men and women across a broad religious spectrum were united by a commitment to rationality and tolerance, by revulsion against Thomas Hobbes, the deists and David Hume, and by a strong religious and devotional instinct. The Rational Dissenters at the end of the eighteenth century can be properly understood only within this context.

In 1866, Anthony Trollope published a set of sketches called *The Clergymen of the Church of England*, the last chapter of which offers a composite portrait of the Broad Churchman. More numerous and more at home in London and in large towns, Trollope wrote, in the country the Broad Churchman was especially upsetting to the traditional clergyman who held to his creeds and articles and unshakeable Bible, ready with his answers because he did not think, while the Broad Churchman was not ready with his answers because he was always thinking of them.

Debonair though he be, and smile though he may, he has through it all some terrible heart-struggles . . . When he resolved that he must give that five pounds to the Colenso fund, – or rather when he resolved that he must have his name printed in the public list, for an anonymous giving of his money would have been nothing, – he knew that his rope was indeed cut, and that his boat was in truth upon the wide water.[34]

The subscribers to John Jebb's collected *Works* in 1787 were far more variously motivated than would be the case with those Victorians who

---

[33] There were limits: compare Robert Hall's eloquent defence of toleration with his strident attack on Theophilus Lindsey and Belsham's memoir of him, *The Works of Robert Hall. A.M. With a memoir of his life by Olinthus Gregory* . . ., 6 vols. (London, 1846; first publ. 1831–2), vol. VI, pp. 370–86, and vol. II, pp. 365–90. For another perspective, see William Enfield, *An Apology for the Clergy, and particularly for the Protestant Dissenting Ministers* . . . (Warrington, 1777), an ordination sermon in which he tells the ordinands that if their study ends in conviction about the 'system of our forefathers', i.e., Calvinism, they can expect indulgence, respect and candour, although adopting liberal views will bring approbation, countenance and support. But it is still evidence for the continuum, however undiscriminating.

[34] Anthony Trollope, *The Clergymen of the Church of England* (London, 1866), pp. 129–30.

cast in their lot with a South African bishop whose honest doubts led him into schism. Besides the expected family connections, there were Jebb's pupils and colleagues at Cambridge and some thirty-six physicians and surgeons representing the profession he joined after resigning from the University, following defeat of the campaigns against subscription and for university reform. At least forty present or future MPs (most, but not all, Whigs and radicals) gave in their names, along with sixty lawyers who presumably shared an admiration for Jebb's reforming politics, as, no doubt, did the forty-five clearly identifiable businessmen and manufacturers and the sprinkling of other professionals. A handful of peers of radical bent made their appearance, but the other laymen whom one can describe as gentlemen, again around fifty in number, seem to be drawn less from the traditional gentry than from merchant wealth of a generation earlier, thus confirming John Seed's characterisation of the Dissenting élite.[35]

What is most impressive for present purposes is the inclusion of nearly 150 clergymen (including dons and schoolmasters) of the Church of England, which Jebb had abandoned, most but not all of them from Cambridge and most in parochial rather than academic careers; a few present or future bishops were among their number. It can be assumed that, almost without exception, these Churchmen shared Jebb's rational Christianity, while stopping short, at least openly, of the Unitarianism to which he eventually came, and the same must be true of the laymen whose Anglicanism can be ascertained, though note should be taken of one clearly identified evangelical clergyman and of the presence of William Wilberforce's name two years after his conversion. The thirty-eight Dissenting ministers were predominantly Unitarian, but they included an Independent and five Arians; it is not possible to be so certain about the theological orientation of identifiable Dissenting laymen; Unitarianism appears to be proportionally dominant, however,

---

[35] From 605 subscribers, I have removed the libraries and book clubs, the handful of foreign admirers, and those entries that were anonymous or consisted only of initials or indistinguishable surnames. I have also omitted the names of dependants, mostly wives or mothers, leaving only one woman, Catherine Macaulay (Mrs Macaulay Graham), who could claim professional standing in her own right. For the remaining 534 names, I have identified the occupation or social status of 410, or about 77 per cent. I relied chiefly on the *Dictionary of National Biography*, the relevant volumes of the *History of Parliament*, the Oxford and Cambridge alumni lists compiled by Joseph Foster and John and J.A. Venn, and the *Gentleman's Magazine*. I consulted *Lowndes's London Directory* for 1786 but did not include identifications for those for whom certainty was elusive. For Dissenting ministers I relied on my own database of the Unitarian ministry, with some additional information from the Surman list in Dr Williams's Library. Compare the admirable analysis of subscribers to Doddridge's *Family Expositor* in Alan Everitt, 'Springs of Sensibility' (fn. 21).

while a few of the laymen can only be described as rationalists with no more than a nominal Christian gloss. This subscription list thus underlines my suggestion of a continuum of rational religion, in which Dissenters are numerically less significant than Churchmen, and in which Unitarians do not entirely exhaust Dissent.[36]

Had Jebb died five or ten years later, the list would probably have been much altered. The Unitarian category might have increased somewhat through the movement of Arians into Unitarianism and through the addition of some numbers of enlightened manufacturers to leaven the mercantile and banking dominance of 1787. But far more would have refused to subscribe because of the changed political climate. The outbreak of the French Revolution increased the hopes of some in radical and rational circles, and eventually, through frustration, brought a few to extreme positions, but among others the threat the Revolution seemed to pose in England led to defections from the reforming ranks, notably among loyal followers of the younger Pitt. Until further study has been done, however, we must remain content to note that such political shifts rarely involved dramatic religious reversals: Richard Watson, Regius Professor of Divinity at Cambridge and Bishop of Llandaff, might have declined to add his name, but he did not see that his opposition to Paine and his support for the war made him a turncoat, as others thought him, and he certainly did not abandon his rational Christianity. Indeed, in 1787, the subscribers to Jebb's *Works* almost certainly displayed a greater certainty and confidence than was to be found among the Broad Churchmen who subscribed to the Colenso fund eight decades later.

In the dark days of the war and for long thereafter, the Unitarians seemed almost the sole open defenders of the legacy from Rational Dissent.[37] What allies they had in other denominations were quietly so. By the end of the nineteenth century, however, with the terms of

---

[36] The subscribers who attended university numbered 200 Cambridge men and 24 from Oxford. The largest numbers at Cambridge, all in the thirties, came from St John's, Trinity, and Peterhouse, the last Jebb's own college and a hotbed of radicalism in those days. Christ's, Clare, Jesus and Queens' weigh in with upward of a dozen each, and the remainder are scattered among ten other colleges. In the occupational calculation, I have lumped barristers and attorneys together as lawyers, but of the subscribers who are identified with one of the Inns of Court, whether or not they practised, Lincoln's Inn is the dominant source, with thirty-one, compared to thirteen each from the Inner Temple and the Middle Temple, and nine from Gray's Inn. On all this, Gascoigne, *Cambridge in the Age of Enlightenment* is enlightening. Note his perception of a spectrum of religious opinion in mid-century, p. 140.

[37] See the over-arch but still remarkable assertion that Unitarians were the sole claimants to the distinction of 'Rational Dissent' in a communication signed W.J., 'Remarks on the Appellation of "Rational Dissenters"', *Monthly Repository*, 2 (1807), 570–5.

debate sharply altered, liberal religion began to emerge once more into prominence, sometimes to the benefit of Unitarians, sometimes not, and in the twentieth century began to press on or to cross boundaries of faith that were mostly unbridgeable for eighteenth-century latitudinarians. The writing of history has, however, dealt less kindly with the Rational Dissenters than did history itself.

In the work of older historians, drawn from the orthodox ranks and embittered by later quarrels, the tone at times verges on hysteria. We can accordingly discount it, though one must feel something stronger than regret for its atavistic re-emergence in a writer like Donald Davie in our own time. But, despite decades of revisionism, even sober and perceptive modern historians have lapsed, with a curious automatism, into the old arguments and rhetoric. In his temperate and balanced discussion of the early eighteenth century, Michael Watts tends to judge the rationalists out of the mouths of their critics. Even Norman Sykes, who more than anyone helped to rescue the eighteenth-century Church from its Victorian detractors, could not resist describing the transition of Presbyterian congregations to Unitarianism as a 'decline', the same language that is found extensively in the pages of J.C.D. Clark, who sees the Rational Dissenters as the most important enemies of a confessional state.[38] By the same token, Unitarian historians have been swift to claim an entire tradition as source and justification for their own theological and denominational position. It is to correcting such usually unconscious biases that the essays in this book are directed, not as special pleading but as a fresh look at what Rational Dissent was and how it functioned.

[38] The best instance of early denunciation is David Bogue and James Bennet, *History of Dissenters from the Revolution of 1689 to the Year 1808*, 3 vols. (London, 1809). Donald Davie combines admirable intention and much insight with an astounding display of prejudice in *A Gathered Church: The Literature of the Dissenting Interest, 1700–1930* (New York, 1978), especially in the notes. Watts, *Dissenters* (fn. 2), pp. 392–3. N. Sykes, *From Sheldon to Secker: Aspects of English Church History, 1660–1768* (Cambridge, 1959), p. 103. Clark, *English Society* (fn. 12), pp. 307–24, 330–46. See also A.D. Gilbert, *Religion and Society in Industrial England: Church, Chapel, and Social Change, 1740–1914* (London, 1976), pp. 36–7 and 40–1

CHAPTER 3

Rational Dissent in early eighteenth-century Ireland

M.A. Stewart

I

The Reformation was as much a rejection of the temporal as of the spiritual authority of the papacy, and it succeeded only in those countries where the ruling power could carry with it enough of the population to ensure the continuance of stable and efficient administration. In Ireland, there had been no such ruling power. The English monarchy had from time to time, since the reign of Henry II, exerted some authority within the Pale, the short coastal tract north and south of Dublin which extended inland for about twenty miles; but most of the country remained in the hands of regional clan lords till the Flight of the Earls in 1607. Henry VIII had been pronounced head of the Church in Ireland as well as in England and Wales; but only in the reign of Elizabeth was there any sort of concerted attempt to enforce the Reformation. It was too little, too late, and it took second place to securing political control over a relatively backward and in places lawless population. A Protestant episcopal administration succeeded to the properties and dwindling wealth of the outlawed Catholic Church, but their first clergy were uncertain converts and the active membership never extended far beyond the ranks of the new immigrants who represented an alien, and frequently token, government.[1] They remained chronically short of committed clergy, and most of those they had did not possess the language to communicate with the native congregations. Buildings went to ruin. Absenteeism was rife. Benefices were combined to an impracticable

Research for this essay was supported by a grant from the British Academy. The writing was completed while I held a visiting fellowship in the History of Ideas Program, Australian National University.

[1] A judicious account of the failure of the Reformation in Ireland is provided by P.J. Corish, *The Irish Catholic Experience: A Historical Survey* (Dublin, 1985), ch. 3.

degree, and the incumbents eked out a living from dubious and unpopular tithes.

This situation was complicated, from the early seventeenth century, by the arrival in Ulster of growing numbers of Scots settlers who were mostly of a different Protestant persuasion. The first may have been fugitives from justice, or from the relative over-population of southern Scotland, taking advantage of the availability of cleared lands after the subjugation of the Catholic clans. But they were increasingly followed by religious refugees, as the monarchy put pressure on Scots Presbyterians to return to episcopacy. In the early 1640s, the posting of a Scottish Covenanting army to Ireland to help preserve the Protestant interest put an end to what had been a marriage of convenience between episcopacy and presbytery in the north, and established what was effectively a Presbyterian hegemony there.

It is the successors of this Scots population who are normally identified as 'Dissenters' in the Irish context, together with a smaller representation of English Dissenters, Presbyterians among them, primarily in the south. The northern Dissenters fell foul of episcopacy as soon as Laudian ceremonial started to be implemented in Ireland; and within a few years fell foul equally of Cromwell's toleration policy, which admitted all peaceful forms of Christian practice except 'Popery or Prelacy' and forbade the use of penalties to extort public professions of faith.[2] This 'Universall Toleration of all Religions' (which it was not) was something the presbytery at Belfast had already previously denounced as 'directly subverting our Covenant, Religion, Lawes and Liberties' and as conducive to 'damnable errors, under the specious pretence of a Gospel-way, and new Light'.[3]

In fact Presbyterians were, on the whole, royalist at heart, particularly since the future Charles II, as a young prince at the end of the Civil War, had prudently subscribed the Covenant before going into exile. In the Declaration from Breda before his return, he had promised 'a liberty to tender consciences, and that no man shall be disquieted or called in question for differences of opinion in matter of religion which do not disturb the peace of the kingdom'.[4] The Dissenters were therefore bitterly disappointed when the restoration of the monarchy

---

[2] *Instrument of Government* (London, 1653), articles 36–7.
[3] 'A Necessary Representation' (1649), reprinted in *Complete Prose Works of John Milton*, 8 vols. (New Haven, 1953–82), vol. III, pp. 296–9. The 'Representation' met with a contemptuous and vitriolic response from Milton.
[4] D.C. Douglas [*et al.*], eds., *English Historical Documents*, 12 vols. (London 1953–77), vol. VIII, p. 58.

re-established episcopacy without the option and, from time to time, they followed the Irish Catholics into a semi-clandestine mode of existence. The King, nevertheless, in 1672 – at a time when he was declaring an Indulgence in England – awarded an annual grant (*regium donum*) towards the stipend of the Dissenting ministers of Ulster.

With the accession of William and Mary, the grant was increased; Presbyterianism was restored to their mother church in Scotland; foreign (i.e. French) Protestants in Ireland were accorded full religious liberty; and in England, Dissenters were granted a legal toleration. This emboldened the Irish Dissenters to push their luck to the limit in the face of a disorganised establishment, for which they suffered afresh under Queen Anne. An Act of the Irish Parliament in 1704 for the suppression – as ever – of 'Popery' was returned from England with a revision excluding from public office all, not just Catholics, who failed to take the sacrament according to the ceremony of the Church of Ireland, and the Dissenters found themselves trapped.[5]

This essay is a study of certain intellectual trends in Irish Presbyterianism from the orthodoxy of the 1690s to sectional heterodoxy in the 1720s. To ecclesiastical historians it marks the rise of a movement that culminates in what is called the 'first subscription controversy' – there were three altogether, over a period of a century and a quarter. The controversy was over whether Presbyterian ministers must be bound, and publicly agree to be bound, by the terms of the Westminster Confession of Faith.[6] The Confession had been the product of an assembly of Puritan divines convened by the English Parliament in the early 1640s, but in course of time it became best known through its adoption by the Church of Scotland. It started to figure in Irish Presbyterian debate with a new Scottish influx after 1690, but only took firm hold in the north as a reaction to the heresy trial of Thomas Emlyn in Dublin in 1703. Those who demurred were eventually herded into a separate presbyterial splinter-group. But the subscription controversy had another and less insular impact: it spilt over

---

[5] 2 Anne c. 6 (Ireland). It should be kept in mind that Presbyterians themselves participated in the power politics of which they were now the victims. They had cheerfully appropriated Church of Ireland parishes when episcopacy was abolished in the 1650s, but 'had so little principle that they joined with their enemies to persecute the Baptists in 1660 and the Roman Catholics in 1704. It is not, therefore, to be wondered at that they persecuted their own brethren later on, and even invoked the help of the bishops to do so' (J. Campbell, *Short History of the Non-subscribing Presbyterian Church of Ireland* (Belfast, 1914), p. 43).

[6] A recent analysis is provided by A.W.G. Brown, 'A Theological Interpretation of the First Subscription Controversy', in J.L.M. Haire *et al.*, *Challenge and Conflict* (Antrim, 1981), pp. 28–45.

to the Scottish universities, contributing to the climate of moderation which we associate with the rise of Francis Hutcheson and his allies. That the beneficiaries of toleration in Cromwellian times had already been typecast as *new light* was prophetic: 'new light' became the catch-phrase of both critics and supporters in the distinctive interplay between religion and philosophy among the Irish Dissenters in the early eighteenth century.[7]

II

Born in 1694, Hutcheson grew up in an Irish manse during the reign of Anne. As a Dissenter, he was debarred from both Irish and English universities, and was educated at the Presbyterian academy at Killyleagh, an institution whose existence was a source of irritation to the Anglican hierarchy. The instruction was in Latin and involved some sort of reformed scholastic curriculum in logic, metaphysics, and moral philosophy.[8] Those who wanted to proceed to final-year studies in natural philosophy could cross to Glasgow if they needed a degree for professional purposes. Hutcheson did this but took an extra year to study language and literature before graduating. It was at Glasgow, he later recalled, that he discovered the pleasures of classical poetry, and read the works of Cicero which were the inspiration for much of his later philosophy; it was there that he mastered natural theology and 'the nature and basis of virtue'.[9]

After continuing on to the Divinity School, Hutcheson returned to Ireland in 1718 and qualified for the ministry, but never took up a charge. In the wake of the Irish Toleration Act of 1719, he accepted an invitation to set up a Dissenters' academy in Dublin. There is enough evidence in correspondence that the majority of ministers in Dublin had new-light sympathies at this time to suggest that the academy which Hutcheson

---

[7] John Malcome revived the term in his pamphlet against John Abernethy, *Personal Persuasion no Foundation for Religious Obedience* (Belfast, 1720). But in a later tract, *The Dangerous Principles of the Sectaries of the Last Age, Revived Again by our Modern New-Lights* (Belfast, 1726), he traced its origin to the seven Dissenting divines, led by Thomas Goodwin, who rejected the propositions on Church government and discipline (chiefly the clause on excommunication) subscribed by the majority of the Westminster Assembly. The phrase occurs twice in John Milton's *Areopagitica* (London, 1644).

[8] A search for student notebooks that were still in circulation earlier this century has so far been unavailing. See M.A. Stewart, 'Abating Bigotry and Hot Zeal', suppt. to *Fortnight*, 308 (1992), 4–6.

[9] Francis Hutcheson, *De Naturali Hominum Socialitate Oratio Inauguralis* (Glasgoviae, 1730), pp. 1–2. Cf. *On Human Nature*, ed. T. Mautner (Cambridge, 1993), p. 125.

was invited to take charge of was intended to be a new-light founda-tion.[10] He taught there for nearly ten years, publishing the works that established his philosophical reputation as a proponent of the Moral Sense tradition.

The orthodox view is that Hutcheson and his generation had picked up dangerously liberal ideas in Scotland and brought them back to con-taminate the faith of the settlers in Ireland.[11] This picture is too one-sided, too dependent on unstable evidence about the quality of the theological training in Glasgow.[12] Irish students did not have to go to Glasgow rather than another Scottish university, and the Irish Dissenters constituted too close-knit a community for it to be plausible to think that a predominantly conservative body of parents should send their offspring over to Scotland, year after year, in total innocence of what would befall them: the presumption must be that at least some came to Glasgow because they knew and wanted what Glasgow could offer. In fact, the movement of ideas is as much a movement from Ireland to Scotland, and its roots lie in the civil disabilities of the Irish Dissenters.

Hutcheson was one of the first of a generation of Irish students who were active in university politics at Glasgow over a period of ten or more years from 1717.[13] Not all the leaders were Irish: in the mid 1720s, one was a nephew of the Duke of Argyll, exploiting the chance to be trouble-some to his uncle's opponents. But it is a period that, significantly, begins towards the end of Hutcheson's student career. It closes with his return from Ireland in 1730 to succeed to the chair of moral philosophy

---

[10] Joseph Boyse (Dublin) to Thomas Steward (formerly of Dublin), c.1725: 'I had lately a free private Conversation with our Lord Chancellor about the Arrears of Regium Donum. He took occasion to enquire about the Distinction of Old & New-light which he had heard mention'd by the Lawyers in a Case before him . . . [He] talk'd wholly on the New-light side, in which you may be sure he met with no Contradiction from me. He inlarg'd on these Topics with a good strain of clear Reasoning, & is no Freind to exorbitant Claims of Church-Power in any Ecclesiastical Synods whatsoever.' (Magee College Library, MS. 46, item 18.) Hutcheson was another of Steward's correspondents (*ibid.*, item 73), and Alexander Gordon, writing in the *Dictionary of National Biography*, had evidence, now lost, that Boyse was Hutcheson's first colleague in his academy.

[11] See W.D. Killen's third volume added to J.S. Reid, *History of the Presbyterian Church in Ireland*, new edn. (Belfast, 1867), pp. 294–300.

[12] The divinity professor, John Simson, may have shown Arminian tendencies, but his main offence was to encourage open discussion. A contemporary source criticises the influence of the rhetoric of the Irish nonsubscribers on Simson, rather than his influence on them: [Allan Logan], *An Enquiry into Professor Simson's Sentiments on the Doctrine of the Trinity* (Edinburgh, 1729), p. 42.

[13] M.A. Stewart, 'John Smith and the Molesworth Circle', *Eighteenth-Century Ireland*, 2 (1987), 89–102; 'Academic Freedom: Origins of an Idea', *Bulletin of the Australian Society of Legal Philosophy*, 16 (57) (1991/2), 1–31.

at Glasgow and to develop the liberal political teaching that is characteristic of his later writings.[14] In the course of the unrest two Irish divinity students were expelled: one became Hutcheson's Dublin publisher and the other had been one of his own former students.

The clarion call of the young radicals was 'Liberty' and, obviously, one did not have to be Irish to believe in that. It was commonplace to construe both political and religious victories as restoring a desirable liberty to the winning side – a liberty from whatever threat was posed by the other side. So the Reformation brought liberty from idolatry, foreign power, etc., and every small-scale re-enactment of the Reformation (the accessions of Elizabeth, William and Mary, George I) was heralded as the restoration of this precarious commodity. But many of those who extolled 'liberty *from*' had relatively little to offer in the way of 'liberty *to*'. For many believers, the path of salvation was narrow, and they frequently sought as much conformity to alternative practices and beliefs as those they had ousted. The Irish students were not of this cast.

The universities still had some legal basis for keeping alive the mediæval notion that they were political societies in miniature, with their own internal forms of civil and ecclesiastical management. This was exploited on more than one occasion in the early eighteenth century when some of the faculty at Glasgow galvanised student support to try to override the autocracy of the Principal and the political appointees who worked with him. As part of the political defences of the period, the classics of early liberal thought like the works of Grotius and Locke were already a staple of the curriculum.[15] In 1716–17, the rebel faculty tried to change the balance of power by urging the students to reclaim their statutory right to elect their own magistrate, the Rector. Gershom Carmichael, the Regent who that year had charge of the logic class, took the leading part in organising the election, and was still remembered five years later for his 'noble Harrangue' to the students 'in one of the publick Halls in Praise of Liberty'.[16] William Forbes, the Professor of

---

[14] Within two years of Hutcheson's returning to Glasgow, James Kirkpatrick, the leading nonsubscribing minister in Belfast, was examined for and awarded two doctorates (Glasgow University Archives, 21320).

[15] A student versifier, James Arbuckle from Belfast, recorded the academic routine, 'In which sad Game their Heads they knock / On Grotius, Pufendorf, or Locke' ('Epistle to Mr Thomas Griffith of Rhual', part of the Arbuckle MS collection in the National Library of Wales, MS PR4116.A47).

[16] [John Smith], *A Short Account of the Late Treatment of the Students of the University of G---w* (Dublin, 1722), p. 10. Earlier in 1716 Carmichael had unsuccessfully lobbied members of the same political management for one of the vacant posts in Aberdeen: R.L. Emerson, *Professors, Patronage and Politics* (Aberdeen, 1992), p. 36.

Civil Law, wrote to the ousted Rector in similar terms: 'we found ourselves under an indispensible necessity to cross a groundless despotick power intollerable to any free agent who hath the least sense of liberty & property'.[17]

A hastily created Royal Commission, dominated by the University's political managers, banned the students from any further elections, but the rebel staff secured lawyers able and willing to draw up defences for the student side. These defences typically revolved round four points: the students' right to elect their governing magistrate was embodied in statutory instruments which had been confirmed by every successive monarch; the warrant which had set up the new commission carried no authority to overturn pre-existing law and could therefore constitute no justification for any act which violated that law; the legality or otherwise of the Rector's appointment was necessarily bound up with the legality or otherwise of any discipline the University could continue to exercise over the students; and 'no Authority, under that of the King and Parliament, can by Law communicate Power to Alter or subvert private Rights'.[18]

When, in late 1717, the administration pushed through a new election without the participation of the students – or, indeed, of half the faculty – the students initiated legal action. A committee of nine, six divinity students and three undergraduates, spent three days collecting signatures and took the University to court; two of their number stayed in Edinburgh over the winter with financial assistance from both staff and students to see the litigation through. Francis Hutcheson was one of the nine and another Irishman, Peter Butler from Waterford, one of the two: he later became a Dublin minister.

The court decided that the University had a case to answer and called for their constitutional papers. The two litigants now found themselves barred, on grounds of unwarranted absence, from readmission to the Divinity School: a notarised record of this further confrontation survives, with Hutcheson as one of four witnesses.[19] The court's assistance had to be sought a second time. The students had seen 'their Rights invaded', and 'knew that the Laws of their Country afforded them Relief'.[20] On the insistence of the court, they were reinstated, but the dispute simmered for several years.

---

[17] Glasgow University Archives, MS 47415.

[18] *Memorial for the Scholars and Other Matriculated Members of the University of Glasgow*, 21 December 1717.

[19] Scottish Record Office, Court of Session papers, CS228/B1/114.

[20] *The Petition and Complaint of Mr. Peter Butler, and John Edmonston, Students of Divinity, and Matriculated Members of the University of Glasgow.* Duncan Forbes, advocate, 20 February 1718.

It flared again in 1722, when news filtered out that the student body at large was supporting a petition to Parliament on the issue of the rectorship. Lord Molesworth, an Anglo-Irish opposition politician, had published a controversial tract in the 1690s, in which he contrasted the ideals of the revolution in England with an alleged political and ecclesiastical tyranny in Denmark, and this had led to a lifelong friendship with the Earl of Shaftesbury. He became a rallying point for the disenchanted minority of Whig supporters for whom the 1688 revolution had gone sour. His reputation was one of hostility to the government in power and to clerical influence in education. He had also written forcefully on the defects of the traditional curriculum and on the need to instil well-informed political understanding and social values.[21] His friendship with Shaftesbury, and with other radical intellectuals like Toland and Collins, identified him with the deists and freethinkers. On both political and religious fronts, therefore, his support for the Glasgow students is likely to have been perceived as a threat to discipline.

Molesworth lost his British parliamentary seat in the election of 1722 and retired to Dublin. But, before the loss was confirmed, some of the Glasgow students had received a false report of his re-election and, with sympathetic townsfolk, organised a commemorative bonfire outside the college bounds. John Smith, a divinity student from Belfast, was expelled for his role in the proceedings, and, like the other divinity students a few years earlier, took the University to court. The University lost the argument wherever they tried to engage with it, but wasted the court's time until the summer recess. Smith then turned from legal to literary recourse, moving to Dublin and the protection of Lord Molesworth, and published a lively pamphlet on the case.[22] This goes beyond the immediate defence of the bonfire into the whole underlying controversy about the rectorship and into broad issues of jurisprudence. Smith identifies a

---

[21] [Robert Molesworth], *An Account of Denmark, as it was in the Year 1692* (London, 1694); the title of this attack on the Protestant administration of Denmark may have been modelled on Pierre Bayle's *Ce que c'est que la France toute catholique, sous le règne de Louis le grand* (S. Omer, 1686). See also Molesworth's preface to the second edition of his translation of F. Hotoman, *Franco-Gallia* (London, 1721). Molesworth supported the radical journalism of Trenchard and Gordon in *The Independent Whig* and *The London Journal*, in which he was widely but wrongly thought to be personally involved. His attack on Denmark was echoed by the Belfast Dissenter, John MacBride, in the preface to his *Animadversions* on the toleration debate in 1697. Like Milton, MacBride rejected the argument that toleration encouraged sectarianism and civil tumults: the true schismatics are those whose unjustified opinions and practices provoke others to dissent. In those Lutheran countries where Dissent had been outlawed, there was as offensive an inquisition as in Catholic Spain.

[22] On Smith's authorship of *A Short Account*, see Stewart, 'John Smith and the Molesworth Circle' (fn. 13).

'happy Resemblance between the Academick and National Constitutions' and appeals to 'A Right that seems not less well founded in natural Justice, than positive Laws. For who is so fit to choose their Governours as those who are to feel the greatest Consequence of the Choice, be they Good or Bad?'

Smith was particularly scathing on the conduct of his former teacher, Carmichael, who had by now switched his loyalties to the University side as a result of favours shown to his family. Having got into a scuffle with Carmichael over the bonfire, Smith had been hauled before a tribunal where Carmichael was witness, juryman and secretary all in one.

> Where the Fundamental Rights of such a Society are violated, and those that oppose such Encroachments sacrificed to the Arbitrary Power they resist, by being punished without Proof, and in the most illegal Manner, for Things contrary to no Law; we need not wonder, that to carry on such projects, the Cause of Learning should be neglected, and ignorant Masters brought in, to Strengthen the Hands of the P[rincipa]l. And certainly if some Measures be not fallen upon in Time, to rectifie these great Abuses, the University must sink under them; since it cannot be supposed, that People will be fond of sending their Children to an Academy, where the Love of Liberty, the first Opening of an honest and generous Spirit, will be sure to be suppressed, and their Minds rendered callous, and insensible of those Motions that stir Men up to the Service of their Country, and Mankind (*A Short Account*, p. 40).

This linking of liberty with patriotism and virtue aligns Smith with Molesworth and his Scottish admirers. He compares the students' role in their *comitia academica* with that of the third estate of the 'Old *Gothick* Rule' idealised by Molesworth,[23] and claims the same rights to have a part in the consultative process. This did not impress the new University Rector, Robert Dundas, the Lord Advocate, who took personal charge of the University's unsuccessful defence, and argued that it was no business of students to be interested in public affairs at all. Any who indulged such an interest to the extent of kindling bonfires at will were setting an example that must plainly be 'dangerous to his Majesty's Person and Government'.[24]

It was the Irish dimension to the case that caused the Advocate particular concern. 'Mr *Smith* is an *Irishman*; and if he, and his *Irish* Brethren take the Liberty to put on Bonefires when they think fit, others may do it upon very unlawful Occasions' (p. 35). Either the student agitators had portrayed the University, or the University was paranoid enough to

---

[23] On this 'Harringtonian interpretation of the ancient constitution', see J.G.A. Pocock, *Politics, Language and Time* (New York, 1971), ch. 4.   [24] Quoted in *A Short Account*, p. 33.

believe it was being portrayed, in the same opprobrious light as the episcopalian regime in Ireland.[25] Smith himself identifies some of the underlying worries as doctrinal. The rebels were perceived as 'a Set of Latitudinarians, Free-thinkers, Non-subscribers, and Bangorians, and in a Word, Enemies to the Jurisdictions, Powers, and Divine Authority of the Clergy' (p. 21). And this brings us to the nub of the issue.

III

When Hutcheson had returned to Ireland in 1718 at the conclusion of his own studies, he had been surprised to find what he called 'a perfect Hoadly mania among our younger ministers in the north',[26] a craze, that is, for the strenuously anti-authoritarian principles of Benjamin Hoadly, then Bishop of Bangor, and subsequently in quick succession Bishop of Hereford, Salisbury and Winchester. Hoadly's sermon on *The Nature of the Kingdom, or Church, of Christ,* preached before the King in March 1717, on the text 'My kingdom is not of this world', had caused a national storm. It went through fifteen London editions in one year, and sundry editions in other cities, including Dublin. Coming within days of a parliamentary debate on the penal laws against the Dissenters, it was quickly construed as supporting their cause. Hoadly at the beginning of his career had taken the conventional latitudinarian line about the desirability of embracing all reasonable views within a comprehensive Church of England, but by 1717 he seemed to his critics to have left that Church with very little constitutional leg to stand on, having effectively challenged the basis of all ecclesiastical forms and judicatures.[27]

To an argument loosely modelled on Locke's on toleration, Hoadly added a semantic theory which masks a series of persuasive definitions. He produced a fusion of Locke's account of the signification and abuse of words with his view of the degeneration of propositional information transmitted through time.[28] 'The Signification of a Word,' Hoadly had written,

---

[25] Their paranoia is plainest in the attempt to stifle two plays which were elsewhere recognised as symbols of loyalty to the Williamite Revolution – Addison's *Cato* and Rowe's *Tamerlane.*

[26] Hutcheson to William Wright, September 1718, cited by Wright in a letter to Wodrow, *The Correspondence of Robert Wodrow,* ed. T. M'Crie, 3 vols. (Edinburgh, 1842–3), vol. II, p. 389 (cf. p. 365). It is worth noting that in the mid 1720s Hoadly took over Molesworth's role as a patron of the rebellious Glasgow students. See R. Wodrow, *Analecta,* 4 vols. (Edinburgh, 1842–3), vol. III, p. 248.

[27] However, in a reply to Andrew Snape, one of the King's chaplains, Hoadly claimed that he had been condemning the authoritarian structures of the Church of Rome, thereby implicitly vindicating the Church of England.

[28] John Locke, *An Essay concerning Human Understanding,* III. ix–xi; IV. xvi. 10.

well known and understood by Those who first made use of it, is very insensibly varied, by passing thro many Mouths, and by being taken and given by Multitudes, in common Discourse; till it often comes to stand for a Complication of Notions, as distant from the original Intention of it, nay, as contradictory to it, as Darkness is to Light.[29]

This reversal of the designated signification of words is an 'Evil', attributable to the 'Ignorance and Weakness of Some, and the Passions and Bad Designs of Others'. The only cure for it is

to have recourse to the Originals of Things: to the Law of Reason, in those Points which can be traced back thither; and to the Declarations of *Jesus Christ*, and his immediate Followers, in such Matters, as took their Rise solely from those Declarations. (p. 4)

This slightly surprising advice, adapted from the distinction between *truths* demonstrable by reason and those above but not contrary to reason, is applied to the term 'religion', which 'in St *James*'s Days, was Virtue and Integrity, as to our selves, and Charity and Beneficence to others'. But

By Degrees, it is come to signify, in most Countries throughout the whole World, the Performance of every thing almost, except Virtue and Charity; and particularly, a punctual Exactness in a Regard to particular *Times*, *Places*, *Forms*, and *Modes*, diversified according to the various Humours of Men. (p. 5)

Again, 'the Worship of God', which once meant 'the Worship of the Father *in Spirit and Truth*', has come to represent

the Neglect, and the Diminution of the Father; and the Worship of other Beings besides, and more than, the *Father*. And this, performed in such a manner, as that any *indifferent Spectator* would conclude, that neither the Consciences nor Understandings of Men, neither *Spirit* nor *Truth* were at all concerned in the Matter. (p. 7)

Similarly, prayer and love have been transformed from what they were in New Testament times into forms of ecstasy and enthusiasm quite alien to the original conceptions.

All this is building up to an account of the original conception of the 'kingdom' of Christ. For Hoadly, Christ as head is the sole authority in the Church, a kingdom not of this world. Those who have set up as his vicegerents and interpreters, with their own subordinate systems of reward and punishment, have done no more than create a rival kingdom of men, in which they have usurped the authentic legislator's role.

---

[29] Benjamin Hoadly, *The Nature of the Kingdom, or Church, of Christ* (London, 1717), p. 3.

So it is, whenever They erect *Tribunals*, and exercise a *Judgment* over the Consciences of Men; and assume to Themselves the Determination of such Points, as cannot be determined, but by *One* who knows the Hearts; or, when They make any of their own Declarations, or Decisions, to concern and affect the State of Christ's Subjects, with regard to the Favour of God: this is so far, the taking *Christ's Kingdom* out of *His* Hands, and placing it in their own. (p. 14)

But in that kingdom where Christ alone is both lawgiver and judge, all are equal subjects, and

No One of them, any more than Another, hath *Authority*, either to make *New Laws* for *Christ's* Subjects; or to impose a sense upon the *Old* Ones, which is the same thing; or to *Judge*, Censure, or Punish, the Servants of *Another Master*, in matters relating purely to *Conscience*, or *Salvation*. (p. 16)

If it is a kingdom not of this world, its honours and punishments are not of this world either, and those that are have nothing to do with religion. Christ enjoined

No Rules against the Enquiry of All His Subjects into his *Original Message* from Heaven; no Orders for the kind and charitable force of *Penalties*, or *Capital Punishments*, to make Men think and chuse aright; no Calling upon the *secular Arm*, whenever the *Magistrate* should become *Christian*, to inforce his Doctrines, or to back his *Spiritual Authority*. (pp. 22–3)

As a corollary of this, Hoadly rejects the idea that any human authority can legitimately require a uniformity of religious profession. This would 'found the *Authority* of the Church of *Christ*, upon the ruins of Sincerity and Common Honesty; and mistake *Stupidity* and *Sleep*, for *Peace*' (p. 29).

It was not just a formality that Hoadly's sermon, critical as it was of all use of temporal power for spiritual regimentation, was 'Publish'd by His MAJESTY'S Special Command'. George I took a personal interest in the rights of Dissenters, not least in Ireland. He tried hard, through the Lord Lieutenant, to secure a more liberal Toleration Act in 1719 than the narrowly Anglican Irish Parliament was prepared to countenance. In 1722, when the Swiss Protestants were as divided as the Irish over confessions and catechisms, he wrote them a public letter pleading for reconciliation, and this circulated as a broadsheet in Ireland.[30]

So what was the significance of Hoadly for the North of Ireland? He might have been read – as he was certainly capable of being read – as criticising the political enforcement of Anglican ceremonial and of subscription to the Thirty-Nine Articles. Hutcheson, in the comment

---

[30] Public Record Office, State Papers (Ireland), S.P. 63/377, esp. fols. 214–21; National Library of Scotland, Wodrow Letters Quarto, vol. 20, no. 161.

previously cited, was puzzled that his colleagues should preach 'as if their hearers were all absolute princes going to impose tests and confessions in their several territories', that is, as if their targets were the government.

However, there were other ways of reading Hoadly. The immediate cause of excitement had been the refusal of one of the prominent northern ministers, John Abernethy of Antrim, to be moved to Dublin against his own and his congregation's wishes.[31] This was an unprecedented challenge to the authority of the General Synod, and fuelled dissension just as the Dissenters were trying to lobby for more favourable legislation. Abernethy was leader of a ginger group known as the Belfast Society, whose liberal tendencies were currently under suspicion. If Hoadly's principles freed them from subscription to the Thirty-Nine Articles, where did they stand on their own Confession of Faith? For if subscription to formularies can only be voluntary, the Westminster Confession might be no more secure than the Anglican Articles.

In fact those who subscribed to the one would find a good deal of common ground doctrinally in the other, and the orthodox on each side would claim that their respective documents were no more than codifications of biblical teaching and practice. Their opponents contended that, if this was so, then the various formularies were redundant and the Bible should be their sole tribunal. A competition ensued as to who was the most authentically biblical, the Anglicans or the Dissenters, and among the Dissenters, those who accepted or those who discounted the Westminster formularies. Opposition to the Confession as a formal institution, widespread in England, was growing among some of the Irish ministers, in line with parallel movements in Switzerland and the Netherlands and in proportion to their knowledge of the latest developments in biblical criticism; and there were real fears that a rejection of 'subscription' would lead inevitably to the dilution of doctrine.[32]

This underlying theological agenda was recognised by friends of the Glasgow students elsewhere in Scotland, who were also in touch with Molesworth. George Turnbull, newly appointed Regent at Aberdeen and the tutor of Thomas Reid, looked forward to the day when the

---

[31] *Records of the General Synod of Ulster, from 1691 to 1820*, 3 vols. (Belfast, 1890–98), vol. i, pp. 427–30, 458–64, 471–2, 476–7, 488–94, 496, 505–6, 532–3.
[32] M.A. Stewart and J. Moore, 'William Smith (1698–1741) and the Dissenters' Book Trade', *Bulletin of the Presbyterian Historical Society of Ireland*, 22 (1993), pp. 20–7.

philosophers would revive the tradition of the ancients and again teach civic virtue as the cornerstone of a university education. But how can this be, he asked,

> while our Colleges are under the Inspection of proud domineering pedantic Priests whose interest it is to train up the youth in a profound veneration to their Senseless metaphysical Creeds & Catechisms, which for this purpose they are daily inured to defend against all Doubters & Enquirers with the greatest bitteness & contempt, in a stiff formal bewildering manner admirably fitted indeed to Enslave young understandings betimes and to beget an early antipathy against all Free thought.[33]

As is usual in such circumstances, when traditional formularies are under rational scrutiny, it was orthodox believers in the Trinity who were the first to look to their defences. Through what may or may not have been a drafting accident, the Irish Toleration Act of 1719 did not require explicit assent to the doctrine of the Trinity as did the corresponding English legislation. It required only that no one publicly impugn it.[34] But there is in fact little evidence that this doctrine was high on the agenda in the early years of the nonsubscription movement in Ireland, though Whiston and Clarke had their admirers and a number of ministers would have been Arian in their tendencies.[35]

It was the bleaker side of Calvinism that was at risk. The 'new light' intellectuals preached and not merely sought toleration, and showed an antipathy to any dogmatic theological stance that could be socially divisive. They developed a humane ethic founded more in natural law than in the decalogue, and soft-pedalled on a certain amount of traditional redemption theology. Central to the new-light philosophy is a more optimistic view of human nature than is found in orthodox Calvinism, a view that mankind is amenable to reason and at heart motivated by benevolence and humanity. Others had already found a biblical basis for such a philosophy, but Hutcheson and his generation drew also on secular writers, notably Shaftesbury. The religion they believed in was the religion, as they perceived it, of the gospels, and they looked back on the Westminster Assembly in the same way as they looked back on the early Councils of the Church: episodes of a particular epoch which were not to be mistaken for the permanent message and living tradition of the Christian Church.

---

[33] Turnbull to Molesworth, 5 November 1722. For full documentation, including evidence of an early connection with Toland, see M.A. Stewart, 'George Turnbull and Educational Reform', in J. Carter and J. Pittock, eds., *Aberdeen and the Enlightenment* (Aberdeen, 1987), pp. 95–103.
[34] 6 Geo. I c. 5 (Ireland).   [35] Cf. Wright to Wodrow (fn. 26).

IV

This return to a strictly biblical form of Christianity, the attempt to ally it with natural reason, and the rejection of all man-made formularies, is in fact more consistent with the whole philosophy of Dissent than the more doctrinally committed traditions of the Dissenting mainstream. For it is simply being consistent with what has always been central to the Dissenting programme – the rejection of the intrusion of human convention in the worship of God. Although their primary target was those conventions that they regarded as idolatrous and superstitious, the argument with which they attacked that target was an argument that no conventions of any kind, either doctrinal or ceremonial, can be binding on the conscience unless they have been voluntarily entered into or have biblical precedent. This had in effect been the position under the pre-Westminster Confession which was still operative in the days of the Covenanters. This old Scots Confession, for all its theological orthodoxy, was antipathetic to the idea of any non-scriptural authority. The Old and New Testament alone contained 'all thingis necessary to be beleeved for the salvation of mankind'.

The interpretation quhairof, we confesse, neither appertaines to private nor publick persone, nether zit to ony Kirk, for ony preheminence or prerogative, personallie or locallie, quhilk ane hes above ane uther, bot apperteines to the Spirite of God, be the quhilk also the Scripture was written. When controversie then happines, for the right understanding of ony place or sentence of Scripture, or for the reformation of ony abuse within the Kirk of God, we ought not sa meikle to luke what men before us have said or done, as unto that quhilk the halie Ghaist uniformelie speakes within the body of the Scriptures, and unto that quhilk *Christ Jesus* himselfe did, and commanded to be done.

The 'plaine Word of God' takes precedence over 'the interpretation, determination, or sentence of ony Doctor, Kirk, or Councell'.[36]

   To illustrate my case I want to refer to a controversy that was familiar to all Irish Dissenters in the early eighteenth century – the controversy over Presbyterian marriage. The Church of Ireland had a monopoly by law in the conduct of marriage services; it considered the ceremony to fall within the scope of those indifferent matters on which the magistrate could harmlessly require uniformity. The Dissenters argued that these were not indifferent matters: their consciences were affronted by a ceremony which appeared to be peppered with popish doctrine and practice.

---

[36] G.D. Henderson, ed., *The Scots Confession 1560* (Edinburgh, 1960), article 18.

In practice, Presbyterian marriages conducted according to the Directory of the Church of Scotland were often connived at, but could be challenged in the ecclesiastical courts, leaving Presbyterian inheritances permanently at risk until well into the nineteenth century. In the eighteenth century the risk was real: the Church of Ireland badly needed the income and might be prepared to forgo the ceremony so long as they got the cash; to the Dissenters this sounded too much like the sale of indulgences. There were several prosecutions of Presbyterians for conducting or contracting marriages outside the Church of Ireland around 1708 and in the period 1714–16; in the latter instances the General Synod agreed to foot the bill.[37]

The primary document in this case is a work by the orthodox Belfast minister, John MacBride, *A Vindication of Marriage as Solemnized by Presbyterians in the North of Ireland* (1702). Already, in his *Animadversions* of 1697, MacBride had attacked the way that ecclesiastical discipline was being used to 'drain men's Purses' and citizens were being deprived of their 'Hereditary Right' to public service. In *A Sermon before the Provincial Synod at Antrim* (1698) he had used natural-law arguments to defend the right of free assembly for worship; and just as there is in civil politics a right for the majority to take decisions for the whole community, and for there to be appeal against disputed judgements, so there is in religious assemblies. They have the same natural right to exist and regulate themselves that a political assembly has.[38] They are properly dependent on the civil power for their protection, but not for their authorisation.

His tract on marriage is similarly combative and similarly founded in natural law. It is aimed, he says, against those members of the established clergy 'whose intemperate Zeal, and others whom the Love of Money, hath engag'd to be thus unseasonably vexatious'.

Marriage on MacBride's account is 'the Conjunction of one Man and Woman marriageable, by their just, full and express Consent; to live as Husband and Wife, in Obedience to these Laws, and for these Ends, which God hath ordained in this Institution'. There is biblical authority for God's role in this, but the solemnity and significance of the marriage process have been apparent to pagan nations since antiquity by the

[37] National Library of Scotland, Wodrow Letters Folio, vol. 51, no. 48 (a petition of the ministers and people in the North of Ireland to the Lord Lieutenant); see also *Records* (fn. 31), vol. 1, pp. 339, 404.

[38] The parallelism between civil and Church administration is repeated in MacBride's *Sample of Jet-Black Pr---tic Calumny* (Glasgow, 1713), citing the *Second Book of Discipline*. It would have been sufficiently commonplace to the Irish students at Glasgow for them to have had little difficulty in placing university discipline in the same perspective.

'Light of Nature'. It is indeed expedient for a minister of religion to be present, to assist the parties 'by Instruction, Exhortation, and Prayers', but there is no biblical requirement that 'Prophets, Priests or Gospel Ministers' should be employed in the conduct of a ceremony 'by vertue of their Office'. The idea that a marriage contract is void unless the parish priest, or an episcopally approved substitute, is present, is a notion traced to the Council of Trent. All that is required is 'a solemn Oath before God and sufficient witnesses'.

The laws by which marriage is attended are either legal or moral; there is no scope for them to be ecclesiastical, and therefore they cannot run to the excommunication of Dissenters. 'As to Ceremonies, or Administration of Sacraments, as necessary to such occasions, neither Scripture, nor Reason directs us to any such.' If it be claimed that the clergy derive the right to conduct marriages by delegation from the civil power, then they are not performing it in their priestly function; so the ceremony should not have become a part of the 'Divine Service of the Church' regulated by ecclesiastical procedure.

But it is not the administration as such, so much as the details of the Prayer Book service that particularly offended MacBride. Most of the critique was not original to him. It derived from the arguments of the Dissenters in their unsuccessful conference with the English bishops in 1661, trying to hammer out revisions to the Prayer Book that would have been acceptable to both sides;[39] and those arguments in turn can be traced back to the reforms proposed within the Church of England by Puritan divines in the reign of Elizabeth.

The first criticism is of the wording that God 'consecrated the State of Marriage to such an high and excellent Mystery, that in it is signified and represented the spiritual Marriage and Unity that is betwixt Christ and his Church'. But, says MacBride, this has no relevance to marriage before the Fall, or to marriage in Old Testament times; and there is no warrant for it in the New Testament. It is a device of the 'Popish Schoolmen' to make a sacrament out of something that is not even a specifically Christian ceremony.

Secondly, it is unreasonable to have people plight their troth 'for better, for worse, from that time forward till Death them do part', because no one can reasonably be expected to predict whether their partner will engage in 'wilful and obstinate Desertion', or worse, 'turn

---

[39] *An Accompt of all the Proceedings of the Commissioners of both Perswasions, Appointed by his Sacred Majesty, According to Letters Patents, for the Reveiw of the Book of Common Prayer, &c.* (London, 1661).

Papist, and fly to a Monastery or Nunnery'. And even if you are tied to your partner 'for better', you cannot be tied 'for worse'; for what happens when your partner becomes a threat to your own welfare?

Thirdly, the marriage ring is accorded a 'mystical signification' which is inconsistent with its having a merely civil function. It is declared to be a 'Token and Pledg of the Vow and Covenant made between the married Persons, and that they may ever remain in perfect Love and Peace together, and live according to God's Laws'. But the vow is effected in the name of the Trinity after the ring has been first placed on the open Prayer Book and then transferred to the fourth finger. There is no biblical warrant for this and it 'tends to no imaginable Edification'. It is a 'Popish Consecration'. The ring is a pagan Roman convention, and therefore ruled out on principle.

Nor can we see, how a Ring doth more natively signify Fidelity than Circumvention, and seeing it hath as few Beginnings as Endings, it may as aptly signify, their Love should never begin, as well as never end.

The use of the fourth finger is a piece of antique folk-physiology about a special nerve passing between that finger and the heart. But 'ocular Inspection' proves there is no such nerve, so 'this way of charming the Wife's Heart by that Finger, doth fail, as oft it doth'.

Finally, MacBride makes merry with the logical difficulties that the attempt to discredit Presbyterian marriages leads to. The Church of Ireland claimed that Presbyterian marriages were null and void. But you cannot inflict penalties on the parties to something that has not happened; neither can you prosecute the minister who performed clandestinely what is deemed to have been no ceremony. You cannot hang a man for murder where no one has died. And while Presbyterian partners might by Church law be deemed fornicators, it must be logically impossible for them to be charged, as some were, with adultery. But the biggest absurdity of all is that the Church is much less bothered about the ceremonies than the money, and when that is paid they will cheerfully ratify the marriage that never occurred. 'So mighty is that Mettal, that it doth not only cleanse from moral Uncleanness, but makes Nullities valid.'

The episcopalian side was not without its able, and exasperated, defenders. Ralph Lambert, later Bishop of Meath, responded with a sixty-four-page *Answer to a Late Pamphlet* (1704); but Edward Synge, then chaplain to the Lord Lieutenant and later to be Archbishop of Tuam, ran to 336 pages a year later, in *A Defence of the Established Church and Laws*. Both stress strongly the legal status of the established Church and claim that divine law enjoins conformity to the civil law, and that the civil law has the right and obligation to specify the conditions under which it will recognise marriages as legally entered into, and at what charges. For Lambert, it is the finances that are important: 'If some will Marry in their own way, must the Establish'd Minister therefore lose part of his legal Salary?' For Synge, it is the engagingly circular argument that we must lay down precisely and unambiguously what is to constitute marriage, since otherwise we will not know who has to be prosecuted for fornication and adultery. Both agree with MacBride that the attendance of a minister of religion is 'expedient' rather than essential to the office, but whereas Lambert argues that the ceremony prescribed by Irish legislation is through and through a religious one, Synge is more concerned to see the minister as strictly the agent of the civil power.

When it comes to the offending ceremonies, neither admits to anything remotely popish. Synge is prepared to take seriously the Dissenters' claim to rights of conscience, so long as there is a 'full perswasion' that is 'built upon clear and solid Evidence'. This turns out to mean that the evidence must be clear and solid, not only to the Dissenters, but to the episcopalians. It involves being able to cite the particular 'Law of God' which, 'either *expressly*, or by a *clear and rational Consequence*' appears to forbid the prescribed practice. Since it is a plain law of God that we should obey the civil power, only where there is 'as plain, and express a Declaration of the Will of God that we should not do it' can this be overridden. Synge seems to have overlooked the contradiction inherent in this advice.

Neither prelate thinks there is a word of substance in MacBride's scruples over the Prayer Book service, which does nothing but introduce quite innocent conventions into a ceremony which could not exist without some such conventions to constitute it. Even the Presbyterians accept the utter conventionality of holding hands. As for being bound to one's partner for life, that is a total misunderstanding. Where there has been adultery, the innocent party can petition Parliament for divorce (Lambert);[40] it is merely inexpedient to take another partner during the life of the first (Synge). A fat lot of comfort that is.

---

[40] The anonymous author of *Thoughts on the Propriety of Preventing Marriages Founded on Adultery* (London, 1800) traces divorce by Act of Parliament effectively to the reign of William III, when there were four cases. There were only two under Anne, two under George I, twenty-four under George II, and then the numbers increase. The figures probably relate only to England and Wales, but it is unlikely that the proportions would be significantly different for Ireland.

Both critics argued that Presbyterian marriages were not in fact void if they could be proved, but the proof rendered the minister liable to prosecution for breach of the law. The great difficulty was therefore to uncover the proof and with it the evidence that would legitimate an inheritance. Neither critic admitted the absurd dilemma in which this placed the Dissenters, but Synge tried to take the sting out of the charge that the episcopalians were in it for the money. The fines imposed by the ecclesiastical court were a benevolent amelioration of worse penalties to which the Dissenters were strictly liable.

This was not the only issue upon which the Dissenters got into a major controversy with episcopacy over the imposition of human convention in matters of conscience, but it is typical of the genre. There was another and earlier controversy in which William King, as Bishop of Derry, tried to turn the tables by proving that the Church of Ireland was the truly scriptural Church and that it was the Dissenters who succumbed to convention (with metrical psalms, extempore prayer, sitting at communion, etc.). His *Discourse concerning the Inventions of Men in the Worship of God* (1694) is a clever and at times outrageous piece of needling, attempting to get the Dissenters out of their overflowing meeting houses into his own largely empty churches. There was, no doubt, as much misinformation and mutual incomprehension in this controversy as in the later one. King was competently, if not decisively, answered by Joseph Boyse, in a dual exchange.

v

I have tried to show that Irish Dissent was founded on the assumption that Church and state operate on similar principles, as voluntary societies – the one protected by the other – that should not impose on the rights and liberties of their members. The same appeal to natural law that one finds in the orthodox MacBride is as much part of the repertoire of John Abernethy, the pioneer of Nonsubscription. The 'Light and Law of Nature', said Abernethy, antecedently to all revelation established the need for civil government, whose sole end is the 'common Safety and Happiness'.[41] Christ did nothing to undermine or overturn this civil

---

[41] John Abernethy, *The Nature and Consequences of the Sacramental Test Considered* (Dublin, 1731), p. 94. See also other polemical pieces posthumously collected in his *Scarce and Valuable Tracts and Sermons* (London, 1751). In addition to these, Abernethy's collected works consisted in two substantial volumes of *Discourses concerning the Being and Natural Perfections of God* (Dublin, 1740–2) and two further volumes of devotional *Sermons on Various Subjects* (London, 1748).

order by vexatious legislation; his teaching is concerned with purity of heart and conscience. But laws which enforce outward conformity enforce hypocrisy and degrade religion. The Test Act lays down a condition for civil and military office – kneeling to receive the sacrament – which is nothing to do with the 'original Interest and Liberty of the Society' and 'plainly inconsistent with the first Principles of Liberty'.[42] The toleration of Dissenters is the natural consequence of the legal limits to royal authority, limits which are themselves the natural consequence of human fallibility – a thesis argued on historical as well as theoretical grounds, citing Saxon and later constitutional landmarks.

The nonsubscription principle is one way of extending a deeply held and longstanding conviction that no human authority can intervene, or convention be imposed, except after proper trial, and within the limits of its imposer's competence, and with the consent of those affected; even then, the role of authority is to advise rather than direct. This attitude is found initially among those who are zealous for revealed religion, but it comes increasingly to typify the new generation of those who are seeking to underpin biblical teaching with more philosophical foundations.

We can conclude by again citing Abernethy. 'Diversity of Judgments is a Natural Consequence from Humane Imperfection, which cleaves to Believers as well as others',[43] so the principle that justifies Dissent in the first place justifies also differences of opinion among the Dissenters. Yet 'our Blessed Redeemer was not wanting in his Care for Necessary Order and Harmony among his Servants'. The dilemma is resolved by peaceable coexistence, every party being guided by his or her own conscience and respecting the conscience of others. What seems at first like a trite get-out is then elaborated with a full philosophical analysis of what it is to be 'Persuaded in one's own Mind'. Everyone, he says,

knows what Difference there is between being *Persuaded*, which is an Assent form'd upon Evidence and Attentive Reasoning, and an indeliberate Determination without Evidence and without Enquiry. It is true in the Assent of our Minds to, or Dissent from any Proposition, we are wholly Passive, being Necessarily and Inevitably Determin'd by the Evidence which Appears to us. It is not in our Power to Refuse, or so much as suspend such an Assent or Dissent, not from any faulty Impotence, but as far as I can see, from the Essential frame of the soul it self, and in that wherein by the very Constitution of our Nature we have no Liberty, there can be neither Moral Good nor Evil. But since we know by Experience, and the Scripture teaches us, we are apt to run into mistakes

---

[42] Abernethy, *Tracts*, p. 33.
[43] Abernethy, *Religious Obedience Founded on Personal Persuasion* (Belfast, 1720), p. 3.

thro' Inattention, and the secret Influence of our Affections and Passions; it must be our unquestionable duty, as it is indeed the best Use we can make of our Reason, to guard against these Springs of Error especially in the Judgments and Resolutions we Form, concerning points of Faith and Obedience to God.

It is thus essential that our persuasion be based on thorough deliberation and be free from prejudice.

When Forreign motives are brought into the Counsels of the Soul, and it inclines to one side of the Question in debate by the Opinions of other Men, by worldly Interest, by the biass of it's own corrupt Affections, by a fond Respect to Preconceiv'd Notions, which render it unwilling thro' Pusillanimity, pride or sloth to undergo the Fatigue of an Impartial Examination, or bear the Reproach of a discover'd Mistake; when any of these things, or others of a like Nature influence the Mind, it fails in its Duty and comes short of that Persuasion upon which alone it can Act with Safety.[44]

Even if our persuasion is wrong after meeting these conditions, we still have the obligation to follow it, since it is the best rule we have.[45] We are judged by our sincerity, not by an unattainable infallibility. To be convinced and be wrong is excusable: to profess anything without conviction is not. It is only on this assumption that the Christian revelation can have been presented to us for acceptance. To grant the assumption and then capitulate to another authority as human and fallible as ourselves is contradictory.

[44] *Ibid.*, pp. 11–13.　　[45] Cf. Bayle, *Nouvelles lettres critiques* (Ville-Franche, 1685), XI. 17.

CHAPTER 4

The Enlightenment, politics and providence: some Scottish and English comparisons

Martin Fitzpatrick

The scientific revolution, Enlightenment humanism, Locke, and the Scottish common sense writers . . . had shifted the emphasis from an interventionist God to one whose greatest gift to human kind was natural reason.

(Patricia Bonomi)[1]

Enlightenment religion can be characterised as rational, tolerant and non-mysterious and the Enlightenment God as a beneficent Newtonian hero who had designed the world as a system of benevolence. When the Romantic reaction began, it was comparatively easy for the Carlyles and the Coleridges to be scornful of the spiritual aridity of Rational Dissent and the Scottish Moderate clergy.[2] It requires a sympathy for the 'moderate and non-insistent faith' of the Enlightenment, which they did not possess, in order to understand it.[3] In this volume, R.K. Webb has shown how sympathy can lead to understanding. My own contribution does not represent a systematic study, but it does have a theme, and a core. My aim is to probe the way in which adherents of enlightened religion viewed and interpreted contemporary affairs, and ultimately to reflect on this, given the general trend away from a mysterious interventionist God to one whose beneficent ways were regularised through the workings of a general providence. It explores this theme comparatively, in relation to what we

I am grateful to Dr D.O. Thomas, Professor E.B. Fryde, Professor Knud Haakonssen and Mrs E.Y. Short for their advice on earlier drafts of this chapter. I would like to thank the Institute for Advanced Studies in the Humanities, University of Edinburgh, and The British Academy for providing me with the facilities and support to make this study possible.

[1] Patricia U. Bonomi, *Under the Cope of Heaven. Religion, Society and Politics in Colonial America* (New York, Oxford, 1986, pbk. 1988), p. 98.
[2] See Ian Campbell, 'Carlyle's Religion: The Scottish Background', in John Clubbe ed., *Carlyle and his Contemporaries: Essays in Honor of Charles Richard Sanders* (Durham, North Carolina, 1976), pp. 9–11; E. H. Coleridge ed., *Anima Poetae, From the Unpublished Note-Books of Samuel Taylor Coleridge* (London, 1895), pp. 26, 151–2, 155, 167–8.   [3] Bonomi, *Under the Cape of Heaven*, p. 101.

are used to call Rational Dissent and Scottish Moderatism as revealed in the correspondence of James Wodrow of Stevenston, Ayr, and Samuel Kenrick of Bewdley, Worcestershire. Differences are revealed by their contrasting reactions to contemporary events from the mid-1770s to the 1790s, especially the American and French Revolutions. I have resisted the temptation to define these too sharply for, despite their strong disagreements, both men shared the same fundamental religious priorities and the contrasts, which initially appear clear cut, are portrayed as consisting of shifting nuances. To convey and to understand their differences one has to examine their correspondence in considerable detail, and place it in the context of their intellectual inheritance and of the ideas of some of the leading thinkers of their day. This investigation is not an attempt to review the field of studies on Scottish Moderatism and Rational Dissent. That would require a different approach. But I believe that there is room for a study of this sort,[4] more especially because religious attitudes are manifest in the reactions to events both great and small, and my source, which forms the core of the study, the Wodrow–Kenrick correspondence, is a wonderfully sensitive litmus for testing them.[5] After studying the attitudes of the correspondents towards the American Revolution, I offer some general reflections on why they might have taken up opposing stances and in so doing examine comparative dimensions of Scottish Moderatism and Rational Dissent. I then return to bring my observations together by studying briefly their reactions to the events of the late 1780s and early 1790s, notably the French Revolution.[6]

I

Revd James Wodrow (1730–1810), of Stevenston in Ayr, was the ninth son of the Scottish clergyman and historian, Robert Wodrow (1679–1734). His friend and contemporary at Glasgow University, Samuel Kenrick (1728–1811), was the son of John Kenrick (d.1745), a Dissenting minister

---

[4] On this point, see C. Camic, *Experience and Enlightenment. Socialization for Cultural Change in Eighteenth-Century Scotland* (Edinburgh, 1983), pp. 50–1.

[5] The correspondence is held in Dr Williams's Library, London. I am grateful to the Trustees of the Library for permission to quote from it and to the Librarian, Mr John Creasey, for many kindnesses in helping me to read it. The correspondence reference is D.W.L. MSS 24: 157. In what follows I refer to it as W–K and then give the letter number. My ultimate aim is to produce a full study as well as an edition of the correspondence.

[6] This is not the first time I have used the correspondence to study aspects of Enlightenment religion. See my 'Varieties of Candour: English and Scottish Style', *Enlightenment and Dissent*, 7 (1988), 35–56. In an effort not to repeat myself, I shall treat that as a complementary study.

at Wrexham, and was destined to spend most of his life as a banker at Bewdley, Worcestershire, where he settled in 1765.[7] By the time the conflict with the American colonies had become the central political issue in Britain, Wodrow and Kenrick had exchanged some fifty letters. These provide indications of their future attitudes, but only incompletely. In the later 1760s and early 1770s, when parliamentary reform and toleration were beginning to emerge as potentially long-playing issues in British political life, their correspondence is patchy,[8] and so it was not until the American Revolution began that we witness a major and lively exchange of views. No doubt the groundwork had been prepared, for almost immediately major differences of opinion and outlook emerged. For James Wodrow, politics was the art of balancing imperatives which were ultimately religious against those of worldly prudence: one needed to follow one's conscience but also to be convinced that that was the right course to take. His unequivocal condemnation of the American colonies' resistance to the British Government was founded on his belief that both politically and morally they were in the wrong. Samuel Kenrick, on the other hand, sympathised with the Americans. Wodrow, in pointing out the error of his ways in a letter of September 1775, articulated his own position with precision:

I am sorry that you shoud think that in Scotland we have forgot or deserted the principles of liberty imbided in our youth. My Dear Sir I have no idea of any civil or political liberty but that which stands on the basis of Law and Legislative Authority when this is shaken and overturned all our rights and priviledges as citizens must fall with it and be buried in its ruins till a new constitution is established. Is there any Liberty just now in America? scarce a spark of it remaining. They have subverted their constitution under which they enjoyed much liberty and payed little for it and in their madness have subjected themselves to a democratical Tyranny.

The indignation did not end there. He predicted that the colonies

will split into factions among themselves and God knows what will be the consequence what a scene of confusion and anarchy may ensue.

Wodrow accepted the right of resistance to oppression, whether of a king or a corrupt legislature, but crucially such a right should only be applied in the very last resort, as when a legislature had become 'so corrupt and tyrannical that the consequences of living under it are likely

---

[7] Colin Bonwick has provided a useful introduction, accompanied by John Creasey's invaluable Calendar, for the microfilm edition of the correspondence, W.E. Minchinton, gen. ed., *British Records Relating to America* (Wakefield, Yorkshire, 1982).

[8] There is a gap between May 1771 and April 1774.

to be worse than the consequence of resistance'. In the meantime account should be taken of the inevitable imperfections of 'human governments' and of the dangers of flying to arms. Rebellion breaks the delicate balance of politics and when, as is likely, it is repressed, offers the government an access of power which also endangers liberty.[9] He was quite clear in his mind that the government had not abused the trust reposed in it, and found repugnant the notion that the Americans were acting as instruments of providence.[10] Generally, Wodrow's position during the War was that of a conservative Whig; while adhering to a belief in Whig freedoms, he also believed that they could only be freedoms within the law; too much was hazarded if one asserted natural rights against a government which had not sunk into abject tyranny. It was, he felt, 'an affront to the common sense of mankind to compare these times to those of Charles I and James II' and thought that firm action against the colonies was justified 'to bring them back to their duty'.[11]

Kenrick's view was the opposite of Wodrow's. From the outset of hostilities he believed that, on the whole, 'the generous and impartial' favoured the American cause.[12] Justice was on the colonists' side and it was the government whose conduct was both wrong and impolitic. In rebelling, the colonists were exercising their right of resistance as justified by the heroes of their education, Locke and Hutcheson. He chided Wodrow for being in the company of Jacobites like Shebbeare and Johnson, and the conservative Sir William Blackstone, who, in his *Commentaries on the Laws of England*, attacked the revered Whig heroes, Locke, Milton and Sidney, and portrayed them as genteel versions of Wat Tyler and Jack Cade.[13] Making play with Blackstone's argument that 1688 was 'entirely a new case in politics, and its true ground was the abdication of King James: whereas the principles of Mr. Locke levelled all distinctions repealed all positive laws & reduced the society almost to a state of nature', Kenrick implied that Wodrow was associating himself

[9] W–K (54), Wodrow to Kenrick, 19 September 1775. Burke, who blamed the government for the rebellion, used a similar argument to support the colonial cause. If Britain triumphed, she would break the very spirit that kept the empire together: 'you impair the object by your very endeavours to preserve it'. 'Speech on Conciliation with the Colonies', *Edmund Burke on Government, Politics and Society*, ed. B.W. Hill (Brighton, 1975), p. 170.

[10] W–K (57), Wodrow to Kenrick, 16 June 1776; cf. (163), Kenrick to Wodrow, 10 June, 1791, in which Kenrick refers to the 'gloomy turn' of the recently deceased Price.

[11] W–K (54), Wodrow to Kenrick, 19 September 1775.

[12] W–K (51), Kenrick to Wodrow, 19 July 1775.

[13] W–K (55), Kenrick to Wodrow, 29 January and 18 March 1776; W. Blackstone, *Commentaries on the Laws of England*, 4 vols. (London, 1765–9, facsim. repr., London, 1966) Book 4 (1769), Ch. 33, p. 427.

with those who came close to denying the right of resistance.[14] He himself had no doubt that the Americans were fighting for their 'natural inalienable rights' and that they were supported by 'a majority of the cool, sedate independent community at large'.[15]

Kenrick's stance aligned him firmly with the majority of Rational Dissenters. While he noted that Job Orton, who was something of a 'metropolitan' amongst the Dissenters, was an ardent supporter of the government, he represented an older generation of liberal Dissenters.[16] The new leaders, and most notably Richard Price, were advocates of the American cause.[17] Kenrick sent Wodrow a copy of Price's *Observations on the Nature of Civil Liberty*, the best British defence of the American right to self-government, although it is likely that Wodrow had already read extracts from the pamphlet in the *Scots Magazine*.[18]

Why should the two friends find themselves so opposed to each other over the American conflict? Kenrick from the outset tended to think that the truly independent-minded would favour the Americans and that those who did not were 'within the circle more or less of the influence of the administration'.[19] He expected the Scots to take an independent line as a result of their education, which inculcated the 'spirit of liberty'. If he did not quite suggest that his friend had lost his ability to think for himself, he certainly made it clear to him that he thought he was betraying his intellectual heritage, namely that of Locke and Hutcheson.[20] Not only had Hutcheson provided justification for the right of resistance, he had also recommended 'the most extensive benevolence'.[21] By depriving

---

[14] *Ibid.*, Book 1 (1765), Ch. 2, p. 157; Ch. 3, pp. 204–7. Kenrick is paraphrasing Blackstone, whose objection to Locke lay essentially in the notion that one cannot make a case *in law* for resistance to the *law*. On Blackstone's opposition to resistance, see H.T. Dickinson, *Liberty and Property. Political Ideology in Eighteenth-Century Britain* (London, 1977), pp. 130–1. Hutcheson's views on resistance would again provide a focus for debate between Wodrow and Kenrick during the French Revolution. See W–K (193), Wodrow to Kenrick, 17 or 18 July 1794.

[15] W–K (55), Kenrick to Wodrow, 29 January and 18 March 1776.

[16] W–K (69), Kenrick to Wodrow, 12 May 1780.

[17] C. Bonwick, *English Radicals and the American Revolution* (Chapel Hill, 1977), esp. pp. 9–10; James E. Bradley, *Religion, Revolution and English Radicalism. Non-Conformity in Eighteenth-Century Politics and Society* (Cambridge, 1990), pp. 123–4, 189.

[18] W–K (55), Kenrick to Wodrow, 29 January and 18 March 1776; *Scots Magazine*, 36 (1776), 101–4.

[19] W–K (51), Kenrick to Wodrow, 19 July 1775.

[20] W–K (53), Kenrick to Wodrow, 30 August 1775, (55) Kenrick to Woodrow, 29 January and 18 March 1776.

[21] F. Hutcheson, *A System of Moral Philosophy* (London, 1754), vol. 1, p. 69; the potentially radical dimensions of Hutcheson's ideas were first discerned by Caroline Robbins, in her 'When it is that colonies may turn Independent', *William and Mary Quarterly*, 3rd ser., 11(2), 214–51 (April 1954), and *The Eighteenth-Century Commonwealthman: Studies in the Transmission, Development and Circumstances of English Liberal Thought . . .* (Cambridge, MA., 1959), esp. pp. 185–96. For a discussion of the subsequent historiography, see N. Waszek, *Man's Social Nature. A Topic of the Scottish Enlightenment in its*

the Americans of their just rights and going to war with them, the British were offending against such Hutchesonian tenets. It was natural for a Rational Dissenter to view things in such a light. The government had done Dissent no favours in the early 1770s, having apparently encouraged a minor measure of toleration for them, and then defeated it in the House of Lords. Rational Dissenters for their part had sympathised with the Wilkite agitation for parliamentary reform and parliamentary reporting. Whether one viewed Wilkes, as Priestley did, as 'a member of a same [sic] community, and a lover of liberty', or took the more disdainful view of Price that, although the man was worthless, his cause was worthy, the trend of Rational Dissenters was generally to take a critical attitude towards a government that opposed political and religious reform.[22] The American issue, above all, exemplified this hostility and enabled Kenrick to feel an identity with fellow Rational Dissenters, while believing at the same time that his stance was in line with his Scottish educational heritage and, for good measure, with his views as a banker, for he believed that the conflict harmed the local economy.[23] Although, in one of his early letters on the topic, there is an echo of Burke in his condemnation of a government whose actions, 'however, justifiable by acts of parliament and metaphysical deductions' were 'to the last degree unpolitical and contrary to the well-being of both states – nay I am afraid impracticable', his views rested essentially on enlightened optimism that reason, nature and utility were in harmony. He followed Price in arguing that the Navigation Acts were mutually beneficial and Hutcheson and Priestley in believing '*salus populi, suprema est lex*'.[24]

Wodrow reacted to Kenrick's criticism by defending his adherence to his heritage. He did not deny the right of resistance, but he did deny that the government was acting tyrannically.[25] Whereas Kenrick admitted that many of his neighbours favoured the government, Wodrow from the experience of his travels in the Lowlands during the summer of 1775 believed that his ideas were broadly in tune with his countrymen. Those few who favoured the Americans were like the English Dissenters 'roused

Historical Setting, European University Studies, ser. xx, vol. CICII (Frankfurt am Main, Bern, New York, 1986), pp. 51–61; Richard B. Sher, 'Introduction: Scottish-American Cultural Studies, Past and Present', in R.B. Sher and Jeffrey R. Smitten, *Scotland and America in the Age of the Enlightenment* (Edinburgh, 1990), pp. 1–27 at pp. 6–23.   [22] B.L. Add. MSS 30877, vol. XI, fo. 66 n.d.

[23] W–K (51) Kenrick to Wodrow, 19 July 1775. Kenrick noted the 'baleful effects' of government policy 'in the iron manufacture particularly nails'.

[24] *Ibid.*; W–K (55), Kenrick to Wodrow, 29 January and 18 March 1776.

[25] W–K (54), Wodrow to Kenrick, 19 September 1775.

into enthusiasm by the very sound of liberty'.[26] He believed that there
were constitutional ways of resolving the dispute and feared that the
habit of flying to arms to procure a remedy of grievances was extremely
dangerous. It could give rise to 'civil comotion' at home, which would
lead to a strengthening of the power of the Crown.[27] In the eighteenth
century debate between those who sought to procure change through co-
operating with circumstance and those who believed in effecting reform
through imposition of will, Wodrow aligned himself with those who were
on the side of co-operation. In his letters of the early 1770s, his sense of
the fragility of order and his fierce hostility to Wilkes is similar to that of
Hume.[28] Hume did not quite conform to type, for he opposed the government in the conflict over America. Like Josiah Tucker in England, his
arguments were distinctive and were not those of the colonists themselves.[29] Moreover, they did not convince his leading contemporaries in
the Scottish Enlightenment. Adam Ferguson, for example, criticised
Richard Price for confusing liberty with the absence of restraint and for
believing that liberty was sustained by 'zeal in behalf of equitable government'.[30] Zeal was not a virtue much recommended by the Scottish
Enlightenment;[31] it was associated with enthusiasm and faction. Wodrow
noted with satisfaction that despite kith and kin in America, the
Scots generally opposed the American cause.[32] Wodrow portrayed
himself as a conformist, and certainly he typified the stance of the
Scottish Moderate clergy.[33] Yet he may have over-stressed the degree of
support for the government because he did not wish to face the
uncomfortable fact that the Popular Party amongst the Presbyterians was

[26] W–K (52), Wodrow to Kenrick, 13 August 1775. Later, in 1778, Wodrow reported that there had
been a falling off of adherents to the American cause. W–K (60), Wodrow to Kenrick, 18 March
1778.   [27] W–K (54), Wodrow to Kenrick, 19 September 1775.

[28] See D.L. Miller, *Philosophy and Ideology in Hume's Political Thought* (Oxford, 1981), pp. 181–4.

[29] See Donald W. Livingston, 'Hume, English Barbarism and American Independence', in Sher
and Smitten, *Scotland and America* (fn. 21), pp. 133–47. On Tucker on America and his criticism of
Price and Priestley, see G. Shelton, *Dean Tucker, Eighteenth-Century Economic and Political Thought*
(London, 1981), pp. 182–239.

[30] R. Price, *Additional Observations on the Nature of Civil Liberty, the Principles of Government and the Justice
and Policy of the War with America . . .* (1777); Adam Ferguson, *Remarks on a Pamphlet Lately Published by
Dr. Price*, in B. Peach ed., *Richard Price and the Ethical Foundations of the American Revolution* (Durham,
NC., 1979), esp. pp. 159, 161, 253–7; A. Ferguson, *An Essay on the History of Civil Society* (1767), ed. with
intro. Duncan Forbes (Edinburgh, 1966), p. 128.   [31] Hutcheson, *System* (fn. 20), vol.II, p. 319.

[32] W–K (52), Wodrow to Kenrick, 13 August 1775.

[33] Richard B. Sher, *Church and University in the Scottish Enlightenment: The Moderate Literati of Edinburgh*
(Princeton, NJ, 1985), pp. 262–97. Wodrow's conservative Whig position during the War was not
unlike that of many of the Anglican clergy who opposed the American cause. See Paul Langford,
'The English Clergy and the American Revolution', in Eckhart Hellmuth, ed., *The Transformation
of Political Culture. England and Germany in the Late Eighteenth Century* (London, 1990), pp. 275–308.

pro-American.[34] Certainly, underlying his dignified defence of liberty under the law was a fear of enthusiasm. This is something that he detected amongst English Dissenters before he became deeply concerned about the American issue. It will be worth following this a little further as it will provide reasons why Wodrow could feel that he was acting in accordance with the traditions of his mentors, Hutcheson and Leechman.

In his comments on English Dissent in the 1770s Wodrow mixes sympathy for their position with criticism of their conduct. In 1771, he thought they were too easily drawn into the 'sentiments of the opposition' and that enthusiasm for their ideals blurred their judgement: 'their enthusiasm for Liberty carries them along with every thing that has the least appearance of it'.[35] Moreover, even when they believed their cause to be just, they ought to act with caution and circumspection, not as if providence were always on their side. The path of providence, even in retrospect, was not always clear; light did not always appear to triumph over the forces of darkness. Caution, prudence and a generally pragmatic approach to the affairs of this world were to be recommended rather an attempt to convert the world into an enlightened paradise in the shortest time possible. Thus, when sympathising with the disappointment of the English Dissenters at their failure to obtain, for their ministers and schoolmasters, the repeal of subscription to the doctrinal articles of the Thirty-Nine Articles,[36] he observed, 'it seems to be the purpose of providence to expose the friends of truth in all ages to much opposition sometimes to much persecution and oppression yet they will prevail and triumph in the end'. In the meantime, he was equivocal as to whether the Dissenters, having been defeated twice, should fight on, concluding, 'Many compliances[?] must be made in this imperfect world & may be made surely without hurting the interests of truth and virtue.'[37]

---

[34] Robert Kent Donovan, 'The Popular Party of the Church of Scotland and the American Revolution', in Sher and Smitten, *Scotland and America* (fn. 21), pp. 81–99.

[35] W–K (49), Wodrow to Kenrick, 22 May 1771.

[36] The English Dissenters, having twice failed to obtain relief from subscription to the Thirty-Nine Articles (in 1772 and 1773 when the attempt had been blocked by the House of Lords) had decided to abandon the campaign for the time being. The leaders of the more radical Rational Dissenters, such as Richard Price, Andrew Kippis, Thomas Amory and Joseph Jefferies, had wanted to continue campaigning, more especially as there was an election in the offing and they wished to use the issue as a means of putting pressure on candidates. See D.W.L. Minutes of the General Body of Protestant Dissenting Ministers of the Three Denominations in and about the Cities of London and Westminster, MS 38.106, ff.146–7; D.W.L. MS 12.44, f.13, Theophilus Lindsey to William Turner, 9 February 1774; J. Priestley, ed., *The Theological and Miscellaneous Works of Joseph Priestley*, J. T. Rutt, 25 vols. (London, 1817–1831), vol. XII, 'Address to Protestant Dissenters' (1774); A. Kippis, *A Vindication of the Protestant Dissenting Ministers with Regard to their Late Application to Parliament* (2nd edn, London, 1773), pp. 106–7. [37] W–K (50), Wodrow to Kenrick, 5 April 1774.

Although Wodrow did not want to minimise the cost of accepting the imperfections of the world, it was one of his charges against the Rational Dissenters that they were both too pessimistic about the world and too optimistic about the prospect of its transformation. He detected such failings in Richard Price. In his response to Kenrick's gift of Price's *Civil Liberty*, he expressed agreement with the latter's view that government was a trust, but differed profoundly in the application of that insight and believed that 'some things thrown out in the Pamphlet . . . discover a mind either provoked by injury or keenly exasperated by Party spirit'. Perhaps more interestingly, he picked up on that deep strain of pessimism about the state of Britain which informed the old Commonwealth tradition, and which in Price's case also betrayed a Puritan background and a spirit that was often gloomy.[38] 'I am grieved', wrote Wodrow, 'for the distress that his and your benevolent hearts must feel from the melancholy imagination that the ruin of your dear Country is fast approaching which seems like a black cloud to hang over your minds and to darken all your views of the public prosperity and felicity.' He came to link Price and his associates not with the sensible revolution of 1688/9 but with the English revolution of the sectarians, whose sense of perspective had been lost by wild aspirations about the coming millennium.[39]

Kenrick and their friends might well regard themselves as Rational Dissenters, but it is clear that in Wodrow's mind they strongly resembled members of the Popular Party in the Kirk who combined radical politics with religious bigotry. The Hutcheson who provided the Americans and maybe also the Rational Dissenters with a radical contractarian justification of resistance, provided Wodrow and the moderate clergy with arguments for trying to maintain a moderate balanced stance in politics and religion. Here the evidence comes from Hutcheson's discussion of the issue which crucially embraced secular and religious concerns, and which proved of perennial concern for moderate clergymen, namely that of patronage.

---

[38] W–K (57), Wodrow to Kenrick, 16 June 1776.

[39] W–K (65), Wodrow to Kenrick, 21 September 1778. His viewpoint is echoed remarkably some fifteen years later, when the Moderate minister, Thomas Hardy, addressed Paine in his *The Patriot addressed to the people, on the present state of affairs in Britain and France* (Edinburgh, 1793), p. 27: 'The Millennium is not yet come; it is not the saints only for whom the governments of the earth are intended, but mankind, in mixed society.'

II

The issue of patronage led to a conflict between rival conceptions of the Church: at one extremity, a proprietorial view of the Church, in which the Crown and the lay patrons would choose their ministers; at the other, a congregational view of the Church, in which the community of the faithful would make the choice. In between there were a variety of compromise positions centring on the assumption that the Church should be a mirror both of society generally and of the faithful themselves. Such an intermediate view had predominated when the Church settlement was made in 1690 following the Glorious Revolution. In that year the Presbyterian Parliament abolished the rights of patronage and placed the election of the ministers in the hands of 'the *heritors* [landowners] *and elders* in the country', and of the '*magistrates, town-council and elders*, in the boroughs'.[40] However, in 1712 lay patronage was restored. Generally, lay patrons exercised their rights with some circumspection until the late 1720s when the courts of the Church began to support them. This led to an attempt in 1732 by the General Assembly of the Church of Scotland to restore the situation which had prevailed between 1690 and 1712.[41] Unwittingly this opened up tensions in the Church between those who favoured the 1690 settlement and those led by Ebenezer Erskine, minister at Stirling, who maintained 'the divine right of the people in the choice of their pastors'. In 1734 the Church Assembly reversed its decision of 1732 and tried to gain a complete reform of patronage, but to no avail. Erskine and three other ministers who had formed their own presbytery were eventually expelled from the Church, and they formed their own secession church.[42]

---

[40] *Considerations on Patronages. Addressed to the Gentlemen of Scotland by Francis Hutcheson (1735). Likewise a state of the Secession in Scotland in the year 1773* (Glasgow, 1774), pp. 5–6.

[41] For the general background, see Callum Brown, *The Social History of Religion in Scotland since 1730* (London, 1987), pp. 29–30; T.C. Smout, *A History of the Scottish People, 1560–1830* (Glasgow, 1969, 9th impress. 1990), pp. 216–17; cf. also Hutcheson, *System*, pp. 5–6.

[42] Following their protest against the Act of 1732, Erskine and three others refused to bow to the disciplinary procedures of the Church and were declared 'no longer ministers of this church'. Whereupon they formally seceded from the Church while maintaining their role as parish ministers. In an attempt to undo the harm caused by their secession, the General Assembly of 1734 repealed the Act of 1732 and 'dispatched Commissioners to address the King and Parliament for a repeal of the Patronage act', and attempted to restore the seceders. Both the attempt to repeal the Patronage Act and to bring in the seceders failed. They formed their own presbytery and were eventually deposed by the General Assembly in 1740. [N. Morren, comp.], *Annals of the General Assembly of the Church of Scotland, from the Final Secession in 1739 to the Origin of the Relief in 1752. With an Appendix of Biographical Sketches* . . . (Edinburgh, 1838–40), vol. I, pp. 1–3. See Henry Reay Sefton, *The Early Development of Moderatism in the Church of Scotland* (Ph.D. thesis, University of Glasgow, 1968), 39–42; and Richard B. Sher, *Church and University*, pp. 45–64, the most comprehensive discussion of Moderate attitudes.

Francis Hutcheson became Professor of Moral Philosophy at Glasgow University in 1730, and was already associated with liberal causes. As in other aspects of his work, over the issue of patronage he articulated the attitudes of the emerging moderate interest in the Church. His views were spelled out in a lucid pamphlet of 1735, *Considerations on Patronage. Addressed to the Gentlemen of Scotland*. His initial plea was that the 'gentlemen of Scotland' had a contribution to make in 'obtaining a wise regulation of this matter'. Indeed, they had more of an interest in the issue than the clergy, yet they had been put off taking an interest by the fuss made by 'some weak zealots of the church'. Since most of the gentry were ignorant of the present 'miserable state' regarding patronage, he offered a brief historical explanation: after being abolished in the English Revolution, patronage was restored by Charles II; abolished again following the Glorious Revolution,[43] it was restored (in 1712) by the last Tory Government of Queen Anne's reign, although it was plainly contrary to the Union.[44] The resulting situation was most unsatisfactory, with extensive powers of patronage in the hands of the Crown and to a lesser extent of the nobility who had no genuine interest in the parishes where they held patronage powers.[45] Out of 950 parishes, Hutcheson estimated that

there are not 150 parishes in Scotland, where the patronage is in any gentleman of considerable estate, or natural interest in the parishes, to whom it is of any real consequence, as to himself, whether the minister be a person of sobriety, diligence, or good abilities in his office, or not.[46]

Yet the 'presbyteries and some heritors' had not proved 'tame enough to quit their rights altogether'. The result was conflict over

[43] Hutcheson, *Considerations on Patronages* (fn. 40), pp. 5–6; Morren *Annals of the General Assembly*, pp. 1–3, 16.

[44] The patrons had been left in the anomalous position after 1690 of still being obliged to provide and allocate stipends. They had been stripped of their rights and left only with duties, hence the acceptability to them of the restoration of lay patronage in 1712. See R. Buick Knox, 'Establishment and Toleration during the Reigns of William, Mary and Anne', *Records of the Scottish Church History Society*, vol. XXIII, pt. 3 (1989), p. 355.

[45] Hutcheson, *Considerations on Patronages* pp. 6, 10. Hutcheson estimated that nearly two thirds of the powers of patronage (over 550 churches out of 950) were in the hands of the Crown and of the remainder near 200 places in the hands of a few absentee Lords, some in the hands of magistrates, leaving 'not 150' in the hands of local gentry (ibid., p. 10). According to Robert Kent Donovan, of the 944 benefices of the Church of Scotland, in 1769 the Crown presented to 334 and the nobility to 309. See his *No Popery and Radicalism. Opposition to Roman Catholic Relief in Scotland, 1778–1782* (New York, 1987), p. 286 fn. 91. Hutcheson was not alone amongst the early moderates in exaggerating crown influence. Revd Robert Wallace thought that half the patronage was in crown hands; his stance over patronage was very close to Hutcheson's. Henry R. Sefton, 'Rev Robert Wallace: An Early Moderate', *Records of the Scottish Church History Society*, vol. XXV, pt. 1 (1966), pp. 5–9.   [46] Hutcheson, *Considerations on Patronages* (fn. 40), p. 6.

presentations in which the qualities of the candidate seemed to be the least concern.[47]

Hutcheson foresaw a situation in which the gentry, tiring of the patronage struggles, would abandon supporting the presbyteries and elders leaving the patrons to hold sway. Unsuitable candidates – time-servers, and the poor and illiterate – would be presented, and the 'Scotch clergy will be the most despicable set of churchmen in *Christendom*'.[48] The gentry, for their part, by accepting patronage were allowing themselves to be deprived of substantial civil and religious rights.[49] Yet the thrust of Hutcheson's argument was prudential. While accepting that Scripture and the practices of the early Church indicate that patronage was wrong, he emphasised considerations of 'common prudence'. The powerful tendency of patronage was towards corruption. In contrast, a system by which ministers were chosen by 'men of property in the several parishes, in conjunction with the elders as representatives of the people' would ensure that worthy characters were selected.[50] Such men would naturally be men of 'learning and manners', generally drawn from the middling gentry.[51] Hutcheson even suggested that too many of the lower sort were obtaining bursaries to train as ministers and that it would be better to amalgamate some bursaries to ensure that only the brightest and best came from the people.[52] His ideal minister was one who would be comfortable in society, and with whom society would be comfortable; and society naturally meant the polite society of the gentry.[53] This is not too far removed from Burke's arguments later in the century for an Anglican hierarchy able to speak to the different levels of society, and for a career open *only* to the most talented.[54] Hutcheson even stresses the desirability of the gentry having a '*natural hereditary influence*'. One can therefore see a strong

---

[47] *Ibid.*, p. 7: 'Tis deplorable, that the populace, who have little judgement about the abilities of men, generally pitch upon as weak candidates as the patrons do, nay, sometimes upon worse: and the gentlemen who oppose the patron, must join them, and allow them greater power than in proportion to their abilities of discernment.'

[48] *Ibid.*, p. 8.   [49] *Ibid.*, p. 10.   [50] *Ibid.*, pp. 10–11.   [51] *Ibid.*, pp. 15–18.

[52] *Ibid.*, p. 15. It is fair to point out that on Sundays at 6 p.m. Hutcheson gave free lectures on 'Grotius de veritate Religionis Christianae', *Autobiography of Rev Dr. Alexander Carlyle*, 2nd edn (Edinburgh, 1860), p. 70.

[53] *Ibid.*, pp. 12–13. The idea that the gentry had a right to have companionable ministers occurred in a later pamphlet favouring reform of patronage. See *A Short History of the Late General Assembly of Scotland, Shewing the Rise and Progress of the Schism Overture* (Glasgow, 1767), p. 33. In fact many in the 'Popular Party' actually favoured the compromise of 1690. Sher, *Church and University* (fn. 33) p. 48.

[54] E. Burke, *Reflections on the Revolution in France 1790*, in *The Writings and Speeches of Edmund Burke* (gen. ed. Paul Langford), vol. VIII: *The French Revolution 1790–1794*, ed. L.G. Mitchell (Oxford, 1989), pp. 101–3, 149–50.

conservative thrust in Hutcheson's thinking, and a relationship between the emerging moderate religion and the growing prosperity of the gentry. Hutcheson wanted change but not democratic Congregational-ism for 'the populace are by no means the fittest and best judges of mini-sterial qualifications'. They favoured demagogic preachers, radical in their attitude towards Church and state and narrow minded in their religion, in sum, 'men of little learning, sense, or moderation, or any other good qualities'. Just as Burke tried to kick-start the aristocracy into life, Hutcheson sought to activate the local gentry. His pamphlet sup-ported a measure which would have transferred the power of patronage to 'the principal men of interest in each parish'.[55] The measure failed, and the tide of secession was not stemmed. When the pamphlet was reprinted in 1773 it included details of secessionist churches. It was estimated that there were, in all, 190 separatist congregations, usually affiliated to one of the five separatist organisations, although some con-gregations were independent.[56]

Despite the failure of Hutcheson's ideas on patronage, his desire to create a more moderate, tolerant and urbane clergy was to a degree ful-filled. According to Dr Alexander Carlyle, a contemporary witness and a future leader of the Moderate Party, Hutcheson and Leechman together produced a clergy in the 'western provinces' of Scotland of 'a better taste and greater liberality of sentiment'.[57] This did not, however, solve the problem of secession, which was moreover exacerbated by evangelical revivalism; the gap widened between a gentrified clergy who were influenced by enlightened ideas and those who clung to the popular old orthodoxies. One of the first effects of this was to create a mini-drama which threatened the career of William Leechman, in an episode which underlined the dangers of giving way to popular senti-ment, and which would have been very familiar to James Wodrow, who wrote an account of Leechman's life and edited his sermons on his death.

William Leechman (1706–85) was educated at Edinburgh University. While acting as tutor to the family of Mure of Caldwell, Renfrewshire, he attended Hutcheson's lectures on natural theology, ethics and

---

[55] *Ibid.*, pp. 11, 13, 15–16.

[56] *Ibid.*, pp. 30–1. The author of the 'State of the Secession' calculated that it cost Scotland £1,236,050 to maintain the seceders. Since it was argued that 'by the over-ruling providence of God this wantonnes in throwing away their money, is likely to be one great mean of preserving the knowledge of the gospel among us', it can be presumed that Hutcheson's pamphlet was reprinted as a still relevant contribution to the debate on the reform of patronage.

[57] Carlyle, *Autobiography* (fn. 52), pp. 68, 84. Carlyle studied Divinity at Glasgow from 1743 to 1745.

jurisprudence, and they became friends.[58] In 1731 he was licensed to preach by the Presbytery of Paisley, but did not receive a call as minister until 1736 when he was ordained minister at Beith.[59] This was a particularly difficult time for the Church of Scotland. With the failure of the attempt to reform patronage, secessions were occurring, and in 1738, through the influence of John Whitefield, a full-scale revival began at Cambuslang, just south of Glasgow and not so many miles away from Leechman's parish. On one occasion, Leechman had a meeting with the evangelicals in order to defend the characters of the ministers of the Kirk from their attacks.[60] He would have been sensitive to such attacks for, during his probationary period he had been warned for his lack of evangelical commitment. He was cautioned by some ministers that his preaching was 'philosophical and abstract',[61] or, as one of his critics later put it, his sermons were 'moral Harangues'.[62] Leechman's response came when, as Moderator of the Provincial Synod of Glasgow and Ayr, he opened the Synod at Glasgow in April 1741 with a sermon on 'The Temper, Character, and Duty of a Minister of the Gospel: a Sermon on 1 Tim. iv. 16'. In this he created a view of the ministry which served as a model for the rising Moderate Party in the Church. His ideal minister was virtuous, educated, unprejudiced and capable of moving easily in society, while remaining untainted by the world.[63] Such a minister, who was aiming always at 'the highest pitch of virtue', would be a

[58] Leechman's charge was William Mure (1718–76), the future MP for Renfrewshire from 1742 to 1761. Initially an opposition Whig, by 1754 Mure was a firm government supporter. In 1757 he became estate manager for Lord Bute, and soon became his principal adviser. He left Parliament when he became a Baron of the Exchequer in 1761. He was a close friend and correspondent of David Hume. His political role is discussed in A. Murdoch, *The People Above Politics. Politics and Administration in Mid-Eighteenth Century Scotland* (Edinburgh, 1980).

[59] Leechman's presentation conformed to Hutcheson's ideal. The right of presentation at Beith resided in the family of Eglinton, but the Countess waived her right and recommended Leechman. This fulfilled the wishes of the Mure family who usually resided in the parish. Leechman, for the seven years of his ministry, lived both in Beith and at Caldwell.

[60] *Sermons by William Leechman D.D. . . . To which is Prefixed some Account of the Author's Life and of his Lectures . . .*, ed. J. Wodrow, 2 vols. (London, 1789), p. 16. According to Wodrow the meeting gave 'a considerable check to the spirit of division spreading fast in that part of the country'.

[61] Morren, *Annals of the General Assembly* (fn. 42), pp. 46–7.

[62] *A Short Essay to Prevent the Dangerous Consequences of the Moral Harangues, Now so Common in Scotland. Especially to Prevent the Dangerous Consequences' of Mr. Leechman's Sermon on Prayer* (Glasgow, 1746). This sort of criticism of the Moderates did not go away. See Thomas Chalmers, *A Sermon Preached at the Opening of the General Associate Synod at Edinburgh, April 29 1789* (Edinburgh, 1790), which pours scorn (p. 45) on the 'splendid descants on virtues and vices'.

[63] W. Leechman, *The Temper, Character, and Duty of a Minister of the Gospel. A Sermon Preached . . . at Glasgow . . . 1741* (Glasgow, 1746). Morren, *Annals of the General Assembly* (fn. 40), p. 46 notes that it was often re-printed. On Leechman's moderate religion see Fitzpatrick, 'Varieties of Candour' (fn. 6), pp. 37–8.

man of 'mild moderate conduct' and, as a teacher and exemplar of
such virtues, would be 'fitted to moderate the desires of worldly things',
and be prepared to meet worldly 'ridicule and contempt', maintaining
'to the last, that the joys of religion are the sun, the light, and the life of
our souls in all states, and amidst all the vicissitudes of human affairs'.[64]
Leechman's informed and reverential piety was already the antithesis of
the direct experiential religion of the evangelicals, and although he did
not labour the point, it was deeply critical of their misguided zeal.[65] His
sermon, therefore, did nothing to allay the fears that he underplayed the
'mysteries of religion, and the peculiarities of Christianity', and these
were subsequently compounded by his sermon on prayer. He was seen
as representing a dangerous trend within the Church of preaching
'sermons without Christ, and consisting of morality, without that relation to the Gospel of Christ which alone can render it acceptable in the
sight of God'.[66] When he was elected to the influential chair of divinity
at Glasgow in 1743 his critics attempted to unseat him. According to
Wodrow's account, Leechman's supporters were those 'who considered
themselves as the people of taste and education'; his opponent, John
Maclaurin, on the other hand, enjoyed widespread popular support.
The election was decided by the casting vote of the Rector, a 'worthy
gentleman', George Bogle of Daldowie.[67] Leechman's opponents first
tried to hold up the proceedings of the Presbytery of Irvine by which he
was to be released from his parochial position. Having failed there, the
following day, when he presented himself to the Presbytery of Glasgow,
they persuaded the court to refuse him enrolment. Believing that his
'election might prove of evil consequence to the purity of doctrine, and
the ministry of the Church',[68] in February the Presbytery was persuaded to institute 'a process of *heresy*' against him, and a committee was
set up to inquire into his sermon on prayer. This committee drew up
eight charges against the sermon which he, Leechman, refuted point by
point. In doing so, he accepted that his sermon contained a 'general
observation on human nature, and true in some respects in all nations
and ages of the world, however different their notions of religion may
be'.[69] At the same time he argued that his remarks were particularly
directed at atheists and sceptics. His aim had been to establish rational

---

[64] Leechman, *Temper, Character, and Duty*, pp. 16, 18, 21, 39.   [65] *Ibid.*, pp. 40, 44.
[66] Morren, *Annals of the General Assembly* (fn. 42), pp. 46–7.
[67] Leechman, *Temper, Character, and Duty* (fn. 60) p. 19. Maclaurin was a minister at Glasgow and was,
   according to Wodrow, 'highly respected for his learning and piety' but with little aptitude for
   teaching.   [68] Morren, *Annals of the General Assembly* (fn. 42) pp. 46–7.   [69] *Ibid.*, p. 48.

grounds for prayer, to show that 'prayer is a duty, even by the light of nature'.[70] The immediate cause of the sermon had been a pamphlet by a Quaker, who had called in question the practice of prayer.[71] Leechman's primary purpose, therefore, was to establish the argument for the theory and practice of prayer rather than to give an exposition of Christian prayer. His defence was accepted neither by the committee nor by the Presbytery. A 'spirit of bigotry' was raised against him; the Presbytery had continued its sittings and kept the issue before the public. Leechman therefore complained to the Synod of Glasgow and Ayr, which, at a very full meeting in April 1745, took the issue out of the hands of the Presbytery. The Synod found unanimously in Leechman's favour and their verdict was confirmed by the General Assembly. Leechman was not to be troubled again and indeed won over many of his adversaries in the ensuing years.

At the time of the Leechman affair Samuel Kenrick had already commenced his studies at Glasgow and he was admitted MA in 1747, the year James Wodrow began his studies with Leechman. Although the Jacobite entry into Glasgow no doubt eclipsed the affair in terms of interest and excitement, it undoubtedly affected the views of the two friends. For Wodrow, it underlined the need for caution and heightened his suspicion of popular politics. Although the Moderates would have preferred a reform of patronage, and continued to criticise the Act of 1712, its reform was relatively low in their priorities. It, in effect, produced the sort of ministry which Hutcheson wanted. For Wodrow, the Leechman affair, following so closely the controversy over patronage in the 1730s, underlined the dangers of participatory democracy. Had the Presbytery of Irvine had its way, Leechman would have been pronounced a heretic and Glasgow would have lost a distinguished teacher and a fine Christian. In such circumstances, liberty under the law even if imperfect, was vastly preferable to conceding claims to rights which, though just in the abstract, would, if conceded, lead to bigotry and injustice. It was better to accept the imperfections of the Patronage Act than to follow the arguments of those like the seceder, Ebenezer Erskine, based on 'the divine right of the people in the choice of their pastors'. That Act, though wrong in principle, was not wholly bad in its operation, for lay patrons generally appointed clergymen in the Moderate interest, who then protected this trend from local evangelical forces, usually in the majority, by organising themselves very effectively in the General

---

[70] *Ibid.*, pp. 51–2.   [71] Leechman, *Temper, Character, and Duty* (fn. 60), pp. 23–4.

Assembly and disciplining local opposition through insisting on its sovereignty.[72] The parallel with the relationship between the colonies and the British Government should be clear enough. As a Scotsman, Wodrow's education and situation led him to view the conflict with the American colonies in a quite different light from that of Kenrick. It was natural for him to believe that the colonies would do better to accept the limitations of their present position than to be led into uncharted waters by following the popular claims to the exercise of natural rights. For Wodrow, the liberties of the colonies had been safe in British hands for a century and a half and were now endangered by 'designing factious Demagogues'.[73]

The worldly constraints on Samuel Kenrick were very different from those on his friend and enabled him to draw out the radical dimensions of his education to justify an alternative way of looking at things. His experience of Scotland (and one must not forget that he had ties of blood with Scotland) left him with feelings of pride in his education and Scotland's achievements.[74] On the other hand, he felt that the forces of bigotry could be taken on with confidence. The cause of Enlightenment did not require one to bend to the winds of enthusiasm and superstition. That betokened a lack of confidence in the progress of truth. Living away from Scotland, and confident that such forces would not disrupt his life, he increasingly adopted the providential politics of the radical English Enlightenment and of leading Rational Dissenters. Whereas in 1771 he condemned the Wilkite mobs and suggested that the English Dissenters were too easily drawn into sympathising with the opposition,[75] a few years later he supported wholeheartedly the outlook of men like Price and Priestley, which allowed a much more limited role for prudence in politics than that of the Moderate clergy of Scotland. The American cause, he argued, should be supported for it was the cause of truth.

It is in my opinion the cause of liberty and truth and I have not the least doubt but the God of truth will defend it and in his own good time make them to flourish in those extensive fertile regions.[76]

---

[72] Callum Brown, 'Religion and Social Change', in T.M. Devine and Rosalind Mitchison, eds., *People and Society in Scotland*. 3 vols. (Edinburgh, 1988–92), vol. I, pp. 147–8; Carlyle, *Autobiography* (fn. 52), pp. 244–8, 255–6.

[73] W–K (57), Wodrow to Kenrick, 16 June 1776. Wodrow conceded that 'two or three' of the leaders of the Americans were 'generous and worthy Patriots'.

[74] Kenrick's mother, Sarah, was the daughter of Revd Archibald Hamilton of Corstorphine near Edinburgh and Sarah Wynne of Denbighshire. Wodrow described him as 'half a Scotsman'. W–K (46), Wodrow to Kenrick, 1 May 1770.

[75] W–K (48)a, Kenrick to Wodrow, 31 March 1771. It was this letter which led Wodrow to condemn the Dissenters' 'Enthusiasm for Liberty' (*ibid.* (49), Wodrow to Kenrick, 22 May 1771).

[76] W–K (55), Kenrick to Wodrow, 29 January, 18 March 1776.

For Kenrick the conflict could be viewed as a struggle between virtue and vice, enlightenment and darkness, in which those on the side of the angels should be prepared to struggle with their antagonists rather than to pray for the enlightenment of their souls. 'We cannot', he declared, 'expect that men of sense will submit to the imperfections of our constitution, because they are fond of its imperfections.'[77] Betraying the same cast of mind which led Priestley to affirm, 'I do not see why, in a judgement of equity ... insolence on one side should not be answered by contempt on the other',[78] he asserted that 'As long as men have spirit or are not slaves they will repel force by force and ill usage by ill usage – and be very good christians too in my opinion.' In 1780, Joseph Priestley moved to Birmingham and became a neighbour of Kenrick. Like many who visited him, including Edmund Burke, Kenrick came away impressed. It would, however, be too tidy to date Priestley's influence on him from that time. Priestley was the most active propagandist for Rational Dissent in the late 1760s and early 1770s and Kenrick would have been aware of his work for a decade or so before he became a neighbour. Although we do not find deep metaphysical discussions in Kenrick's letters, his reaction to events and his political outlook are very close to those of Priestley.[79]

III

At the end of the American War of Independence, Kenrick could not resist a final triumphal throw. Using a distinction made by Priestley,[80] he offered some closing reflections in which he suggested that the attitudes of the Scots caused them to lag behind the van of Enlightenment.

The great difference between Scotland and England, with regard to their notions of government, lies in the former having no political liberty – you enjoy

---

[77] *Ibid.*

[78] J. Priestley, *An Essay on the First Principles of Government, and on the Nature of Political, Civil, and Religious Liberty*, 2nd edn (London, 1771), p. xiv.

[79] Kenrick in 1781 described Priestley as 'this wonderful man'. At the time he had been reading his *Letters to a Philosophical Unbeliever* (1780) in which Priestley attacked Hume's scepticism (W–K (72), Kenrick to Wodrow, 15 August 1781). In the letter he shows his familiarity with Priestley's earlier attack on the common sense philosophies of Reid, Beattie and Oswald, *An Examination of Dr. Reid's Inquiry into the Human Mind...* (1774).

[80] Priestley, *Letters* (fn. 79), pp. 9–10. For a valuable discussion of the contemporary context of Priestley's distinction and its originality, see J. Dybikowski, *On Burning Ground: An Examination of the Ideas, Projects and Life of David Williams* (Oxford, 1993), pp. 166–75; and D.O. Thomas, 'Progress, Liberty and Utility: The Political Philosophy of Joseph Priestley', in R.G.W. Anderson & Christopher Lawrence eds., *Science, Medicine and Dissent: Joseph Priestley (1733–1804)* (London, 1987), pp. 75–9.

civil liberty and are satisfied with it. So is the Dane, the Swede, the Frenchman and the Spaniard. They all enjoy civil liberty and are governed by established laws and customs.

One suspects that Kenrick had had this critique up his sleeve ever since Wodrow had asserted the importance of liberty within the law in 1775, but, more immediately, he was replying to Wodrow's '"apprehensions that the Americans by their high degree of political liberty have hurt their civil liberty and that their lives and fortunes are not so safe &c."'.[81] This was not a juxtaposition that Kenrick would accept, for, following Priestley, he believed that civil liberty was made secure through political liberty.[82] Of course the implication of this was that it was more secure in England than in Scotland. In England, he argued, 'the commonest mechanic' exerted himself in jury service 'with all the zeal, of one whose life and death depended [sic] – neglecting all their private business'. To rub salt into the wound, he declared that he was not holding up the English as paragons: the Americans had exceeded them in their standard of political liberty. Like Wodrow he had read the American Constitutions, 'those of Massachusetts bay, and the rest – where I find literally verified the principles of government laid down by Dr Price – wch have so often been termed visionary and impracticable'. True, in conclusion he welcomed the fact that the 'spirit of liberty' had reached Scotland, meaning that moves were afoot for reform of the Burghs, but one could hardly be sanguine about the outcome. Scottish representation was too inadequate and too corrupt to carry through reform: 'you will as soon see bishops stand forth in behalf of the civil and religious rights of mankind as your representatives'.[83]

This sort of epistolary confrontation might lead one to the conclusion that it is possible to delineate with some clarity the divide between the world of the Scottish Moderate and the Rational Dissenter. It would go as follows: the Scottish Moderates were prudential in their politics, non-dogmatic in their theology, moralistic in their teachings, and anxious that virtue would be maintained so that their good lives and virtuous country would draw on them the blessings of providence; the Rational Dissenters elevated truth over expediency in politics, were anxious to eliminate the errors of orthodox theology, proclaimed the virtues of candid free inquiry in all aspects of life and were confident that

---

[81] These were expressed in a letter of 26 December 1782, which unfortunately is not extant, in which Wodrow appears to have mounted a final defence of his position over America. Kenrick is quoting him verbatim. (W–K (77), Kenrick to Wodrow, 9 May 1783.)
[82] Priestley, *Essay* (fn. 78), pp. 59–60.   [83] W–K (77), Kenrick to Wodrow, 9 May 1783.

Providence would secure the triumph of truth over error. It would see Kenrick, the Rational Dissenter, as typical of the radical Enlightenment and Wodrow, the Scottish Moderate, as typical of the moderate Enlightenment. But that would be making too much of their correspondence, or at least of the episode on which we have focused. It would also be using it falsely to magnify their personal differences and simplify the contrasts between their respective worlds. In particular, there were divergences as well as contiguities *within* Rational Dissent, which need to be explored further before conclusions can be drawn.

If we begin with their leading figures, Price and Priestley, we can see that they shared similar political aspirations, similar hopes for progress, and similar attitudes to the great events of their time. Price's justification of resistance and of natural rights led him to be cited by the anti-patronage camp in 1790.[84] Yet not only are there important prudential dimensions to his politics, but also he shared something of the Moderates' belief that only rigorously moral lives and a virtuous nation can expect to win divine favour. Even his most celebratory performances retain the character of a jeremiad.[85] At the height of British successes in the Seven Years War, he preached a sermon which glorified all aspects of British achievements, but still cautioned:

'Tis to God we owe all that makes us happy . . . All events are subject to his superintendency, *and he doeth whatsoever he pleaseth in the armies of heaven and among the inhabitants of the earth* . . . We ought to ascribe all our successes to his goodness, and, with grateful hearts, to direct our regards to his providence, and to fix our dependence upon his favour, as the original sources of all prosperity and bliss.

He went on to indicate that improvements could still be made in the nation and to warn:

'Tis *possible* that we may lose the advantages we have gained, and our joy and triumph be suddenly changed to misery and despair. Let us then rejoyce with trembling, and suppress carefully in ourselves all vain confidence, placing our chief trust in God, and discovering, in all events, that regard to the common welfare of mankind and those equitable, reasonable, and pious dispositions, which are the best proofs of true magnanimity, and the best means of securing the continuance of the divine protection.[86]

---

[84] R. Park, *Defence, of the Rights and Liberties of the Church, against the Pretended Right and Usurpations of Patronage* 2nd edn (Glasgow, 1789, repr. 1790), advert.

[85] On the jeremiad and providential views, see Richard B. Sher in his 'Witherspoon's *Dominion of Providence* and the Scottish Jeremiad Tradition', in Sher and Smitten, *Scotland and America* (fn. 21), pp. 46–64 at pp. 50, 61.

[86] R. Price, *Britain's Happiness and the Proper Improvement of it* (1759), in *Richard Price. Political Writings*, ed. D.O. Thomas (Cambridge, 1991), pp. 1–13 at pp. 7–8, 12.

By the time Price came to preach his famous *Discourse on the Love of Our Country* (1789), he had witnessed the success of the American cause which he had supported, and publicly became more enthusiastic than ever about the general development of the Enlightenment, although ever more critical about the British Constitution. For the most part he confined his worries to his own shorthand diary.[87] But the importance of behaving well, sticking to one's principles *and* depending on providence was still a theme in the *Discourse*. In celebrating the anniversary of the Glorious Revolution, he viewed it as the source of Britain's special blessings. He enjoined his audience, 'Let us, therefore, offer thanksgivings to God, the author of all our blessings', and immediately went on, '*Had he not been on our side, we should have been swallowed up quick, and the proud waters would have gone over our souls.*'[88]

In some respects therefore, Price's outlook is closer to that of Wodrow than it is to Priestley, for whom whatever happened was God's will. Kenrick, with his devotion to the value of muscular controversy and profoundly influenced by Priestley's optimism and necessitarianism, was committed to believing in a rather simple doctrine of providential progress. Price, on the other hand, in his debate with Priestley published as *A Free Discussion of the Doctrines of Materialism, and Philosophical Necessity* (1778), worried about Priestley's belief that even acts of wickedness could be seen as part of the providential plan. He asked him whether he could 'believe easily that in all those crimes which men charge *themselves* with, and reproach *themselves* for, God is the agent; and that (speaking philosophically) *they*, in such instances, are no more *agents*, than a *sword* is an agent when employed to commit murder?' Priestley's response was that 'It does require *strength of mind* not to startle at such a conclusion; but then it requires nothing but strength of mind.'[89] Price's reservations about the effect of Priestley's Unitarian metaphysics were expressed in a letter to Lord Monboddo in which he considered Priestley's 'system as most dangerous in its tendency'.[90] Although both Price and Priestley believed life to be permeated by the divine presence, for Price, as John

[87] See 'Richard Price's Journal for the Period 25 March 1787 to 6 February 1791 Deciphered by Beryl Thomas with an Introduction and Notes by D.O. Thomas', *The National Library of Wales Journal*, 26 (4) (1980), 366–413.
[88] R. Price, *Discourse on the Love of Our Country* (1789), in *ibid.*, pp. 176–96, at p. 189.
[89] J. Priestley, *A Free Discussion of the Doctrines of Materialism, and Philosophical Necessity, in a Correspondence between Dr. Price and Dr. Priestley* ... (London, 1778), pp. 158–61.
[90] *The Correspondence of Richard Price*, ed. W.B. Peach and D.O. Thomas (in progress): vol. 2: March 1778–February 1786, ed. D.O. Thomas (Cardiff and Durham, NC, 1991), p. 87, Price to Lord Monboddo, 11 December 1780.

Stephens has noted, 'God directs us by presenting choices to our minds: in responding to them we develop our capacity to grow in virtue'.[91] If we failed to heed the teachings of our divine master, we could not expect to continue in his favour. The world, in this view, was a school of virtue. Wodrow may or may not have understood or agreed with Price's underlying philosophy, but his *outlook* was similar.

Despite these affinities, Price and Priestley were much closer to each other over political issues and tactics than Price was to Wodrow; broadly speaking, they were for will rather than circumstance.[92] But not all Rational Dissenters were so hostile to the *status quo*. If Kenrick had accepted the offer to teach modern languages at Warrington Academy, he would have had as a colleague William Enfield, whose teaching emphasised moral virtues and gentlemanly conduct in a way thoroughly consonant with the ideals of Scottish Moderatism.[93] As Enfield wrote to his friend, Dr Nicholas Clayton, 'I set out in life upon the plan of *moderation*, and neither my temper nor my principles will suffer me to desert it.'[94] John Aikin admirably summed up his ideals and qualities:

Religion was to him rather a principle than a sentiment; and he was more solicitous to deduce from it a *rule of life*, enforced by its peculiar sanctions, than to elevate it into a source of sublime feeling. Despising superstition, and fearing enthusiasm, he held as of inferior value everything in religion which could not ally itself with morality, and condescending to human uses. His theological system was purged of every mysterious or unintelligible proposition; it included nothing which appeared to him irreconcilable with sound philosophy, and the most rational opinions concerning the divine nature and perfections.[95]

Enfield was both a friend and critic of Priestley. He objected to Priestley's constant attacks on the Anglican establishment, because he believed that an established religion was justified on utilitarian grounds, although his preference would have been for an establishment reformed

---

[91] John Stephens, 'Price, Providence and the *Principia*', *Enlightenment and Dissent*, 6, (1987), pp. 77–93 at 88.

[92] There were prudential elements in Price's politics and moderate dimensions in Priestley's. The relationship between Rational Dissent and radicalism was complex, see my, 'Heretical Religion and Radical Political Ideas in Late Eighteenth-Century England', in Hellmuth, *Transformation of Political Culture* (fn. 33), pp. 339–72.

[93] Kenrick refused an offer to teach modern languages at Warrington Academy (W–K (53), Kenrick to Wodrow, 30 August 1775). On Enfield, see Fitzpatrick, 'Varieties of Candour'(fn. 6), at pp. 46–7.

[94] Liverpool Record Office, Nicholson Papers, 920 NIC 9/12/3, Enfield to Clayton, 15 March 1789. Nicholas Clayton was a contemporary of Priestley at Daventry Academy and subsequently studied at Glasgow University. See Anne Holt, *Walking Together. A Study in Liverpool Nonconformity, 1688–1938* (London, 1938), pp. 140, 148.

[95] W. Enfield, *Sermons on Practical Subjects . . . To Which are Prefixed Memoirs of the Author by J. Aikin*, 3 vols., 2nd edn (London, 1799), vol. I, pp. xiv–xv.

according to Unitarian principles. He did not believe that controversy furthered the cause of truth, rather it might have the opposite effect of 'rousing the sleeping lion' of prejudice. His attitude towards truth was both more sceptical and ecumenical than that of Priestley. He objected to the latter's belief that the Dissenting cause was 'the *cause of truth, religion* and *liberty*'.[96] Indeed, he was the translator of Johann Jakob Brucker's *Historia Critica Philosophiae* (1766) in which Brucker's eclectic attitude towards truth is indicated by his method of writing the history of modern philosophy without acknowledging divisions into different schools.[97] More profoundly, he differed from Priestley in believing that many aspects of religion were open to doubt and indeed always would be. He quoted Charron's view that 'nous sommes nais à questre la verité; la possèder appartient à une plus haute et grande puissance'.[98] That undercut Priestley's belief in the value of truth-seeking through vigorous controversy. Enfield believed that errors and prejudice were best left to die away; for the most part they did little harm, provided due emphasis was placed on 'those principles which are obvious and certain'.[99] Even when he praised Priestley's *Letter to Pitt* (1787), which upbraided Pitt for failing to support the repeal of the Test and Corporation Acts, he hoped that the outcome of the publication would be to convince 'the world that all polemical disputes are futile and unsatisfactory . . . and that it is high time for us all to meet on the broad ground of Common Sense'.[100] It is, I hope, not too fanciful to link this with Enfield's notion that it would be better for English speakers if the rough edges of their provincial dialects were worn away so that individuals could meet on the broad ground of plain, modest, speaking.[101] Certainly his faith was one which accepted the value of being at ease with oneself and the world.[102] When, in 1774,

[96] W. Enfield, *Remarks on Several Late Publications Relative to the Dissenters in a Letter to Dr. Priestley* (London, 1770), p. 12.

[97] W. Enfield, *The History of Philosophy from the Earliest Periods: Drawn up from Brucker's 'Historia Critica Philosophiae'* (London, 1837); R. Tuck, 'The "Modern" Theory of Natural Law', in A. Pagden, ed., *The Languages of Political Theory in Early-Modern Europe* (Cambridge, 1987), pp. 99–100.

[98] Enfield (fn. 96), pp. 68–9, citing *De La Sagesse* (1601).   [99] *Ibid.*, pp. 70–1.

[100] Liverpool Record Office, Nicholson Papers. 920 NIC 9/12/1, Enfield to Revd Dr Clayton, 2 May 1787. See also, Enfield, *Remarks* (fn. 96), p. v: 'Possibly, the time may not be far distant when an end will be put to fruitless controversy, by distinctly ascertaining the limits of the human understanding.'

[101] When Kenrick discussed dialect with Wodrow, he noted that Joseph and especially Mary Priestley had retained their provincial dialects, Yorkshire and Westmoreland respectively, and that Joseph's preaching was marked by his 'Yorkshire pronunciation'. Kenrick commented: 'perhaps it [vulgar dialect] is most attended to and guarded against by people of the most superficial minds' (W–K (85), Kenrick to Wodrow, 2 December 1784).

[102] W. Enfield, *The Speaker* . . . (London, 1774), p. xxv. The parallel with the desire of the Scottish Moderates from Robert Wallace and William Leechman on, to purge their work of Scotticisms is obvious. See Sefton, *Early Development* (fn. 42), p. 22; and Sher, *Church and University* (fn. 33), pp. 168–9.

he published a book on elocution, *The Speaker*, he struck a responsive chord and its popularity continued well into the nineteenth century. In its sequel, *Exercises in Elocution* (1780), he admitted, as a subsidiary purpose, that it would serve as an anthology which would help to shape the literary taste of the young as well as impressing upon their minds 'sentiments of honour and virtue'.[103] It was appropriate that when Enfield left Warrington in 1785, he became minister at the Octagon, in Norwich, a fine example of classical taste and the munificence of liberal Dissenters.[104]

There were, however, limits to Enfield's conformity to the world, to his bowing to circumstance. Theologically he can be placed amongst the more radical Rational Dissenters who made the transition to Unitarianism.[105] Like Priestley, there is a primitivist dimension to his thought. In the preface to Brucker's work he argued that the study of the history of philosophy would lead to the discovery of 'the origin of many notions and practices, which have no other support than their antiquity, and consequently to much important reformation and improvement'.[106] Finally, he remained a Dissenter, critical of the constitution in Church and state and a firm supporter of the rights of humanity violated by the slave trade. During the troubled years of the 1790s he adhered to his principles, hoping forlornly that some path might be found between the increasingly reactionary government and the increasingly revolutionary desires of radicals. He refused to hide his opinions on the need for radical reform,[107] he resisted wilder currents of thought, mesmeric or millenarian, and there is an impressive integrity about his clear-headed adherence to moderation and the quiet religious optimism which informed his views.[108]

---

[103] W. Enfield, *Exercises in Elocution*, a new edn (London, 1794), advert.

[104] See G. Hague, J. Hague, *The Unitarian Heritage. An Architectural Survey of Chapels and Churches in the Unitarian Tradition in the British Isles* (Sheffield, 1986), pp. 62–3. The chapel cost £5,174 to build. John Wesley remarked of its finery, 'How can it be thought that the coarse old gospel should find admission'. It was not only evangelicals who had reservations about Rational Dissenting display; Revd George Walker wrote of Paradise Street Chapel, Liverpool, 'finery without superstition will not do . . . commodious and neat but plain, suits best with the chaste character of Presbyterianism' (Liverpool Record Office, Nicholson Papers, 920 NIC 9/20/1 Revd George Walker to Revd Dr Clayton). Walker, like Clayton, was a graduate of Glasgow University.

[105] *Ibid.*, 9/12/3, same to same, 15 March 1789. He declared that he could not conform to the Established Church until it became 'perfectly unitarian'.

[106] Enfield, *History of Philosophy* (fn. 98), pp. v–vi.

[107] Bodleian Library, Griffiths Correspondence, ff. 65–7, Enfield to Griffiths, 6 December 1792.

[108] *Ibid.*, f. 60, same to same, 5 August 1791. Enfield, in the aftermath of the Birmingham riots, wrote, 'let us persevere in well doing: every meritorious exertion has its effect – a phoenix will arise out of the ashes of our Birmingham conventicles'.

To a degree, therefore, even being a moderate amongst Rational Dissenters was not the same as being a Moderate Scottish clergyman, and the fact of Dissent is the clearest difference. But this is not the whole truth, for Moderatism was under pressure in the later eighteenth century. The leadership of Moderatism was aging and a new generation of leaders was faced with the defence of moderation at a time when the centre ground was shifting and increasingly difficult to hold.[109] Moderate fears of popular enthusiasm had been fuelled by the antics of the Popular Party over the Catholic Relief Act of 1778.[110] When the Popular Party then revived the issue of patronage,[111] Revd Thomas Hardy, who was soon to become Professor of Ecclesiastical History at the University of Edinburgh, defended the Moderate interest with a robust re-statement of the principles of Moderation, but in suggesting that the patronage issue was the only source of division within the Church he was being piously over-optimistic.[112] Moreover, his articulation of the Moderate argument for abiding by the *status quo* coexisted uneasily with his advocacy of the reform of the Patronage Act. In Wodrow's case, at least, one can see how the failure of the Moderate stance over the American conflict led him to re-appraise his political position, and drew him closer to Rational Dissent, more especially of Enfield's brand. It was inevitable that he should wonder why the American revolt had been successful, and that for an answer he should look within. Maybe it was a case not of virtue being unrewarded, but of the British lacking the virtue to deserve reward. He was critical of the failure of the government to take advantage of the martial spirit aroused by the surrender of Burgoyne at Saratoga (October 1777) and of its discouragement of schemes for a militia, believing that an armed citizenry would act as a guarantor of law and order and an effective means of self-defence.[113] Wodrow, indeed, became infected by the sort of gloom that he detected in Richard Price; he came to believe that a militia scheme 'seems necessary to prolong the existence of this Country'.[114] Thus events had led him to concede, to a degree, the pessimistic evaluations of

---

[109] Sher, *Church and University* (fn. 33), pp. 298–333.   [110] *Ibid.*, 277–97.

[111] Donovan, *No Popery* (fn. 45), p. 290.

[112] T. Hardy, *The Principles of Moderation Addressed to the Clergy of the Popular Interest in the Church of Scotland* (Edinburgh, 1782), pp. 1–5.

[113] W–K (74), Wodrow to Kenrick 23 May 1782. Wodrow favoured the scheme of arming the people, which involved 'training and disciplining the better sort among them to arms'. It is unclear whether he was referring to a specific scheme, but his own proposals are close to those emanating from the Poker Club in July of the same year. See J. Robertson, *The Scottish Enlightenment and the Militia Issue* (Edinburgh, 1985), esp. pp. 140–7.

[114] W–K (74), Wodrow to Kenrick, 23 May 1782.

the corruptions of the constitution with which his friend had belaboured him. In the 1780s we find him looking for moderate reform in order to restore Scottish virtue. He now found himself on the side of his friend Kenrick, despite continuing differences in outlook. Moreover, although Kenrick could feel vindicated in his support of the American Revolution, the reform causes at home, which he supported on the same principles, did not have much success. Although those principles generally led him to take a more favourable stance towards the French Revolution than Wodrow, the hand of Providence was sufficiently hidden to cause puzzlement and uncertainty, feelings reinforced by the profoundly divisive impact of the French Revolution in Britain. In consequence the French Revolution did not cause the friends to re-play their differences of the 1770s which would have placed Wodrow in the camp of Burke and Kenrick in that of Price and Paine. The re-shaping of the ideas and their relationship in the later 1780s and early 1790s is worth looking at in a little more detail.

IV

James Wodrow's failure to predict the consequences of the American Revolution for both Britain and America wore down some of the assertiveness that he had displayed when he had been arguing the issue with his friend and left him in a depressed mood. Worse than that, just when things were settling down and some reconciliation of views seemed possible, his friend launched an attack on the state of Scottish liberty. Worse still, his friend seemed to be right. Every issue to which Wodrow was committed in the 1780s and early 1790s was either an outright failure or had a mixed outcome. The Burgh Reform Movement of the early 1780s had failed and, although the issue had not gone away, the increasing ascendancy of Henry Dundas made success only a fairytale possibility. Similarly, the movement to repeal the Test Act as it applied to Scotland, stimulated by the English campaign for the repeal of the Test and Corporation Acts, was defeated.[115] Wodrow need not have felt particularly defensive about these failures, for the English campaigns for parliamentary reform and for the repeal of the Test and Corporation Acts were equally ineffectual. However, an issue particularly close to his heart, and also close to him in proximity, forced him on to the defensive.

---

[115] See G.M. Ditchfield, 'The Scottish Campaign Against the Test Act, 1790–1791', *Historical Journal*, 23 (1980), 37–61, which *inter alia* discusses the attitudes of Wodrow and Kenrick.

This was the threatened prosecution for heresy of Revd William M'Gill of Ayr. It served as a reminder that the confidence of Thomas Hardy (if it *really* was confidence) in the essential unanimity of the Church was misplaced and that Moderatism had to work as hard as ever to keep the forces of prejudice and persecution at bay.[116]

The proceedings against M'Gill were triggered by an issue of which Wodrow could have felt justly proud, Scotland's celebration of the centenary of the Glorious Revolution. The Scots, unlike the English, set aside a day for a national commemoration of the event, and leading dignitaries of the Scottish Enlightenment celebrated it while the aristocracy lent its support.[117] Among the sermons published to commemorate the event was one by M'Gill. The sermon itself was not contentious, but it contained an appendix in which he replied to a critic of his liberal theology as expounded in a work entitled *The Death of Christ*. Published in 1786, this had immediately attracted the hostile attention of the orthodox, but no action had been taken against him. M'Gill wisely did not reply to his critics, but when a neighbouring clergyman, Dr William Peebles (of Newton-on-Ayr), whom M'Gill considered to be his friend,[118] attacked him in his own commemoration sermon,[119] his patience snapped, and, without consulting those advisers, such as James Wodrow, who had assisted with the publication of *The Death of Christ*, he issued a sharply polemical rebuttal.[120] This gave his enemies the opportunity they needed. The Synod of Ayr, on the prompting of the General Assembly (which in turn was responding to an initiative taken by the Synod of

---

[116] See Hardy, *Principles* (fn. 112), pp. 4–5, in which he specifically noted 'that our people are in no danger of being distracted by jarring theories from the pulpit, in their most momentous concerns; that the word *heresy* is not once mentioned among us; and that we do not meet in our church-courts, to discuss articles of faith, or to divide on the orthodoxy of opinions'. In fact, there was a heresy proceeding in the late 1760s in Wodrow's neighbourhood against Alexander Fergusson (1689–1770) minister of Kilwinning. Wodrow was disturbed by the case, which appears to have been a forerunner of that of M'Gill (W–K (45), Wodrow to Kenrick, 25 January 1769, and *ibid.* (46), same to same, 1 May 1770).

[117] Henry Beaufoy was designated by the London Revolution Society to propose a motion in the Commons that 16 of December, the day on which the Bill of Rights was passed, should become a day of national thanksgiving. The motion was carried in the Commons and defeated in the Lords, 23 July 1789. B.L. Add. Ms. 64814, Minutes of the London Revolution Society, ff. 14 & 53; *Parliamentary History*, vol. xxvii. col. 1332, and vol. xxviii, cols. 294–7; A. Goodwin, *The Friends of Liberty: The English Democratic Movement in the Age of the French Revolution* (London, 1979), p. 86.

[118] W. M'Gill, *The Benefits of the Revolution: a Sermon preached at Ayr on the 5th of November, 1788 ... to which are added, Remarks on a Sermon, preached on the same day, at Newton upon Ayr* (Kilmarnock, 1789), pp. 25–6.

[119] W. Peebles, *The Great Things which the Lord hath done for this Nation, Illustrated ... in two sermons, preached ... for a National Thanksgiving in Commemoration of the Revolution 1688* (Kilmarnock, 1788), pp. 34–8.

[120] Fitzpatrick, 'Varieties of Candour' (fn. 6), p. 42; W–K (146), Wodrow to Kenrick, 8 March 1789.

Glasgow and Ayr), investigated his writings and found them erroneous on five counts.[121] M'Gill was forced to take a conciliatory tack: while he did not actually withdraw anything he had said in response to these charges, he regretted any expression which 'may appear improper' and reaffirmed his belief in the doctrines of the Kirk as laid down in the Westminster Confession.[122] Wodrow himself was a member of the committee of ministers which produced this settlement.[123] But the whole affair did not die down completely until the end of 1792.[124] Yet, if Wodrow had incurred some criticism over the M'Gill affair – we find him complaining, with perhaps a touch of self pity, that in Scotland the settlement had been regarded 'as a proclamation of an open indemnity to Socinianism; and in England as an open and severe persecution of it'[125] – his friend had to cope with the outbreak of violence in neighbouring Birmingham against his hero, Joseph Priestley, in July 1791.

In sum, the views of both Wodrow and Kenrick on the French Revolution were undoubtedly coloured by their growing realisation that the age they lived in was not as enlightened as they had hoped, that political reform was unlikely, that toleration was incomplete, that bigotry had not been conquered and that the fires of persecution in both England and Scotland had been rekindled, and, one might add, by their friendly rivalry over the relative stages of advancement that their two countries had reached. Consequently, we do not find that there are long stretches of even longer letters devoted to the French Revolution; rather the Revolution is discussed in relation to a series of other events and causes that were dear to them. In this respect, neither could feel very happy about the progress of Enlightenment at home and abroad, as a brief discussion of their reactions to events in France will show. Kenrick in a letter of 16 December 1789, which discussed the M'Gill affair, rejoiced that the issue had come fully out into the open. He predicted that it would lead to Christianity being established on a true Biblical foundation, but he warned that if the Scots did 'not look sharp the French – and the Spaniards for what I know will have the start of you, in religious as

---

[121] The five counts were: 'The original and essential dignity of the Son of God: the doctrine of the Atonement by His sufferings and death; the priesthood and intercession of Christ; the method of reconciling sinners to God; and subscription to the Confession of Faith'. See A. McNair, *Scots Theology in the Eighteenth Century* (London, 1928), pp. 96–7. McNair argues that M'Gill had 'flatly denied' three other articles of the Westminster Confession, namely, those of 'The Covenant of Works', 'Predestination' and 'Effectual Calling'.

[122] *Ibid.*, pp. 99–100; *Proceedings of the Very Reverend The Synod of Glasgow and Ayr . . . 13 & 14th April 1790, Relating to some late publications of the Revd Dr William McGill, with the final decisions in that cause* (Glasgow, 1790), pp. 6–12. [123] *Ibid.*, p. 5. [124] McNair, *Scots Theology* (fn. 121), pp. 104–7.

[125] W–K (159), Wodrow to Kenrick, 28 March 1791.

well as civil liberty'. This was not the usual points scoring, for he added, 'We poor dissenters are left far behind you all.'[126]

It was, of course, a common reaction amongst English Dissenters to fear that British liberties would soon pale in comparison with those being introduced in France. Yet it was Wodrow, not Kenrick, who first mentioned the Revolution in their correspondence in a letter of 5 August 1789; he confessed that initially he had hoped that 'a grand and glorious revolution in favour of liberty would have been effected without bloodshed and that it would have made the tyrants of Europe tremble on their thrones', but he now feared that the Third Estate had lost control and there was a danger of returning to the outrages of the 'days of the League'.[127] Later he recovered his composure and, in a letter of 1790, he wrote what Kenrick described as 'your warm panegyric on the French Revolution'.[128] Wodrow's attitude was nonetheless more cautious than Kenrick's. Although no defender of Burke, whom he described as having 'too much respect for the prejudices of mankind', he thought Priestley's reply to *The Reflections* erred in the opposite direction: it treated the prejudices of mankind 'with too much contempt'.[129] Kenrick leapt to the defence of his hero, pointing out that the controversy had begun with Burke's scurrilous, sarcastic, abusive and unprovoked attack on Richard Price. His essential point, however, was rather different; it was that the controversy would further the cause of truth. He declared, 'I look upon Burke . . . as co-operating with all his able antagonists in bringing forwards the great work of improvement.'[130]

It was this expectation that progress somehow would take place which made the two friends men of the Enlightenment. But they were also Protestant Christians, although of a thoroughly liberal sort, and so they were continually trying to relate that expectation to their religious ideas. A constant theme of their letters is how contemporary happenings might be seen as part of the plan of providence. This clearly posed problems when events like the September Massacres and the execution of Louis XVI were viewed by both as casting dark shadows over the bright ideals of the Revolution.[131] Kenrick, with his devotion to the value of energetic

---

[126] W–K (152), Kenrick to Wodrow, 16 December 1789.

[127] W–K (149), Wodrow to Kenrick, 5 August 1789.

[128] W–K (155), Kenrick to Wodrow, 25 September 1790. Wodrow's letter of 23 July 1790, to which Kenrick refers, is not extant.   [129] W–K (159), Wodrow to Kenrick, 28 March 1791.

[130] W–K (160), Kenrick to Wodrow, 20–1 April 1791.

[131] A useful introduction to their attitudes towards the French Revolution can be found in J. Creasey, 'Some Dissenting Attitudes Towards The French Revolution', *Transactions of the Unitarian Historical Society*, 13 (1966), 155–67. Wodrow, while considering himself as of the same party as Kenrick 'in all material points', still distanced himself from his friend's radicalism and adhered to what he considered to be the moderate centre ground. W–K (193), Wodrow to Kenrick, 17 or 18 July 1794.

controversy, and profoundly influenced by Priestley's optimism and necessitarianism, was committed to a rather simple doctrine of providential progress; Wodrow, who remained attached to the doctrine of free will, placed greater emphasis upon the role of virtuous human action as a prerequisite for providential rewards. Both, however, in their adherence to scriptural revelation, expected that the end would be most glorious. Thus in September 1794 we find Wodrow enquiring further about Priestley's views on general judgement and the end of the world.[132] He had been reading Priestley's Fast sermon preached on 28 February of that year, shortly before he departed for America, in which he suggested that the calamitous state of affairs in Europe indicated that the Second Coming of Christ and the inauguration of the millennium were at hand.[133] Almost a fortnight earlier, on 17 February, Wodrow had preached two Fast sermons on the measures of providence as they applied to the affairs of Britain and France. Apart from his edition of the sermons of William Leechman, these sermons were to be his only published work and therefore they offer us a special insight into the way his ideas and experiences had been shaped by those events that he had discussed so frequently with his friend. Whereas Priestley's focus was on revelation and the overall plan of providence as foretold there, Wodrow looked more closely at the fortunes of the two countries and tried to make sense of these in providential terms. His sermons do not present a straight contrast between British virtue and French folly and vice, however tempting that might have been as the Terror moved into its last menacing phase. Wodrow chose to examine Britain and France separately. The French Revolution, he argued, began full of promise and would have fulfilled that promise had not the French revolutionaries begun to act in evil ways.[134] They had created not a republic but a despotism. Although the patriotic spirit of the French people was 'rather to be admired',[135] the 'blind zeal or

[132] W–K (195), Wodrow to Kenrick, 10 September 1794.
[133] J. Priestley, *The Present State of Europe Compared with the Antient Prophecies* (London, 1794), p. 2. For a discussion of the sermon see my 'Joseph Priestley, Politics and Ancient Prophecy', *Enlightenment and Dissent*, 10 (1991), 104–9.
[134] J. Wodrow, *The Measures of Divine Providence towards Men and Nations . . . applied to the present state of the British and French nations: in two sermons . . . 1794* (Glasgow, 1831), pp. 23, 30. In relation to the religious dimensions of the Revolution, Wodrow argued that had 'they satisfied themselves with retrenching the oppressive power and enormous revenues of the higher orders of their clergy, and increasing those of the lower order, more useful in their office; with abolishing religious tests; and establishing a full liberty of conscience: – thus opening to the Protestants, equally with the Catholics, a share in the protection and in the offices of state. Had they stopped there, the reformation must have been useful to the community.'
[135] cf. Hutcheson, *System* (fn. 21), vol. I, p. 81: 'we honour sometimes what we conceive directly to be detrimental; as patriotism or courage, in a foreigner, or an enemy'.

enthusiasm of a multitude' had been manipulated 'by a few artful men' to create a new species of Inquisition. Providence had therefore visited on them a 'civil war . . . one of the most tremendous judgments, which the provoked severity of Heaven ever inflicted upon a guilty nation'.[136] The French would not recover from this easily; they required not merely political but moral regeneration which was more dearly bought, yet was essential if the wounds within the community were to be healed. The French example was, therefore, not one to be followed, and popular clamour for reform should be resisted for

improvements, especially in a free government like ours, can only be safe, solid, and permanent, when they come on in a very gradual way, by the slow and silent working of wisdom, reason, and experience; producing a full conviction of their necessity or utility upon the public mind.[137]

This was, of course, the British way, and one which they should hold to; but he warned against loyalist jingoism. In condemning the French, 'we should not be so presumptuous as to justify ourselves; standing as we do this day, before an impartial God'.[138]

In his first sermon, he accepted that providence had shone on Britain: the last century had been 'one of the most distinguished seasons of mercy and goodness ever vouchsafed unto any people'.[139] The Glorious Revolution had 'fixed and increased the securities for our liberty'.[140] And he reiterated his belief that the essence of liberty was *civil liberty*:

the protection or security which the whole people, – all the members of the state, high and low, – enjoy, under the *restraint* of wise and equal laws, under a well-regulated and well-executed public authority; which leaves every individual as much power as possible to do good, in his own station, and to enjoy it; but, at the same time, ties up his hands, and restrains him as much as possible from doing evil, either to others or himself.[141]

Was this his final riposte to his friend after all those fiery arguments of the 1770s? Not quite. For Wodrow civil liberty did not embrace participation as it did for Price, nor did it require political liberty to guarantee its perpetuation, as it did for Priestley; its survival depended upon the maintenance of virtuous conduct.[142] Britain had recently had a sharp

---

[136] Wodrow, *Measures of Divine Providence* (fn. 134), pp. 26–7, 29.   [137] *Ibid.*, p. 25.
[138] *Ibid.*, p. 32.   [139] *Ibid.*, p. 15.   [140] *Ibid.*, p. 15.   [141] *Ibid.*, p. 8.
[142] *Ibid.*, p. 13. Wodrow argued that 'nations and societies of men are placed in a state of trial, as to the enjoyment of their temporal and religious blessings, even in this world. The divine goodness continues to be exercised towards them, as long as they continue to be good, to do good, or to be useful to mankind.'

reminder of that truth. If Wodrow did not modify those ideals he had so fiercely defended in the 1770s, he now publicly acknowledged that the American War was not waged in their defence, declaring that 'By means of an unjust and very expensive war with our Colonies, we were then brought to the very brink of ruin.'[143]

Reading his Fast sermons as in a sense concluding a long debate with his friend, it is typical of James Wodrow, the man, that in his summing up, he could now be so dispassionate, remaining firm to his principles and accepting that, on the great issue of the American Revolution, he had been fundamentally mistaken in their application.[144] The text for his sermon can perhaps be seen as a warning against the over-confidence of intellectuals in politics: it was Romans 11, 20–3, which begins 'Be not high-minded, but fear'. It is this sense of the active involvement of God in daily events, punishing the wicked and rewarding the virtuous that is usually missing in the providential optimism of Kenrick. Instead there is a generally cheerful acceptance that, one way or another, all is for the good. Yet this is not the whole story. Kenrick was not a natural business-man. His optimistic view of human nature led him to be too trusting, and in consequence he suffered a number of losses. On such occasions he confessed that, 'in spite of all my philosophy – I still read Boëthius and Seneca', he became depressed and suffered from lassitude. One can therefore create patterns that are too neat and draw distinctions too finely. There can be strong elements of agreement even where philosophical and theological differences are profound. Kenrick's mentor in such matters, Priestley, concluded his Fast sermon: 'It is "righteousness that exalteth a nation", and "sin" only is the reproach, and will be the ruin, "of any people".' Wodrow would have disagreed with the latter half of the statement, for him, sin was wilful disobedience to God's commands, rather than a divine reproach, yet he would have heartily endorsed the former, indicating that he, too, looked at the world for signs of providential dispensation. Moreover, Priestley conceded that there were elements of mystery about the providential plan. Here one needs to distinguish between his optimistic belief that all things were and are part of God's providential plan, and his acceptance that the unfolding of that plan contains elements of mystery beyond our

---

[143] *Ibid.*, p. 19.

[144] One should add that in sending his sermons to his friend, Wodrow invited him to 'Take the same Liberty with them in controverting every exceptionable point as you woud do with my Letters: only making some allowance for the ignorance and party spirit of those to whom they were addressed' (W–K (193), 17 or 18 July 1794).

comprehension.[145] In different ways, impossible to categorise, the providentialism of Wodrow and Kenrick, of Scottish Moderates and Rational Dissenters, sustained them through the difficult closing decades of the eighteenth century. In public matters, we can see the polarities between those who emphasised individual will while accepting the constraints of circumstance, and those for whom choice was a matter of rational necessity and who yet emphasised the power to change circumstances. But there were many intermediate stages between them and when one comes to private matters one can be even less confident in making patterns. This is particularly true of attitudes towards tragic personal events. There were undoubtedly doctrines and formulas that would help, notably the Christian stoicism of Hutcheson and other members of the Scottish Enlightenment, and the consolations of meeting again in heaven.[146] But it is one thing to find comfort and exemplary conduct in stoic resignation at the end of a full life, and quite another to find meaning in unexpected bereavement and in blighted hopes. Wodrow suffered the double bereavement of his only surviving sons, Gavin and Pate, who died from what he described as fever.[147] It was perhaps a mercy that providence had spirited Gavin away, for his father believed that he had contracted a fatal combination of a nervous derangement and religious bigotry. In a consoling letter, Principal Leechman of Glasgow University, with whom Gavin had lived for eight years, wrote,

---

[145] See J. Priestley, *The Proper Constitution of a Christian Church* (1782) in Priestley, *Works* (fn. 36), vol. 15, p. 24. On Priestley's millennialism, see my 'Joseph Priestley and the Millennium', in R.G.W. Anderson and Christopher Lawrence, ed., *Science, Medicine and Dissent: Joseph Priestley (1733–1804)* ... (London, 1987), pp. 29–38; Jack Fruchtman, Jr., *The Apocalyptic Politics of Richard Price and Joseph Priestley. A Study in Late Eighteenth-Century English Republican Millennialism, Transactions of the American Philosophical Society*, 73 (4) (Philadelphia, 1983).

[146] Hutcheson, *System* (fn. 21), pp. xxxiv–xxxv, 174–226. See also Leechman, *Temper, Character, and Duty* (fn. 63), p. 39; R. Price 'On the reasons for expecting that virtuous men shall meet after death in a state of happiness', the third of his *Four Dissertations* (London, 1767). Price cited (p.138), for other purposes, Robert Wallace's *Various Prospects of Mankind, Nature, and Providence* (London, 1761), but it may be no coincidence that Wallace included a section on 'Proof of a future state of mankind after death, on the principles of reason and philosophy' [Prospect XI]; Wodrow believed that he would meet his old acquaintance 'in the Kingdom of God', W–K (46), Wodrow to Kenrick, 1 May 1770; cf. Sher, *Church and University* (fn. 33), pp. 175–86; John A. Dwyer, *Virtuous Discourse: Sensibility and Community in Late Eighteenth-Century Scotland* (Edinburgh, 1987), pp. 46–51; a fine example of the employment of the various aspects of consolation – God's mysterious intentions, his wisdom and integrity, the promise of redemption – can be found in Edward Pickard's letter to his nephew, Thomas Belsham, following the suicide of Belsham's father in 1770 and at the time of the imminent death of his brother. John Williams, *Memoirs of the Life of ... Thomas Belsham, Including a Brief Notice of his Published Works* ... (London, 1833), pp. 70–1.

[147] W–K (71), Wodrow to Kenrick, 31 July 1781; (73) Kenrick to Wodrow, 29 November 1781. Wodrow had lost his eldest son at an early age, when Kenrick was still living in Scotland and in 1768 his wife had a stillborn child; *ibid.* (45), Wodrow to Kenrick, 25 January 1769.

His disease seemed to threaten, not only a stop, but a decay in Moral improvement. It had begun to diminish his Esteem even for his best friends, and coolness of Affection to them would have quickly followed, and would have gradually extended to all persons, who did not espouse his sentiments on religious subjects. Candour, Charity the chief virtues would have been greatly confined. Besides his Usefulness in the World and his own happiness in the Line of Life he had fixed on was very uncertain.[148]

Kenrick found Leechman's letter both elevating and consoling, though he wished that it had 'pleased Providence to have spared Gavin', who was due to visit him at Bewdley. Though grief was the lot of ordinary mortals, he was confident that

Were we raised ever so little above our present sphere, so as to be able to take in a larger compass of the works and ways of our beneficent creator, I make no doubt of our seeing things in a very different light. Numberless analogies in nature illustrate this. The sentiments of the wise and virtuous do daily confirm it.[149]

Such Olympian sentiments could not survive the loss of Wodrow's other son, Pate, who had neither suffered mental illness nor declined into bigotry. Kenrick simply confessed that he did not know what to say to his friend.[150] William Enfield also suffered a tragic bereavement when his eldest son Richard died at the beginning of what appeared to be a promising career as town clerk of Nottingham. In talking of his loss to his friend, Nicholas Clayton, he referred to this 'mysterious world'. A few years later, he found himself having to console his old friend, Ralph Griffiths, on the death of his eldest daughter. He, too, was at a loss as to the meaning of such deprivation. Yet, in a sense, his acknowledgement was a type of consolation:

Your affliction is indeed one of the heaviest that falls to the lot of mortals. *How* heavy it is, I am, alas, too well able to judge, for not long ago, as you well know, I lost a son, at a time when he was entering upon life with the brightest prospects, and when I assure myself he would be a lasting pillar of my house, and would fulfil all a parent's fondest wishes and hopes. Why such events are part of a system, which on the whole appears to be wise and good, it is not in your power,

---

[148] Leechman's letter was cited by Wodrow in his letter to Kenrick, 31 July 1781.

[149] W–K (72), Kenrick to Wodrow, 15 August 1781.

[150] W–K (73), Kenrick to Wodrow, 29 November 1781. Wodrow's letter conveying the news of the death of Pate is not extant. What makes it even more difficult to assess Kenrick's feelings is that his letter went on to discuss other personal news and the wider political issues, including a jibe about American affairs. This should not be seen as unfeeling; Wodrow had not confined himself to his personal grief in the letter conveying the news of the death of Gavin, and indeed he responded to the jibe. W–K (71), Wodrow to Kenrick, 31 July 1781, W–K (74) same to same, 23 May, 1782.

or mine, to explain. All that remains for us, in such circumstances, is silent submission. I will not repeat to you the beaten topics of consolation: as far as they
are of any value, they have, I am sure, presented themselves to your reflections.

Instead, Enfield offered simple practical advice, which was that Griffiths
should, 'as soon as the first natural grief is paid', return to work in order
to occupy his mind.[151] Enfield and Wodrow could still share the optimism that out of tragedies like the Birmingham riots, which devastated
Priestley's life, good would still triumph.[152] If Priestley or one of his
family had been killed, one suspects that such a view would not have
been articulated so readily. Providentialism was easier to apply to public
events. Once evil and suffering cast their shadows over one's own life and
those of one's friends, schematic accounts located in philosophical and
theological beliefs were barely operative. The various accounts of the
workings of providence no doubt proved useful in seeking for meaning in
contemporary events, despite involving a certain amount of posturing,
detectable even in the private correspondence of such sincere friends as
Wodrow and Kenrick. This is, no doubt, a condition of life, but in those
accounts we have discussed, we see some of the conditions of *eighteenth-
century* life and especially its religion. The historical imagination needs to
be closely engaged to understand them. But in understanding the more
private feelings of those we have studied another kind of imagination is
required. Their belief in God's providence was certainly not skin deep,
although in confronting private problems a different sort of faith was
needed. That lies beyond words. Here the historical account breaks
down, yet in witnessing the often silent testimonies of grief, one senses
the vitality of their public faith.

[151] Griffiths Correspondence, f. 84, Enfield to Griffiths, 3 November 1794.
[152] Griffiths Correspondence, f. 60, Enfield to Griffiths, 5 August 1791. The text for Theophilus
Lindsey's sermon preached in the aftermath of the Birmingham riots, and attended by Priestley,
was on St John, 16: 3, 'And these things will they do unto you, because they have not known the
Father, nor me.' Liverpool Record Office, MS. 23/4/61, Mary Nicholson's Diary.

CHAPTER 5

The contribution of the Dissenting academy to the emergence of Rational Dissent

David L. Wykes

The purpose of this chapter is to examine the contribution made by the Dissenting academy to the emergence of Rational Dissent. It has long been accepted that academies were responsible for the spread of heterodox opinions within English Presbyterianism through the ministers they trained. Nevertheless, the process by which many Presbyterians came to hold rational religious beliefs, and which by the beginning of the nineteenth century had seen most of the leading urban congregations embrace Unitarian opinions, is still little understood. It is generally argued that Presbyterian congregations were converted from orthodox Calvinism by their ministers, who, having adopted heterodox opinions at the academies, descended upon their unsuspecting congregations and proceeded to carry them into Unitarianism. Presbyterians were especially vulnerable, it is claimed, because unlike the Independents the appointment of the minister was in the hands of a few wealthy trustees rather than the whole church meeting.[1] Such arguments, however, ignore the fact that the academies reflected and had to respond to the intellectual and religious concerns of society in general, and whatever the role of the academies in sending forth ministers with heterodox opinions, it is clear that a significant part of the membership of the leading Presbyterian congregations during the eighteenth century was willing to

I wish to express my thanks to Professor R.K. Webb, the Revd Dr G.F. Nuttall, Dr G.M. Ditchfield, Mr Rupert Evans and Dr Ruth Watts for all their detailed suggestions and comments. Part of the research for this chapter was funded by the Arts Budget Centre Research Committee, University of Leicester. I am grateful to the Committee for its financial assistance. I am also glad to be able to acknowledge the permission of my fellow trustees to quote from the manuscripts in the keeping of Dr Williams's Library and to record my thanks to the Librarian and his staff for their assistance.

[1] M. Watts, *The Dissenters: From the Reformation to the French Revolution* (Oxford, 1978), pp. 465–7; C.G. Bolam, J. Goring, H.L. Short and R. Thomas, *English Presbyterianism: From Elizabethan Puritanism to Modern Unitarianism* (London, 1968), pp. 21–6, 177–8. Cf. A.P.F. Sell, 'Presbyterianism in Eighteenth-Century England: The Doctrinal Dimension', *Journal of the United Reformed Church History Society*, 4 (4) (1990), 378–82.

support ministers who had departed from orthodox Calvinism. Nevertheless, the nonconformist academy played a crucial role in maintaining an educated ministry and, additionally, in educating future generations of lay leaders. By giving ministerial students a training in logic and philosophy, together with a thorough grounding in Scripture and doctrine, academies enabled ministers not only to defend and expound the Scriptures, but also to study and investigate the main theological questions for themselves.

Many favourable references have been made to Dissenting academies by historians, but this interest has concentrated on the eighteenth century and a few outstanding institutions, most notably Warrington Academy.[2] There has been no recent study of their general history nor of the contribution they made to religious Dissent. Herbert McLachlan's *English Education Under the Test Acts*, published in 1931, remains the standard history of the academies themselves, while in many respects Irene Parker's much earlier work, *Dissenting Academies in England*, still offers the best assessment of their contribution to modern education.[3] Recent studies have been undertaken by historians of education rather than of Dissent, who believe that Dissenting academies made a significant contribution to educational development. In these academies, it is suggested, lie the roots of modern teaching philosophy and practice, and research has therefore focused on questions of curricula content and innovation.[4] Although the study of the nonconformist academy has undoubtedly benefited from this interest, it has focused on the contribution made to lay rather than ministerial education. Moreover, such studies are expressed in terms of modern educational concerns and ideas of progress. By concentrating on the teaching of science, foreign languages and other 'modern' subjects as the precursors of contemporary educational priorities, the historical understanding of the role of the nonconformist academy has been distorted. All noncon-

[2] T.S. Ashton, *The Industrial Revolution, 1760–1830* (London, 1948), pp. 19–21; P. Mathias, *The First Industrial Nation: An Economic History of Britain, 1700–1914*, 2nd edn (London, 1983), p. 142; P. Langford, *A Polite and Commercial People: England, 1727–1783* (New Oxford History of England) (Oxford, 1989), pp. 85–6; F. Crouzet, *Britain Ascendant: Comparative Studies in Franco-British Economic History* (Cambridge, 1990), p. 31.

[3] I. Parker, *Dissenting Academies in England: Their Rise and Progress, and their Place among the Educational Systems of the Country* (Cambridge, 1914); H. McLachlan, *English Education Under the Test Acts, Being the History of the Nonconformist Academies, 1662–1820* (Manchester, 1931). There is some assessment of the nonconformist academy in Michael Watts's general history of Dissent (*Dissenters* (fn. 1), pp. 367–71).

[4] J.W. Ashley Smith, *The Birth of Modern Education: The Contribution of the Dissenting Academies, 1660–1800* (London, 1954); B. Simon, *Studies in the History of Education, 1780–1870* (London, 1960), pp. 26–30; J. Lawson and H. Silver, eds., *A Social History of Education in England* (London, 1973), pp. 205–6.

formist academies, even where the provision of an education for the sons of laymen was particularly stressed, were established with the object of educating students for the ministry. A proper assessment of the nonconformist academy will have to await a full-scale investigation. Nevertheless, consideration of their contribution to the development of Rational Dissent is possible. Although it is recognised that academies had an important role in educating laymen, this study will concentrate on the education provided for the ministry.

ORIGINS

The earliest nonconformist academies were established following the Restoration of Charles II as a result of the 1662 Act of Uniformity. Nearly a thousand ministers (perhaps a sixth of the total) gave up their livings, and in all just over two thousand clergymen and teachers were displaced or ejected in England and Wales between 1660 and 1662 as a consequence of their refusal to conform to the Anglican religious settlement.[5] Despite the penalties involved many continued to preach and minister where they could; others chose to follow secular employments, principally in medicine and teaching. Nearly 150 ministers were ejected from school posts and university fellowships, and a number of others had taught privately. For the period after 1662 there is evidence for over a hundred ejected ministers, at some time or other, keeping schools, and, in over twenty cases, conducting academies involved in the training of ministers.[6] Teaching, like preaching, could only be undertaken by nonconformists at the risk of prosecution. Since the Middle Ages schoolteachers had been subject to ecclesiastical control and, by a series of Elizabethan and early Stuart statutes and injunctions, they had to be licensed by the bishop or his official. The Act of Uniformity introduced a number of new requirements. In addition, as graduates of Oxford and Cambridge, many tutors were technically in breach of the 'Stamford Oath' (1334), by which they were bound not to lecture *tamquam in universitate*. Most nonconformist ministers, however, refused to accept this interpretation of the oath.[7] During the

---

[5] *Calamy Revised: Being a Revision of Edmund Calamy's Account of the Ministers and Others Ejected and Silenced, 1660–2*, ed. A.G. Matthews (Oxford, 1934), pp. xii–xiv; Watts, *Dissenters* (fn. 1), pp. 218–19.

[6] *Ibid.*, pp. xiii–xiv, lvi; N. Hans, *New Trends in Education in the Eighteenth Century* (London, 1951), p. 58. For the number of ejected ministers conducting academies, *v. infra*.

[7] E. Calamy, *A Continuation of the Account of the Ministers, Lecturers, Masters and Fellows of Colleges, and Schoolmasters, who were Ejected and Silenced*, 2 vols. (London, 1727), vol. I, pp. 177–97, vol. II, pp. 732–5; A. Gordon, *Addresses Biographical and Historical* (London, 1922), pp. 69–70; McLachlan, *English Education* (fn. 3), pp. 2, 76–7. For an exception, see *Calamy Revised* (fn. 5), p. 385, *s.v.* William Pell.

period under the penal laws, nonconformist tutors were not only prosecuted for conducting private schools and academies, but many had their work disrupted by the threat of prosecution. Richard Frankland, who opened his celebrated academy at Rathmell near Settle in Yorkshire in 1672, was forced to move it more than four times before returning to Rathmell in 1689. Thomas Doolittle, who established one of the leading academies in London after 1662, moved six times before 1687.[8]

Although Protestant Dissenters were granted freedom to worship in public after 1689 by the Toleration Act, it did not remove but merely suspended the earlier penal laws against nonconformity leaving in place the restrictions on nonconformist teaching.[9] Attempts were made to prosecute tutors for teaching without a licence: Frankland in 1690, again in 1692, 1695 and 1697.[10] The growth in High Church feeling during Queen Anne's reign led to a more rigorous enforcement of the existing statutes against unlicensed schoolteachers, as well as the enactment of new legislation, in particular the Schism Act in 1714. The Act was a threat to the continued existence of Dissent since it sought to create an Anglican monopoly in education by excluding Dissenters from teaching. If it had been successfully enforced it is probable that Dissent would have disappeared as a significant political and religious force within a generation or two. At least one academy closed its doors for a time as a result of the threat, and a number of tutors were prosecuted for teaching without a licence. In addition, there are examples of laymen who were teachers, and in particular Quakers, being harassed and even imprisoned during the two decades after the Toleration Act. Nevertheless, by the beginning of the eighteenth century subscription seems to have been widely ignored in the case of all but grammar schools. The attempted prosecution of Philip Doddridge in 1733 for conducting his academy at Northampton without a licence appears to have been the last attempt of this kind.[11]

---

[8] F. Nicholson and E. Axon, *The Older Nonconformity in Kendal* (Kendal, 1915), pp. 122–74; *DNB*, *s.v.* Doolittle.

[9] For a consideration of the Act and of its limitations, see D.L. Wykes, 'The Tercentenary of the Toleration Act of 1689: A Cause for Celebration?', in *Papers from the 1989 International Symposium on Truth and Tolerance, McGill University*, ed. E.J. Furcha (ARC Supplement no. 4, Faculty of Religious Studies, McGill University), (Montreal, 1990), pp. 60–82, 82a–d; *ibid.*, 'James II's Religious Indulgence of 1687 and the Early Organization of Dissent: The Building of the First Nonconformist Meeting-House in Birmingham', *Midland History*, 16 (1991), 86, 97–8.

[10] A.T. Hart, *The Life and Times of John Sharp, Archbishop of York* (London, 1949), pp. 136–8; N. Sykes, *From Sheldon to Secker: Aspects of English Church History, 1660–1768* (Cambridge, 1959), p. 93. For other examples, see Bolam *et al.*, *English Presbyterianism* (fn. 1), p. 124.

[11] D.L. Wykes, 'Religious Dissent and the Penal Laws: An Explanation of Business Success?', *History*, 75 (1990), 47–8, 52.

It has been argued that Dissenters founded their academies because they were excluded from Oxford and Cambridge by the Act of Uniformity and the Test Acts. Although nonconformists could not hold university or college teaching posts unless they conformed, during the period under the penal laws many Dissenters, even students intended for the ministry, continued to be educated at one of the English universities, especially before any alternative tradition of higher education had developed. There were no legal barriers to Dissenters studying at Oxford or Cambridge (though there were against receiving a degree), but there were many practical reasons against the practice: both universities upheld values hostile to Dissent. Oxford, in particular, was conscious of its role in defending Anglican orthodoxy. In addition, many parents, including Anglicans, were deeply uneasy about the moral standards that prevailed at the universities.[12] Nevertheless, those Dissenters who did study there usually refused, on conscientious grounds, to take the oaths necessary to obtain a degree.

ACADEMIES UNDER THE PENAL LAWS

Evidence on nonconformist academies and the education of ministers is, not surprisingly, difficult to obtain for the period before toleration. Moreover, the informal and personal nature of many of the earliest efforts makes it difficult to identify those tutors who educated students for the ministry. There is evidence for twenty-three, maybe twenty-four, ejected ministers providing university learning during the period under the penal laws.[13] In addition, a further eight, possibly ten men who entered the ministry after 1662, were also involved in educating students before 1689.[14]

---

[12] *The History of the University of Oxford*, vol. v: *The Eighteenth Century*, ed. L.S. Sutherland and L.G. Mitchell (Oxford, 1986), pp. 356–7, 402, 424, 12–13. It was necessary to subscribe to the Thirty-Nine Articles at Oxford on matriculation and at Cambridge on graduation, but even the restrictions on matriculation at Oxford were no barrier to studying there privately. For a discussion of the legal position of Dissenters studying at the universities, see Wykes, 'Religious Dissent' (fn. 11), p. 46.

[13] Doubts centre on whether Samuel Jones was teaching at Brynllywarch, near Bridgend, before 1689. T. Richards, *Wales under the Indulgence, 1672–5* (London, 1928), p. 173, suggests that the academy was not opened until 1688, though it is possible it began as early as 1672/3.

[14] These figures are based on a detailed examination of the evidence, using in particular the biographical card index of Congregational ministers compiled by the Revd Charles Surman, now kept at Dr Williams's Library. The index consists of the names of about 30,000 ministers together with their dates, parentage, place of education and ministries, where known, and covers the period from the mid-seventeenth century to 1956. It also includes details on Presbyterian and Unitarian ministers up to about 1800. Cf. 'Early Nonconformist Academies', *Transactions of the Congregational Historical Society*, 3 (1907–8), 273–4. A.G. Matthews identified nine tutors who were ejected ministers, see *Calamy Revised* (fn. 5), p. 597, *s.v.* academies.

The greater freedom promised by toleration was to give a fresh impetus to the establishment of nonconformist academies, as well as to the realisation of the urgent need to train men for the ministry. Many of the early academies were short-lived, modest undertakings, educating one or two students at a time, and in all only a handful for the ministry. Historians have drawn attention to their private personal nature, depending upon the efforts and location of the individual tutors. When they died, or were prevented from teaching, the academy closed, though there is evidence for a surprising degree of continuity, with academies and their pupils continuing under a new tutor, or cases where former pupils opened their own academies following the death of their old teachers, thereby often maintaining the educational ideas and traditions that they themselves had been taught. There were, however, one or two substantial undertakings, which trained significant numbers of students, and which, in terms of their standard of teaching and range of activities, compared very favourably with later institutional academies. Undoubtedly the greatest was the academy established at Rathmell by Richard Frankland, where just over 300 students (two-thirds of whom followed lay careers) were educated between 1670 and Frankland's death in 1698, including a majority of the ministers in the north. The other major academy serving the Midlands and the North of England was opened in about 1675 by John Woodhouse at Sheriffhales in Shropshire. He is said to have had between forty and fifty students in some years, though the total number of students he educated is unknown.[15] Both Frankland and Woodhouse had assistants to help with the teaching, evidence of the number of students and range of subjects taught. In London, the principal academy for the Presbyterians was conducted by Thomas Doolittle, and for the Congregationalists by Charles Morton. According to a former student, Morton's academy was one of the largest in England, responsible for educating 'some hundreds'. Doolittle is said by the same source to have taught between twenty and thirty students in a year.[16] Another large academy was conducted in the West Country by Matthew Warren at Taunton. The majority of academies in this period were typically much more modest than Rathmell or Sheriffhales. Indeed, some hardly qualify for the name. Dr Henry Langley, it is recorded, 'took sojourners into his house, and taught them

[15] J. Toulmin, *An Historical View of the State of the Protestant Dissenters in England* (Bath and London, 1814), p. 2.
[16] [Samuel Wesley], *A Letter from a Country Divine . . . Concerning the Education of the Dissenters in the Private Academies . . .* (London, 1703), pp. 7–8, 9; S. Wesley, *A Defence of a Letter Concerning the Education of Dissenters in their Private Academies . . .* (London, 1704), pp. 14–15.

logic and philosophy'. Ralph Button was 'Tutor to Young Men in his own House'. Because of the troubled times John Shuttlewood only educated 'a Few, (and it was but a Few)', students at his academy at Sulby in Northamptonshire in the 1680s.[17]

There are no reliable estimates for the number of students taught during this period. Professor Stone, relying on Parker and McLachlan and, as he admitted, having 'little concrete evidence', concluded that there were about 50 entrants a year before 1669, 100 from 1670 to 1689, and 150 from 1690 to 1699.[18] This is certainly too high a figure, even for lay as well as ministerial students. The Common Fund Survey in 1690 records the names of only forty-two ministerial students, and this was after toleration had been granted. During the period before toleration ministerial candidates often had to be prepared privately, and many of those who entered the ministry during the period under the penal laws are known to have been educated by a father or some other relative who was a nonconformist minister. Lay as well as ministerial students were taught at most of the early academies, and until at least the mid-eighteenth century they included the sons of Anglican parents as well. The first student admitted by Frankland was the son of an Anglican, Sir Thomas Liddell of Ravensworth. The son was intended for a lay career, and 'went to Rathmell just as he would have gone to Oxford, to receive a learned education'.[19] Financial and political pressures encouraged the teaching of those intended for lay careers; not only were their fees crucial, but the support of the local gentry, that teaching their sons gave, could be invaluable in a time of persecution.

TOLERATION AND THE DEVELOPMENT OF MODERN DISSENT

By 1689, after twenty-five years of persecution, the need to provide a succession of competent ministers had acquired considerable urgency as the ejected ministers died or retired from active preaching. The invaluable survey on the state of Dissent undertaken by the Common Fund immediately after toleration reveals the legacy of nearly three decades of persecution. Many of the original ministers who had suffered ejection were still preaching and, though 'wonderfully preserved to this time, are aged'. Under 400 (about a fifth) of the ministers silenced in 1662 were still living in 1690, of whom only 330 were recorded in the Survey, and

---

[17] Edmund Calamy, *A Funeral Sermon for the late Reverend Mr John Sheffield* (London, 1726), p. 34.
[18] L. Stone, 'The Educational Revolution in England, 1560–1640', *Past and Present*, 28 (1964), 56.
[19] A. Gordon, 'Early Nonconformity and Education,' in *Addresses* (fn. 7), pp. 73, 74; Nicholson and Axon, *Older Nonconformity* (fn. 8), p. 534.

not all of those were still active in the ministry.[20] They were, however, supported by a new generation of men who had begun to preach since 1662. Their importance is clear from the return for the West Riding of Yorkshire. Only nine ejected ministers, including the celebrated Oliver Heywood, were still active, and one of their number, Richard Frankland, according to the Survey was, in 1690, training ministers rather than preaching. In contrast, there were fourteen younger men active there. A similar pattern is evident for Derbyshire, where there is evidence for fourteen individuals who had entered the ministry after 1662, together with a further three students preparing for the ministry, compared with only eleven ejected ministers, of whom several were described as aged. There remained, however, a considerable shortage of ministers, and the North of England was undoubtedly better supplied with the new generation of trained men than other parts of the country, largely, it appears, because of the efforts of Frankland. He had not only taught ten out of the fourteen 'of ye younger sort' in the West Riding of Yorkshire who had entered the ministry since 1662, but his influence extended beyond the North of England. The congregation at Tetney in Lincolnshire expressed the hope that they might be able to obtain a minister 'out of Yorkshire educated by Mr Frankland'.[21] In Leicestershire there were ten silenced ministers and only eight new ministers, and in Nottinghamshire seven silenced and seven new men.[22]

If the efforts of individual tutors during the period under the penal laws had kept the idea of an educated ministry alive, the nonconformist academy was responsible for helping to bring about a remarkable transformation in the state of religious Dissent in the generation after 1689. The two decades following toleration were to witness the development of Dissent from a series of harassed, often informal meetings, into settled, organised congregations, with their own place of worship, regular services and minister. The Evans List, drawn up between 1715 and 1717 to assess the numerical and political strength of Dissent, attests to the achievements of the generation of ministers and laity after the Toleration

---

[20] In addition to 330 ejected ministers recorded in the Common Fund Survey, the names of a further sixty survivors are also known, see *Calamy Revised* (fn. 5), p. xvi.

[21] A. Gordon, ed., *Freedom After Ejection: A Review (1690–1692) of Presbyterian and Congregational Nonconformity in England and Wales* (Manchester, 1917), p. 71. Gordon identified Telney, recorded in the Survey under Lincolnshire, with Tilney in Norfolk. I am grateful to Dr Nuttall for suggesting Tetney, near Grimsby, as the likely identification.

[22] *Ibid.*, pp. 25–9, 66–9, 82–4; C.G. Bolam, 'The Changes and Development Within Presbyterianism in the Counties of Derby, Leicester and Nottingham from its Organisation in the Commonwealth to the Transformation to Independency and Unitarianism c.1780', unpublished MA thesis (Nottingham, 1957), pp. 321–30.

Act in settling ministers and congregations. The great majority of congregations recorded in the Evans List had a fixed minister, and many are known to have built their own meeting-houses despite the political uncertainty Dissenters faced during much of Queen Anne's reign.

Toleration undoubtedly encouraged individual tutors to undertake the preparation of ministerial candidates, and indeed families to consider the nonconformist ministry as a possible career for their sons. Nevertheless, in helping Dissent to provide a more coherent response to the problem of ministerial education, the Common Fund and its denominational successors, the Presbyterian and the Congregational Fund Boards, played a crucial role. The Common Fund Survey referred to a significant number of students who had been forced to give up their studies for lack of funds.[23] After toleration Dissenters established a number of charities to support poorer students during their period of education, of which the most important were the Presbyterian and Congregational Boards, but private benefactions, such as the Lady Hewley Trust in the north of England, Dr Williams's Trust, and the earliest, the Throckmorton Trotman Trust, also made a significant contribution. Additional funds were established from the middle of the eighteenth century, of which the most important was the Coward Trust. Individual students continued to be educated at the expense of their own families or through the generosity of private individuals. Bequests were also left for the purpose by wealthy Dissenters.[24] Nevertheless, the largest number, perhaps even a majority, owed their education to the support of the Common Fund and its successors. Without doubt many candidates from poorer families, and in particular the sons of nonconformist ministers, would never have been educated for the ministry without this support.[25] The contribution made

---

[23] Gordon, *Freedom After Ejection*, pp. 111, 125, 133, 134, 270; Dr Williams's Library [hereafter DWL], MS OD67, Presbyterian Fund Board [hereafter PFB] minutes, I, 1 July 1690–26 June 1693, fo.27. Cf. Edmund Calamy's comments to George Benson in 1726, on the obstacles facing candidates from poor families: John Rylands University Library of Manchester, Unitarian College Collection, Benson Correspondence III, B/1/11, Calamy to Benson, 5 October 1726.

[24] *A History of the Family of Holland, of Mobberley and Knutsford in the County of Chester . . .*, ed. W.F. Irvine (Edinburgh, 1902), pp. 54, 152; Gordon, *Freedom After Ejection* (fn. 21), pp. 28, 29, 41, 64–5; 'A Short Account of the Life of Mr. Richard Stretton', in 'Miscellanea', *Publications of the Thoresby Society*, 11 (1904), 329–30, 331; A. Peel, 'The Throckmorton Trotman Trust, 1664–1941', *Trans. Congregational Historical Society*, 14 (1940–44), 70–93, 168–71.

[25] Gordon, *Freedom After Ejection* (fn. 21), pp. 111, 125, 134; PFB, I, fo.27, 79; PFB, II, pp. 199–200, 204 (Joseph Allen of Worcester, £5: this sum 'with what his friends could advance is like to furnish him with a comfortable subsistance in his education': 6 February 1709/10). Jeremy found evidence for the Board having supported more than 1,300 students between 1690 and 1885, see W.D. Jeremy, *The Presbyterian Fund and Dr Daniel Williams's Trust: with Biographical notes of the Trustees, and some Account of their Academies, Scholarships and Schools* (London and Edinburgh, 1885), pp. 12–16.

by the trust funds was not just financial. The Congregational Fund sought to promote the Congregational interest and took care to examine the sentiments of the students it supported. The King's Head Society was established to defend Calvinist orthodoxy; the students it supported had to provide evidence of their evangelical orthodoxy, and the Coward Trust dissolved the academy at Northampton in 1798 because of doubts about the orthodoxy of its tutor, John Horsey. The academy was re-established at Wymondley by the trustees the following year.

THE NONCONFORMIST ACADEMY AND LATE SEVENTEENTH-CENTURY TEACHING

Historians are no longer so ready to dismiss the intellectual and educational contribution of the two English universities during the century after the Restoration, or to give unqualified praise to the Dissenting academy and thereby exaggerate the contrast in educational standards in favour of the latter. Over forty years ago Hans challenged the supposed superiority of the education provided by the nonconformist academy. He noted for the eighteenth century that many of the innovations thought to be uniquely associated with Dissent had also been introduced at Anglican and other private institutions. Recent work on seventeenth- and early eighteenth-century universities invites a similar re-evaluation. The teaching and scholarship of Cambridge in this period has always been better regarded than that of Oxford, particularly in the sciences. Modern studies of the history of Oxford University, however, have done much to rescue its reputation from the worst calumnies. Nevertheless, despite the evidence for certain areas of excellence, notably the Bodleian Library and the undergraduate teaching found in some colleges, the overall impression by the early eighteenth century remains one of decline, especially in the teaching undertaken by the University itself. Though modern subjects were studied at Oxford, many of the main contributions to scholarship were made outside the formal structure of the University and not taught to undergraduates. Recent research on Cambridge also suggests that the standards of teaching and scholarship declined in the eighteenth century. Newton's work, though not adopted until after he left the University, came to dominate undergraduate teaching. As a result it 'became the new orthodoxy and, once it was established within the curriculum', the system of tutorial teaching helped to ensure that 'there was little incentive to break new scientific ground.'[26] It is, however, equally important to avoid assuming that the standards of the best nonconformist tutors, which were often very good indeed, were representative of all nonconformist academies. There is plenty of evidence to suggest wide variations in the range of subjects taught, the content of the curriculum (whether it reflected the latest advances in scholarship) and the quality of the teaching.

Although the first generation of tutors included many excellent scholars and teachers, such as John Bryan sen., Theophilus Gale and Charles Morton, it must be accepted that in terms of their resources early academies compared poorly with the universities, lacking proper libraries and often having only limited accommodation for teaching and study. Morton's academy at Newington Green was an exception. According to Samuel Wesley, who studied there, it had 'annext a fine Garden, Bowling Green, Fish-pond, and within a Laboratory, and some not inconsiderable Rarities, with Air Pumps, Thermometers, and all sorts of Mathematical Instruments'.[27] Historians have often commented on the evidence for experimental philosophy that Wesley's description provides, but Morton's academy was clearly exceptional for this period. Save for the largest academies, teaching depended upon the efforts of a single tutor with perhaps the assistance of a senior student. Although the corpus of necessary knowledge was smaller than it is for modern scholarship, few men could master the whole course of lay and divinity studies, let alone be knowledgeable about every subject.[28] In addition, a poor library limited the learning that a student could acquire to what was provided by the tutor and, whereas a lack of books might be compensated for by a tutor of real scholarship, the ideas and subjects he covered would inevitably reflect his own opinions and beliefs. Students at Sheriffhales, for example, were directed to further reading, which included subjects such as history on which Woodhouse did not lecture.[29]

From the mid-eighteenth century a number of nonconformist academies funded by private subscription were established on a much more ambitious scale, with their own buildings and libraries, and with separate tutors responsible for the main subjects. Warrington Academy (1757–86), New College, Hackney (1786–96), and Manchester College, York

---

[26] Hans, *New Trends* (fn. 6), pp. 54–62; Sutherland and Mitchell, *History of the University of Oxford*, vol. v (fn. 12), see section 'Academic Life in the University', pp. 760, 683; J. Gascoigne, *Cambridge in the Age of Enlightenment: Science, Religion and Politics from the Restoration to the French Revolution* (Cambridge, 1989), pp. 179, 58, 68, 142–5, 177–9.

[27] McLachlan, *English Education* (fn. 3), pp. 2, 17, 18–19, 21, 22, 23–4, 42; [Wesley], *Letter* (fn. 16), p. 7.

[28] Nevertheless see the comments of Gordon, *Addresses* (fn. 7), pp. 78–9.

[29] Toulmin, *Historical View* (fn. 15), p. 227.

(1803–40) could rival, and, in terms of educational standards, surpass Oxford and Cambridge. But until the development of the institutional academy with three or four tutors offering a full range of subjects, it was not uncommon for students to migrate from one academy to another to benefit from the particular scholarship of a tutor, or, in the case of the better students and those with private means, to complete their studies outside England, usually in Scotland at Glasgow University, though occasionally at Utrecht or Leiden in the Dutch Republic.[30] Thomas Emlyn left John Shuttlewood's academy at Sulby in 1679 after only a year because of his dissatisfaction with Shuttlewood's library, which consisted of 'very few books, and them chiefly of one sort'. John Shower, the son of an Exeter merchant, began his studies under Matthew Warren at Taunton, but he also studied at Exeter, at Newington Green under Morton, and with Edward Veal at Wapping. Thomas Secker, the future archbishop, studied first at Attercliffe under Timothy Jollie, about whose abilities he was uncomplimentary, believing that under Jollie's tutorship he lost what knowledge of the classics he had previously acquired. He then returned home intending to proceed to Glasgow, but instead went to London where he studied mathematics under John Eames for a year, before moving to Samuel Jones's academy at Gloucester, which was transferred the following year to Tewkesbury. 'There I recovered my almost lost Knowledge of Greek & Latin; and added to it that of Hebrew, Chaldee & Syriack.' He also studied logic, mathematics, geography and 'a Course of Lectures, Preparatory to the Critical Study of the Bible'. At least 43 of the 300 or so students educated by Frankland proceeded to university, including, in a number of cases, Cambridge.[31]

The nonconformist academy was intended to provide students with a higher education similar to that provided by the universities, and therefore to follow on from grammar-learning. In some of the earliest

[30] G.F. Nuttall, '"The Sun-shine of Liberty": The Toleration Act and the Ministry', *Journal of United Reformed Church History Society*, 4 (1989), 249 and n.32; G.F. Nuttall, 'English Dissenters in the Netherlands, 1640–1689', *Nederlands Archief voor Kerkgeschiedenis*, 59 (1979), 37–54; O.M. Griffiths, *Religion and Learning: A Study in English Presbyterian Thought from 1662 to the Foundation of the Unitarian Movement* (Cambridge, 1935), p. 34. During the period 1700–25, the Presbyterian Fund supported twenty-five students at Glasgow, ten at Edinburgh and nine at Utrecht. There was an attempt by the English Presbyterians to establish a hall and library as a place in which English students could reside while studying at Edinburgh, see *ibid.*, p. 33, and ch. v, p. 54. Dr Williams's bursary was attached to Glasgow, evidence of the benefactor's high regard for the University.

[31] For other examples, see McLachlan, *English Education* (fn. 3), pp. 23–4, 43, 70, 72; *DNB*, *s.v.* Emlyn; *The Works of Mr Thomas Emlyn . . . To the whole are prefixed, Memoirs of the Life and Writings of the Author*, 4th edn, 3 vols. (London, 1746), vol. I, p. vi; 'The Autobiography of Thomas Secker, Archbishop of Canterbury', ed. J.S. Macauley and R.W. Greaves, *University of Kansas Library Series*, 49 (1988), 3; A. Brockett, *Nonconformity in Exeter, 1650–1875* (Manchester, 1962), p. 76.

academies this distinction was almost certainly not made, though Rathmell and Sheriffhales, two of the leading academies, taught only university subjects. The Common Fund, and later the Presbyterian Fund and the Congregational Fund Boards, would only support students in university learning and refused to consider candidates whose knowledge of the classics was inadequate.[32] It is difficult to establish the length of study, particularly for the earliest academies. At Rathmell, the only seventeenth-century academy for which a detailed list of students survives, ministerial candidates appear to have studied for four years. Because of the difficulties facing Dissenters during the period under the penal laws, it is likely that the period of formal education for many students was much shorter and, owing to the interruptions suffered, was in many cases incomplete.[33] Lay students generally attended for a shorter period than ministerial candidates as they did not follow the theology course. They often proceeded to the Inns of Court or even to university. The period of study increased with time as academies became institutionalised, their courses more comprehensive, and the range and level of knowledge expected of students grew. By the mid-eighteenth century most ministers received their education at a single academy, and increasingly the trend was for the course to last for five years.

PHILOSOPHY, LOGIC AND THE TEXT-BOOKS STUDIED

Because the first nonconformist tutors were nearly all graduates of one or other of the two universities, and in many cases had actually taught there, it is likely that the earliest academies were little different in terms of their curricula and teaching methods from either Oxford or Cambridge. Thus like the universities, the principal subjects taught were philosophy and logic, which formed the main intellectual concerns of the late seventeenth century, as the older schemes of thought derived from Aristotle were undermined by the ideas of Descartes, Ramus and Locke.[34] Evidence on the instruction the earliest tutors gave to candidates for the ministry comes mostly from accounts by the students

---

[32] PFB, I, fo. 50v. Cf. fos. 31r, 26r, 33v; 'The Exeter Assembly: The Minutes of the Assemblies of the United Brethren of Devon and Cornwall, 1691–1717', ed. A. Brockett, *Devon & Cornwall Record Society*, n.s. 6 (1963), 3, 31, 76. For accounts of the grammar education of students who attended the early academies, see 'Autobiography of James Clegg' in 'The Diary of James Clegg of Chapel en le Frith, 1708–55, Part 3', ed. V.S. Doe, *Derbyshire Record Society*, 5 (1981), 905, 907–10; 'Seventh Report of the Committee on Devonshire Records: The Fox Memoirs – Worthies of Devon', *Transactions of the Devonshire Association*, 28 (1896), 130–1.

[33] Nicholson and Axon, *Older Nonconformity* (fn. 8), pp. 532–612.   [34] Gordon, *Addresses* (fn. 7), p. 77.

themselves. During the mid-1690s Clegg, in his first year at Frankland's academy at Rathmell, read logic. The next two years were spent studying metaphysics and pneumatology, but Frankland died before Clegg had completed his course. John Ashe, a student at Rathmell a decade before Clegg, went 'thro' the usual Course of Logick, Metaphysicks, Somatology, Pneumatology, natural Philosophy, Divinity, and Chronology'. At Bridgwater under John Moore, John Peirce followed a course of philosophy 'and the preparatory studies usual, . . . he hath also read a body of Theology'.[35] Evidence concerning the academic attainments expected of ministerial students comes from the examination of candidates for ordination. In September 1692, the ministers of the Cheshire Classis met to examine six candidates. 'After the Reading of their Th[ese]s They were all Distinctly Examined concerning their Knowledge in the Tongues, Philosophy &c.' Each candidate was expected to defend a thesis involving some theological question in Latin on a subject chosen for him.[36]

Latin appears to have been the main language used for teaching as well as for examining until the early eighteenth century. Nevertheless, Morton and a number of other tutors certainly used English for at least part of their instruction before Doddridge, who is said to have been the first to abandon Latin even in his theology lectures. It is claimed that the change in language led to the neglect of older traditional texts in Latin in favour of more modern works, and that English was more suited to theological study as well as to the new sciences. The replacement of Latin by the vernacular in publications throughout Europe served to reduce, rather than encourage, the exchange of ideas. Students from England also had little difficulty attending lectures in Holland while Latin was still the language of instruction. The use of English for teaching was not matched by the availability of text-books in that medium. Moreover, the decline in the significance of Latin can be exaggerated. The tutors at Manchester College, York, in the early nineteenth century, still maintained the traditional stress upon the classics (without which it would have been impossible to have claimed to be sending forth educated men), as well as providing the instruction in history, political economy and the

---

[35] J. Clegg, 'Autobiography' (fn. 32), pp. 910–11; Nicholson and Axon, *Older Nonconformity* (fn. 8), p. 131; Brockett, 'Exeter Assembly' (fn. 32), p. 94. Somatology was the branch of knowledge concerned with the general properties and characteristics of the body. Pneumatology was the theory of the mind. Dr Nuttall points out that there appear to be no other references to somatology as a subject taught in nonconformist academies, whereas there are many references to pneumatology.

[36] *Cheshire Classis Minutes, 1691–1745*, ed. A. Gordon (London, 1919) p. 11; cf. pp. 12, 13, 127–34; Brockett, 'Exeter Assembly' (fn. 32), pp. 29, 31.

new sciences which helped place the College in the forefront of contemporary education.[37]

The tutors of the leading academies during the early period were certainly open to the new intellectual concerns of the period. Both Frankland and Woodhouse used Ramist and Cartesian text-books. The most complete account of the range of texts used and the subjects taught is available for Woodhouse, whose papers were still available in the early nineteenth century. In logic Woodhouse was using Ramus together with Downame's *Commentary*, for the natural sciences Descartes's *Principia*, and in physics the works of the Cartesian authors Rhegius and Rohault. Although Frankland was a Ramist, it is clear he was not wedded to a single system of logic, for Clegg spent his first year reading 'the Logick both of Aristotle and Ramus'.[38] There are no lists of the texts used by Frankland, but the books owned by one of his last students, Reginald Tetlaw, 'which we made use of at the University', suggests that the other texts used included Descartes on philosophy, and, like Woodhouse, the Cartesian Rohault on physics. Tetlaw also had a copy of the Aristotelian Smiglecius' *Logica*.[39] Both Woodhouse and Frankland used more traditional text-books, the Cartesian Heereboord on ethics, and Burgersdijk's *Institutiones Logicae* (first published in 1644 and popular at Cambridge), together with Heereboord's *Commentary* on the latter. Tetlaw's library did, however, include the Platonist Henry More's *Enchiridion Ethicum* (1669), perhaps recommended by Frankland, which represented a movement away from Cartesianism.[40] William Bilby, while a student at Mansfield under John Billingsley jun. in the early 1680s, also read Downame's *Commentary* on Ramus as well as the logic of Smiglecius. In addition to studying Greek and Latin at the Free

---

[37] Ashley Smith, *Birth of Modern Education* (fn. 4), p. 128, cf. pp. 89, 95, 105, 119–20; Gordon, *Addresses* (fn. 7), pp. 212–13; McLachlan, *English Education* (fn. 3), pp. 21–2, 78–9; R. Watts, 'Manchester College and Education, 1786–1853', in B. Smith, ed., *Truth, Liberty, Religion: Essays Celebrating Two Hundred Years of Manchester College* (Oxford, 1986), pp. 90–3.

[38] Toulmin, *Historical View* (fn. 15), pp. 226–8; J. Clegg, 'Autobiography' (fn. 32), p. 911; P. Ramus, *Dialecticae libri duo . . . cum commentariis Georgii Downami annexis* (Londoni et Cantabrigiae, 1669); R. Descartes, *Principia philosophiae* (Amstelodami, 1664; first publ. 1644); Henricus Regius, *Fundamenta physices* (Amstelodami, 1646); Jacques Rohault, *Traité de Physique* (Paris, 1671).

[39] Tetlaw did not study at one of the ancient universities; by 'the University' he meant Rathmell. After Frankland's death he studied at John Chorlton's academy in Manchester, see Nicholson and Axon, *Older Nonconformity* (fn. 8), p. 610.

[40] Rather more detail is available for Woodhouse, see Toulmin, *Historical View* (fn. 15), pp. 226–8, who had access to Woodhouse's own papers, *ibid.*, p. 230 m*; 'Lancashire and Cheshire Wills and Inventories at Chester', ed. J.P. Earwaker, *Chetham Society*, n.s. 3 (1884), pp. 192–3. Tetlaw died in December 1745. Adrianus Heereboord, . . . ἑρμηεια logica, seu Explicatio, tum per notas, tum per exempla, synops. logicae Burgersdicianae . . ., 3rd edn (Lugduni Batavorum, 1657).

School, he had read Burgersdijk's *Logicae*, 'which prepared me for Academical learning'.[41]

Tutors were restricted by the books that were available, which explains the continued popularity, amongst both nonconformist tutors and their university contemporaries, of such traditional texts as those by Burgersdijk and Heereboord. The earliest tutors would have been directly influenced in their choice of texts by their own experience as undergraduates at Oxford and Cambridge before the Restoration. Nevertheless, there is evidence to suggest that tutors encouraged their students to adopt new texts as they became available. Rohault's *Physics*, which Frankland and Woodhouse used, was published in 1671 after they had left Cambridge, though it was also adopted at Cambridge as the main text before Newton. Tetlaw's library included Samuel Clarke's translation of Rohault published in 1697. It is, of course, possible that Tetlaw purchased the work after he had left Rathmell. Nevertheless, although the text-books used by their students suggest that Frankland and Woodhouse kept abreast of current thinking, it should be noted that the works of Ramus and Descartes were already well known at Cambridge during the early 1650s and 1660s when Frankland and Woodhouse were themselves students there.[42]

Until the early eighteenth century there were few differences in the text-books used at the leading academies from those found at Oxford and Cambridge. The books used by Henry Fleming, who matriculated at Queen's College, Oxford, in 1678, differed little from those found at Sheriffhales, with the exception of Ramus, who was apparently not read at Oxford. In 1690, however, Fleming's younger brother, George, told his father that his tutor had recommended books on 'the new Philosophy'. He had already read Aristotle's ethics and Smiglecius' *Logica* for himself.[43] At Cambridge after the Restoration the new Cartesian philosophy came to be adopted as part of the undergraduate curriculum and by the early eighteenth century had in turn been replaced by Newtonian philosophy. Recently it has been argued that the universities were not

---

[41] Nottingham Subscription Library, Angel Row, Nottingham, 'Some Remarkable Passages in my life' by William Bilby [Typescript copy, DWL, MS12.62], Cap.1 §5, appendix. Marcin Smiglecki, *Logica*, 2 vols. (Oxonii, 1658). Cf. C.G. Bolam, 'Some Remarkable Passages in the Life of William Bilby (1664–1738), with an Appendix', *Transactions of Unitarian Historical Society*, 10 (3) (1952), 123–41.   [42] Ashley Smith, *Birth of Modern Education* (fn. 4), p. 20, see Appendix A, pp. 269–86.

[43] 'The Flemings in Oxford. Being documents selected from the Rydal papers in illustration of the lives and ways of Oxford men, 1650–1700', ed. J.R. Magrath, vol. I, *1650–1680*, Oxford Historical Society, 44 (1904), 250–5, 295, 321–6; vol. II, *1680–1690*, ibid., 62 (1913), 252, 273–4, 296–7; Parker, *Dissenting Academies* (fn. 3), pp. 74–5; Sutherland and Mitchell, *History of the University of Oxford*, vol. v (fn. 12), pp. 588–9.

hostile to science or the spread of new ideas, though it was studied mainly as a graduate subject, and usually without official encouragement;[44] nevertheless, they reflected the political concerns of the period. Thus, after the Restoration they were seen to have a key role in providing intellectual defences against the threats to the Church from papists, Dissenters and atheists. They were, therefore, 'the guardians of a body of traditional learning on which religious orthodoxy, political obedience and social order were thought to depend', and the ideas of Aristotle and the ancient schoolmen thus retained their authority over the new ideas.[45]

Although there is convincing evidence for acceptance of the new thinking by a number of early nonconformist tutors, it is important not to exaggerate its extent, or to date it too early, but rather to note the continuing persistence of traditional texts and logical methods. According to one student in the late 1660s, Thomas Cole, the former Principal of St Mary's Hall at Oxford, 'read to us Aristotle's *Philosophy*, and instructed us in the Classicks, and Oratory': presumably the same curriculum he had taught at the university until his ejection.[46] Matthew Warren, a graduate of Oxford, whose academy at Taunton was the largest in the West Country, had himself been educated 'in the Old Logic and Philosophy, and [was] little acquainted with the improvements of the New'. Grove, who was a former pupil of and eventually presided over Warren's academy, went to London to complete his education under two of the leading tutors following the new learning, Thomas Rowe and John Eames.[47] It was said of Doolittle that 'tho' a very worthy and diligent divine, yet [he] was not eminent for [his] compass of knowledge or depth of thought'. There are few details relating to Doolittle's system of logic, but a notebook of one of his students survives containing notes on Aristotle's rhetoric.[48]

If a number of the leading tutors during the earliest period were open to the new ideas in philosophy, logic and the sciences, in theology they were strictly orthodox. Frankland, for example, opposed any departure

---

[44] Gascoigne, *Cambridge in the Age of Enlightenment* (fn. 26), pp. 7, 52–5, 142–7; M. Hunter, *Science and Society in Restoration England* (Cambridge, 1981), pp. 136, 141–3.

[45] G.V. Bennett, 'University, Society and Church, 1688–1714,' in Sutherland and Mitchell, *History of the University of Oxford*, vol. v (fn. 12), pp. 3, 359; Gascoigne, *Cambridge in the Age of Enlightenment* (fn. 26), p. 53.

[46] William Hamilton, *The exemplary life . . . of James Bonnell . . .* (Dublin, 1703), pp. 11–12.

[47] *Sermons . . . by the late Revd Mr Henry Grove*, ed. T. Amory, 2nd. edn, 6 vols. (London, 1741), vol. i, p. xiv; Ashley Smith, *Birth of Modern Education* (fn. 4), p. 48.

[48] Emlyn, *Works* (fn. 31), vol. i, p. vii; *DNB*, *s.v.* Doolittle. DWL, MS28.56, commonplace book re-used by Thomas Emlyn and his son Solomon. The original [unknown] owner was a student at Doolittle's academy. Some of his entries are dated January 1689/90, see fo .1, pp. 203–25.

from Calvinism. His only published work was an answer to a plea for moderation towards those who rejected the Trinity. The books Tetlaw used at Rathmell included such orthodox authors as Ames (or Amesius), Windelius and Wollebius. Again, more detail is available for Woodhouse, who, for the doctrinal works in his course on theology, used the Westminster Assembly's *Confession of Faith* and the *Larger Catechism* together with Calvin's *Institutes*.[49] Charles Morton, in his *Advice to Candidates for the Ministry*, encouraged students to read the 'Advice' found in the Westminster Assembly's *Directory*, as well as such conventional religious works as Oliver Bowles's *Evangelical Pastor* and William Fenner's *Christ's Alarm to Drowsie Saints* (1646). According to one of his students, he also recommended Ames.[50] Such details are not available for the other tutors during the first period and the only evidence comes from their own writings. Theophilus Gale, who established one of the earliest academies in London, at Newington Green, was a strict predestinarian and included in the fourth part of his *Court of the Gentiles*, published in 1678, a powerful effort 'to rescue the Calvinist doctrine of predetermination from moral difficulties'.[51] Further evidence is available as a result of the divisions within Dissent caused by the controversy over Richard Davis of Rothwell in 1692. Thomas Cole, whose instruction in philosophy and logic followed the traditional Aristotelian method, took the side of the high Calvinists in the dispute, which led to the break-up of the Happy Union. Other tutors who took the side of the high Calvinists included Stephen Lobb, who, together with Glascock and Wickens, gave private lectures to Morton's students after Morton had sought asylum in America. In 1697 Lobb published *The Growth of Error; or Rise and Progress of Arminianism and Socinianism*. Doolittle was also an orthodox Calvinist in doctrine. 'He look'd on the Assembly's Catechism particularly as an excellent Summary of Christian Doctrine.' His *Complete Body of Practical Divinity*, published after his death in 1723, was 'a painstaking and prolix expansion of the assembly's shorter catechism', which Alexander

---

[49] R. Frankland, *Reflections on a Letter Writ by a nameless Author to the Reverend Clergy of both Universities, And on his bold reflections on the Trinity* (London, 1697); cf. Nicholson and Axon, *Older Nonconformity* (fn. 8), pp. 180–6, 137; Toulmin, *Historical View* (fn. 15), pp. 226–9. Among the commentaries that Woodhouse used was T. Vincent's *An Explicatory Catechism: or, An Explanation of the Assemblies Shorter Catechism* (London, 1701 and numerous repr.). Gordon, *Freedom After Ejection* (fn. 21), pp. 81, 82.

[50] Calamy, *Continuation* (fn. 7), vol. I, pp. 198–210; [Wesley], *Letter* (fn. 16), p. 11.

[51] T. Gale, *The Court of the Gentiles: or a Discourse touching the Original of Human Literature, both Philologic and Philosophic, from the Scriptures, and Jewish Churches*, 4 pts (London, 1669–78), Pt IV, Book III; 'Early Nonconformist Academies', *Trans. Congregational Historical Society*, 3 (1907–8), 276. *DNB*; N.H. Keeble, *The Literary Culture of Nonconformity in Later Seventeenth-Century England* (Leicester, 1987), pp. 168–70.

Gordon described as 'more remarkable for its conscientiousness and unction than for its intellectual grasp'.[52] It was subsequently claimed that Thomas Emlyn, who was convicted of blasphemy in 1703, acquired a distaste for 'narrow schemes of systematic divinity' as a result of his studies under Doolittle.[53]

The most complete account of the range of texts used and subjects taught by the generation of tutors who were active after 1689 is available for John Ker's academy at Bethnal Green, provided by one of his students, Samuel Palmer, in his defence of the nonconformist academy against the attacks of Samuel Wesley. The four-year course covered logic in the first year, metaphysics in the second, ethics in the third and natural philosophy in the fourth. The main text-book used in logic was the Cartesian Heereboord's, but his system was compared with that of the Aristotelian Smiglecius and the Newtonian Le Clerc, whose *Logica* had been published in 1692. Heereboord's *Logic* was the standard text in general use in other academies and also at Cambridge, and had come to replace Aristotle by this date but Ker, through his use of Le Clerc, was clearly open to the latest thinking. In metaphysics his main text was Frommenius's *Synopsis Metaphysica* (1669). His students also read Suarez's *Metaphysicarum Disputationum* (1605), Baronius's *Ethica Christiana* (1666) and Colbert's [i.e. Du Hamel] *Philosophia* for themselves. The works of Baronius, Colbert and Frommenius had all been in use at Rathmel. In ethics Ker followed Heereboord's *Collegium ethicum* (1658), a traditional system, and such ageless texts as Epictetus's *Enchiridion, Solomon's Proverbs*, the *Meditations* of Marcus Aurelius Antoninus and *Tully's Offices*, but he also recommended the Platonist Henry More's *Enchiridion Ethicum* (1669) and 'the Moral Works of the great' Pufendorf, presumably his *De Officio Hominis et Civis* (1682). In natural philosophy Ker followed Le Clerc, whose ideas were compared with 'the Antients and the other Moderns', Aristotle, Descartes, Colbert and Stair.[54]

---

[52] T. Doolittle, *A Complete Body of Practical Divinity being a new Improvement of the Assembly's Catechism . . . To which are prefix'd Some Memoirs of the Author's Life . . .* (London, 1723), 'Commending dedication'. Doolittle's personal covenant, based on the Assembly's *Shorter Catechism*, was dated 18 November 1693, see his memoirs above. His *The Young Man's Instructor and The Old Man's Remembrancer . . .* (London, 1673) also used the Assembly's Catechism.

[53] Emlyn, *Works* (fn. 31), vol. I, p. vii; *DNB*, s.v. Emlyn.

[54] [Samuel Palmer], *A Defence of the Dissenters' Education in their Private Academies in Answer to Mr W---y's Disingenuous and Unchristian Reflections upon 'em . . .* (London, 1703), pp. 4–6; [Wesley], *Letter* (fn. 16), pp. 50–1. Colbert can be identified with Jean Baptiste Du Hamel, *Philosophia vetus et nova*, 4th edn (London, 1685; first publ. Paris 1678), which was dedicated to (and the authorship often confused with) Jacques Nicolas Colbert; *Tull. de Off.* with M. Tullius Cicero, *De Officiis*; and Stair with [James Dalrymple, Viscount Stair], *A Vindication of the Divine Perfections* (London, 1695), with a preface by John Howe and William Bates, two nonconformist ministers in exile in Holland at the same time as Stair; *DNB*, s.v. Dalrymple.

The only details on the textbooks used by John Rowe, Theophilus Gale's successor in 1679, are provided by Isaac Watts, who studied under Rowe between 1690 and 1693. Watts had, among the manuscript notes he made as a student, a Latin volume of 'Logical Questions' drawn largely from Burgersdijk's *Logicae* and Heereboord's *Commentary* on the latter. Rowe, however, was an early supporter of Descartes, and later of Locke, though he was to remain a Cartesian in physics despite the growing influence of Newton. Rowe also recommended Pufendorf's *De Officio*.[55] Other tutors open to the new learning included James Owen, who conducted an academy at Oswestry and later at Shrewsbury, where he moved in 1700. Among the authorities he used were Burgersdijk, Heereboord and the Cartesian Ramus in logic, Eustachius in metaphysics, who followed the old method, but in philosophy Le Clerc and in ecclesiastical history Frederick Spanheim, who had taught at Leiden. The textbooks he used in theology included the Calvinist Wollebius.[56] After Owen's death in 1706 the academy was continued by Samuel Benion who had been persuaded to open an academy at Broad Oak following Frankland's death in 1698. Benion died within two years of moving to Shrewsbury, at the early age of 35, but he had devised his own system of logic instead of following the traditional method of teaching, in which the tutor commented on a set book.[57]

The greatest influence in the development of the new thinking was exerted by Locke, though Newton came in time to rival Locke in the estimation of Rational Dissenters. Not only did Locke's *Essay concerning Human Understanding* become one of the main texts used by Rational Dissenters in their academies, but his ideas were to dominate their thinking. Presbyterians were already greatly influenced by Locke's *Letter concerning Toleration* but they, and indeed scholarship in general, were subsequently profoundly affected by Locke's whole philosophical outlook and ultimately by the new scientific ideas and scepticism that in time were to dominate the early eighteenth century. Doddridge, during his first ministry at Kibworth, drew up for his own use an 'analytical

---

[55] T. Gibbons, *Memoirs of the Rev. Isaac Watts, D.D.* (London, 1780), pp. 21, 59; Gordon, *Addresses* (fn. 7), pp. 203–4; DWL 564.C.19, for Watts's annotations to his copy of Wilkins, *Ecclesiastes*, [7th edn, 1693] opposite p. 183. For further details of Watts's annotations, see W.E. Stephenson, 'Isaac Watts's Education for the Dissenting Ministry: A New Document', *Harvard Theological Review*, 61 (1968), 263–81; Stephenson, 'Isaac Watts and Bishop Wilkins' "Ecclesiastes"', *Notes and Queries* (December 1966), 454–5.

[56] [Charles Owen], *Some Account of the Life and Writings of . . . James Owen, Minister of the Gospel in Salop*, [ed. J. Evans, D.D.] (London, 1709), pp. 70–1, 87–93.

[57] Benion previously assisted Philip Henry in teaching gentlemen's sons. Matthew Henry, *A Sermon Preach'd at the Funeral of Dr Samuel Benion . . .* (London, 1709), pp. 42, 47, 49, 68.

scheme' of the contents of the epistles of the New Testament. As he told Samuel Clark, 'I make use of those few commentators which I have. I find Locke of far greater service to me than any of the rest.'[58]

By the first decades of the eighteenth century the new learning had been widely adopted. Samuel Jones, one of the best of the early eighteenth-century tutors, covered all Heereboord and the greater part of Locke's *Essay on the Art of Thinking* in his lectures on logic. Although he was 'no great admirer of the old *Logic*, yet he has taken a great deal of pains both in explaining and correcting Heereboord, and has for the most part made him intelligible, or shewn that he is not so'.[59] Jones also used the notes he had made as a student at Leiden, where he had attended the lectures of Perizonius and Gronovius. In addition, he taught his students Hebrew so that they could study the Scriptures for themselves.[60] Joshua Oldfield, who established his academy at Coventry before moving to London in 1699, made Locke the authority in all his teaching.[61] The leading academy in the North of England during the early eighteenth century was established at Whitehaven in 1708 by Thomas Dixon, and removed to Bolton in 1723 when Dixon became minister there. Three volumes of lecture notes taken by one of his students at Whitehaven, Henry Winder, survive: two contain lectures on mathematics and astronomy, the latter in Latin; the third has extracts from the writings of the Fathers, and from contemporary authors such as Newton, Bishop Burnet and Limborch, the Dutch Remonstrant and correspondent of Locke. Winder knew Greek and Hebrew, which he had presumably been taught at Whitehaven. A notebook of Ralph

---

[58] Doddridge to Clark, 22 October 1724, in *Correspondence and Diary of Philip Doddridge*, ed. J.D. Humphreys, 5 vols. (London, 1829–31), vol. 1, p. 425.

[59] Thomas Secker, Gloucester, to Isaac Watts, 11 November 1711, in Gibbons, *Memoirs* (fn. 55), pp. 347–52; Secker, 'Autobiography' (fn. 31), pp. 3–4. Jones's students included Joseph Butler as well as Thomas Secker, the future archbishop.

[60] Gibbons, *Memoirs* (fn. 55), pp. 347–52. The following volumes of lecture notes taken by his students survive: DWL, New College Library MS L38, 'In Dionysii Orbis Descriptionem Notae Quaedam, 1713: Autore Do. Sam Jones', (with the owner's signature: 'S. Shaw's Book, 1717'). (Dionysius's *Periegesis* was also used by Ker's students at Bethnal Green as part of their geography lectures, cf. Palmer, *Defence* (fn. 54), p. 5. Ker had studied at Leiden); DWL, MS24.3, 4 'Samuelis Jonesii, Academiae inter Fratres Dissententientes Archididascali, in Godwini Mosen et Aaronem Annotationes'; DWL, Congregational Library, MS I g 1–6, 'Annotationes in Godwini Mosen & Aaronem Autore Sam: Jones' (1719) 6 vols.; Bristol Baptist College, 'Notae Gronovii et viri clarissmi', see Griffiths, *Religion and Learning* (fn. 30), p. 36 n.2; McLachlan, *English Education* (fn. 3), p. 292. Jones had studied under Gronovius at Leiden. For an account of Semitic studies in nonconformist academies, see H. McLachlan, 'Semitics in the Nonconformist Academies', in his *Essays and Addresses* (Manchester, 1950), p. 183.

[61] Joshua Oldfield, *An Essay Towards the Improvement of Reason* . . . (London, 1707); Bolam *et al.*, *English Presbyterianism* (fn. 1), p. 140.

Astley, who was a student of Dixon's at Bolton in the mid-1720s, also survives. His emphasis on the use of reason in theological interpretation is striking. 'Reason must enable us to judge of ye Evidences of any Revelation pretended to be divine, & to understand it.' Astley on several occasions listed why he would not subscribe to any 'human confessions of Faith'. Nevertheless, the volume also includes the orthodox arguments against Socinianism.[62] Doddridge's tutor, John Jennings, at the academy he established at Kibworth in Leicestershire in 1715, devised his own system of logic, 'a great deal of which was taken from Mr Locke', though 'we first skimmed over Burgersdicius in about six lectures'. In the volume of lectures he published in 1721 for the use of his students, Jennings devoted a chapter to Ramus. The recommended textbooks included Locke's *Essay concerning Human Understanding* and Oldfield's *Essay towards the Improvement of Reason*, which embodied Locke's ideas, Newton's *Principia* and Le Clerc's *Logica*. In addition to logic, the four-year course covered physics (using texts by Le Clerc and Rohault), mathematics, mechanics, languages (French as well as Hebrew, Greek and Latin) and divinity. The academy closed on Jennings's death in 1723, following his move to Hinckley the year before, but both his methods and his lectures were used by Doddridge at Northampton.[63]

There were, however, a number of tutors who disregarded and in some cases rejected the new learning. Timothy Jollie at Attercliffe not only ignored the new philosophy but, it was alleged, went so far as to forbid mathematics 'as tending to scepticism and infidelity'.[64] Warren

[62] Manchester College, Oxford, MS Winder 1, Papers of Henry Winder (1693–1752) 1 (i–iii), three notebooks kept by Winder when a student at Whitehaven Academy, 1708–12; British Library Manuscripts Department, Add MS 45,978, Heywood Papers, 'Notebook of the Revd Ralph Astley, 1724–27', fos. 25v, 27r, 27v, 31r, 35r, 34r; H. McLachlan, 'Thomas Dixon, M.A., M.D., and the Whitehaven–Bolton Academy, 1708–29', *Essays and Addresses*, pp. 136, 137, 140; McLachlan, *English Education* (fn. 3), pp. 126, 293; PFB, II, pp. 242–3, 271, 273.

[63] DWL, MS24.179 (4), Doddridge to Thomas Saunders, 16 November 1725; J. J[ennings], *Miscellanea in Usum Juventutis Academicae*, 2 vols. (Northamptoniae, 1721), vol. 1 No. IV; vol. II, p. 3. Samuel Clark of St Albans told his protégé Doddridge that Locke's *Essay concerning Human Understanding* 'is so useful to direct the mind in its researches', and suggested that it ought to have been read before Doddridge began the study of pneumatology. Samuel Clark, St Albans, to Doddridge at Kibworth, 3 October 1721 in 'Calendar of the Correspondence of Philip Doddridge DD (1702–1751)', ed. G.F. Nuttall, *Historical Manuscripts Commission*, JP26 (1979), p. 1. For Doddridge's use and annotations of Jennings's *Miscellanea*, see G.F. Nuttall, *New College, London and its Library: Two Lectures*, Friends of Dr Williams's Library Lectures, (London, 1977), pp. 33–4. For Isaac Watts's comments on Doddridge's description of Jennings's teaching plan, see DWL MS24.180 (3).

[64] DWL MS24.59, 'An Account of the Dissenting Academies from the Restoration of Charles the Second', pp. 31–3; McLachlan, *English Education* (fn. 3), p. 108; Secker, 'Autobiography'(fn. 31), p. 3; John Barker, *A Sermon Occasioned by the Death of the Reverend Benjamin Grosvenor . . .* (London, 1758), p. 27.

at Taunton was said to have had little knowledge of the new ideas in logic and philosophy, and used Burgersdijk's *Logicae* and Eustachius's *Ethica* (London, 1677); the latter, according to Isaac Watts, was 'read as a system in most academys, & it is well-writt after the Old method'.[65] Nevertheless, Warren's students read Locke, Le Clerc and the rationalist ethics of Cumberland for themselves, for 'he encouraged his pupils in a freedom of enquiry, and in reading those books which would better gratify a love of truth and knowledge, even when they differed widely from those writers on which he had formed his own sentiments'.[66]

DOCTRINAL DIVISIONS

The religious orthodoxy that prevailed amongst the early tutors was to break down after 1689. Their successors were profoundly influenced both by the intellectual developments of the period and by the doctrinal divisions that emerged within Dissent, particularly over the Trinity. The break-up of the Happy Union in 1692, partly as a result of the activities of Richard Davis, minister of the Independent Church at Rothwell in Northamptonshire, shattered the theological consensus between Presbyterians and Congregationalists. Denominational differences, which had originally involved mainly differences in church order, were increasingly focused on doctrine. Richard Baxter, anxious to lessen the number of disputed points dividing Protestants, had sought to reduce to a minimum the fundamental doctrines required of believers by appealing to the sufficiency of Scripture and relying upon reason as the sole means by which to distinguish revealed truth.[67] Presbyterians, through the influence of Baxter, came to moderate traditional Calvinist doctrine by appealing to reason in matters of controversy. The decision to exalt reason was to prove fundamental in the development of Presbyterian thought, for this appeal to reason and personal conscience inevitably led Presbyterians to tolerate a wide divergence in belief. Thus the refusal of a majority of Presbyterians to subscribe to the declaration in support of the Trinity at the Salters' Hall debate in 1719 was concerned with the

---

[65] DWL 564.C.19, for Watts's annotations opposite p. 141.

[66] Grove, *Sermons* (fn. 47), vol. I, p. xiv; Richard Cumberland, *De Legibus Naturae Disquisitio Philosophica* ... (Londini, 1672). Care has to be taken, when using Grove as a source for Warren's attitudes, not to read back the sentiments of a later period.

[67] G.F. Nuttall, *Richard Baxter and Philip Doddridge: A Study in a Tradition*, Friends of Dr Williams's Library Fifth Lecture (London, 1951), pp. 6–7.

principle of subscription rather than doctrine.[68] Baxter's dislike of
extreme forms of Calvinism, which he labelled Antinomianism, was
matched by many orthodox Calvinists, who in turn detested the
Arminian tendencies they associated with Baxter's 'Middle Way'; as a
result they came frequently to equate an appeal to reason with
Socinianism. The acceptance of Locke's philosophical ideas also
encouraged the use of reason to test revealed truth.

The establishment of a separate Congregational Fund in 1695 with
the design of promoting the Congregational interest helped to accentu-
ate denominational differences within Dissent, and to stress the growing
division between orthodox Calvinists and those who used reason to
interpret Scripture. The Congregational Fund Board was to appoint its
own tutors to instruct its students. In April 1696 the Board wrote to John
Langston 'about takeing young Students', and a few months later to
Thomas Goodwin, whose academy at Pinner in Middlesex was for many
years the principal academy for the instruction of the Board's students.
The Board also sent students to William Payne jun. at Saffron Walden,
Timothy Jollie at Attercliffe, James Forbes at Gloucester and Thomas
Rowe in London.[69] The Board's decision to appoint its own tutors was to
further the breach with the Presbyterians. All the tutors chosen by the
Board were orthodox. Rowe, one of the original managers of the
Congregational Fund, was certainly doctrinally sound. According to
Watts, Rowe considered Calvin's *Institutes* 'a most excellent, Scripturall,
argumentative, and elegant System of Divinity'. Wollebius, 'a neat short
Logicall method of Calvinistic divinity', also seems to have been read at
Rowe's academy together with a number of other Calvinist systems of
divinity. Watts's manuscript volumes included an abridgement of Gale's
The Court of the Gentiles.[70] Of the other tutors patronised by the Board,
Forbes, who supported the Happy Union, was of a 'catholic temper',

---

[68] R. Thomas, 'The Non-Subscription Controversy Amongst Dissenters in 1719: the Salters' Hall
Debate', *Journal of Ecclesiastical History*, 4 (1953), 174–5, 183–5; Bolam *et al.*, *English Presbyterianism*
(fn. 1), p. 168.

[69] After 1704 there is a break in the minutes, see DWL, OD401, Congregational Fund Board [here-
after CFB] minutes, vol. I, 17 December 1695 to 5 February 1699/1700, pp. 17, 28 (13 April, 29
June 1696); OD402, minutes, II, 5 February 1699/1700 to 18 December 1704. For a useful
summary of the students supported by the Board and the names of their tutors, see DWL, New
College collection, MS487, Extracts from Congregational Fund Board minutes (1695–1800)
made by Henry Rutt, *s.v.* 'List of Students educated by the Congregational Fund Board', fos.
68–83.

[70] CFB, minutes, I, p. 2; DWL 564.C.19, for Watts's annotations to his copy of Wilkins, *Ecclesiastes*,
opposite pp. 112, 146, cf. opposite p. 113; Joannes Wollebius, *Compendium Theologiae Christianae . . .
Editio nova prioribus correctior* (Londini, 1647); Gibbons, *Memoirs* (fn. 55), pp. 21, 59.

and the ministry of Langston was described as conciliatory 'towards people of different perswasions'; both, however, were Calvinists.[71] Timothy Jollie, who had rejected the new philosophy, was clearly conservative in his doctrine and teaching.[72] No evidence survives on Goodwin's teaching or the texts he used, but he was a strong supporter of the High Calvinist side in the controversy over the re-publication of Tobias Crisp's sermons in 1689.[73] Not only were all the tutors Calvinists and orthodox in doctrine but none appear to have accepted students from the rival Presbyterian Board, despite having previously received students from the Common Fund.

By 1700 there are increasing references in the minutes to the Board's concern that only candidates holding Congregational principles should receive support.[74] Unfortunately, the loss of the Fund's minutes between 1705 and 1738 makes it impossible to trace the Board's growing insistence on the doctrinal orthodoxy of those they supported. Nevertheless, the policy was certainly established by the 1720s, following the Salters' Hall debate. Under the regulations adopted in 1738 (the date the minutes resume), it was agreed that

Satisfaction be given to this Board, if required, that all those to whom any Exhibitions are allowed are Sound in the Faith, particularly as to the Doctrine of the Blessed Trinity as revealed in the Holy Scriptures and explain'd in the Assembly's Confession of Faith and Catechism, and that every Member of this Board has a right to desire this Satisfaction.[75]

This regulation, however, was only confirming what had already clearly been the Board's policy for a decade or more. A collection of testimonies detailing the orthodoxy of the ministers receiving grants from the Fund is available from 1724. Mr Robert Pierson was described in 1726 as 'a good Man sound in the Doctrine of the Holy Trinity & orthodox in all other Articles of Faith contain[e]d in the Savoy Confession,

[71] Gordon, *Freedom After Ejection* (fn. 21), p. 266; John Browne, *History of Congregationalism, and Memorials of the Churches in Norfolk and Suffolk* (London, 1877), pp. 370–1; *DNB, s.v.* Langston.

[72] Gordon, *Freedom After Ejection* (fn. 21), p. 263; 'The Attercliffe Academy', *Transactions of the Congregational Historical Society*, 4 (1909–10), 341. Although Jollie had received Presbyterian ordination, he was undoubtedly a Congregationalist like his father.

[73] Gordon, *Freedom After Ejection* (fn. 21), p. 273; *DNB*.

[74] CFB Minutes, I, pp. 19, 35, 61, 81, 95, 102, 103 (27 April, 19 October 1696, 1 November 1697, 3 October 1698, 1 May, 20 & 27 November 1699).

[75] DWL, OD404, CFB, 'Rules & Orders relating to the Meetings of the Ministers and other Messengers of the Congregational Churches in London, for encourageing the Preaching of the Gospell in England and Wales, agreed upon heretofore, and now revised Febr^y 5th 1737/8', part II 'Concerning the Churches or Congregations and Ministers who desire any Distribution from this Board', p. 7, §4.

Congregational in discipline'.[76] A few years earlier, Joseph Dodson of Penruddock was struck out by the Board from the list of ministers receiving grants, after being accused of Arianism because of the sermon he preached before the general meeting of ministers at Keswick in April 1719.[77]

The managers of the Presbyterian Fund, unlike their Congregational brethren, attempted to maintain a broader, non-sectarian outlook, but they were forced to adopt a narrower interpretation as a result of the rival Fund's tactics. In 1695, following the withdrawal of the Congregational members from the management of the Common Fund, the opportunity was taken with the opening of a new volume of minutes to set out the revised policy of the Fund. It was agreed to 'take care of such as were formerly provided for of this Fund. Except such as were recommended by those that have deserted this good Work'.[78] This new policy did not involve attempts to encourage those they supported to adopt heterodox opinions, but rather a refusal by the managers to enquire into the religious principles of any they assisted. In December 1719, Edmund Calamy, the biographer of Dissent, was successful in proposing that the question of subscription should be ignored by the Board when considering grants. The motion was passed following the celebrated Salters' Hall debate, but appears to have been drawn up because of the dismissal of John Cox for Arian sympathies by the congregation at Kingsbridge in Devon.[79] This refusal to demand any religious subscription, together with a willingness to allow individuals the right of private judgement, was to become one of the fundamental principles characterising Rational Dissent.[80]

[76] DWL, OD455, CFB 'Book of Memoranda on places ministers and students', p. 116 (no.71). Cf. pp. 111, 114–5, 118 (nos. 2, 13, 45, 57, 96).

[77] The sermon was published, with details of the dispute, by Joseph Dodson, see *Moderation and Charity, Recommended in a Sermon Preach'd at Keswick, to the Associated Protestant Dissenting Ministers of Cumberland and Westmoreland* (London, 1720); J.H. Colligan, 'The Provincial Meeting of Cumberland & Westmorland', *Transactions of the Congregational Historical Society*, 4 (1909–10), 162; Bolam et al., *English Presbyterianism* (fn. 1), pp. 135–6, 165. A number of ministers in Cumberland and Westmorland had lost their allowances in 1713. Among those who received an extraordinary grant from the Presbyterian Fund on this occasion were Samuel Bourn, who had refused to subscribe to the Assembly's Catechism out of 'christian liberty', and Dodson. Nicholson and Axon, however, suggest this grant may have been connected with the inability of the Lady Hewley Trust to make grants owing to litigation. PFB, II, pp. 242, 243 (4 May, 8 June 1713); J. Toulmin, *Memoirs of . . . Samuel Bourn* (Birmingham and London, 1808); Nicholson and Axon, *Older Nonconformity* (fn. 8), pp. 259–61.   [78] PFB, II, p. 3, rule 5.

[79] DWL, OD68, PFB minutes, II, 5 February 1694/5 – 4 June 1722, pp. 357, 356; Bolam et al., *English Presbyterianism* (fn. 1), p. 165; Brockett, 'Exeter Assembly' (fn. 32), p. 137 s.v. Cox.

[80] M. Fitzpatrick, 'Toleration and Truth', *Enlightenment and Dissent*, 1, (1982), 3–31. Explicit denominational references in the Presbyterian Fund minutes are rare.

The insistence of the Congregational Fund in maintaining a clear denominational identity, to which the managers of the Presbyterian Fund found themselves forced to respond, was to widen the division between Presbyterians and Congregationalists. Nevertheless, it was the Trinitarian controversy, which resulted in the Salters' Hall debate of 1719, that proved to be the watershed between liberal and orthodox Dissent. Although the division between those who subscribed to the declaration on the Trinity and those who refused was far from being determined on denominational lines, Salters' Hall does appear to have encouraged those who were Calvinist and favoured orthodoxy to iden- tify with the Congregational interest, and those who prized freedom of enquiry with Presbyterians. English Presbyterians, from being the most orthodox and conservative body of Dissenters in 1662, had, by the early nineteenth century, become a 'body which refused to impose any test or creed and whose only formula was a heterodox insistence upon the single personality of God and the proper humanity of Christ'.[81]

Although the managers of the Presbyterian Fund did not seek to influ- ence the religious principles of those they assisted, some of the policies they adopted did help encourage the growth in heterodoxy. In 1725 the managers agreed to patronise only the academies at Taunton and Findern, together with the academy at Carmarthen, resolving that 'the two places in England be reduc'd to One as soon as shall be thought Convenient by this Board'. This resolution appears to have been prompted by administrative considerations, but all three academies were conducted on liberal principles. The author of the 1732 survey of London Dissent, who though anonymous was clearly an Independent, blamed Findern and Taunton for the fact that most of the ministers edu- cated by the Presbyterians, and who 'have of late years been called to the ministry, are Inclined to the arminian scheme'. Carmarthen also became notorious as a nursery of heterodoxy under Thomas Perrot, who was tutor there between 1718 and 1733.[82]

Concern over the spread of Arminianism and the threat to orthodox Calvinism led to the establishment of the King's Head Society in 1730, to promote evangelical Dissent and to provide students with an orthodox

[81] Griffiths, *Religion and Learning* (fn. 30), p. 3.
[82] DWL, Minutes of the Presbyterian Fund Board, III, (1722–1751), pp. 50–1; DWL, MS38.18, 'A View of the Dissenting Interest in London of the Presbyterian & Independent Denominations, from the year 1695 to the 25 of December 1731, with a Postscript of the present state of the Baptists', p. 90; G.H. Jenkins, *The Foundations of Modern Wales, 1642–1780* (Oxford, 1988), pp. 314, 384.

education for the ministry. Every candidate supported by the Society was required to subscribe to *A Declaration as to some controverted points of Christian Doctrine*, and by means of a formal examination every three months attempts were made to ensure the continued orthodoxy of the Society's students. In 1753 the members of the Society declared that

they would take none under their care but such as give the most satisfying Evidence, in a Judgment of Charity, that they have received the Grace of God in Truth; whose hearts God had inclined to the work of the Ministry; and who appear to have natural Abilities for that sacred Work.

Additional support for the defence of orthodox Calvinism was given by William Coward, who left considerable property in trust for the education of students for the ministry. Trustees were enjoined to take care that the students were instructed according to 'the assembly's catechism, and in that method of church discipline which is practised by the congregational churches'. The Northern Educational Society, established in London in May 1756, had similar objectives, and the maintenance of Calvinism and the promotion of evangelical piety owed much to the Yorkshire academies it established.[83] Although orthodox Dissenters introduced religious tests and subscriptions in order to preserve the continued orthodoxy of their students, even academies that regulated their students strictly could not guarantee their religious faith. All suffered a small but embarrassing number of expulsions or withdrawals. Academies that rejected religious subscription were no more successful. The students they educated included ministers who became High Calvinists, and some who even conformed.

THE ACADEMY AND HETERODOX OPINIONS

The new learning in philosophy and the sciences was adopted in a number of academies with the use of texts by Locke and Newton, but the most significant advance for the development of Rational Dissent was not so much doctrinal (involving the encouragement of heterodox opinions), as the willingness of tutors to allow their students the right of private judgement, a principle which can be traced back to Baxter. Samuel Benion used the Assembly's *Confession of Faith* and the Calvinist

---

[83] DWL, New Coll. MS105/1, King's Head Society Minute book, 25 October 1737 to 27 October 1747, pp. 5–6, 15, 30–1, 35; DWL, MS38.30, printed advertisement: '[King's Head] Society for educating for ministry of Protestant Dissenters' (1753); New Coll. MS239/5–9 correspondence concerned with changes in sentiment of students; *DNB*, *s.v.* William Coward; R.T. Jones, *Congregationalism in England, 1662–1962* (London, 1962), pp. 140–1, 177.

William Ames's *Medulla Theologica* (originally published in 1623) to methodise his students' studies, but he was a Baxterian in his dislike of theological schemes and in placing the emphasis on the sufficiency of Scripture and reason: 'the Bible was the System he read, and the Genuine Expositions of that he thought the most profitable Divinity Lectures he could read to his Pupils; To that onely he was devoted, and not to any Man's Hypothesis'.[84] Caleb Rotheram, a student of Dixon, who opened his academy at Kendal in 1733 after Dixon's death, 'was an impartial lover of truth, he incouraged the most free and unbounded inquiry after it, in every branch of science'. Rotheram's academy became one of the leading institutions patronised by liberal Dissent.[85] It was said of Warren that he was 'never Vehement, nor Rigid to his own Opinion, but Receptive of, and Yielding to Reason, Preferring the Judgement of Others to his own. So he allow'd his Pupils Freedom of Thought, and never denied 'em the Use of any Authors'. This freedom, however, should not be exaggerated. Warren was careful 'to establish his Pupils against those Erroneous Principles that undermine the Fundamentals of our Religion, and to strengthen their Minds against the Licentious'. Owen insisted that the student presenting the heterodox position did so in the third person.[86]

It has generally been argued that ministers acquired heterodox opinions as a result of being exposed to such ideas at nonconformist academies. Certainly the example of John Fox, who attended Hallett's academy in Exeter between 1708 and 1711, supports this contention. Fox was first introduced to Arian opinions by the eldest son of his tutor, who lent him a number of books that questioned the Trinity.[87] Nevertheless, the significance of the nonconformist academy in encouraging heterodox ideas amongst their students can be exaggerated. Few tutors, if any, deliberately taught heterodox opinions. Even those tutors who later held Unitarian opinions, because of their fundamental commitment to the principle of free enquiry, refused to teach Unitarianism or indeed any other system of beliefs as doctrine, despite

---

[84] Henry, *Sermon* (fn. 57), p. 69.
[85] James Daye, *The Christian's Service, Compleated with Honour: A Sermon Occasioned by the Death of the Reverend Caleb Rotheram . . . Preached at Kendal, June 14 1752* (London, [1752]), p. 19; McLachlan, *English Education* (fn. 3), p. 191.
[86] John Sprint, *A Funeral Sermon for the Reverend Mr Warren . . .* [with] *A Character of the Late Reverend Mr Matthew Warren By another Hand* (London, 1707), p. 46; [Owen], *Account* (fn. 56), pp. 70–1.
[87] 'The Fox Memoirs: Worthies of Devon', *Devonshire Association*, 28 (1896), 131. Cf. Brockett, 'Exeter Assembly' (fn. 32), pp. 78–9. It was the reputation that Hallett's academy acquired for heterodoxy that led to its closure. Cf. Clegg, 'Autobiography' (fn. 32), p. 913.

the risk of serious misunderstanding.[88] Academies did however encourage the spread of heterodox ideas amongst students, if unintentionally. With respect to controversial questions of doctrine, the method of instruction adopted by the tutors involved presenting defences of both the orthodox and heterodox positions. Exposing students to the different arguments, however, encouraged some to question the very doctrines that the teaching was intended to defend. Perhaps more important than the ideas themselves was the encouragement given to the principle that students should discover the truth for themselves. According to Doddridge, Jennings, an Independent, always encouraged 'the greatest freedom of inquiry' and 'inculcates it as a law, that the scriptures are the only genuine standard of faith'. As a result Jennings did not follow 'the doctrines or phrases of any particular party; but is sometimes a Calvinist, sometimes an Arminian, and sometimes a Baxterian, as truth and evidence determine him'. But

He furnishes us with all kinds of authors upon every subject, without advising us to skip over the heretical passages for fear of infection. It is evidently his main care to inspire us with sentiments of Catholicism, and to arm us against that zeal which is not according to knowledge.

Doddridge also tried to present his students with the arguments for both sides, leaving them to form their own judgement after reading the different authorities for themselves.[89] In later academies the method of disputation became formalised, with the tutor and his assistant taking up opposing sides. At Daventry, according to Priestley, Ashworth took 'the orthodox side of every question, and Mr Clark, the sub-tutor, that of heresy'. Moreover, 'we were referred to authors on both sides of every question, and were then required to give an account of them'.[90] Inevitably some students, after having heard the arguments against, found it impossible to return to the orthodox position.

The academy was not, however, the only place of heterodox opinions or indeed of intellectual study. Ministers continued to read and study throughout their careers. Samuel Bourn first settled at Crook near

[88] See D.L. Wykes, 'Dissenting Academy or Unitarian Seminary? Manchester College at York (1803–1840)', *Transactions of Unitarian Historical Society*, 18 (1988), 102–4 *et seq*.

[89] Doddridge to Samuel Clark, [22] September 1722, and Doddridge to his brother-in-law, John Nettleton, 27 February 1722/3 in Doddridge, *Correspondence and Diary* (fn. 58), 1, pp. 155–6, 198–9; 'Doddridge', ed. Nuttall (fn. 63), letter no. 35; A.V. Murray, 'Doddridge and Education', in G.F. Nuttall, ed., *Philip Doddridge, 1702–51: His Contribution to English Religion* (London, 1951), pp. 103–6; R. Thomas, 'Philip Doddridge and Liberal Religion', in *ibid.*, pp. 132–5, 152–3.

[90] *The Theological and Miscellaneous Works of Joseph Priestley*, ed. J.T. Rutt, 25 vols. in 26 (London, 1817–31) vol. 1, pt 1, pp. 23–4.

Kendal in 1711, and in this 'retired situation he spent nine years in a close application to his studies'. He had originally accepted the orthodox interpretation of the Trinity, but in 1719, as a result of the Salters' Hall debate, he 'determined to enter into a diligent and thorough examination' of the issues and read Samuel Clarke's *Scripture Doctrine of the Trinity* (1712) together with the various replies. As a result of his reading he became an Arian. Hubert Stogdon, later notorious for his part in the Exeter heresy, had originally accepted the doctrine of the Trinity, and 'conceived it to be of such importance, as to make a departure from it extremely dangerous', but after 'long and deliberate reading' his opinions were to change: 'he came into it by slow degrees, laborious and humble enquiries, with many prayers and tears'. James Peirce, who was also at the centre of the Exeter controversy, claimed that many of those who came to question the orthodox interpretation of the Trinity came to their conclusions as a result of studying the Bible for themselves. Peirce had studied at Leiden, but he was still a Calvinist when he published his *Vindication of the Dissenters* in 1710. Lardner claimed not to have read any of the controversial tracts on the Trinity, but to have arrived at his interpretation of the Logos as a result of his own studies. His work was to influence, among others, Priestley, who declared that he 'became what is called a Socinian' after reading Lardner's *Letter on the Logos*.[91]

Although many Presbyterians came to have doubts about the doctrine of the Trinity as a result of Clarke's work, the new standards of biblical criticism he set by his thorough investigation of the scriptural evidence were, perhaps, to prove more important. Locke's *Paraphrases of Pauline Epistles* and Le Clerc's *Five Letters* (first translated into English in 1690), together with William Whiston's *Essay upon the Apostolical Constitution* (1708), also encouraged the questioning of existing interpretations by challenging the assumption that orthodox doctrine was necessarily in accordance with Scripture. Many who were led by the controversies of the period to examine the evidence and arguments for themselves found that their studies, rather than buttressing their existing faith, led them to question the very orthodoxies they had set out to defend. Nevertheless, it should be noted that many of those who did study the arguments for

---

[91] Toulmin, *Memoirs of … Samuel Bourn* (fn. 77), pp. 16, 17–18; Samuel Blyth, *The Good Soldier of Jesus Christ Characterized in a Sermon … Occasioned by the Sudden and Much-Lamented Death of the Reverend Mr S. Bourn …* (London, 1754), pp. 13–14; Nicholas Billingsley, *A Sermon Occasioned by the Death of the late Reverend Mr Hubert Stogdon … With Memoirs of his Life and Character* (London, 1728), pp. 20–1; James Peirce, *The Western Inquisition, or a Relation of the Controversy … among the Dissenters in the West of England* (London, 1720), p. 11; Gordon, *Addresses* (fn. 7), p. 126; Griffiths, *Religion and Learning* (fn. 30), pp. 121, 147; Priestley, *Works*, vol. 1, pt 1, p. 69.

themselves were not persuaded that a departure from the orthodox line was justified.

Although it was intended that the academy should provide ministers with the same type of education found at a university, to give them the scholarly skills with which to expound and explain the Scriptures to their congregations and to defend the main doctrinal tenets,[92] it also gave them the techniques and skills to pursue an independent study of the Scriptures. Students were introduced by their tutors not only to the different branches of knowledge and to new ideas, but to a training in logic and philosophy that provided them with the principal techniques of intellectual study and the fundamental concepts and methods of analysis which, together with a knowledge of Greek and Hebrew, enabled them to study the original texts and assess controversial points of doctrine for themselves. It is important to understand, therefore, that the intellectual and doctrinal development of a minister did not end with the period of formal academic instruction. Surviving letters for the period, in particular the Benson correspondence, provide evidence for the considerable interest of many ministers in contemporary theological questions. Moreover, such interest was widespread, involving ministers not only of leading urban congregations, but also those of small rural meetings.[93]

LATER ACADEMIES

The insistence by orthodox Dissenters on the use of religious tests in order to prevent the spread of error forced Rational Dissenters to support their own academies. There is evidence of the anxiety felt by Rational Dissenters during the early 1750s, following the demise of those academies where, free from religious subscription, the majority of their ministers had been educated. The death of Doddridge in 1751 was followed within three years by those of Rotheram and Latham.[94] Throughout the second half of the eighteenth century there were always

---

[92] See, for example, Theophilus Lobb, *A Sermon Preach'd at the Ordination of the Reverend Mr John Greene*... (London, 1708), pp. 21–5.

[93] See John Rylands University Library, Benson Correspondence B/1/15–16, letters addressed to Benson from Joseph Chandler, 29 January 1722/3, T. Payne, 11 August 1729, John Dolland, 20 May 1748. See also Bodleian Library, Oxford, MS Eng. lett. c.352, 'Letters of the Astley Family', fo. 1r, John Leland to Ralph Astley, 12 December 1720, Liverpool Record Office, Nicholson Papers, 920 NIC 3/8/2, Thos Farrer, Westfield, to Samuel Nicholson, at Rotheram's Academy, Kendal, 26 November 1735. It is also evident that ministers were encouraged to pursue their studies, even concerning the doctrinal confession they made on ordination, see Gordon, *Cheshire Classis Minutes* (fn. 36), p. 133.   [94] Bolam *et al.*, *English Presbyterianism* (fn. 1), pp. 192–3, 195.

two, and usually three, leading academies educating students on liberal principles: Daventry, Warrington and Hoxton, and, following their closure, New College Hackney and the Manchester Academy. After Doddridge's death in 1751, his academy moved to Daventry where Caleb Ashworth, named by Doddridge as his successor, was minister. On the resignation in 1789 of Thomas Belsham, following his adoption of Unitarian opinions, the academy returned once more to Northampton where John Horsey, the new tutor, was minister. At the insistence of the Coward trustees, who supported the academy, no lay students were admitted under Horsey.[95] All the tutors at Daventry, including initially Belsham, were orthodox in theology, but no religious test was ever required of students studying at the academy. Warrington Academy was established in 1757 by a public subscription amongst the supporters of Rational Dissent, because of the concern that, following the closure of Kendal in 1753 and Latham's Academy at Derby (previously at Findern) in 1754, there was for the first time in nearly a century no academy in the north of England. Nevertheless, the concern amongst the promoters of Warrington over the absence of any institution conducted by tutors on liberal principles is also evident. Hoxton Academy under Samuel Morton Savage, who had succeeded the orthodox David Jennings in 1762 as theology tutor, became the main place of liberal education in London, particularly with the appointment of Andrew Kippis and Abraham Rees as tutors.

Warrington Academy closed in 1782, due to financial difficulties arising from a decline in the number of students and subscribers supporting it, but the underlying causes of this decline were problems over student discipline and doubts about the principles of the institution. Warrington Academy was finally dissolved in 1786 and the remaining funds applied to New College Hackney and the Manchester Academy. Although Hackney came to be regarded as the main successor to Warrington, its promoters had originally sought to persuade the Coward trustees to continue their academy at Hoxton. When they failed they established their own academy in London.[96] The younger divinity students supported on the Coward Trust Foundation at Hoxton completed

---

[95] DWL, New College MSS, CT2, 'Minutes of the Trustees of William Coward, 9 March 1779 to 2 February 1813, p. 61. At the meeting of 28 July 1789, it was agreed to inform Horsey that 'though the trustees are determined to admit no *new* lay students into Mr Coward's Academy', they have no objection to those who came under Belsham finishing their studies at Northampton.

[96] DWL, CT2, pp. 32, 33, 37, 38, 41, 44, 45, 47; New College MSS, 187/2/3–12, letters and memoranda of Joseph Paice concerning dissolution of Hoxton Academy, 1785–6; DWL, MS38.14, 'Hackney College Minutes, 1765–1791', pp. 1–6; McLachlan, *English Education* (fn. 3), p. 122.

their studies at Daventry, but attempts to save Warrington Academy by uniting the institution at Daventry under Belsham came to nothing.[97] The academy established at Manchester in 1786 was a conscious attempt to provide an academy for the north of England and to continue the work of Warrington. Its first promoters and tutors all had strong connections with Warrington: many had been educated there, and of the remainder a majority were former subscribers and benefactors. The college at Hackney closed in 1796, having become encumbered with debt as a result of an over-ambitious building project and poor financial management. The underlying factor, however, was the same crucial loss of support that had destroyed Warrington, due to the indiscipline of its students and the political radicalism with which the academy had become associated. Timothy Kenrick opened an academy at Exeter in 1799, but it was short-lived due to his premature death in 1805. After the closure of Hackney and Exeter during the very difficult political conditions liberal Dissent faced as a result of the conservative reaction to the French Revolution, the academy at Manchester was liberal Dissent's only remaining place of education free from religious subscription. The academy struggled on, very nearly closing on at least two occasions, in 1797 and 1803. Uncertainty over the academy's survival remained until after the move to York in 1803, when the political conditions for Rational Dissenters improved and there was renewed support from parents and subscribers.[98]

Warrington has acquired a reputation as the greatest of the non-conformist academies, indeed, as one of the leading educational establishments of the eighteenth century. Although recent studies (of Oxford in particular) have qualified earlier assessments of the eighteenth-century university as educationally moribund, Warrington's reputation as 'the Athens of the North' still remains largely intact.[99] Some qualification of the contribution the academy made, both to religious Dissent and to educational development, is, however, necessary. Although historians have established the excellence of the education

---

[97] John Williams, *Memoirs of the late Thomas Belsham, Including a Brief Notice of his Published Works and ... Extracts from his Diary ... and Letters ...* (London, 1833), pp. 308–19.

[98] D.L. Wykes, 'Sons and Subscribers: Lay Support and the College, 1786–1840', in Smith, *Birth of Modern Education* (fn. 37), pp. 44–5; *ibid.*, '"The Spirit of Persecutors Exemplified": The Priestley Riots and the Victims of the Church and King Mobs', *Transactions of the Unitarian Historical Society*, 20 (1991), 30–1.

[99] McLachlan, *English Education* (fn. 3), p. 209; H. McLachlan, *Warrington Academy: Its History and Influence*, Chetham Society, n.s. 107 (Manchester, 1943). The most recent study, which follows this laudatory tradition, is P. O'Brien, *Warrington Academy, 1757–86: Its Predecessors and Successors* (Wigan, 1989).

provided, the scholarship of the tutors and, through the introduction of new subjects and methods of instruction, the innovative nature of the teaching (at least when the academy was at its zenith), the significance of Warrington's achievements for modern education seems less certain. The isolation of Warrington and nonconformist academies generally from the mainstream of society, and from other places of higher education, suggests that the direct influence of their ideas and methods was probably minor, particularly as the number of students educated there was too small to have had any significant impact on society. It is true that some of the tutors, most notably Priestley, disseminated their ideas and teaching methods by later publishing the texts of their lectures, but in a number of cases only some years after Warrington's demise.[100] The reputation the academy acquired, together with the subsequent notoriety of Priestley, is unlikely to have encouraged emulation, particularly as it was believed that one of the main causes of the disorders at Warrington was the principles upon which it was founded.

Nor was the contribution made by Warrington to Dissent itself perhaps as great as has often been claimed. The academy's reputation was founded on the excellence of its instruction in secular subjects: the teaching of science, languages and history. Its course in theology was solid rather than inspiring, involving the detailed examination of Scripture and the application of reason to test revealed truth, an approach adopted first in the early eighteenth century. John Taylor, the first theology tutor, was a distinguished Hebraist and had written a controversial and highly influential work on Atonement. He was, however, old when appointed and he found it difficult to adapt to the demands of his new post. His period at Warrington was not made any happier by disagreements with his colleagues. His successor, John Aikin, was a good scholar but can hardly be considered innovative. He used Doddridge's lectures, except in ethics, where he generally followed his own scheme, though in the fourth year he made an important addition with a course on Church history. By the time Nicholas Clayton succeeded Aikin in 1780, the academy was in decline and only a few years from dissolution. Clayton, though he was appointed as theological tutor, was noted more for his scholarship in mathematics and natural philosophy. The strength

---

[100] Priestley's theories on education were set out in his *An Essay on a Course of Liberal Education for Civil and Active Life. With plans of lectures . . . To which are added Remarks on a Code of Education proposed by Dr Brown . . .* (London, 1765; 2nd edn, 1771) and *Miscellaneous Observations relating to Education* (Bath, 1778; 2nd edn, Birmingham, 1788).

of teaching in the languages and sciences only served to stress the secular bias of the academy.[101]

Less than 400 students passed through the academy. Although this was a significantly higher total than for its main rival, Daventry, or for Doddridge's earlier academy at Northampton, the overall numbers were still small when compared with Oxford or Cambridge. During the twenty-six years of the academy's active life between 1757 and 1782, a total of 393 students were educated there, but only 53 followed the divinity course (less than one in seven), even though the education of students for the ministry had been one of the main objects of the original founders.[102] The reasons for the small numbers were in part financial. The trustees were unable to continue their divinity exhibitions after June 1776. Only seven students who attended Warrington after that date entered the nonconformist ministry.[103] No other Dissenting academy had so high a proportion of lay students. By comparison, nearly three-fifths of the 254 students who attended Daventry were divinity students, a very similar proportion to that found at Doddridge's earlier academy at Northampton. Two-thirds of the students at Kendal were also intended for the ministry, but the period of the academy's existence was shorter (1733–53). The academy was also more isolated from the main centres of Dissenting population.[104] Only a quarter of the forty-eight students educated at the second Exeter Academy, the main liberal rival to Warrington, entered the ministry, but the academy was much smaller than either Daventry or Warrington and lasted only eleven years (1760–71).[105]

Warrington's reputation for scholarship and its non-denominational outlook found favour with many parents who were not Dissenters, perhaps because the academy was never intended as a seminary for the training of Dissenting ministers, but rather as a rival to Oxford and Cambridge free from religious subscription. Gilbert Wakefield, a tutor

[101] H.L. Short, 'Warrington Academy', *Hibbert Journal*, 56 (1957–8), 3; *A Report of the State of the Academy at Warrington. Drawn up by the Trustees at their annual Meeting July 10.* MDCCLX; J. Fulton, 'The Warrington Academy (1757–1786) and its Influence Upon Medicine and Science', *Bulletin of the Institute of the History of Medicine*, 1 (2) (1933), 60, 62, 64.

[102] The student figures are derived from a fresh study of the evidence and involve a number of new identifications of individual students. The figures therefore differ slightly from those of McLachlan, *Warrington Academy* (fn. 99) and Parker, *Dissenting Academies* (fn. 3), p. 159.

[103] McLachlan, *Warrington Academy* (fn. 99), p. 99.

[104] See John Rylands University Library, Benson Correspondence B/1/15, John Hodgson, Lincoln, to Benson, 11 December 1751.

[105] H. McLachlan, *The Unitarian Movement in the Religious Life of England*, vol. 1; *Its Contribution to Thought and Learning, 1700–1900* (London, 1934), pp. 87–93. [No more publ.]

during the final years, estimated that at least a third of the students in his time were Anglicans.[106] The extent of the academy's non-denominational character becomes even clearer when the fifty-three students who followed the divinity course are examined in detail. Eleven proceeded to either Oxford or Cambridge and took holy orders. They included the eldest son of Archdeacon Blackburne, Theophilus Lindsey's father-in-law, and Nathaniel Alexander, subsequently Bishop of Clonfert.[107] A further six conformed or took holy orders, including four who had followed the lay course: in all, seventeen ultimately entered the Church.[108] There were, in addition, at least three lay students who were Quakers, though their families had either resigned from the Society of Friends or were disowned.[109] A number of the men Doddridge trained entered the Baptist and Presbyterian as well as the Independent ministry, some of whom were to become Methodists.[110]

Whilst evidence that a significant proportion of the students at the academy were members of the Church of England attests to the reputation of Warrington academically, it is clear that the academy experienced difficulties in recruiting both students and subscriptions from liberal Dissent. The Academy also did little to preserve the nonconformist principles of those it educated. The sons of the nonconformist gentry generally proceeded to Oxford or Cambridge and in time conformed to the Church of England. 'For them the Academy was at most little more than an excellent and economical substitute for private tuition or the schools where nonconformist youths were unwelcome.'[111] After the mid-1760s a significant proportion of the students educated at Warrington had no connection with Dissent, as financial difficulties forced the tutors to be less selective. The five-year period between 1767 and 1771 saw a dramatic peak in the number of students from the West Indies, as well as an increase in the students from Ireland and Scotland. It was some of these students who were to cause the most serious problems over discipline.

If some of the wilder claims that historians have made in the past concerning the contribution of Warrington Academy cannot be sustained, there is no doubt that the education it offered, particularly in secular

---

[106] *Memoirs of the Life of Gilbert Wakefield... Written by Himself* (London, 1792) p. 199.
[107] William Turner, *The Warrington Academy (1757–1786)* ..., ed. G.A. Carter (Warrington, 1957), pp. 54, 56, 61, 66, 70, 73, 74, 77, 78.   [108] *Ibid.*, pp. 56, 66, 71, 73, 74, 78, 80.
[109] They include the Whig MP Henry Beaufoy, who played a leading role in the campaign for the repeal of the Test and Corporation Acts between 1787 and 1790, *ibid.*, pp. 62, 65, 73.
[110] McLachlan, *English Education* (fn. 3), p. 150.
[111] McLachlan, *Warrington Academy* (fn. 99), p. 13.

subjects, was exceptional by the standards of the second half of the eighteenth century. Its demise was a major blow for Rational Dissent and helps explain the efforts made by the supporters of New College Hackney and of the Manchester Academy in promoting a replacement. Although the direct contribution of Warrington Academy to Rational Dissent must be qualified, John Yates, writing in November 1784, thought the academy could justify itself 'in the gentlemen educated there', and in the 'dissenting ministers settled in some of the most respectable congregations in the kingdom'.[112] The number of ministers the academy educated may have been small, but they included some of the leading figures in late eighteenth-century Rational Dissent. Thomas Barnes and Ralph Harrison were the first tutors of Manchester Academy. Other ministers included Thomas Astley, John Simpson, Philip Taylor, James Pilkington, William Turner, William Hawkes and John Coates. The academy may have been short-lived and may only have educated a comparatively small number of Dissenters, but its influence was to be felt in later academies. The two main academies supported by liberal Dissent in the late eighteenth century, New College Hackney, and Manchester New College, built directly on the traditions of Warrington.

The academy at Daventry was the main rival to Warrington. The latter has acquired the higher reputation amongst historians, largely because of the excellence of the lay education it provided, but Daventry was the more important for liberal Dissenters, despite the closer management of the academy by the Coward trustees after 1752. Between 1752 and 1788 a total of 254 students attended Daventry, of whom 151 were divinity students, three times the number educated at Warrington. The contrast is even more striking when the ministers themselves are examined. Out of ninety-four Presbyterian ministers who belonged to the Provincial Assembly of Lancashire and Cheshire in the second half of the eighteenth century, nearly two-fifths (thirty-six) had attended Daventry, against under a fifth (seventeen) educated at Warrington. The academy at Warrington, of course, lay within the area covered by the Assembly. A further nine had attended Horsey's academy at Northampton, the successor to Daventry. Manchester Academy was only established in 1786, but by 1799 it had already educated fourteen ministers belonging to the Provincial Assembly. In the West Midlands,

---

[112] John Rylands University Library, Unitarian College Collection, 'Papers &c relating to the Warrington Academy from its Institution', p. 94, John Yates, Everton, to Samuel Heywood, 27 November 1784.

twenty-nine out of fifty-six ministers (over half) who served Presbyterian (later Unitarian) congregations there, had attended Daventry, together with three more at Horsey's academy and another three at New College Hackney. Only five had been educated at Warrington and none at Manchester.[113]

Daventry may not have matched Warrington in the teaching of languages and the sciences, but in theology, metaphysics and ethics it was superior. Admittedly, under Ashworth the teaching appears to have been thorough rather than inspired. He was not a great scholar, but by virtue of much effort he was said to have 'acquired a store of theological learning not often exceeded'. In divinity both he and his successor, Robins, relied on Doddridge's lectures. The method of instruction they used tended to discourage individual enquiry, which, when combined with the way that Doddridge's lectures were structured, served 'to bring orthodox sentiments into fuller view than any other tenets'. Nevertheless, none of the tutors sought to dictate on matters of individual conscience. Belsham proved to be much more innovative than either of his predecessors. In the final two or three years of his tutorship at Daventry, he introduced 'an elaborate and a far more impartial plan of lecturing' on controversial subjects, which proved to be a great improvement over the previous text-book type of lecturing. His lectures on materialistic and necessarian philosophy, based on his study of the philosophy of David Hartley, were the first in a Dissenting academy. Belsham, following his resignation from Daventry, was appointed theological tutor at Hackney, where he influenced a generation of Unitarian ministers.[114] By the end of the eighteenth century the majority of academies, in order to secure their continued orthodoxy, enforced religious tests and subscriptions and had as a consequence taken on the distinctive appearance of denominational seminaries intent upon providing a sectarian education.

The contribution made by the nonconformist academy was not to educational advancement or to the evolution of society, but to the development of religious Dissent. Its main role was in maintaining the tradition of an educated ministry amongst Dissenters. The first

---

[113] These figures are based on a detailed analysis of the ministers recorded in George Eyre Evans, *Record of the Provincial Assembly of Lancashire and Cheshire*, vol. II (Manchester, 1896); *idem, Midland Churches: A History of the Congregations on the Roll of the Midland Christian Union* (Dudley, 1899).

[114] *DNB, s.v.* Caleb Ashworth; 'Review of Robert Hall's *Memoir of the Rev. T. Toller*', *Monthly Repository*, 19 (1824), 230, 232 (the reviewer, 'N', apparently a student under Belsham, cannot be identified from the evidence available); T. Coleman, *Memorials of the Independent Churches in Northamptonshire . . .* (London, 1853), p. 197; McLachlan, *English Education* (fn. 3), pp. 153, 162–3, 156; Williams, *Memoirs of … Thomas Belsham* (fn. 97), p. 328.

generation of tutors played a vital part in keeping this principle alive before 1689. The opportunities for ministerial training, and in many cases the standard of education available, were, however, limited during the period because of the difficulties tutors and their students faced under the penal laws. In the decades following toleration, with the settling of the earlier informal meetings into permanent congregations, Dissent underwent a remarkable transformation. It is clear that as part of this transformation an increasing proportion of ministers had received their education at an academy; among the Presbyterians there were only a very few exceptions to this by the end of the eighteenth century. Caution is needed in assessing the standard of education provided by the nonconformist academy, particularly in comparison with the English universities. Whilst the best academies were excellent, wide variations always existed, and most of the claims to excellence involve the later institutional academies, notably Warrington. The early tutors, in particular, had only limited resources and their work suffered accordingly. Although recent studies of Oxford and Cambridge have done much to rehabilitate their reputation for the century after the Restoration, the impression still remains that in terms of both scholarship and teaching they stagnated during the eighteenth century. It is also difficult to escape the conclusion that whilst the standard of education provided in secular subjects at Warrington Academy was outstanding, its work took place in isolation from the main educational developments of the period. In addition, the contribution made by Warrington to Dissent was more limited than past studies have admitted, not least because of the small number of ministerial students educated there, many of whom indeed did not enter the Dissenting ministry. Admittedly, the ministers who were educated at Warrington included some of the leading figures of the second half of the eighteenth century. Nevertheless, the academy at Daventry made a more important contribution to the development of Dissent than Warrington; it not only trained three times the number of theological students, the majority of whom went into the Dissenting ministry, but the education it provided in theology, metaphysics and ethics was superior.

It is also necessary to qualify the claims for the contribution made to the emergence of Rational Dissent by the nonconformist academy. Rational Dissent developed after 1689, and its origins are to be found in the general intellectual advances of the period, advances which must be sought outside the academies themselves. In their acceptance of the importance of reason, Rational Dissenters were to be greatly influenced by Baxter and Locke. The efforts to moderate Calvinist orthodoxy were, however, perceived by many as an attack upon fundamental Christian truths. These differences over doctrine came to a head in the Salters' Hall debate of 1719. The first generation of tutors, though open to the new scholarship, were strictly orthodox in doctrine. Their successors were influenced by the growth in biblical criticism and the novel methods of rational scientific investigation which encouraged the questioning of existing interpretations. Once exposed to ideas that challenged the accepted orthodoxies it was inevitable that some individuals found it impossible to hold to the former doctrines. The new learning in philosophy and the sciences was adopted in most of the leading academies, but the most significant advance for the development of Rational Dissent was not the airing of heterodox opinions, nor that such opinions should have been encouraged, but the willingness of tutors to allow those they taught the right of private judgement. As a result tutors who were themselves orthodox came to be responsible, though unintentionally, for encouraging some of their students to depart from orthodoxy. Nonetheless, academies were not the only source of heterodox ideas or of intellectual study. By providing instruction in logic, philosophy, semitics and the classical languages, academies gave ministers the skills to investigate theological questions in depth. There is widespread evidence that many ministers continued their studies throughout their careers, and that they examined the main controversies for themselves. The clearer denominational identity adopted by the Congregational Fund Board, and the growing doctrinal divisions within Dissent which involved the introduction of religious subscriptions by many academies, forced Rational Dissenters to respond by setting up their own establishments. Because of the wealth and scholarship of Rational Dissenters, the handful of academies that they founded – Warrington, Exeter, New College Hackney and the Manchester Academy – proved to be the most brilliant of all. The action of the Rational Dissenters was, however, largely a defensive response to the pressure of orthodox Dissent. Although Warrington, Hackney and the other institutional academies, in providing an education free from religious subscription, performed a crucial role in sustaining a liberal religious tradition, they were not responsible for the emergence of Rational Dissent, which took place during the early eighteenth century. The evidence does support claims that academies encouraged the spread of heterodox ideas, though in a different and rather more limited way than has traditionally been argued.

CHAPTER 6

'A set of men powerful enough in many things': Rational Dissent and political opposition in England, 1770–1790

John Seed

It is difficult to avoid the question of Rational Dissent in late eighteenth-century English political history: J.H. Plumb claimed that Rational Dissenters 'dominated the first movement for radical reform'.[1] Whether the historian's focus is on national campaigns to reform the Church of England or to repeal discriminatory legislation against Dissenters or Roman Catholics, on concerted opposition to the war with the American colonists, on radical political pamphleteering of the period, on campaigns against slavery and the slave trade, on the various bodies campaigning for parliamentary reform, or on the victims of state repression in the early 1790s, many of the same names recur. Time and again, whether the focus is metropolitan or local, on the Rockinghamite Whigs or the circle around Shelburne, on the membership of the Society for Constitutional Information or the Revolution Society or the 'Honest Whigs' or the Yorkshire Association, there are multiple connections to the circles of Rational Dissent.

Contemporaries recognised this too, not least some of the representatives of the state Church who, in numerous sermons and tracts from the late 1770s, poured down vituperation on Rational Dissenters as a clique of conspirators undermining the established order. William Hunter, Oxford Fellow and vicar of St Paul's in Liverpool, fulminated in 1780 against 'the seditious demagogue and envious Presbyter . . . the hydra-headed monster, which now assumes every shape and explores various regions to rob us of our civil and religious rights'.[2] This is a single instance of an extensive propaganda war – which long antedated the

I would like to thank Knud Haakonssen, Wilf Prest and especially Martin Fitzpatrick for useful comments on an earlier and longer draft. This essay covers some of the same ground and exploits some of the same material as John Seed, 'Gentlemen Dissenters: The Social and Political Meanings of Rational Dissent in the 1770s and 1780s', *Historical Journal*, 28: 2 (1985).
[1] J.H. Plumb, *England in the Eighteenth Century*, Pelican History of England, 7 (Harmondsworth, 1950, repr. 1971), p. 133.   [2] Quoted in *Monthly Review*, 58 (1778), 324–5.

storming of the Bastille, Burke's *Reflections* and the demise of the French monarchy.

Burke had originally been sympathetic, however grudgingly, to the campaigns of Dissenters for increased toleration.[3] Even at the end of the 1780s he was urging Fox to gain permission for Priestley to dedicate one of his scientific books to the Prince of Wales:

I cannot conceive what objection the Prince can have to be considered as an encourager of science. Besides this consideration, Dr Priestley is a very considerable leader among a set of men powerful enough in many things, but most of all in elections; and I am quite sure that the good or ill humour of these men will be sensibly felt at the general election.[4]

Only a matter of months later, in his *Reflections on the Revolution in France*, Burke no longer acknowledged Priestley as the leader of a wider body of men 'powerful enough in many things'. Rather, one of his primary strategies was to portray Dissenting English reformers – Joseph Priestley and especially Richard Price were his central targets – as an unrepresentative coterie of intellectuals. He described Price as 'a man much connected with literary caballers and intriguing philosophers, with political theologians and theological politicians both at home and abroad'. They were, he said, 'petty cabals, who attempt to hide their total want of consequence in bustle and noise, and puffing, and mutual quotation of each other' and, in a famous extended metaphor, he compared them to a few noisy grasshoppers.[5]

Some recent historians have similarly portrayed Rational Dissent as a fairly small, unrepresentative and in many ways politically insignificant body. Roy Porter describes them as 'a hothead minority'.[6] John Brewer has argued that the group around Price and Priestley and 'the small, snug, dissenting coterie of Newington Green' were of marginal political significance.[7] Ian Christie proposes that there was little radical opposition among the middling and lower classes of the late eighteenth century in the earlier part of the reign of George III:

[3] See for instance 'Speech on the Second Reading of a Bill for the Relief of Protestant Dissenters, 17 March, 1773', in Edmund Burke, *Works* (with introductions by W. Willis, F.W. Raffety and F.H. Willis), World's Classics, 6 vols. (London, 1906–7), vol. III, pp. 304–16.

[4] Charles James Fox, *Memorials and Correspondence . . .*, ed. Lord John Russell, 4 vols. (London, 1853–7), vol. II, pp. 359–60.

[5] Edmund Burke, *Reflections on the Revolution in France, and on the Proceedings in Certain Societies Relative to that Event . . .* (1790), ed. with intro. by J.G.A. Pocock (Indianapolis, IN, 1987), pp. 10, 74–5.

[6] Roy Porter, *English Society in the Eighteenth Century* (London, 1982), p. 196.

[7] J. Brewer, 'English Radicalism in the Age of George III', in J.G.A. Pocock, ed., *Three British Revolutions: 1641, 1688, 1776* (Princeton, NJ, 1980), pp. 342–3.

The alarmists were members of a fairly restricted circle of young lawyers and intellectuals, some of them also caught up in the development of Unitarianism at this time. Their influence was strictly limited.[8]

Jonathan Clark, though devoting considerable attention to religious heterodoxy in this period, finally calls them 'this small radical intelligentsia'.[9]

This essay questions the proposition that such ministers of Rational Dissent as Price, Priestley, Kippis, Towers and so on, were no more than a noisy metropolitan clique of intellectuals of little influence on, or connection to, the wider political culture. They, and other ministers of Rational Dissent, were intellectual representatives of a wider body of men, especially in major commercial centres, which was capable of exerting considerable influence on the political process in the 1770s and 1780s.

I

Perhaps the most striking fact about Rational Dissent at the end of the eighteenth century is that it was merely the vestige of a once major religious organisation, the English Presbyterians. By the 1790s it was a body in massive and irreversible decline.[10] The situation in eighteenth-century London was particularly acute and here there are some grounds for seeing the circles of Rational Dissent as merely an isolated coterie of intellectuals. Richard Price, for instance, may have been an eminent

---

[8] Ian R. Christie, *Stress and Stability in Late Eighteenth-Century Britain: Reflections on the British Avoidance of Revolution* (Oxford, 1984), p. 46.

[9] J.C.D. Clark, *English Society 1688–1832: Ideology, Social Structure and Political Practice During the Ancien Regime* (Cambridge, 1985), p. 345.

[10] I should note that Martin Fitzpatrick, in private correspondence, dissents from these comments on the irreversible decline of Rational Dissent. The process of theological change and its difficult relationship to numerical decline in this period is discussed further in John Seed, 'Theologies of Power: Unitarianism and the Social Relations of Religious Discourse, 1800–50', in R.J. Morris, ed., *Class, Power and Social Structure in British Nineteenth-Century Towns* (Leicester, 1986), pp. 113–21.

In lieu of further debate on this question, the comments of one minister of Rational Dissent in Leeds in 1811 are worth considering: 'When I came hither, six and thirty years ago, there were four or five and twenty congregations within no very extended miles around this town, loosely united together under the name of Presbyterianism, with ministers attached to them of almost every diversity of common opinion, except High Calvinism. Their sole bond was the right and duty of private judgement.' In the intervening years, he went on, more than half of these congregations had gone to the Independents, three or four had collapsed, a couple were more or less Arian and the rest had become Unitarian: 'While pure Unitarianism is dispensed at York, Halifax, Bradford and Selby to little more than walls and pews; at Leeds and Wakefield it is preached to declining numbers and in short the cause . . . is rapidly sinking into nothing' (Joseph Bowden to Thomas Belsham, 6 December 1811, Dr Williams's Library MSS 24.107 (16a and b)).

intellectual figure of the period but only a handful of people gathered at his Newington Green Chapel on a Sunday. Theophilus Lindsey was surprised in 1774 at 'the comparative smallness that attend on the preaching of so excellent and eminent a person as Dr. Price', and a London Unitarian minister of a later generation said that Price had often preached his 'immortal discourses' to a congregation of ten or so.[11] Even in the heartlands of Old Dissent – the South-West, the Midlands and the North of England – Rational Dissent was sustained by small and declining numbers in the closing years of the eighteenth century.

Yet power and influence were never a matter merely of numbers. The considerable electoral influence of eighteenth-century Dissenters has begun to be thoroughly documented in recent years, notably in the work of Bradley, Philips and O'Gorman.[12] There is little point in reiterating this material at any length here but a few points are worth making. First, we have to make distinctions about the relative power of different sectors of eighteenth-century Dissent. Many constituencies included Independents and Baptists who met the diverse qualifications to possess the vote in parliamentary elections. But it was the smallest sector of old Dissent – the former Presbyterians, now the Rational Dissenters – that provided the essential political strength of Dissent (and continued to do so until the mid-nineteenth century). Though in steady numerical decline, they monopolised the parliamentary representation of Dissent.

John Brooke identified nineteen Members of Parliament in the period 1754–90 who were Dissenters.[13] Affiliation to religious Dissent is often difficult to pinpoint and his figures are certainly an underestimate – but probably not by very much. He omits several MPs who were members of Lindsey's Essex Street Chapel – though admittedly its status as primarily an ex-Anglican Unitarian congregation makes its position within Dissent ambiguous. There were other MPs who were definitely aligned with Rational Dissent, though direct membership of a specific congregation cannot be substantiated. Henry Beaufoy for instance, MP for Yarmouth, was by upbringing a Quaker and nominally a

[11] Theophilus Lindsey, *The Letters of Theophilus Lindsey* (Extracts, with a commentary) by H. McLachlan (Manchester, 1920), p. 31; George Kenrick, *Divine and Human Aids in the Christian Ministry . . . A Farewell Discourse* (London, 1845), Appendix, p. 12.

[12] See James E. Bradley, *Religion, Revolution and English Radicalism: Nonconformity in Eighteenth-Century Politics and Society* (Cambridge, 1990); Frank O'Gorman, *Voters, Patrons and Parties: The Unreformed Electoral System of Hanoverian England, 1734–1832* (Oxford, 1989); John A. Philips, *Electoral Behavior in Unreformed England: Plumpers, Splitters, and Straights* (Princeton, NJ, 1982).

[13] Sir Lewis Namier and John Brooke, *The History of Parliament. The House of Commons 1754–1790*, 3 vols. (London, 1964), vol. I, Introductory Survey (by J. Brooke), p. 115.

Churchman. Yet he was educated at Warrington Academy and moved within the circles of Rational Dissent in London, for example serving on the committee of Hackney Academy. He also put forward the first two motions in the Commons for the repeal of the Test and Corporation Acts.[14] All these MPs were affiliated, or in one or two cases linked, to Rational Dissent.

The electoral strength of Dissent in the later eighteenth century had implications at the level of *national government*. In many constituencies they were a considerable presence and could materially influence the outcome of a general election. This is indicated by the panic with which North and his cabinet greeted the bill, initiated by Rational Dissenters, to relieve Dissenting ministers of particular restrictions in 1772. 'The ministers,' Horace Walpole commented, 'afraid of disobliging the dissenters before the general election, suffered the bill to pass the House of Commons.'[15] The Duke of Richmond had urged the Marquis of Rockingham to support this bill: 'your giving it a warm support will greatly recommend you to that weighty body of men the Dissenters, who all over England are very powerful and who stick pretty much together.'[16] In 1787, when repeal of the Test and Corporation Acts was first raised, a Somerset MP noted that 'many Members . . . will not dare to oppose it'. More than one hundred MPs voted consistently for repeal over the next few years and even a 1792 petition to relieve Unitarians specifically from legal restrictions received substantial parliamentary support.[17]

Theophilus Lindsey's London chapel was a particularly important focus of Rational Dissent's political influence. His Essex Street congregation included among its trustees two important Yorkshire MPs, both on the reforming wing of the Rockinghamite Whigs: Sir George Saville and John Lee.[18] Among the subscribers in the 1780s were a former

[14] *Ibid*, vol. II, pp. 72–3.

[15] Quoted in Edward Porritt, *The Unreformed House of Commons: Parliamentary Representation before 1832*, facsim. repr. of Cambridge, 1903 edn, 2 vols. (New York, 1963), vol. I, p. 277.

[16] Quoted in George T. Keppel, 6th Earl of Albemarle, *Memoirs of the Marquis of Rockingham and his Contemporaries . . .*, 2 vols. (London, 1852), vol. II, p. 224.

[17] Quoted in Brooke, Introductory Survey, in Namier and Brooke, *History of Parliament* (fn. 13) vol. I, p. 114. Aspects of Dissenting parliamentary influence are examined in three articles by G.M. Ditchfield: 'The Parliamentary Struggle on the Repeal of the Test and Corporation Acts, 1787–90', *English Historical Review*, 89 (1974), 551–77; 'Anti-Trinitarianism and Toleration in Late Eighteenth Century British Politics: The Unitarian Petition of 1792', *Journal of Ecclesiastical History*, 42(1) (1991), 39–67; 'Public and Parliamentary Support for the Unitarian Petition of 1792', *Enlightenment and Dissent*, forthcoming. I am grateful to Dr Ditchfield for sending me a copy of this last prior to publication.

[18] 'A Lawyer', 'The Deeds of Essex Street Chapel', *Transactions of the Unitarian Historical Society*, 1(3) (1918), 261–2.

Prime Minister, the Duke of Grafton, the Earl of Surrey and a number of MPs, including William Wilberforce (for a while), James Adair, Thomas Whitmore, James Martin, Joshua Grigby and John Sargent.[19] Both Charles James Fox and Shelburne had promised £100 on the chapel's foundation.[20] Though the latter's contribution failed to materialise, Shelburne's brilliant coterie at Bowood in the 1770s and 1780s always included a number of Rational Dissenting ministers. Richard Price was a long-term adviser and even a friend; Shelburne signed his letters to him 'yours affectionately', apparently a very unusual expression on his part. Joseph Priestley was his librarian from 1773 to 1780 but also accompanied him on journeys and had at least some involvement in political affairs.[21] Thomas Jervis, later minister at Priestley's old Leeds chapel, was tutor to Shelburne's son from 1772 to 1783.[22]

Men such as Price, Priestley and Lindsey had entrée to the inner circles of the Whig élite around both Rockingham/Fox and Shelburne. Lindsey's correspondence makes it clear that he was sometimes privy to sensitive political information – about secret treaty negotiations with the Americans in 1779, about military strategies and failures during the American War, about divisions and alliances within political parties – which he disseminated to other Rational Dissenters.[23] He was even a source of political information for a politician as powerful as Shelburne. Priestley wrote to the latter in 1776: 'Mr Lindsey, whose intelligence is generally pretty accurate, says he is informed from the very best authority, that there is an irreconcilable difference between Lord Gower and Mr Rigby.'[24]

The political influence of Rational Dissent involved more than a degree of influence at election time, a scattering of Members of Parliament and the occasional minister who had the ear of Whig grandees. In a number of towns congregations of Rational Dissenters

---

[19] Lindsey mentions the MPs in his congregation in a number of letters, for instance those to William Tayleur, 13 January 1780, and to William Rowe, 13 February 1791, both in Unitarian College MSS, John Rylands Library, University of Manchester. The membership of Essex Street Chapel is thoroughly examined in G.M. Ditchfield, 'Some Aspects of Unitarianism and Radicalism, 1760–1810' (University of Cambridge Ph.D. thesis, 1968).

[20] Lindsey, *Letters*, (fn. 11) p. 29.

[21] The complex relations between Priestley and Shelburne are discussed in John Seed, 'The Role of Unitarianism in the Formation of Liberal Culture, 1775–1851: A Social History' (University of Hull Ph.D. thesis, 1981), pp. 140–3.

[22] See W.L. Schroeder, *Mill Hill Chapel, Leeds, 1674–1924: Sketch of its History* . . . (Leeds, 1924), pp. 52–4.

[23] See Lindsey, *Letters*, (fn. 11) pp. 84–5; and Lindsey to William Turner, 30 January 1777, Turner MSS, Newcastle Literary and Philosophical Society.

[24] Quoted in Anne Durning Holt, *A Life of Joseph Priestley* . . . (London, 1931), pp. 75–6.

had considerable local power. Though in most cases town corporations, where they existed, were controlled by a close-knit oligarchy of Churchmen, there were instances where Rational Dissenters were capable of taking control. In the two major cities outside London –Bristol and Norwich – Rational Dissenters wielded a measure of local power for extensive spells during the eighteenth century.[25] In some towns they even became the dominant faction. This was the case at Bridgwater, Bridport, Portsmouth and Nottingham. At Bridgwater, for instance, the members of the old Presbyterian meeting-house 'gradually became highly respectable for fortune and numbers and at length included the whole of the civic magistracy' so that in 1788 a special pew for the mayor and the whole corporation was constructed.[26] At Portsmouth, too, the mayor and corporation generally belonged to the old High Street Chapel. The mayoral mace was ostentatiously placed in a socket in front of the gallery and members of the congregation attended public worship in their corporation regalia.[27]

Such local Dissenting élites could cock a snook at government authority. The ruling Rational Dissenters of Nottingham's High Pavement Chapel were disaffected over the war with the Americans and in July 1776 the corporation presented the freedom of the town to the radical pro-American Major John Cartwright. An Admiralty agent complained in the following year:

This town is without any exception the most disloyal in the kingdom, owing in a great measure to the whole corporation (the present mayor excepted) being Dissenters, and of so bitter a sort that they have done and continue to do all in their power to hinder the service by preventing as much as possible the enlistment of soldiers.[28]

At Portsmouth, too, Rational Dissenters used their local power to challenge government policy. Another Admiralty agent warned against the attempt to canvass support for a government address in the town: 'We should meet with great opposition, if not a defeat. We are beset with Presbyterians and Dissenters of every kind.'[29] In 1783 the Dissenting

[25] See Nicholas Rogers, *Whigs and Cities: Popular Politics in the Age of Walpole and Pitt* (Oxford, 1989), pp. 269, 272–4, 308.

[26] C.E. Pike, *Our Ancient Meeting House: Some Account of the Fabric of Christ Church, . . . Bridgwater* (n.p., n.d.), p. 4; Sir Jerom Murch, *A History of the Presbyterian and General Baptist Churches in the West of England . . .* (London, 1835), pp. 178ff.

[27] Namier and Brooke, *History of Parliament* (fn. 11), vol. I, pp. 297–9; N.W. Surry and J.H. Thomas, eds., *Portsmouth Record Series: Book of Original Entries* (Portsmouth, 1976), Appendix; Victor Bonham-Carter, *In a Liberal Tradition: A Social Biography, 1700–1950* (London, 1960), pp. 17–19.

[28] Quoted in Namier and Brooke, *History of Parliament* (fn. 13), vol. I, p. 355.

[29] Introductory Survey, in *ibid.*, vol. I, p. 15.

corporation unanimously voted in favour of shorter parliaments and 'a more Equal representation of the People'.[30] The leading Rational Dissenting family in the town, the Carters, also controlled Portsmouth's parliamentary representation: 'this borough is now in the family of the Carters', John Robinson noted in 1783.[31] Their influence persisted. Thomas Erskine, the town's Foxite MP and former defence counsel for Paine, Thelwall, Horne Tooke and other radicals in the early 1790s, explained his hesitant negotiations with the new Addington administration in 1801 as a consequence of pressure from his patron: 'I have had a letter from Sir John Carter on whom my whole dependence is at Portsmouth in favor of the system prevailing so that independently of my own opinion I should feel more disposed to support the present government than to oppose it.'[32] Fox told Holland three years later that one of Bridport's MPs 'maintained his parliamentary interest . . . by professing to be a DISSENTER'.[33]

Even where congregations of Rational Dissenters had not captured the corporation or parliamentary representation they were often capable of wielding considerable local power. In many larger urban centres, especially in northern and midland England, the chapels affiliated to Rational Dissent were centres of considerable wealth and influence. 'The dissenters are some of the most wealthy merchants and manufacturers here', an American visitor to Manchester commented in 1777.[34] Cross Street Chapel, the oldest, largest and most important Dissenting congregation in the town, numbered among its supporters in the 1770s and 1780s leading physicians such as Thomas Percival and John Ferriar; the Jones family and the Heywoods, owners of the town's two banks; a number of prosperous merchant families with substantial mansions, such as Robert Hibbert at Stocksfield House, Josiah Birch at Failsworth Lodge, James Touchet at Broome House in Pendleton, John Jackson at Clowes Court.[35] The Touchet family were a particularly

[30] Christopher Wyvill, *Political Papers Chiefly Respecting the Attempt . . . to Effect a Reformation of the Parliament of Great Britain*, 6 vols. (York, 1794–1802), vol. IV, pp. 255–6.

[31] W.T. Laprade, ed., 'Parliamentary Papers of John Robinson, 1774–1784', *Transactions of the Royal Historical Society*, 3rd ser., 33 (1922), 88.

[32] Thomas Erskine to Charles Grey, December 1801, Papers of the Second Earl Grey, Durham University Library.

[33] Fox, *Memorials and Correspondence* (fn. 4), vol. IV, p. 57. See also Basil Short, *A Respectable Society: Bridport 1593–1835* (Bradford-on-Avon, 1976).

[34] Samuel Curwen, *The Journal of Samuel Curwen, Loyalist*, ed. Andrew Oliver, 2 vols. (Cambridge, MA, 1972), vol. I, p. 366: Saturday, 7 June 1777.

[35] Sir Thomas Baker, *Memorials of a Dissenting Chapel . . . Being a Sketch of the Rise of Nonconformity in Manchester . . .* (London, 1884).

important Dissenting merchant dynasty. Thomas Touchet had set up in Manchester with little capital. By the time of his death in 1745 he was described as 'the most considerable Merchant and Manufacturer in Manchester' and left his four sons the sum of £20,000, one of them becoming a City of London magnate and a Whig MP in the 1760s.[36]

Manchester was riven by animosities throughout the eighteenth century. Cross Street Chapel was destroyed by Jacobite crowds in 1715 and 1745 and was attacked by a Church and King crowd in 1792. Nevertheless its members exerted considerable influence in the town in the 1770s and 1780s. They served as town constable, were represented on the Court Leet Jury, on the Committee for the Protection and Encouragement of Trade, on the committee of the Society for the Detection and Prosecution of Felons and on Improvement Commissions; they were among the officers of the Manchester Military Association set up in 1782; they were members of the exclusive Billiards Club and the Assembly Rooms; they dominated the prestigious Literary and Philosophical Society. Cross Street Chapel even included two landed gentlemen, Henry Norris and Thomas Butterworth Bayley, who were also magistrates. Bayley was particularly influential: a Deputy Lieutenant of Lancashire and an ardent supporter of Wilkes, Collector of the King's revenue under the Chancellor of the Duchy of Lancashire and an important prison reformer.[37]

Cross Street Chapel in Manchester was not unique in the wealth or status of its leading families in the late eighteenth century. In other major commercial towns in late eighteenth-century England – Liverpool, Bristol, Norwich, Nottingham, Leicester, Birmingham, Hull, Newcastle-upon-Tyne – the upper echelons of Rational Dissent exhibited the same profile. Their chapels were dominated by families of substantial merchants and manufacturers, some of them on the edge of county society and occasionally serving on the magistrate's bench, plus a scattering of professional men, especially physicians. Of course, this *haute bourgeoisie* was only the ruling élite in congregations where all kinds of tradesmen, shopkeepers, small-scale manufacturers and lesser professionals made up the majority. However, it was this élite that was decisive in shaping the culture of Rational Dissent. It was their pew rents and donations that

---

[36] For the Touchets see E. Axon, 'Harrison Ainsworth's Maternal Ancestors', *Transactions of the Lancashire and Cheshire Antiquarian Society*, 21 (1911), 111–13; Alfred P. Wadsworth and J. de Lacy Mann, *The Cotton Trade and Industrial Lancashire, 1600–1780* (Manchester, 1931), pp. 244–7.

[37] For Bayley see [Thomas Percival], *Biographical memoirs of the late Thomas Butterworth Bayley . . .* (Manchester, 1802); E. Axon, 'The Bayley Family of Manchester and Hope', *Transactions of the Lancashire and Cheshire Antiquarian Society*, 7 (1889), 194–9; Margaret DeLacy, *Prison Reform in Lancashire, 1700–1850: A Study in Local Administration* (Stanford, CA, 1986) esp. pp. 70–3.

maintained the chapel and paid the minister's stipend. They generally constituted a self-selecting oligarchy of trustees, appointing the minister and, with their families, sitting in judgement on his preaching.[38]

II

Focusing on the social and economic status and the political role of Rational Dissenters in West Yorkshire illuminates their capacity to penetrate into the circles of Whig power. There were two influential congregations in the textile districts of the West Riding in the late eighteenth century. At Wakefield, the congregation on Westgate was described by its minister in these years as composed 'for a considerable part, of persons of fortune and genteel life'.[39] Among its leading men were the town's principal physician, Dr James Richardson, and a number of important woollen merchants. The latter included Benjamin Heywood, a substantial merchant and the town's Chief Constable in 1785, the Lumbs, the Holdsworths and the Burrells, and the Naylors, who were, by the end of the century, buying around 12 per cent of the total cloth production of West Yorkshire.[40]

Towering above them all were the different branches of the Milnes family. Their capital dominated the woollen industry in the region as their four substantial houses dominated the town's main thoroughfare, Westgate.[41] Their ostentatious carriages and fine horses were a feature of the district. A tax return of 1780 indicates that these four households had sixteen men servants, one-third of the total for the whole town. John Milnes's mansion was particularly imposing, with massive gardens, a suite of ballrooms with ceilings decorated by Italian artists and a valuable collection of paintings, notably by Joseph Wright.[42] According to

[38] The issue of institutional power within congregations is investigated in Seed, 'Theologies of Power' (fn. 10), esp. pp. 142–6.

[39] William Turner, quoted in *Memoirs and Correspondence of Joseph Priestley*, in J. Priestley, *The Theological and Miscellaneous Works of Joseph Priestley* ed. John Towill Rutt (hereafter *Works*), 25 vols. in 26 (London, 1817–31), vol. I, pt. II, p. 85n.

[40] See Minute Book of Westgate Chapel, Wakefield, Archives Department, Wakefield Central Library.

[41] James Pope-Hennessy, *Monckton Milnes: The Years of Promise 1809–51* (London, 1949) provides a useful outline of the family's history. See also R.G. Wilson, 'The Denisons and Milneses: Eighteenth-Century Merchant Landowners', in J.T. Ward and R.G. Wilson, eds., *Land and Industry: The Landed Estate and the Industrial Revolution* . . . (Newton Abbot, 1971), pp. 145–72 at pp. 162–5.

[42] Henry Clarkson, *Memories of Merry Wakefield: An Octogenarian's Recollections* . . . (Wakefield, 1887), pp. 83–5; John W. Walker, *Wakefield: Its History and People*, 3rd edn, 2 vols. (Wakefield, 1966), vol. II, p. 466.

the travelling actor, Tate Wilkinson, in 1795: 'The spirited John Milnes, Esq. has one of the most elegant furnished houses of any private gentleman in the kingdom.'[43]

A few miles further north, in Leeds, the sister congregations at Call Lane and Mill Hill gathered congregations of substantial merchants and manufacturers in the late eighteenth century. Of the one million pounds's worth of the region's woollen cloth that passed through the hands of Leeds merchants in 1781, at least one quarter was handled by such leading firms as the Bischoffs, Thomas Lee and Jeremiah Dixon, the Oates family, Wolrich and Stanfield – all, with their families, affiliated to Rational Dissent.[44] Here, as elsewhere, these merchants were beginning to penetrate county society. Several owned or rented substantial mansions standing in acres of land outside Leeds: Thomas Wolrich at Armley House, Joseph Oates at Weetwood Hall, George William Oates at Low Hall and Carr House, Richard Lee on Woodhouse Lane, and so on. Others, such as Hans Busk and James Fenton, married into landed families; the former even maintained a private Unitarian chaplain, Thomas Halliday, on his Yorkshire estate at Bull House, Penistone.[45]

To the south of the woollen district, Sheffield's Upper Chapel was the oldest and largest in the district throughout the eighteenth century. It lacked the solid phalanx of 'gentlemen merchants' to be found among the Dissenters in the woollen districts of the West Riding and its trustees in 1781 included a butcher, a shoemaker and several linendrapers. However, its trustees and membership in these years included several cutlers, a substantial brewer, a number of doctors and surgeons and an attorney.[46] Dominant in the congregation, in terms of wealth and local influence, was the Shore family, whose rise had been as meteoric as any Manchester or West Riding textile merchant. The first Samuel Shore (1676–1751) had accrued considerable capital, first as an ironmonger, then as owner of an iron works, diversifying into some shrewd land purchases and canal shares. His son's marriage to a Liverpool heiress

---

[43] T. Wilkinson, *The Wandering Patentee; or, A History of the Yorkshire Theatres, from 1770 to the Present Time...*, facsim. repr. of York, 1795 edn, 4 vols. in 2 (London, 1973), vol. I, p. 200.

[44] See *Minute Book 1771–1858*, in vestry of Mill Hill Chapel, Leeds; a list of trustees of Call Lane Chapel can be found in *Papers of William Lupton and Co.*, VII/131, Special Collections, Brotherton Library, University of Leeds. See also Richard G. Wilson, *Gentlemen Merchants: The Merchant Community in Leeds, 1700–1830* (Manchester, 1971), pp. 239–40.

[45] See Wilson, *Gentlemen Merchants*, pp. 69, 150, 243–5.

[46] See J.E. Manning, *A History of Upper Chapel, Sheffield* (Sheffield, 1900), p. 189, for list of trustees. For wider membership see Upper Chapel Baptismal Registers in Sheffield Central Library, HC29.

increased the family's capital and his son, in turn, the third Samuel Shore (1738–1828), married into minor Derbyshire gentry, inheriting an estate of several hundred acres at Norton. At the same time the family – notably Samuel, John and William, all three trustees of Upper Chapel in 1781 – maintained its Sheffield interests, playing a key role in initiating the town's major bank.[47]

The wealth and leisure of these Dissenters in Northern England enabled some of them to frequent fashionable resorts such as Scarborough, Matlock and Buxton. Services were held annually at the least throughout 'the season', such were their numbers regularly taking the waters, though none were resident in the town.[48] In 1787 Thomas Christie was astonished by the circle of worldly Dissenters gathered at the Wakefield house of William Turner, friend of Benjamin Franklin, Price and Priestley and minister of the Westgate Chapel. Turner, he noted, was 'a man profoundly skilled in the law, and in the Hebrew Language and in the History of the Antient people of God'. But this young and earnest Unitarian, a few years later an intimate of Paine and Mary Wollstonecraft and, by 1792, a Citizen of the French Republic, was disappointed:

I found him encompassed with gay young friends who had come there from different parts on a visit and amongst whom the old man was to me quite lost, for instead of philosophy and theology we talked of I can scarce tell thee what and we spake of Matlock and Buxton and of what dashing youths were there and of the lords and dukes and of their equipages and of their horses and of their lacqueys and of their dogs.[49]

Dr Johnson once remarked, 'An English Merchant is a new species of Gentleman'.[50] These northern Dissenters were also a new species of gentleman, taking the waters at Buxton and Matlock, campaigning for parliamentary reform and repeal of the Test and Corporation Acts, riding to hounds, sitting at the feet of men such as Joseph Priestley and Richard Price.

Some of these West Yorkshire Rational Dissenters had accumulated considerable political capital by the 1770s. At Wakefield, Richard Milnes

[47] See Lady Stephen, 'The Shores of Sheffield and the Offleys of Norton Hall', *Transactions of the Hunter Archaeological Society*, 5 (1943) and footnote 58 below.

[48] E. Axon, 'Buxton Chapel', *Transactions of the Unitarian Historical Society*, 3 (4) (1926).

[49] Quoted in J. Nichols, *Literary Anecdotes of the Eighteenth Century . . .*, 9 vols. (London, 1812–15), vol. IX, p. 379.

[50] James Boswell, *Life of Johnson*, ed. R.W. Chapman, 3rd edn corr. J.D. Fleeman (Oxford, 1970, repr. 1980), p. 348.

had been a loyal supporter and adviser of the first Marquis of Rockingham. In 1745 he led the organisation of a county subscription to fund military resistance to the Jacobite invasion and was responsible for distributing the money to loyal Hanoverians in the area.[51] The next generation of the Milnes family became influential political figures in county politics and supporters of the second Marquis of Rockingham. Pemberton Milnes, son of Richard, was a frequent correspondent of Rockingham and his successor, Earl Fitzwilliam. As the head of a major woollen firm, a Dissenting leader and owner of land in several counties, he used his influence to mobilise electoral support for the Whigs. 'My Nottinghamshire Interest and Vote', he asked Fitzwilliam to assure the Duke of Portland, 'are at his command whenever they are wanted.'[52] In return Pemberton Milnes was privy to the tactical manoeuvres of the leadership nationally.[53] He was appointed a county magistrate, even advising on who in his area should be excluded from the bench, and managed to combine being the recognised leader of Yorkshire Dissent, a merchant, banker and landowner, and reputedly the largest consumer of port in the county.[54]

Another woollen merchant and a trustee of Mill Hill Chapel in Leeds, Thomas Lee, was rewarded with the profitable post of receiver of the East Riding land taxes for his loyal political services to Rockingham.[55] His younger brother, John, a barrister, was an especially strategic individual for the political network between Rational Dissent in Yorkshire and London and its penetration into the circles of the Whig magnates. Called to the bar, he followed the Northern circuit for several years, became Attorney-General of the County Palatine of Lancashire and Recorder of Doncaster. He made his

[51] Richard Milnes to Rockingham, 15 January 1745, and Rockingham to Milnes, 13 October 1746: Crewe MSS Ms/362 and 409–10, Archives Dept., Sheffield Central Library.

[52] Pemberton Milnes to Fitzwilliam, 24 February 1784, Wentworth Woodhouse MSS F34/43, Archives Department, Sheffield Central Library. This collection is subsequently abbreviated to SCL: WW MSS.

[53] In February 1780 Rockingham wrote to him expressing his anxieties about the current political situation in terms that were quite clearly not those of master and servant: 'I could say much more to you if I had the opportunity of seeing you, I may perhaps have already wrote more to you or stated opinions to you, which your mind might not concur in. I write nevertheless with the fullest confidence that if your Sentiments differ with mine, you as an old and esteemed friend wil point out to me wherein you differ from me, or wherein you doubt.' (Rockingham to Pemberton Milnes 28 February 1780, SCL: WW MSS RI–1881).

[54] P. Milnes to Fitzwilliam, 17 February 1784, WW MSS F34/38. See also: Andrew Chalmer's Manuscript History of the Chapel, Westgate Chapel MSS., SCL; Clarkson, Merry Wakefield (fn. 42), p. 45; J. Hewitt, The History and Topography of the Parish of Wakefield (Wakefield, 1862), p. 158.

[55] Wilson, Gentlemen Merchants (fn. 40), pp. 150, 245.

name in April 1769 as counsel for the petitioners against Colonel Luttrell, Wilkes's opponent in the Middlesex elections, and was provided with a seat in Parliament by Rockingham. Wraxall was willing to acknowledge 'the sincerity and independence of his natural character' and called him 'a man of upright principles'. But he was appalled by 'that coarse, strong and illiberal species of invective which usually accompanied his addresses to the House, and which always appeared to me more befitting the Robin Hood Society than accommodated to a legislative assembly'.[56] Dr Johnson told Boswell that the best way of speaking at the Bar of the Commons was not to be studied: 'Be as impudent as you can, as merry as you can, and say whatever comes uppermost. Jack Lee is the best heard there of any Counsel; and he is the most impudent dog, and always abusing us.'[57] As companion, speech-writer and general man of business, Lee's loyalty to Rockingham was unswerving and he was one of the trustees of his will. After his death in 1793 his bust was placed alongside Rockingham's statue at the Rockingham mausoleum at Wentworth Woodhouse, though he was politically inactive after his patron's death in 1783, partly through serious ill-health.[58]

Lee had been a member of Priestley's congregation as a young man in the 1760s but, subsequently based in London, he was a member of Lindsey's Essex Street Chapel from its foundation and was in constant contact with leading figures of Rational Dissent. He seems to have kept his distance from metropolitan radical bodies, but was certainly a useful patron and adviser for Rational Dissenters. For instance, he procured an invitation for Priestley to accompany Cook as ship's astronomer on his second voyage in 1771 and provided effective legal advice on the foundation of Lindsey's chapel when local magistrates were creating obstructions.[59] Lee was also an important mediator between Whig leaders and the circles of Rational Dissent in London and Yorkshire. He called himself 'a Vehicle of Communication' between Rockingham and his Yorkshire supporters.[60] Thus in 1779 Lee was urged to use his nephew in Leeds to mobilise political support: 'some of your excellent

[56] Sir Nathaniel Wraxall, *The Historical and Posthumous Memoirs, 1772–1784*, ed., with notes and additional chapters by H.B. Wheatley, 5 vols. (London, 1884),vol. II, p. 370, vol. III, pp. 99, 112.

[57] Boswell, *Life of Johnson* (fn. 50), p. 896.

[58] N.B. Penny, 'The Whig Cult of Fox in Early Nineteenth-Century Sculpture', *Past and Present*, 70 (1976), 96.

[59] Priestley, *Memoirs*, in *Works*, vol. I, pt. I, pp. 86, 157, 209, 216; Thomas Belsham, *Memoirs of the late Reverend Theophilus Lindsey...*, (London, 1812), pp. 109–10.

[60] John Lee to Rockingham, 18 September 1769, SCL: WW MSS R1–1229.

Hints convey'd to him might have a good effect in stirring up others at
that place to exert a proper spirit.'[61]

A number of other substantial West Riding merchants affiliated to
Rational Dissent played an important role in opposition politics, notably
through the Yorkshire Association after 1779. This organisation is often
seen as a body of Yorkshire gentry and clergy and certainly these were a
major element.[62] E.C. Black, at least, has noted that Wyvill made a place
in his movement for 'new propertied elements, particularly the new
industrialists'.[63] However, he mentions only Samuel Shore and describes
him as an exception. Black is right to note the importance of Samuel
Shore. In fact he was not a 'new industrialist' but was involved in
banking, property development in Sheffield and owned a small landed
estate and he was an important figure in the Yorkshire Association from
the beginning. He was one of the three Yorkshire deputies who attended
the General Meeting of County Associations in the City of London in
March 1781. In April 1782 he was a member of the committee which
drafted a report on the activities of the Association to be presented to a
general meeting of the county and he was a particularly trusted confi-
dant of Wyvill.[64] Shore had been High Sheriff of Derbyshire in 1761
and for several years a magistrate. He refused the offer of a parliamentary seat though he and his brother John remained politically
influential in the Sheffield area throughout this period.[65] But Shore
was by no means an exception. There was a significant number of
these West Riding Dissenting merchants actively involved in the
Yorkshire Association. Eight Wakefield Rational Dissenters, all woollen

[61] Rockingham to Lee, 19 December 1779 – this letter and one hundred others to and from John Lee
are in the William Clements Library, University of Michigan. Some of the contents are detailed
in *Appendix to Handlist of Correspondence of Charles, Second Marquis of Rockingham*, SCL: WW MSS.

[62] For Carl Cone, 'The political aims of the Yorkshire Association reflected the social philosophy of
country gentlemen, albeit country gentlemen who admitted that the electoral system was too narrowly based' (Carl Cone, *The English Jacobins: Reformers in Late 18th Century England* (New York,
1968), pp. 59–60). John Osborne talks about the Yorkshire Association as 'a group of sober
Yorkshire gentry and clergy' and then oddly goes on to describe them as 'beef-eating, port wine-
drinking squires and parsons' (John W. Osborne, *John Cartwright* (Cambridge, 1972), p. 24). Ian
Christie struggles to make any sense of its origins, lamely concluding that perhaps it had something to do with 'a peculiar provincial solidarity' and a degree of hostility to London, which is to
come full circle to the original question (Ian R. Christie, *Wilkes, Wyvill and Reform: The Parliamentary
Reform Movement in British Politics, 1760–1785* (London, 1962) p. 230).

[63] E.C. Black, *The Association: British Extraparliamentary Political Organization, 1769–1793* (Cambridge,
MA, 1963), pp. 61–2.

[64] See Wyvill's letter to Shore in June 1783 in Wyvill *Political Papers* (fn. 30), vol. IV, pp. 286–95.

[65] 'Obituary of Samuel Shore', *Gentleman's Magazine*, 98,(2) (1828), 639; Robert E. Leader, *Sheffield in
the Eighteenth Century*, 2nd edn (Sheffield, 1905) pp. 71–3, 113–15; Lady Stephen, 'The Shores of
Sheffield' (fn. 47), pp. 1–3, 6–7.

merchants, were subscribers to the Association.[66] Pemberton Milnes played a decisive role in getting the Association off the ground, as Wyvill acknowledged, and was extremely active. At Leeds a number of the woollen merchants of Mill Hill Chapel were also active in Association politics, chief among them the Oates family, Milnes Rayner, the Lees, Obadiah Dawson and Thomas Wolrich. They were so closely identified with the Yorkshire Association, in fact, that William Denison, Conservative, Churchman, member of Leeds Corporation and merchant of immense wealth, was profoundly suspicious. He supported some of the Association's principles but, he grumbled in 1780, 'the chief promoters of it in this County are the Oates who were Promoters and Supporters of the American rebellion and are consequently the cause of our present distress'.[67]

These Rational Dissenting merchants were not merely subordinate and deferential junior partners alongside the country gentlemen and clerics. Without their activities the Yorkshire Association would have had little impact in the textile districts of the West Riding. The Milnes family, especially, were crucial in getting signatures, since in a country almost entirely of clothiers, as John Milnes himself commented, 'none but Merchants have much interest', and as major buyers the different branches of the Milnes family had immense influence over the clothiers.[68] In April 1780 Milnes remarked on canvassing clothiers for a Yorkshire Association petition: 'As we purchase at least one half of the White cloths don't doubt getting them all to a man.'[69] Of the 10,000 signatures on a county-wide petition in 1783, for instance, around, 1,500 were procured by the Milnes circle alone in the clothing districts between Wakefield and Huddersfield.[70]

Rational Dissenters were also important agents of Rockingham's political influence in the textile districts of West Yorkshire and, after his death in 1782, of his successor Earl Fitzwilliam. When Fitzwilliam was involved in the cynical and short-lived Fox–North coalition of 1783 and then supported both the East India Bill and the receipt tax, that support was alienated. One of Fitzwilliam's aides found the Wakefield merchants furious with him and the receipt tax: 'they were all to a man very clear

---

[66] See list of subscribers in Wyvill, *Political Papers* (fn. 30), vol. II, pp. 322–4.
[67] Quoted in Wilson, *Gentlemen Merchants* (fn. 44), p. 168.
[68] John Milnes to Holmes, 13 July 1780, Yorkshire Association Papers, M25/291, York City Library, Archives Department. This collection is hereafter abbreviated to YAP/YCA.
[69] John Milnes to Holmes, April 1780, YAP/YCA: M25/271.
[70] Wyvill, *Political Papers* (fn. 44), vol. II, pp. 249–51.

that Ld. Rockingham had so great a respect for the trade of this country, that he would never have persisted in it.'[71] At a seven-hour meeting of around 4,000 freeholders of the County, the Foxites, led by Fitzwilliam and Lord John Cavendish, were severely defeated. One of the leading opposition speakers was Richard Slater Milnes, another member of the Westgate Chapel in Wakefield, who saw the Fox–North coalition as a betrayal of principle for mere power, everything that the Rockinghamite idea of party claimed to oppose:

I am very sorry to rise against many of those men, whose principles I have been accustomed to revere; but, Sir, we have, with regret, seen their pernicious tendency; the Coalition, the Coalition must not be forgotten, I hope it shall be remembered to immortality, and posterity have a lesson, that the most amiable men, in private life, could not resist temptation when public advantage was set in opposition to interest.[72]

The Yorkshire Association split and the bulk of the key Rational Dissenters – but not Pemberton Milnes – went into opposition to Fitzwilliam and the Foxites. They played a role in the debacle of the 1784 general election for the Foxites.[73] One of the successful candidates for the City of York, defeating Fitzwilliam's candidate, was the Wakefield Rational Dissenter Richard Slater Milnes. He told the electorate: 'I have this day the unspeakable Happiness of being at once the Instrument of your Emancipation from the Influence of an Aristocratical Faction, combined to annihilate your importance in the national scale.'[74]

The substantial political influence of Rational Dissenters in Yorkshire, one of the major arenas of national politics in the late 1770s and 1780s, is clear. Their role was never merely that of deferential supporters, subordinated to patronage. Their support for Rockingham and Fitzwilliam was contractual. It was to do with the trading of mutual support and mutual benefits. Fitzwilliam's failure to live up to that contract in 1783 was punished and he, like other Foxites, had to labour long and hard to redeem their support.

[71] One anonymous pamphlet represented the receipt tax as a tax laid on trade by the landed interest: *A Serious Address to the Public concerning the Tax on Receipts: with a few Observations on the Present Critical Situation of this Country, with regard to Trade, Revenues, National Debt, and Principles of Government* . . . (London, 1784). [72] Wyvill, *Political Papers* (fn. 44), vol. II, pp. 337–8.

[73] See John Cannon, *The Fox–North Coalition: Crisis of the Constitution, 1782–4* (London, 1969), ch. II.

[74] Quoted in N.C. Phillips, *Yorkshire and English National Politics, 1783–1784* (Christchurch, NZ, 1961), p. 49. Richard Slater Milnes was also an Alderman of York, Deputy Lieutenant of the West Riding, Provincial Grand-Master of the Freemasons of Yorkshire, a substantial landowner, a convinced Unitarian and during the 1790s a warm Foxite and reformer. His sister married Henry Thornton, MP for Hull.

Did the religious tenets and moral values of Rational Dissent make a significant contribution to the political dispositions of its adherents? In his 1792 speech against Fox's unsuccessful motion for the repeal of certain statutes specifically affecting Unitarians, Burke argued that the latter were not merely a religious sect. They were, he said, a 'political faction' dedicated to the destruction of the Church of England, the subversion of the state and the creation of a political regime modelled on that of revolutionary France.

The principle of your petitioners is no passive conscientious dissent on account of an over-scrupulous habit of mind; the dissent on their part is fundamental, goes to the very root; and it is at issue not upon this rite or that ceremony, on this or that school opinion, but upon this one question of an establishment, as unchristian, unlawful, contrary to the Gospel and to natural right, popish and idolatrous. These are the principles violently and fanatically held and pursued – taught to their children who are sworn at the altar like Hannibal. The war is with the establishment itself, no quarter, no compromise.[75]

There is some hyperbole here. Nevertheless religious Dissent, especially Rational Dissent, did involve an oppositional political content in eighteenth-century England. Whether 'sworn at the altar like Hannibal' is the appropriate metaphor, religious identity did involve a commitment to a whole family and community history of heroic principle, internal exile and persecution. The very existence of their chapels, often tracing their origins back to 'the Great Ejection' of 1662, testified to their continuing adherence to an oppositional political and intellectual tradition. History was a nightmare from which Rational Dissenters, more than most, were trying to awake. Generation after generation their religious affiliation involved confronting the repressive powers of the state. Several thousand Dissenters had died in prison during the 1670s and 1680s.[76] If the coup which removed James II from the throne and the Toleration Act of 1689 marked the end of that brutal period, at least in England, anti-Dissenting laws remained on the statute book, notably the Test and Corporation Acts. Hardwicke's Marriage Act of 1753, ostensibly targeting clandestine marriages, forced all Dissenters to go through the Anglican ceremony in an Anglican church. Their dubious legal status made Dissenters continuously vulnerable to acts of petty

---

[75] 'Speech on a Motion for Leave to Bring in a Bill to Repeal and Alter Certain Acts Respecting Religious Opinions, 11 May 1792', in Burke, *Works* (fn. 3) vol. III, p. 330.
[76] See Gerald R. Cragg, *Puritanism in the Period of the Great Persecution 1660–1688* (Cambridge, 1957).

victimisation by local figures of authority – a magistrate refusing to license a chapel or offer the protection of the law, a clergyman refusing to conduct the marriage or the funeral of a Dissenter. The Dissenting deputies published a report in 1796 documenting many hundreds of cases of Dissenters suffering such discrimination or experiencing physical assault or damage to property.[77] Poorer and orthodox Dissenters in the countryside or small market towns were much more vulnerable to this kind of harassment than Rational Dissenters of wealth and influence in large towns. Nevertheless the latter's sense of insecurity and injustice, of symbolic exclusion and victimisation by the state was undoubtedly real.

Those who denied the Trinity, hence the divinity of Christ, were specifically unprotected by the Toleration Act of 1689 (1 William and Mary c.18) and the Blasphemy Act of 1698 made them liable to loss of civil rights and imprisonment for up to three years (9 and 10 William III c.32). If by the 1770s this threat was apparently in abeyance, the sentencing in 1762 of Peter Annet to the pillory and a year's hard labour for some mildly deist writings was a chilling reminder of the dangers of heterodoxy. According to Priestley, Rational Dissenters no longer felt secure in the moderation and good sense of the nation's rulers after their handling of the Wilkes case. The spectre of a Jesuitical court once more began to haunt them.[78] These anxieties were exacerbated from the late 1770s by the extreme anti-Dissenting aggression of a vociferous section of the Church of England.

The very conditions of their existence as religious communities made Dissenters alert to the threat which the state, including the Church of England, always posed to their autonomy. Of civil rights and the freedom of the individual, it was noted in 1796, Dissenters 'more than any other class of the subjects of this realm, are led by their peculiar situation to study the nature and appreciate the value'.[79] The conviction that the state's involvement in the affairs of civil society should be minimal was not a matter of abstract economic theory for Rational Dissent. The belief that the independent action of rational individuals should be left to regulate matters in everyday life; that the individual should be free to read or write whatever he wished, to worship at whatever church he chose, to

---

[77] *An Abstract of Proceedings of the Deputies and Committee Appointed for the Support of Protestant Dissenters from the Commencement of the Institution* (London, 1796), pp. 8ff.

[78] Priestley, *Remarks on some Paragraphs in the Fourth Volume of Dr Blackstone's Commentaries on the Laws of England, Relating to Dissenters* (London, 1769), in *Works* (fn. 39), vol. XXII, pp. 302–28 at pp. 302–3.

[79] *Abstract of Proceedings*, p. iii.

educate his children in whatever way he wished, had become not only their ideal but also their practice.

This is where Rational Dissent's break from doctrinal authority, its tolerance of diversity and difference, moved beyond the Dissenting tradition and had new and radical political implications. The most advanced and Rational Dissenters, Enfield argued in 1778, based their Dissent from the state Church on the grounds of absolute individualism: 'the natural right every man possesses of framing his system of religious faith, and choosing his form of religious worship for himself'.[80] Rational Dissent was not a unified and coherent doctrinal position but a voluntary association of individuals who recognised the rights of others to absolute religious liberty. This was reflected in Rational Dissent's increasingly self-conscious ideal of a free public sphere, beyond the control of the state. Rational Dissenters argued for liberty not just for themselves but for all who suffered state interference. They even began to move towards support for the relief of Roman Catholics, a commitment which some-times attracted the hostility of other sections of Dissent and generated some uncertainty within the ranks of Rational Dissent.[81] Priestley argued: 'whether we be called, or call ourselves, Christians, Papists, Protestants, Dissenters, Heretics, or even Deists, (for all are equal here, all are actuated by the same spirit, and all engaged in the same cause,) we stand in need of the same liberty of thinking, debating, and publish-ing.'[82] Rational Dissent not only accepted absolute religious and intellec-tual freedom within the walls of its chapels but actively campaigned for a similar freedom throughout civil society.

Some leading voices of Rational Dissent deployed this language in effective political polemic on specific issues. Joseph Priestley's pamphlet, *The Present State of Great Britain and her Colonies* (1769), gained him the friendship of Sir George Savile and the good opinion of Rockingham.[83] It was published in several cheap and widely distributed editions. His *Address to Protestant Dissenters* (1774), defending the American cause and

[80] William Enfield, *The Principles and Duty of Protestant Dissenters Considered, in a Sermon Preached at the Ordination of Rev John Prior Estlin* . . . (London, 1778), p. 8.

[81] See Colin Haydon, *Anti-Catholicism in Eighteenth-Century England: A Political and Social Study* (Manchester, 1993), pp. 182–3; M. Fitzpatrick, 'Joseph Priestley and the Cause of Universal Toleration', *Price–Priestley Newsletter*, 1 (1977).

[82] J. Priestley, *An Essay on the First Principles of Government, and on the Nature of Political, Civil, and Religious Liberty* . . ., 2nd edn, corr. . . . (London, 1771), in *Works* (fn. 39), vol. XXII, pp. 1–144 at p. 137. This has been reprinted in J. Priestley, *Political Writings*, ed. Peter N. Miller, (Cambridge Texts in the History of Political Thought) (Cambridge, 1993), pp. 1–127.

[83] [J. Priestley], *The Present State of Liberty in Great Britain and her Colonies*, by an Englishman (London, 1769), in *Works*, XXII, pp. 380–98; reprinted in *Political Writings*, pp. 129–44.

written and published in close co-operation with Benjamin Franklin, was again successful and widely distributed. Franklin even wondered if it had contributed to the early dissolution of Parliament. A member of the government, Lord Suffolk, had justified the dissolution a year early in order to prevent public opinion 'being poisoned by artful and dangerous publications'.[84] Two years later Price's *Observations on Civil Liberty and the Nature and Justice of the War with America*, not only supporting the American rebels but calling for parliamentary reform, rapidly went through fourteen editions – more than 60,000 copies in London alone.[85]

More important, however, were the ways in which political values were reinforced within the Rational Dissenting congregation itself. If the ministers' sermons were, by and large, concerned with things moral, spiritual and theological they were, on occasion, explicitly and aggressively political. Two sermons, both preached in Yorkshire on a government-proclaimed fast-day in the early stages of the war with the American colonies, will illustrate this point. At Westgate Chapel in Wakefield, William Turner subjected his congregation to a vehement denunciation of the corruption of rulers. Ostentatious self-mortification on such a political fast-day fitted well, he said, with 'pride, vanity, self-confidence and even the basest sensualities and most odious debaucheries in secret, as well as of morousness, haughtiness, censoriousness, hardness of heart, oppression, fraud, falsehood, and cruelty towards others'.[86] It is not hard to imagine some of the congregation, ready to indulge in a little self-mortification, already stirring in their cosy box pews. But his focus shifted elsewhere. It was necessary, he went on, that some individuals should – 'by common consent' – be invested with the power to govern, but this was for the common good, not for the particular interests of a narrow group. Yet, he said, in all countries at all periods there have been men, 'blinded by avarice and ambition, hardened against the feelings of humanity, and having perverted or lost all principles of fear of God, and righteousness to man', who confuse power and right. Finding themselves possessed of the power, they assume the right

---

[84] [J. Priestley], *An Address to Protestant Dissenters of all Denominations, on the Approaching Election of Members of Parliament, with Respect to the State of Public Liberty in General, and of American Affairs in Particular* (London, 1774), in *Works* (fn. 39), vol. XXII, pp. 483–98; J. Priestley, Letter to the Editor of *The Monthly Magazine*, 1 February (1804), in Appendix XXIV, *Works*, vol. XXV, pp. 395–8 at p. 396.

[85] Priestley, *Memoirs*, in *Works* (fn. 39),vol. I, pt 1 p. 289n; Peter D. Brown, *The Chathamites: A Study in the Relationship between Personalities and Ideas in the Second Half of the Eighteenth Century* (London, 1967), p. 148.

[86] William Turner (1714–94), *The Whole Service as Performed in the Congregation of Protestant Dissenters at Wakefield on Friday December 13th 1776, Being the Day appointed for a General Fast* (Wakefield, 1777), p. 23.

'to invade, and make a property of their fellow-creatures, and use them for their own advantage, pleasure or caprice, though it were to their bitter suffering and cruel oppression, both in body, mind and outward estate'. Though the whole sermon remains at this pitch of generality, the immediate context of the British Government's attempt to repress the American rebels haunted everything Turner said. He concluded with biblical fury:

> whoever shall persist in the commission of unrighteousness, oppression, and cruelty to their brethren, and, at the same time attempt, by fastings, however solemn, to bribe the righteous ruler of the world to connive at the wickedness, will only bring down on themselves his heavier vengeance for the aggravated insult.[87]

This sermon was not simply a confirmation of the already-formed view-point of his congregation. Some of the woollen merchants looking up to Turner in his pulpit were hostile to the American cause, seeing a speedy and effective defeat or capitulation of the rebels as the best way of protecting their lucrative trading links with the colonies. Turner's fast-day diatribe was an open challenge to his hearers. Theophilus Lindsey in London was most impressed, noting that its moral vindication of 'the just rights of men . . . might be of service to those that attended however averse to the Americans'.[88] He was in receipt of several copies and undertook to distribute them at 'our club', presumably the fortnightly club of 'Honest Whigs' whose membership included John Lee, Price and Priestley, Benjamin Franklin, other leading London Dissenting ministers such as Abraham Rees and Andrew Kippis, Jonathan Shipley, Bishop of St Asaph, and William Rose, co-editor of the *Monthly Review*. Turner remained active in oppositional politics, writing a paper in 1780 explaining the principles and political strategy of the Yorkshire Association.[89]

At St Saviourgate Chapel in York on the same fast-day, Newcome Cappe delivered a sermon that was even more of a political polemic against the nation's rulers and in fact against the moral ethos of Britain as a whole. He pointed to widespread electoral corruption, a legal system 'unrighteous and oppressive'; everywhere 'public virtue' was 'trampled underfoot by interested ambition, consumed by party zeal, or suffered to

---

[87] *Ibid.*, pp. 26, 34.
[88] Lindsey to Turner, 30 January 1777, Turner MSS, Library of Newcastle Literary and Philosophical Society.
[89] Unfortunately I have been unable to trace this text. See the Memoirs in William Wood, *A Sermon Preached . . . on Occasion of the Death of the Rev. William Turner . . . To which are added, Memoirs of Mr. Turner's Life and Writings* (Newcastle-upon-Tyne, 1794), p. 44.

die away through a cold and careless sensibility'. Every aspect of social life was exposed as decadent – religion, family, education and business – and all classes in society, rich and poor, shared in the profligacy. The political message was hardly disguised. Under its present rulers the nation had gone to the dogs. There could be no moral legitimacy for action against the Americans, especially not the spurious term 'patriotism'.[90]

Cappe had made something of an impact in London circles as a young man in 1757 with a sermon praising Frederick the Great's victory at Rosbach; this had rapidly gone through thirteen editions, brought him praise and attention from leading political figures and a brief moment of fame.[91] His 1776 fast-day sermon similarly pushed him into the political spotlight. It quickly went through two editions and, via the ubiquitous John Lee MP, was brought to the attention of various members of the Whig opposition. Lee wrote to Cappe early in 1777:

Sir George Savile, happening to call on me a fortnight since . . . I showed him your sermon, and read him several parts of it. He was delighted beyond measure with it, insisted on taking it away with him . . . I have seen him frequently since, and he has never failed repeating his admiration, in terms that do him and you equal honour. He sent to Johnson for seven or eight copies, but none are to be had; and he was strongly disposed to take a liberty with you, by giving orders to print a new edition of it, without your knowledge.

Savile and Lee canvassed it around. Burke had read it and spread its fame around the benches of the Commons. Lee told Cappe: 'last night the Duke of Portland sent me a card, to desire I would give him an opportunity of reading it'.[92] Subsequently Cappe was invited to the Yorkshire Association's founding meeting. 'Had he been a Freeholder in this County', he replied, 'he could not have lost a moment to have done himself honor, by annexing his to so respectable a list of names, associated, on so urgent an occasion, for so laudable a purpose.'[93]

---

[90] Newcome Cappe, *A Sermon Preached on the Thirteenth of December, the Late Day of National Humiliation* . . ., 2nd edn (London, 1777).

[91] N. Cappe, *Discourses, Chiefly on Devotional Subjects . . . To which are Prefixed Memoirs of his Life*, by Catharine Cappe, 2nd edn (York, 1816), p. xxxiv.

[92] *Ibid.*, vol. 1, li.

[93] Cappe to Holmes, 16 December 1779, YAP/YCA: M25/89. Cappe (1732/3–1800) was in fact a gentleman of some property and related to Dr Secker, Archbishop of Canterbury. He refused to conform to the Church and accept the lucrative patronage of his family connections. He was a correspondent not just of the leading figures within Rational Dissent but also of Adam Smith, Archdeacon Blackburne and Edmund Burke. William Wood, minister at Mill Hill Chapel in Leeds, made this blunt and illuminating observation at his funeral in York in 1800: 'He carried an aversion to public life, and a love of studious retirement, to a somewhat blameable excess. With natural and acquired capacities for extensive usefulness, in the course of five-and-forty years he was seldom absent from this city.' See 'Memoirs' by C. Cappe (fn. 91), pp. xviii–xxi, 419.

Burke made much of the impropriety of Dissenting ministers dabbling in political affairs: 'politics and the pulpit are terms that have little agreement'.[94] Many orthodox Dissenters in the late eighteenth century were similarly critical of ministers of Rational Dissent who neglected religious duties for political causes, 'who are zealous for liberty, but the souls of their flocks are neglected', as Job Orton grumbled.[95] But the Rational Dissenter no longer distinguished the religious and the secular with such rigour. Thus Priestley argued:

As it is expressly asserted, that Christ came 'to bless mankind, in turning them away from their iniquities' . . . I think I am authorized to consider the Christian religion as a means to an end; and therefore, if the great end of it, namely the reformation and virtue of man be, in fact, attained by another means, the benevolent author of it will not be offended.[96]

For George Walker, minister at the High Pavement Chapel in Nottingham, political activity was an extension of his religious and moral principles. Politics, he wrote, 'is a branch of morals, it involves the character and happiness of a people, and to think and act aright in it must forever be a serious duty of man'.[97] Walker was a member of the Society for Constitutional Information. He drafted petitions against the American War and was a prominent speaker on the platform of a number of Nottinghamshire county meetings in the early 1780s in the cause of parliamentary reform.[98] He remained politically active, speaking on platforms, drafting petitions, chairing meetings during the 1780s and 1790s. In 1811, four years after his death and thirteen years after his departure from Nottingham, Major John Cartwright, his friend and business partner, told Lord Holland:

I lament to observe, that since the loss of that excellent man, George Walker, Nottingham seems with him to have lost somewhat of its decision of character, and that a leader, authoritative from wisdom, virtue and energy, is wanting.[99]

---

[94] Burke, *Reflections* (fn. 5), p. 10.

[95] Job Orton, *Letters to Dissenting Ministers and to Students for the Ministry . . . To which are prefixed, Memoirs of his Life*, by S. Palmer, 2 vols. (London, 1806), vol. II, p. 4.

[96] Quoted in John J. Tayler, *A Retrospect of the Religious Life of England: or, The Church, Puritanism and Free Inquiry . . .*, 2nd edn (London, 1876), p. 296.

[97] George Walker, 'The Duty and Character of a National Soldier', in *Sermons on Various Subjects*, 2 vols. (London, 1790), vol. II, p. 437.

[98] See for instance, G. Walker, *Substance of the Speech of the Rev. Mr Walker . . . at Mansfield, 28 Feb. 1780* (London, 1780), printed and distributed by the Society for Constitutional Information.

[99] Frances D. Cartwright, *The Life and Correspondence of Major Cartwright*, ed. by his niece, 2 vols. (London, 1826), vol. II, p. 19. Subscribers to Walker's two volumes of sermons in 1790 included five MPs – Henry Beaufoy, Henry Duncombe, Robert Smith, Samuel Smith and William Wilberforce.

Walker was unusual in the extent of his political activities but many other ministers of Rational Dissent saw their proper role as involving secular activities devoted to 'the reformation and virtue of man', in which politics had a significant part to play.

To what extent did the political values and activities of ministers have the sanction of the wider body of laymen? Ministers did have a privileged status. As teachers, the intellectual voices or even moral consciences of their congregations, they spoke with a measure of autonomy. But, as Priestley indicated, they were representatives of a small community and responsible to its values, its anxieties and its problems:

> Among the *Dissenters*, if a minister introduce principles and practices which the people condemn, they dismiss him from their service, and choose another more agreeable to them. If his difference of sentiment occasion any debate, the subject of the debate is thereby more thoroughly understood; and the worst that can happen is, that some of them separate, and form themselves into a new society, or join another in their neighbourhood, that is more to their liking . . . A minister seldom chooses to be connected with a society whose general sentiments are much different from his own, nor do societies often invite a person to officiate among them without having previously sufficient reason to depend upon his being agreeable to them.[100]

Burke and other ideologues of the established order were quite right to identify Rational Dissent as a dangerous political grouping, a 'hydra-headed monster'. Their involvement in a range of campaigns and organisations, their commitment to an anti-state position on civil and religious liberties, struck at powerful vested interests. What it did not threaten, however, was the rule of property and existing social hierarchies and inequalities.

IV

In *Reflections on the Revolution in France*, Edmund Burke's sharp eye noticed that Richard Price in his sermon to the Revolution Society had referred to the corrupt electorate as 'the dregs of the people':

> You will smile here at the consistency of those democratists who, when they are not on their guard, treat the humbler part of the community with the greatest contempt, whilst, at the same time, they pretend to make them the depositories of all power.[101]

---

[100] Priestley, *First Principles of Government*, in *Works* (fn. 39), p. 100; *Political Writings* (fn. 82), p. 92.
[101] Burke, *Reflections* (fn. 5), p. 49.

It is a shrewd and significant point, though of course, characteristically, it distorts Price's meaning. He was not referring to 'the people' as a whole but to that minority in particular constituencies who blatantly sold their votes. Nevertheless Burke points to some important questions here about the character of late eighteenth-century political radicalism among these Rational Dissenters. If they were committed to parliamentary reform and implacably opposed to the state Church they were not, generally, democrats. Price stated in 1787: 'I know not one individual among them who would not tremble at the thought of changing into a Democracy our mixed form of government . . .'[102]

Here we need to remind ourselves of the social ethos of Rational Dissent. The ruling élite of their congregations were employers of servants and often had their small retinues of footmen and coachmen, chamber maids and scullery maids, gardeners and messengers and clerks. Like the propertied classes in general in late eighteenth-century England, these gentlemen of property confronted, or at least perceived, these servants as idle and impertinent in periods of economic prosperity and in recurring periods of depression experienced rising poor rates, pilfering and vandalism, and the ever-present danger of riot and violence.[103] Dissenters, whether or not employers, had particular reason for anxiety about 'the crowd'.

'But what is the promiscuous throng, which generally fills up the lower orders of life?' Hugh Worthington asked a London congregation in 1778:

Look into the streets, and let their words and actions decide their prevailing character. Will not breaking the sabbath, despising the ordinances of religion, using the name of God in sport or blasphemy, together with horrid imprecations, drunkenness and obscenity – will not these justify the application of that Scripture phrase, 'They live without God in the world'.[104]

Theophilus Lindsey's dramatic resignation from the Church of England in 1774, to establish the first explicitly designated Unitarian

---

[102] Richard Price, *The Evidence for a Future Period of Improvement in the State of Mankind . . .* (London, 1787), p. 31. Priestley, in 1769 and again in 1791, rejected universal suffrage on grounds of the vulnerability of the poor to electoral corruption; see *Present State of Liberty*, in *Works* (fn. 39), vol. XXII, p. 385; and *A Political Dialogue on the General Principles of Government* (London, 1791), in *Works*, vol. xxv, pp. 81–108 at p. 103. See also Martin Fitzpatrick, 'Heretical Religion and Radical Political Ideas in Late Eighteenth-Century England', in Eckhart Hellmuth, ed., *The Transformation of Political Culture: England and Germany in the Late Eighteenth Century* (Oxford, 1990), pp. 339–72 at pp. 353ff.

[103] Some of the ways in which relations between masters and servants were handled by Unitarians in the first half of the nineteenth century are examined in Seed, 'Theologies of Power' (fn. 10), esp. pp. 136–8.

[104] Hugh Worthington, *The Progress of Moral Corruption: A Sermon . . .* (London, 1778), p. 24.

congregation, involved no populist appeal to his Yorkshire parishioners. In fact they were vigorously instructed in the duty of obedience they owed to their superiors, rebuked for their misuse of the sabbath in working or in 'all those noisy and riotous games, always accompanied with profane oaths, and generally ending in the ale-house or worse'.[105]

Addressing an assembly of northern Dissenting ministers at Newcastle-upon-Tyne in 1786, the young Unitarian minister of the town's wealthy and prestigious Hanover Square Chapel inveighed against the 'deplorable ignorance and stupidity' and the 'profligacy' of the labouring poor. 'They are not taught the importance of industry and frugality':

They learn, too frequently, from the example of their parents and others with whom they converse, to repine at their lot, to murmur at their difficulties, to grudge at and envy their superiors, and to consider every mean artifice of fraud and deceit, by which they may hope to obtain anything, as perfectly fair and allowable, provided they can only avoid detection and escape punishment.

'Can we wonder', he went on to ask, 'that our persons and properties are growing daily less secure from the violent attacks of the idle and debauched?'[106] Priestley himself pronounced on the lack of industry and foresight of the labouring poor, among whom any 'extraordinary gain', rather than being put to profitable use, was immediately 'spent in ale-houses, where they contract the worst habits, and often encourage one another in every kind of vice and licentiousness'. He spoke of 'the lowest and most illiterate of our common people, who can never have any degree of influence in the state'.[107]

An identity of social priorities emerges, whether we are looking during the 1770s and 1780s at a London Presbyterian of liberal ilk such as Hugh Worthington; or Theophilus Lindsey, the central figure in the Unitarian schism from the Church of England; or a younger representative of the Priestleyan wing of Rational Dissent such as William Turner; or indeed, at Priestley himself. The leading voices of Rational Dissent descanted on the themes of working-class insubordination,

[105] Theophilus Lindsey, *A Farewell Address to the Parishioners of Catterick* [Another ed.] (London, 1774), p. 17.

[106] William Turner (1761–1859), *Sunday Schools Recommended, in a Sermon Preached . . . at Morpeth. . . . To which is added, an appendix, concerning the formation, conduct, and expence of these schools* (Newcastle-upon-Tyne, 1786), pp. 12–15.

[107] J. Priestley, *Some Considerations on the State of the Poor in General, prefixed to An Account of a Society for Encouraging the Industrious Poor* (Birmingham, 1787), Appendix XII, in *Works* (fn. 39), vol. XXV, pp. 314–19 at p. 315; and *First Principles of Government*, Sect. V, in *Works*, vol. XXII, p. 65 (*Political Writings* (fn. 82), p. 60).

indiscipline and immorality and this begins to indicate some of the political uncertainties of Rational Dissent during the 1790s.

In 1794 Thomas Walker, a founding member of Lindsey's Unitarian Society, reflected in Manchester on the failures of the English reform movement and pointed to the timidity of Dissenters:

> The Dissenters of this kingdom have been at the commencement of almost every object of liberal discussion of late years. But, however consistently and disinterestedly many of them have acted, they have, as a body, constantly fallen short of their own principles; they have excited opposition which they have never compleatly supported; and through fear, or some other motive, they have been so strongly the advocates of an overstrained moderation, that they have been rather the enemies than the friends of those who have ventured the most for the rights of the people.[108]

Five years later Charles Wellbeloved, ex-student of Hackney Academy and Cappe's successor as Unitarian minister at York, answered Walker's implicit question with a different set of questions (he was rebutting the charges of Bishop Horsley that Unitarians were 'levellers' and 'regicides'):

> Have Unitarians then alone no interest in the peace and the prosperity of their country? Have they no property to lose? Have they not among their number manufacturers and merchants of the first name and credit, whose whole substance depends upon the preservation of public tranquility and subordination, and who have, therefore, as powerful motives to support the constitution of this country as any one who sits upon the episcopal bench?[109]

Many Rational Dissenters in the 1790s inhabited the political space between these two sets of questions, between Walker's 'ought' and Wellbeloved's 'is'. Intimidated by the repressive measures of government and by Church and King mobs, outflanked by the egalitarianism and strident anti-Christianity of Painite organisations, appalled by events in France, political and economic security seemed threatened from all sides, from a vengeful government, from an insubordinate working class, from a French invasion. Some Rational Dissenters migrated to North America, others drifted back to the Church of England and political respectability, but most withdrew into an uneasy stoicism. This was not, as has sometimes been argued, a failure of political nerve, a collapse into the arms of the dominant regime, a profound

---

[108] Quoted in Archibald Prentice, *Historical Sketches and Personal Recollections of Manchester, intended to illustrate the Progress of Public Opinion from 1792 to 1832*, (London, 1851), pp. 20–1.

[109] Charles Wellbeloved, *The Principles of Roman Catholics and Unitarians Contrasted: A Sermon ...* (York, 1800), p. 34.

compromise with the established order. In a situation of political defeat and confusion, between the Scylla of High Church Toryism and the Charybdis of popular radicalism, strategy and tactics dictated political withdrawal for a while. 'The real friends to liberty in this Country are very few', Richard Slater Milnes wrote to Wyvill in 1800; 'from repeated trials we know them well; and from the experience we have had, it does not appear to me a judicious proceeding to persist in objects that rather revolt than conciliate the Public Mind.'[110]

But there was more involved than merely tactical considerations. This withdrawal marked the point at which the radical rhetoric of propertied Dissenters reached its real limits, limits established by the property relations within late eighteenth-century English society. To understand the political location of Rational Dissent in this period it is not sufficient to examine only the language and action directed against the existing state.[111] It is important to look at the other, less assured, face of Rational Dissent, the face that looked down at the servant and the employee and 'the promiscuous throng' that filled the streets. In 1798 that ex-student of Gilbert Wakefield and Warrington Academy, Thomas Robert Malthus, was to provide a language which gave that limit a name and a justification.[112]

[110] Wyvill, *Political Papers* (fn. 44), vol. VI, p. 168.
[111] For an important discussion of the rhetoric of radicalism in the 1790s and the complexities of its connections to political practice or 'belief' see Mark Philp, 'The Fragmented Ideology of Reform', in M. Philp, ed., *The French Revolution and British Popular Politics* (Cambridge, 1991), pp. 50–77.
[112] [Thomas Robert Malthus], *An Essay on the Principle of Population as it Affects the Future Improvement of Society, with Remarks on the Speculations of Mr Godwin, M. Condorcet, and Other Writers* (London, 1798). This was published by the doyen of radical and Dissenting publishers, Joseph Johnson.

CHAPTER 7

Law, lawyers and Rational Dissent

Wilfrid Prest

Dissent was at very least defined, and in one sense actually created, by a body of statute law. For more than a century and a half after 1660, legislation and litigation (both civil and criminal) modulated dealings between Protestant nonconformists, the Established Church, society and the state. Yet apart from denominational chroniclers of the sufferings of Protestant nonconformists during the 'Great Persecution' between 1660 and 1688, historians have paid surprisingly little attention to the nature and significance of the relationship between Dissent and the law.[1] Neither modern students of the history of crime and criminal justice, nor those of legal doctrines and institutions, have sought to explore how lawyers and the courts dealt with such ideological offences, or the whole range of what has been termed 'religious criminality'.[2] This last phrase comes from the first detailed study of the interaction between English law and religious Dissent after 1660, whose author possesses an unusual combination of interests and skills in legal and religious history.[3] While there is scope for further work on similar lines, looking at denominations other than the Quakers and periods after the Glorious Revolution, this chapter does not seek to fill that gap. It aims merely to outline the legal status of Dissent from 1660 until the repeal of the

For help of various kinds, I would like to thank Barry Smith, Paul Langford, Knud Haakonssen and fellow contributors, Christine Churches and Martin Holt; all faults remaining are my own.
[1] Cf. E. Calamy, *An Abridgement of Mr Baxter's History of His Life and Times. With an Account of the Ministers who were Ejected after the Restoration of King Charles II*, 2nd edn, 2 vols. (London, 1713); J. Waddington, *Congregational History, 1567–1700, In Relation to Contemporaneous Events and the Conflict for Freedom, Purity and Independence* (London, 1874), pp. 571–697; G.L. Turner, ed., *Original Records of Early Nonconformity*, 3 vols. (London, 1911–14). The list could easily be extended.
[2] The subject is completely untouched by the two standard modern works, J.H Baker, *An Introduction to English Legal History*, 3rd edn (London, 1990), and J.M. Beattie, *Crime and the Courts in England 1660–1800* (Oxford, 1986).
[3] C.W. Horle, *The Quakers and the English Legal System 1660–1688* (Philadelphia, 1988), p. ix; as Horle himself points out, his interest in assessing the enforcement of anti-Quaker legislation was to some extent anticipated by Barry Reay, 'The Authorities and Early Restoration Quakerism', *Journal of Ecclesiastical History*, 34 (1983), 69–84.

Corporation and Test Acts in 1828, and then to examine two hitherto neglected aspects of the relationship between Rational Dissent and the law, *via* a mini-prosopography of Dissenting lawyers and a discussion of Joseph Priestley's writings on English law and legal institutions.

THE LEGAL STATUS OF DISSENT 1660–1828

Attempts to constrain religious belief and practice by Act of Parliament go back to the Henrician Reformation and before. Under Elizabeth I and the early Stuarts, penal legislation compelling regular attendance at services in the local parish church and proscribing other forms of religious worship was based on the assumption of a national Protestant Church embracing all subjects, apart from an incorrigible papist minority. Even after – and to some extent because of – the proliferating sects and *de facto* religious pluralism of the Civil War and Interregnum, when Charles II claimed his own again many ministers and lay people assumed that a comprehensive Church of England could and should be restored with him. However, despite efforts by the King, his chief minister and some leading latitudinarian and Presbyterian clergy, Anglican exclusiveness and resentment triumphed over Protestant ecumenicism. The result was a formidable legislative battery, the notorious 'Clarendon Code', which both excluded and penalised those who could not accept the doctrines, liturgy and system of episcopal government set out in the 1662 Book of Common Prayer.[4]

As is well known, the general coolness of Protestant nonconformists to James II's attempts to win their political co-operation was rewarded in 1689 by the passage of an 'Act for Exempting Their Majesties' Protestant Subjects, Dissenting from the Church of England, from the Penalties of Certain Laws'. Equally notoriously, while the Toleration Act provided 'some ease to scrupulous consciences in the exercise of religion', it did not place Dissenters on a footing of absolute civil equality with adherents of the Established Church. In particular, the discriminatory provisions of the Corporation Act (1661) and the Test Act (1673) remained fully in force. These statutes dealt respectively with the holders of municipal office, that is to say, members of the governing bodies of incorporated urban boroughs, and persons enjoying 'offices of trust', whether

[4] Cf. R. Bosher, *The Making of the Restoration Settlement: The Influence of the Laudians, 1649–1662* (London, 1951); I.M. Green, *The Re-Establishment of the Church of England 1660–1663* (Oxford, 1978); T. Harris, P. Seaward and M. Goldie, eds., *The Politics of Religion in Restoration England* (Oxford, 1990).

civil or military, under the Crown. Their most important clauses, so far as the later history of Dissent is concerned, made the tenure of such posts conditional upon the holder receiving the sacrament of holy communion according to the rites of the Church of England.[5] In addition, nonconformists continued liable to pay tithes and 'other parochial duties' to the Established Church. They were free to worship, but only behind unlocked doors in a registered meeting place, led by a minister prepared to subscribe his acceptance to those of the Church of England's Thirty-nine Articles of Religion which dealt with matters of theological doctrine rather than Church government.[6] The Act of Toleration applied the same subscription requirement to Dissenting schoolmasters, while in 1698 a further Blasphemy Act disabled persons who denied the doctrine of the Trinity, the truth of the Christian religion or the authority of the Bible from holding any public office.[7]

Until recently historians have tended to assume that the limited nature of the concessions provided to Dissenters in 1689 ensured their continued exclusion from large areas of public life until well into the nineteenth century. While the reality of occasional conformity (the practice of taking the Anglican sacrament solely in order to qualify for office) can hardly be ignored, its extent and overall significance are less readily apparent.[8] Indeed, one historian has argued that the main purpose of the Indemnity Acts passed from 1726 onwards was rather to protect negligent Anglican office-holders who had accidentally failed to comply with the sacramental requirement than to provide a 'nonconformist's backdoor to public office'.[9] But whether or not such loopholes were greatly utilised by Dissenters, the mere fact of their existence was no bar to attempts to secure repeal of the Test and Corporation Acts.

---

[5] 13 Car. II, stat. 2, c.1, 'An Act for the Well Governing and Regulating of Corporations'; 25 Car II, c.2, 'An Act for Preventing Dangers which may happen from Popish Recusants' (1673). C.F. Mullett, 'The Legal Position of Protestant Dissenters, 1660–1689', *Virginia Law Review*, 22 (1935–6), 495–526; and 'The Legal Position of Protestant Dissenters, 1689–1767', *Virginia Law Review*, 23 (1936–7), 389–418; D.R. Lacey, *Dissent and Parliamentary Politics in England, 1661–1689* (New Brunswick, NJ, 1969), pp. 19, 30, 35–7, 77, 233; W.A. Speck, *Reluctant Revolutionaries: Englishmen and the Revolution of 1688* (Oxford, 1988), pp. 26–9, 186–7.

[6] 1 Will. & Mary, c. 18, cl. 2, 5–7.

[7] 'An Act for the more Effectual Suppressing of Blasphemy and Prophaneness' (9 & 10 Will. III, c. 32).

[8] The Occasional Conformity Act, passed by a High Tory Parliament in 1711 (10 Anne, c. 2, 'An Act for Preserving the Protestant Religion'), threatened all holders of office under the Crown and members of corporations who attended a 'conventicle' after having once received the Anglican sacrament, with loss of office and a fine; generally held to have been of limited practical effect, the statute was repealed in 1719 by the Act for Quieting and Establishing Corporations (5 Geo. I, c. 6).

[9] K.R.M. Short, 'The English Indemnity Acts 1726–1867', *Church History*, 42 (1973), 366–76.

Coordinated from 1732 onwards by the Protestant Dissenting Deputies, England's first permanent extraparliamentary political lobby group, and backed by an intermittent barrage of published pamphlets and tracts, unsuccessful campaigns for repeal were mounted during the 1730s and 1770s. One minor victory came in 1779, with the 'Act for the further Relief of Protestant Dissenting Ministers and Schoolmasters', which permitted substitution of a declaration of belief in the Scriptures as the revealed word of God for subscription to the Anglican Articles of Religion. But further attempts to gain repeal of the Test and Corporation Acts in the late 1780s were checked by the wave of political reaction following the outbreak of the French Revolution.[10]

Many Dissenters chafed under their civil disabilities, especially in the second half of the eighteenth century. More probably resented the petty legal bias in favour of the Established Church which compelled them to pay parochial church fees, rates and tithes, in addition to supporting their own denominational meeting-houses and ministers. Following Hardwicke's Marriage Act in 1753, Dissenters could only be lawfully married in a parish church by a clergyman of the Church of England, while on occasion even their rights to burial in the parochial churchyard might be denied. But how far did the failure to grant full civil equality to Protestant Dissenters effectively exclude these men from the mainstream of national life after 1689?

The question is important, and not merely for historians of religion. It has been widely held that the prominence of Dissenters among the entrepreneurs who led Britain into the world's first industrial revolution may at least partly reflect their lack of comparable opportunities for personal advancement in the armed forces, the learned professions and the public service. Two recent contributions by James Bradley and David Wykes have questioned this conventional wisdom.[11] In essence, they argue that the barriers facing Dissenters who wished to participate in politics or local government, to attend a university, to qualify for and practise a profession or to hold an office under the Crown were far less

---

[10] Cf. Bernard, Lord Manning, *The Protestant Dissenting Deputies*, ed. O. Greenwood (Cambridge, 1952); N.C. Hunt, *Two Early Political Associations: The Quakers and the Dissenting Deputies in the Age of Sir Robert Walpole* (Oxford, 1961), pp. 113–29; R.B. Barlow, *Citizenship and Conscience: A Study in the Theory and Practice of Religious Toleration in England during the Eighteenth Century* (Philadelphia, 1964); J.E. Bradley, *Religion, Revolution and English Radicalism: Nonconformity in Eighteenth-Century Politics and Society* (Cambridge, 1990), pp. 49–61; A. Lincoln, *Some Political and Social Ideas of English Dissent* (Cambridge, 1938), ch. 6; G. M. Ditchfield, 'The Parliamentary Struggle over the Repeal of the Test and Corporation Acts, 1787–1790', *English Historical Review*, 89 (1974), 551–77.

[11] Bradley, *Religion, Revolution and English Radicalism*, chs. 1–2; D.L Wykes, 'Religious Dissent and the Penal Laws: An Explanation of Business Success?', *History*, 75 (1990), 39–62.

formidable than contemporary Dissenting spokesmen claimed or later historians have believed. Bradley and Wykes support their revisionism with a detailed scrutiny of the various institutions and vocations from which Dissenters were supposedly excluded, demonstrating that the extent of exclusion has been greatly exaggerated, and that in so far as it was a fact, the prime causes tended to be economic, political or social rather than legal. As Wykes remarks:

the majority of assumptions concerning the penal laws disqualifying dissenters from a university education, officeholding, politics or a professional career are exaggerated, and in a number of cases – because the statutes did not apply – simply erroneous. It is also clear that dissenters were not so completely excluded from public life, the learned professions, crown office or the universities, as has been claimed. Instead, because the barriers were social and economic rather than legal, nearly all the dissenters represented belonged to the wealthiest denomination, the Presbyterians. In general, dissenters were not members of the social groups that provided recruits for public office and the professions. Similarly, politics were monopolized by the most influential families, which in municipal government meant the leading tradesmen and manufacturers, who included many Presbyterians, and in national affairs the gentry and great county families, who were very largely Anglican.[12]

DISSENTING LAWYERS

So, despite the Test and Corporation Acts, Dissenters could and did become members of borough corporations, aldermen and mayors, justices of the peace, sheriffs, members of parliament, customs, excise and militia officers, attorneys, barristers and judges. Yet the fact that some succeeded in avoiding or evading the provisions of the penal legislation obviously tells us nothing about the numbers who may have been deterred or failed in the attempt. Nor should it be supposed that the legal disabilities of Dissent were or were felt to be mere nominal formalities rather than substantial grievances. On the contrary, much of the Dissenters' self-image and political solidarity derived from the shared sense of labouring under a yoke of unjust discrimination imposed upon them by the law and the Established Church.[13]

Of course discrimination hardly needed a statutory basis: the insistence by grammar schools and universities on student subscription to the Thirty-Nine Articles is the most notable case in point. The four Inns

---

[12] Wykes, 'Religious Dissent', p. 61.
[13] Bradley, *Religion, Revolution and English Radicalism*, pp. 84–90. Cf. P. Langford, *Public Life and the Propertied Englishman 1689–1798* (Oxford, 1991), pp. 75–8.

of Court, which controlled entry to the upper branch of the legal profession, also imposed a religious test on candidates for call to the Bar during at least part of the period with which we are concerned, albeit in no very consistent fashion. According to the Unitarian barrister, Samuel Heywood, until 'some time in the reign of George the Second, all students of the law were obliged to receive the sacrament, according to the rites of the Church of England, before they were admitted to the bar'. Writing in 1787, Heywood credited Lincoln's Inn with being the first to abandon this practice, followed by the Inner Temple and Middle Temple; 'but, to the disgrace of Gray's Inn, it is still required there'.[14] The Pension or governing body of Gray's Inn did indeed order in January 1786 that a book should be provided 'in which such gentlemen as petition to be called to the Bar, their having received the sacrament being a previous requisite thereto, shall at the time they receive the same write their names therein, and that the Preacher or Reader, or any other Minister administering the same, and the Clerk of the Chapel subscribing their names in testimony thereof, shall be deemed sufficient evidence thereof'.[15] This elaborately phrased provision sounds very much like a tightening-up on previous practice, although the sacramental requirement does seem to have been operative at Gray's Inn in the early 1730s, when it was also endorsed by the rulers of the Inner Temple. At Lincoln's Inn, on the other hand, the last positive evidence for such a practice in the governing body's minutes is an order of November 1714 which excuses a student who had been unable to take the sacrament due to sickness, on condition that he deposit the sum of £5 with the Treasurer as 'caution money', to be redeemed after he had communicated in Lincoln's Inn Chapel on the last Sunday of Michaelmas term. Such an arrangement parallels the compositions by cash payment for failure to fulfil formal academic requirements which foreshadowed and accompanied the collapse of the Inns' traditional system of legal education by 'learning exercises' during the middle years of the seventeenth century.[16]

---

[14] [S. Heywood], *The Right of Protestant Dissenters to a Compleat Toleration Asserted* (London, 1787), p. 1. In 1794, however, Daniel O'Connell claimed that he had sought admission to Lincoln's Inn rather than the Temple, in order to avoid having to sign a bond or undertaking to receive the Anglican sacrament: cf. *The Correspondence of Daniel O'Connell, 1792–1847*, ed. M.R. O'Connell, 8 vols. (Dublin, 1972–80), vol. I, p. 14.

[15] *The Pension Book of Gray's Inn (Records of the Honourable Society) 1669–1800*, ed. R.J. Fletcher (London, 1910), pp. 347–8.

[16] *A Calendar of the Inner Temple Records*, vol. IV: *1 George I (1714)-24 George II (1750)*, ed. R.A. Roberts (London, 1933), p. 272; *The Records of the Honourable Society of Lincoln's Inn: The Black Books*, vol. III: *from A.D. 1660 to A.D. 1775*, ed. W.P. Baildon (London, 1899), pp. 199, 244. W.R. Prest, *The Inns of Court under Elizabeth I and the Early Stuarts 1590–1640* (London, 1972), pp. 135–6. Further research in the unpublished eighteenth-century archives of the Inns might modify some of these tentative inferences.

Use of the communion service as a test of religious orthodoxy at the Inns of Court dated back to the Elizabethan struggle against Catholic recusancy. By 1583 communion at least once a year in the church or chapel of their house was required of all resident members, on pain of expulsion; similar provisions appear in the general orders for the government of the societies issued by the common-law judges in 1636 and 1664.[17] It is not entirely clear how and when this universal obligation of membership was converted into a specific pre-requisite for call to the Bar, although at Gray's Inn such a provision was tacked on to a Pension order of November 1661 reviving the communion requirement for all resident members.[18] A similar requirement appears to have operated on a *de facto* basis at Lincoln's Inn from the early 1660s, although not until April 1673 did the bench order that 'all gentlemen of this Society shall receive the Sacrament in the Chappell of this Society before they shalbe called to the Barr'.[19] The timing of this edict, just after the parliamentary session which saw the passage of the first Test Act, might suggest their common origin in anti-papist paranoia. But, like the Test Act, such a measure was a two-edged sword, which in the right political circumstances could and would be employed also against Protestant nonconformists, like the son of John Thurloe, Cromwell's Secretary of State, whose call at Lincoln's Inn in 1672 had been made subject to the explicit condition that he should receive the sacrament.[20]

Because the religious history of the Inns of Court and legal profession in post-Restoration England remains largely unwritten, it is hard to say whether in practice the sacramental test was actually directed more often against papists than Dissenters. Following the Glorious Revolution Catholics were probably its prime target; in 1690, for instance, William Dunch was called to the Bar at Lincoln's Inn when several members of the governing body had satisfied their colleagues that he was 'a very

---

[17] Prest, *Inns of Court*, pp. 180, 183; W. Dugdale, *Origines Juridiciales* (London, 1666), p. 320; Baildon, *Records of … Lincoln's Inn*, vol. III p. 446.

[18] *The Pension Book of Gray's Inn (Records of the Honourable Society) 1569–1669*, ed. R.J. Fletcher (London, 1901), p. 440.

[19] Baildon, *Records of … Lincoln's Inn*, vol. III (fn. 16), pp. 31, 75, 81, 82, 88. The early seventeenth-century Black Books record a few isolated instances of calls to the Bar being made dependent on an individual receiving communion as a proof of Protestant, that is, non-popish orthodoxy, but no settled requirement of this nature: cf. *Records of the Honourable Society of Lincoln's Inn: The Black Books*, vol. II: *from A.D. 1586 to A.D. 1660*, ed. W.P. Baildon (London, 1898), pp. 73, 219, 220.

[20] J.R. Jones, *Country and Court: England 1658–1714* (London, 1978), pp. 177–8; Baildon, *Records of … Lincoln's Inn*, vol. III (fn. 16), pp. 81, 82. In the following decade Henry Care's popular handbook of *English Liberties: Or, The Free-Born Subject's Inheritance* (London, 1680? and numerous later editions) protested that 'It is an abuse, and utterly Illegal, to Prosecute Protestants on such laws as were made solely and wholly against Papists' (p.177).

good Protestant, notwithstanding that it is not certified on his behalfe that he hath received the Sacrament at the Chappell of this House according to the usage of the Church of England'. Their counterparts at the Middle Temple made a still larger concession in 1694, when they agreed that henceforth no person should be called to the Bar until he had produced a certificate indicating 'when he last received the Sacrament in some *Protestant* congregation, signed by the minister thereof' (my italics).[21] Even so, in our present state of ignorance, the possibility that the religious climate within each Inn and the attitudes of their respective governing bodies varied considerably over the next century and a half, as they had done during the previous century or so, cannot be entirely discounted.[22]

Both contemporaries and later historians may have exaggerated the strength and pervasiveness of broadly Puritan sentiment at the post-Reformation Inns of Court. Yet the sermons and pastoral influence of Walter Travers, William Crashaw, Thomas Gataker, John Preston, Richard Sibbes, Joseph Caryll and Edward Reynolds – to mention only the most notable of the godly preachers who served the Inns under Elizabeth I and the early Stuarts – did not fall on entirely barren ground. Their teaching and personal example influenced not only several generations of devout students and practising lawyers, but also men of a much more heterodox cast, like Thomas Helwys, founder of the Pinners' Hall General Baptist congregation, or Thomas Fell, better known as Margaret Fell's husband, who lent his house, Swarthmore Hall, for Quaker meetings in the 1650s.[23]

Richard Baxter's friend and the protector of other persecuted non-conformists, Sir Matthew Hale, despite having served as Justice of Common Pleas under the Cromwellian Protectorate, was created Lord

---

[21] Cf. D.F. Lemmings, *Gentlemen and Barristers: The Inns of Court and the English Bar 1680–1730* (Oxford, 1990); Baildon, *Records of ... Lincoln's Inn*, vol. III, p. 173; *Middle Temple Records: Minutes of the Parliament of the Middle Temple*, ed. C.H. Hopwood and C.T. Martin, 3 vols. (London, 1904), vol. III, p. 1421.

[22] Cf. Prest, *Inns of Court* (fn. 16), chs. 8–9. The influence of individual preachers and masters of the Temple Church would be well worth investigating; John Tillotson, preacher at Lincoln's Inn from 1663–90, and perhaps Thomas Sherlock, Master of the Temple from 1705–53, may have encouraged more tolerant attitudes than the two Henry Stebbings, father-and-son guardians of Anglican orthodoxy, who monopolised the pulpit at Gray's Inn from 1731 until 1787.

[23] Cf. *ibid.*, ch. 9; W.T. Whitley, 'Thomas Helwys of Gray's Inn and of Broxtowe Hall, Nottingham', *Baptist Quarterly*, n.s., 7 (6) (1935), 241–55 (I am grateful to Christopher Hill for this reference); *DNB*, s.v. Fell, Thomas. Cf. *The Writings of Henry Barrow, 1587–1590*, ed. L. Carlson (London, 1962), p. 99 for Robert Lacy, a separatist barrister of Gray's Inn. On the religion of pre-Civil War common lawyers, cf. W.R. Prest, *The Rise of the Barristers: A Social History of the English Bar 1590–1640* (Oxford, 1986), ch. 7.

Chief Baron of the Exchequer in 1660 and Chief Justice of the King's Bench in 1671.[24] Quite a few other less famous common lawyers also managed the post-1660 transition from religiously pluralist republic to intolerant monarchical Church-State, and, like Hale, succeeded in reconciling latitudinarian or Dissenting religious principles with the exigencies of their worldly calling. Revisionist claims that after 1660 'Dissenters were free to take up the practice of law', and that 'no religious disabilities were involved' in 'admissions to the bar' are slightly exaggerated, as we have just seen.[25] Nevertheless, Dissenters did indeed continue to enter the Inns of Court, gain call to the Bar, practise as counsellors and even rise to high legal office throughout the later seventeenth and eighteenth centuries.

The outstanding and best-documented case in point is that of Sir Dudley Ryder (1691–1756), who after studying at the nonconformist Hackney Academy and the Universities of Edinburgh and Leyden was admitted to the Middle Temple in 1713, called to the Bar in 1719 and capped a distinguished forensic career with appointment as Lord Chief Justice of the King's Bench in 1754. Ryder probably owed his early professional success to the patronage of Lord Chancellor Sir Peter King (1689–1734), John Locke's cousin and another Leyden graduate of Dissenting stock.[26] In the diary that Ryder kept as a law student he records the formation of 'a club of dissenters about the Temple, in order to encourage the cause and make those that might come to the Temple not ashamed to own themselves dissenters'. At the first meeting of this group in April 1716 only four students were present, including Ryder himself: 'our conversation turned upon the state of the nation, the influence of the clergy, and law affairs . . . We agreed to meet every Thursday between 7 and 8 and to admit none but such as should be agreed by the company and none but dissenters.' Ryder reports attending only two more meetings of the Dissenters' club; in December, concerned to hear of reports that he had joined 'a club set up upon a religious account', he noted that 'I believe I shall not so commonly frequent the club upon that account'.[27]

---

[24] A. Cromartie, *Sir Matthew Hale, 1609–1676* (Cambridge, 1995).
[25] Cf. above, pp. 174–6. Bradley, *Religion, Revolution and English Radicalism* (fn. 10), p. 83; Wykes, 'Religious Dissent' (fn. 11), p. 47. However, the situation of Protestant Dissenters in England was clearly never as desperate as that of Catholics seeking to practise the law in Ireland between 1692 and 1792. Cf. C. Kenny, 'The Exclusion of Catholics from the Legal Profession in Ireland, 1537–1829', *Historical Studies* 25 (1986–7), 350–7.
[26] *DNB*, s.v. Ryder, Sir Dudley and King, Sir Peter.
[27] *The Diary of Dudley Ryder 1715–1716*, ed. W. Matthews (London, 1939), pp. 226, 233, 361, 374.

Such prudent renunciation foreshadows Ryder's subsequent abandonment of his religious heritage and lapse into conformity with the Established Church, a trajectory followed not only by his patron King, but also by a Middle Templar of slightly earlier vintage, Sir Joseph Jekyll (1663–1738). Jekyll, who served as Chief Justice of Chester and Serjeant-at-law under William III, was appointed Master of the Rolls in 1717; during a long parliamentary career he introduced bills against state lotteries, stage plays and spirituous liquors, as well as for relieving Quakers from tithe, and at his death bequeathed part of his large fortune to advance the Dissenting cause: 'In religion he was probably a freethinker like his friends Whiston, Clarke and Onslow'.[28] Yet two original fellow-members of the Temple Dissenters' club who, like Ryder, also rose to the judiciary, Thomas Abney (d. 1750) and Michael Foster (1689–1763), may well have managed to avoid such a compromise, given that both were founder members of the Protestant Dissenting Deputies, the pressure group of laymen that worked to repeal the Test and Corporation Acts and protect the existing legal rights of Dissenters.[29] Finally, and closer to our present purposes and theme, Sollom Emlyn, the son of England's first avowedly Unitarian minister, was admitted to Lincoln's Inn in 1714 after studies at Leyden and called to the Bar seven years later; a legal author and reporter, proponent of law reform and 'chamber counsel', Emlyn also edited his father's works and was the 'very worthy Christian friend' of the Arian William Whiston.[30]

We have seen that Dissenters were by no means wholly excluded from the the upper branch of the legal profession during the later seventeenth and first half of the eighteenth century. Rational Dissent, as it matured over the first thirty years of George III's reign, also seems to have attracted a significant body of support from members of the Bar. In an

---

[28] *DNB*, s.v. Jekyll, Sir Joseph; C. Robbins, *The Eighteenth-Century Commonwealthman* (Cambridge, MA, 1959) p. 280. P. Clark, 'The "Mother Gin" Controversy in the Early Eighteenth Century', *Transactions of the Royal Historical Society*, 5th ser., 38 (1988), 75–6.

[29] Cf. above, pp. 171–2; Wykes, 'Religious Dissent' (fn. 11), p. 47, n.26. Although Thomas Abney's kinsman by marriage, the Presbyterian John Shute, Viscount Barrington (1678–1734), who was active in securing the repeal of the Schism and Occasional Conformity Acts, has been described as a barrister of the Inner Temple, no entry of his call appears in the printed records of the house: *DNB*; *A Calendar of the Inner Temple Records*, Vol. III: *12 Charles II (1660) – 12 Anne (1714)*, ed. F.A. Inderwick (London, 1901). On the prominence of lawyers among the Protestant Dissenting Deputies and the effectivness of these last in mounting legal actions to defend nonconformist interests, see Manning, *Protestant Dissenting Deputies* (fn. 10), pp. 41–2, 98.

[30] *The Records of the Honourable Society of Lincoln's Inn. Admissions (and Chapel Registers)*, 2 vols. (London, 1896), vol. I, p. 376; *DNB*, s.v. Emlyn, Sollom; *Memoirs of the Life and Writings of Mr William Whiston*, 2nd edn, 2 vols. (London, 1753), vol. I, p. 318.

important recent article John Seed draws attention to the presence of 'wealthy merchants on the edge of county society and a scattering of professional men' among the 'congregations of rational dissent'; these 'gentlemen dissenters', he argues, 'hardly conform to the stereotype of a ghettoised community of dour shopkeepers and petty capitalists'. In particular, Seed notes the presence of the barrister-MPs James Adair, Joshua Grigby and John Lee, together with other legal identities, among those who gathered at the Revd Theophilus Lindsey's Unitarian Essex Street Chapel from 1774 onwards. Having resigned his north-country parish the previous year, Lindsey had moved to London, where he lodged in 'Featherstone Buildings, Holborn', close to the heart of London's legal quarter, and established his first temporary meeting in 'a room that may do for a chapel . . . in Essex House, Essex Street, Strand, near the Temple'.[31] So it was perhaps not entirely surprising that the congregation at his first service on 17 April 1774 included what one of their number described as 'a few barristers'.

Among those lawyers who attended the Essex Street services or acted as trustees of the Essex Chapel after Lindsey bought the site in 1779 were Samuel Benyon, called to the Bar of Lincoln's Inn in 1787, who later rose to the rank of KC; the philanthropist Sir Thomas Bernard, who became a barrister of the Middle Temple in 1780 and subsequently practised as a conveyancer, before retiring to devote himself to good works; Michael Dodson, that 'eminent barrister and student of scripture' (as Lindsey termed him), who had practised as a special pleader after his admission to the Middle Temple in 1754, was called to the Bar in 1783, served as Commissioner of Bankruptcy from 1770 until his death in 1799 and still managed to publish *A New Translation of Isaiah* (1790) and other theological works; Samuel Pipe-Wolferstan, the Staffordshire antiquary and indefatigable diarist, who practised on the Midland circuit after his call to the Bar at the Inner Temple in 1776; John Pemberton Heywood, conveyancer and counsel for the City of York, who was called to the Bar at Lincoln's Inn in 1780, and Serjeant Samuel Heywood, the son of a Liverpool banker, educated at Warrington Academy and Trinity College, Cambridge, admirer and friend of Charles James Fox, and

---

[31] J. Seed, 'Gentlemen Dissenters: The Social and Political Meanings of Rational Dissent in the 1770s and 1780s', *Historical Journal*, 28 (1985), 302–7 and ch. 6 in this volume; T. Belsham, *Memoirs of the Late Revd Theophilus Lindsey . . . together with . . . a General View of the Progress of the Unitarian Doctrine . . .* (London, 1812), p. 97; *Letters of Theophilus Lindsey*, ed. H. McLachlan (Manchester, 1920), p. 22; L.B. Namier and J. Brooke, eds., *The House of Commons 1754–1790 (History of Parliament)*, 3 vols. (London, 1964), vol. II, p. 556.

author of *The Rights of Protestant Dissenters to a Complete Toleration Asserted* (1787).[32]

Some barristers whose religious outlook was compatible with Lindsey's doubtless found it convenient to worship at Essex Street during term because of its proximity to their chambers. Others, who do not appear from the surviving evidence to have formed part of the Essex Chapel congregation, are nevertheless identifiable as Rational Dissenters. Among these were Sir William Jones, Orientalist, political radical and correspondent of Richard Price; Capel Lofft, who delivered the funeral oration for John Jebb at Bunhill Fields in 1786, was one of the founders of the Society for Constitutional Information, and wrote *An History of the Corporation and Test Acts* (Bury, 1790) and other antiquarian, legal, literary and political works; and Francis Maseres, the reformer, mathematician, historian, translator, Cursitor Baron of the Exchequer, treasurer of the Inner Temple and Fellow of the Royal Society.[33] To this distinguished trio we might perhaps add the names of the radical Utopian, Thomas Day (1748–89), Jones's friend at Oxford and the Middle Temple, where he was called in 1775, although he never actually practised at the Bar; Manasseh Dawes (d. 1829), who in addition to legal writings dedicated his edition of a poem by John Stuckey to Joseph Priestley and published some *Philosophical Considerations* (1780) on the controversy between Priestley and Price; and George Tierney (1761–1830), another non-practising barrister, who graduated from Peterhouse during Edmund Law's mastership, sat as an MP and served as treasurer of the Society of Friends of the People.[34]

Should this cohort of fifteen barristers be regarded as insignificantly small or remarkably large? There is no easy answer to such a question.

[32] 'The Deeds of Essex Chapel', by A Lawyer, *Transactions of the Unitarian Historical Society* 1 (1918), 260–5; *DNB, s.v.* Bernard, Sir Thomas; Dodson, Michael; Heywood, Samuel; McLachlan, *Letters of Theophilus Lindsey*, p. 28. J. Money, 'Provincialism and the English "Ancien Regime": Samuel Pipe-Wolferstan and the "Confessional State", 1776–1820', *Albion*, 21 (1989), 389–425. Lindsey's friend William Tayleur of Shrewsbury, although a long-time member of the Inner Temple, was apparently not called to the Bar; nor was the senior trustee of the Essex Chapel, 'Robert Martin Leake, Esquire, the present worthy Master of the Report Office in the Court of Chancery': Belsham, *Memoirs of … Theophilus Lindsey*, p. 122; cf. Seed, 'Gentlemen Dissenters', p. 305. Other non-barrister legal practitioners associated with Lindsey's meeting-house were John Hett, Master in Chancery, and the solicitors Godfrey Kettle, James Pearson and Thomas Logan.

[33] *DNB*; *The Works of Sir William Jones* (Edited by A.M. Jones, i.e. Anna Maria Jones, with a discourse on the life and writings of Sir William Jones, by Lord Teignmouth), 6 vols. (London, 1799), vol. VI, p. 719; Lord Teignmouth, *Memoirs of the Life, Writings and Correspondence of Sir William Jones*, 2nd edn, 2 vols. (London, 1806), vol. I, p. 340; J.C.D. Clark, *English Society 1688–1832* (Cambridge, 1985), pp. 312, 339; R.V. Holt, *The Unitarian Contribution to Social Progress in England* (London, 1938), p. 78.

[34] *DNB*. Although Day's political and social principles are better known than his religious views, he appears to have 'esteemed meetings of Quakers and dissenters as best' and invited neighbours to

The only obvious basis of comparison along occupational lines is with medical men of similarly liberal politico-religious disposition, such as John Aikin, James Currie, John Jebb and Thomas Percival, who certainly do not seem to have been overwhelmingly more numerous.[35] Further research might help to clarify this point, as well as uncovering more legal Rational Dissenters. In the meantime we can at least suggest some reasons why barristers should have been attracted to Rational Dissent. To begin with, as Seed argues, this creed tended to appeal to the well-to-do and well-educated. It may also have tapped a traditional vein of legal anti-clericalism, without seriously compromising the barrister's claims to superior social status, as adherence to the forms of Old Dissent, let alone Wesleyan enthusiasm, might have done.[36] Rational Dissent also seems to have appealed to self-consciously advanced thinkers, like William Jones, who prided themselves on their enlightened, up-to-date attitudes in all spheres, and deprecated the common law's antiquated absurdities, the 'gabble of feudal lawyers'; thus Jones claimed in a letter of 1782 to Major John Cartwright that 'though I have been somewhat conversant with the minute practice of the courts, yet I have sometimes risen to the high principles of rational jurisprudence'.[37] There was plainly considerable congruence and overlap between post-1760 political radicalism (in which the prominence of lawyers has been highlighted by John Brewer) and religious heterodoxy, which doubtless led to some cross-fertilisation, although whether religion determined politics or vice versa is difficult to say, either in general or particular cases.[38] (The problem with attributing

prayer meetings at his own home, where he spoke on the morality of the New Testament; cf. G.W. Gignilliat, *The Author of Sandford and Merton: A Life of Thomas Day, Esq.* (New York, 1932), pp. 252–3. Clark classifies Tierney as a religious radical, but it is not clear on what grounds, other than his Peterhouse connection: Clark, *English Society*, p. 312. John Baynes (1758–87), whose heterodox religious position is incontrovertible, studied at Gray's Inn and practised as a special pleader, but was not called to the Bar: *DNB*; J. Gascoigne, *Cambridge in the Age of the Enlightenment: Science, Religion and Politics from the Restoration to the French Revolution* (Cambridge, 1989), pp. 198, 224.

[35] Cf. Robbins, *Eighteenth-Century Commonwealthman* (fn. 28), pp. 353–5, 370–2. Surgeons and physicians of Rational Dissenting principles might have been more plentifully distributed in country towns, and hence less readily identifiable, than the more predominantly London-based barristers. On the prominence of 'medical doctors' in Priestley's radical circle, see I. Kramnick, 'Eighteenth-Century Science and Radical Social Theory: The Case of Joseph Priestley's Scientific Liberalism', *Journal of British Studies* 25 (1986), 1–30 at p. 25.

[36] Cf. Gascoigne, *Cambridge in the Age of Enlightenment*, pp. 48–9, for patronage by lawyers of latitudinarian clergy, 'since their conciliatory views on church authority naturally appealed to a profession which had long contested the power of the church courts'.

[37] F.D. Cartwright, ed., *The Life and Correspondence of Major Cartwright* (London, 1829), p. 151.

[38] J. Brewer, 'The Wilkites and the Law, 1763–74: A Study of Radical Notions of Governance', in J. Brewer and J. Styles, eds., *An Ungovernable People: The English and their Law in the Seventeenth and Eighteenth Centuries* (London, 1980), pp. 131–2; Clark, *English Society* (fn. 33), p. 277.

causal primacy to religion is that a number of politically radical lawyers, such as Robert Morris, secretary to the Society of Supporters of the Bill of Rights, or Serjeant John Glynn, counsel to John Wilkes and recorder of London, seem to exhibit no distinguishing religious stance whatever.) Finally, the broadly favourable attitudes towards English law and legal institutions expressed by such leading spokesmen of the movement as Joseph Priestley and Richard Price are also significant in this context.

RATIONAL DISSENTERS ON LAW AND LAWYERS

Price and Priestley, like John Jebb and Theophilus Lindsey, seem to have favoured some moderate measure of law reform, and not merely in terms of repealing discriminatory legislation against Dissenters.[39] But their overall stance towards the common law and the legal system was anything but antagonistic. Both viewed the law, along traditional Whiggish lines, as the chief bulwark of English liberties and the rights of man. In a sermon preached just before George III's accession, Price claimed that while the 'greatest part of the rest of mankind are slaves', Britons could rejoice in

the possession of liberty and independency. Our rights and properties are, in general, secured to us beyond the possibility of violation . . . The meanest of our fellow-subjects cannot have the least injury done him without being able to find redress. No life can be taken away or any punishment inflicted on anyone without a fair and equitable trial.[40]

Yet for all his confidence in the benefits of the rule of law, Price hardly showed more than a passing interest in legal issues as such. The polymath Joseph Priestley, on the other hand, had a good deal to say about the nature and role of law in society, past and present, and also seems to have been remarkably well versed in legal technicalities. It is tempting to link his keen interest in and knowledge of English common law with his generally determinist philosophical outlook, and consequent view of the entire created universe as having been originally organised and subsequently controlled by the edicts of divine providence.[41] While Priestley's legal concerns were fostered and supported by his close

---

[39] Cf. Robbins, *Eighteenth-Century Commonwealthman* (fn. 28), pp. 330, 372.

[40] Richard Price, *Britain's Happiness and its Full Possession of Civil and Religious Liberty, Briefly Stated and Proved* ...(London, 1791), pp. 12–14; cf. Clark, *English Society* (fn. 33), p. 316. Publication of this work after the outbreak of the French Revolution, with a preface pointing to the further constitutional gains Englishmen had achieved over the previous thirty years, was obviously intended to embarrass its author and undermine the radical cause. But I have seen no evidence that Price's attitude to the law had changed over the whole period.   [41] I owe this point to Alan Tapper.

friendship with the prominent Unitarian barrister, John Lee, they clearly antedate his move to Leeds and first meeting with Lee in 1767.[42] Priestley's memoirs recount his arriving at Warrington Academy in 1761 to find most students there 'young gentlemen designed for civil and active life', although the curriculum that they followed was 'almost entirely adapted to the learned professions'.[43] (So much for the notion that Dissenting academies provided a form of modern, practical, relevant and up-to-date education otherwise unobtainable in eighteenth-century England.) Seeking to remedy this deficiency, Priestley prepared three courses of lectures, designed to give his pupils at least an acquaintance 'with such branches of knowledge as would be of more immediate use to them when they should come into life'.[44] The subjects of these lectures were history in general, English history and 'the laws and constitution of England'.

Thirty years later, Priestley thought only the first set of lectures worth printing; the appearance of Blackstone's *Commentaries* and Sullivan's *Law Lectures*[45] had made it 'unnecessary' to bring out the third, although (Priestley added) 'my plans will be seen to be, in several respects, more comprehensive than theirs, especially than that of Dr Blackstone' – in itself a striking assertion.[46] There may be some element of rationalisation here, since his manuscript copies of the two unpublished lecture series had actually been destroyed in the Birmingham riots of 1791, although draft outlines fortunately survived. Of these two schemes, that summarising the course on English history is quite concise, for the simple reason that Priestley's plan of campaign was 'to divide the whole into separate periods, and to digest all the materials relating to each under certain important heads, pretty much in the manner of Gordon's Geographical Grammar'. Even so, it would seem that, in accordance with his belief in the mutual interdependence of law and history (discussed further below), a bloc of lectures on '*Laws*, including the general state of Law, shewing our gradual removal from a state of barbarism' comprised the largest single subject group of the whole conspectus,

---

[42] Joseph Priestley, *The Theological and Miscellaneous Works of Joseph Priestley . . .*, ed. J.T. Rutt, 25 vols. in 26 (London, 1817–31; repr. New York, 1972), vol. I, pt I, p. 36 (hereafter cited as *Works*).

[43] J. Priestley, *Lectures on History and General Policy, To which is Prefixed An Essay on a Course of Liberal Education for Civil and Active Life*, 2 vols. (London, 1793), vol. I, sig. A3 (hereafter cited as *Lectures*).

[44] *Ibid.*, p. vi.

[45] F.S. Sullivan, *An Historical Treatise on the Feudal Law, and the Constitution and Laws of England . . . in a Course of Lectures read in the University of Dublin* (London, 1772).

[46] Priestley, *Lectures*, vol. I, p. vi; cf. Kramnick 'Eighteenth-Century Science' (fn. 35), pp. 21–4, for some perceptive comments on Priestley's urge to simplify the laws and government in general.

which ranged from '*Religion and Church History*' and '*Government*, Civil, Military', to '*Agriculture*', '*Commodities*', '*Numbers of Inhabitants*', and '*Manners. Sentiments*'. Thus in the synopsis there are separate sub-headings for '*Administration of Law*, comprising the history of the courts of law. *Feudal System*. *Tenures*, Military, Socage. *Fruits of Tenure*. *Descent of Lands*. *Alienation* of land property; involuntary, with the history of personal execution; voluntary, testamentary. *Entails*. *Forms of conveyance*. *Corporations. Criminal Law. Trials.*'[47]

A still fuller treatment of contemporary English law and legal institutions appears in the extensive 'Account of a Course of Lectures on the Constitution and Laws of England, and a Syllabus of the Course'. This detailed outline of chapter headings and contents is preceded by an interesting 'Introductory Address', which makes specific reference to William Blackstone's inaugural Vinerian lecture 'On the Study of the Law' delivered at Oxford in 1758 and subsequently incorporated in volume I of the *Commentaries on the Laws of England*, first published in 1765. Priestley echoes Blackstone's arguments for the practical benefits of a knowledge of law in any man's private or public capacities. But a distinctive note appears with the assertion that 'the study of the constitution and laws of our country ... exhibits a scene which justly challenges the attention of a philosopher, and promises him the most rational entertainment'. 'Philosophy and legislation were originally the same study', and rightly so, given that human happiness is largely dependent upon 'government and laws'. Moreover, if philosophy is concerned with 'the properties of great objects', and 'with respect to things which are in a state of perpetual fluctuation, to trace the causes of their present state, and judge of their progress in futurity'; and if 'variety joined with uniformity contribute to recommend a subject to a philosopher, this subject of laws and government is a proper field for philosophical speculation'.[48] Unlike the works of nature, which are both enormously various and yet exhibit 'a perfect uniformity reigning through the whole', from the philosopher's viewpoint 'too much contrariety and inconsistency' exists in the legal systems of 'human societies'. Nevertheless, Priestley insists that there is

so much uniformity in these systems, such a connexion of parts, and such a tendency to the same great end in the construction of the several parts of this machine of government, particularly in our constitution, and the tenor of our

---

[47] Priestley, *Works*, volume XXIV, pp. 439–45. Cf. P. Gordon, *Geography anatomized: or, a compleat Geographical Grammer* (London, 1693 and later editions).   [48] *Ibid.*, pp. 445–9.

laws, that, notwithstanding some real inconsistencies, the contemplation of them cannot fail to be highly entertaining to a philosophical mind; especially if the progress of our laws and constitution be attended to, as having arisen from the common principles of human nature, having varied with a natural succession of circumstances, and these, in an almost uninterrupted series, growing more favourable to improvements and to happiness.[49]

These remarks suggest that in the early 1760s Priestley was thinking along the lines of a positivist analysis of the legal and constitutional 'machine of government'. The accomplishment of such a project might well have earned him no less posthumous reputation as pioneering social scientist than he currently enjoys as moral and natural philosopher. So intriguing a possibility is hardly negated by the fact that the surviving syllabus of his lectures falls short of such a goal, since their declared purpose was merely to give a student audience 'what may be called, the outline of the constitution of the English government . . . and to remove the first obstructions which lie in the way of this study, in order to encourage and enable you to enter more thoroughly into the subject in your own private researches'.[50]

The 'syllabus' of the course of sixty-four lectures explains that 'in laying down what relates to the civil state of the kingdom', the lecturer was 'guided by a view to the great objects of all civil policy; relating, in the first place, those institutions which tend to make us *happy*, and consequently *populous*, at home; then those which tend to make us *formidable* abroad'. Priestley begins with the general administrative and social divisions of the country, including descriptions of the royal family and court, the nobility and gentry (lectures 1–3), and the legislative and executive arms of government (lectures 4–5). The judicial branch (the courts) and the laws they administer are then dealt with in the following fifty-three lectures, and the course concludes with accounts of the armed forces, the fiscal regime and (in a single final lecture) 'The ecclesiastical state of the kingdom'.[51] This plan does not follow the scheme of organisation that Blackstone had used in his lectures at Oxford since 1753 (first published in 1756 as 'An Analysis of the Laws of England' and in expanded form as the *Commentaries*),[52] but rather proceeds from public law (concerned with 'the preservation of the government itself . . . trade and commerce' and 'public convenience of various kinds' – that is, social welfare) to 'Laws relating to the conduct and mutual obligation of individuals in society'. This latter bloc of lectures (by

---

[49] *Ibid.*, p. 449.   [50] *Ibid.*, p. 450.   [51] *Ibid.*, pp. 450–63.
[52] W. Blackstone, 'An Analysis of the Laws of England', in his *Tracts Chiefly Relating to the Antiquities and Laws of England*, 3rd edn (Oxford, 1771, first publ. 1756).

far the largest of the series) discusses 'the provisions which our laws have
made to guard our lives, limbs, reputation, and property, real and personal; also those which relate to the commerce of the sexes and the domestic relations'. A further eight lectures deal with the law of actions and
another three are concerned with equity.[53]

While it is obviously difficult to assess their content and merits from
the topic headings that now survive, Priestley's lectures do not seem to
have shrunk from the technical complexities inherent in even a brief discussion of such arcane matters as the rules of descent, franchises, annu-
ities or possessory actions.[54] At the same time, his overall approach is
notably less influenced than Blackstone's was by traditional legal categories of analysis or previous institutional works, and much more sensitive to the law's social functions; in this last sense Priestley's claim to have
been more 'comprehensive' than Blackstone seems entirely justified.
Further evidence of his innovative approach to the law's social dimensions is provided by the one Warrington lecture series that does still exist
in its entirety, the *Lectures on History and General Policy*. Here again law
occupies a prominent place, as the synopsis of lecture 9 indicates:
'Connexion of History and Law . . . Use of Laws in tracing the original
Genius and Manner of Life of a People. Changes in Laws corresponding with a Change of Manners, exemplified in the feudal system of
England'. This discussion opens with an affirmation of the law's social
centrality, and hence its vital importance for historians:

The laws of a country are necessarily connected with every thing belonging to
the people of it; so that a thorough knowledge of them, and of their progress,
would inform us of every thing that was most useful to be known about them;
and one of the greatest imperfections of historians in general is owing to their
ignorance of law . . . it is greatly to be lamented that things so nearly connected
as *law* and *history* should have been so seldom joined. For though the history of
battles and state intrigues be more engaging to the bulk of readers, who have no
relish for anything but what interests the *passions*; from the knowledge of the
progress of laws, and changes of constitution, in a state, a politician may derive
more useful information, and a philosopher more rational entertainment, than
from any other object he can attend to.[55]

---

[53] Priestley, *Works* (fn. 42), vol. XXIV, pp. 457–62.
[54] There are a few minor slips, however, including references to Blackstone's eight (*recte* seven) rules
of descent, and to the explanation of maxims of equity by 'Harris's treatise on that subject', presumably a mistake for R. Francis, *Maxims of Equity* (London, 1727, and later edns): Priestley, *Works*
(fn. 42), vol. XXIV, pp. 456, 462.
[55] Priestley, *Lectures* (fn. 43), vol. I, pp. 155–6; for a later example of the use of law as evidence in an
historical narrative, cf. Adam Smith, *An Inquiry into the Nature and Causes of the Wealth of Nations*, 2
vols. (London, 1776), Bk III, ch. 2.

Priestley's invocation of a rationalist, systematic, theoretical history of progress doubtless owed a good deal to Voltaire, Montesquieu and the Scottish Enlightenment. But his emphasis on the law's value as a source of historical evidence seems entirely original.

The remainder of this chapter provides a series of contemporary and historical examples, with the aim of demonstrating how a particular country's laws and customs reveal 'what was the manner of living and the occupation of the original inhabitants of it'. Thus primogeniture is characteristic of a feudal and militaristic monarchy, partible inheritance marks 'a state having been addicted to husbandry and inclined to a popular equal government', and where the youngest succeeds (as with borough English), 'we may take it for granted that the people formerly lived a pastoral and roving life, in which it is natural for the oldest to be provided for, and disposed of, the first, and the youngest to take what is left.' The relationship between 'change of laws' and 'change of manners' is also discussed, together with the problems caused by legal atavisms, despite an approving reference to Montesquieu's observation 'that the tediousness and expense of law suits is the price of liberty'.[56] Lecture 48 further develops the general notion of law as an index of social development, discussing (albeit in somewhat abstract, *a priori* terms) 'The Theory of the Progress of Law, exemplified in the History of the Criminal Law, and the Progress of Men's Ideas and of Laws concerning Property'.[57]

Similar notions underpin lecture 29, which surveys the primary sources for English history, both ecclesiastical and legal. Next after works of a 'directly historical' nature, 'law books' are said to be the most useful for the historian: 'In these we may trace both the greater and more minute changes in the internal constitution of the nation, with innumerable other important articles of which general historians take but little notice.' Priestley provides a brief but seemingly well-informed 'account of all our most ancient law books, nearly in the order in which they are written'. This takes the form of a summary catalogue, outlining the form and content of each work, beginning with the *Coustumier de Normandy* and proceeding through Glanville, Bracton (oddly misnamed 'John'), Hengham, the *Mirror of Justice*, Briton, Fortescue, *Novae Narrationes*, Statham's *Abridgement*, Littleton (together with Coke's first *Institutes* and

---

[56] *Ibid.*, vol. I, pp. 158–62. Note, however, the rider (vol. I, p. 161) that 'both the laws of a country, and the administration of them, may be rendered much less complex than they are with us, without any diminution of general liberty.' Cf. *ibid.*, vol. II, p. 161: 'this price of liberty itself may be too dear; for when law suits are very expensive, they are ineffectual'.   [57] *Ibid.*, vol. II, pp. 180–8.

the *Complete Copyholder*), *Doctor and Student*, and the *New Natura Brevium*. There is little reference to more recent legal literature, other than Spelman's *Treatise of Feuds and Tenures by Knight-service in England* (1698), the year book reprint edition of 1679–80 and Wood's *Institutes*, first published in 1720 (which although mentioned in the chapter synopsis does not appear in the text itself). All the above, together with the modern reports, are 'necessary to be studied by a person who would enter minutely into the state of the kingdom with respect to those things to which they relate'. However, Priestley's hearers were assured – doubtless to their considerable relief – that 'a person may understand our general historians very well' with the aid of Blackstone's *Commentaries*, Sullivan's *Lectures*, and Dalrymple on feudal property, plus 'some' of Kames's law tracts, backed up by Jacob's *Law Dictionary* and Brady's *Glossary*: 'But without some knowledge of the English law, it can be but a very lame and imperfect idea that any person can get of the English history'.[58]

Like Price, Priestley emphasised the benefits arising to both individual and society from the orderly, predictable and uniform rule of law, rather than the capricious rule of men. At the same time, he recognised that excessive reliance on legal formalities could produce absurdities and inconveniences, as where courts followed ancient precedents 'when the very ideas and maxims of law on which they were founded are vanished. There are many signal instances of this in English law.' One that Priestley cites is the inability of a creditor to seize more than half of a defaulting debtor's lands in satisfaction of his just debt: 'by thus strictly adhering to the form without regarding the substance, law, instead of a rational science, becomes a heap of subterfuges which tend insensibly to corrupt the morals of those persons who make it their profession'.[59]

Similar warnings on the moral danger, both to the individual and society, from the 'habit of pleading indifferently for or against right', are also expressed in Priestley's later *Miscellaneous Observations Relating to Education* (1778). Here the profession of law is compared unfavourably with those of medicine and theology, as 'much inferior, in real value and importance . . . especially with respect to the discipline of the mind'. Nevertheless, Priestley readily admits that 'an able and truly upright lawyer is a most valuable character in any country . . . and though the practice of the law for a livelihood be attended with the danger above mentioned, the study of it is essential to any person who would serve his country in a civil capacity.'[60] Apart from these caveats, Priestley

---

[58] *Ibid.*, vol. I, pp. 365–77.   [59] *Ibid.*, vol. II, pp. 161–2.   [60] Priestley, *Works* (fn. 42), vol. XXV, pp. 21–2.

expresses no general prejudice against lawyers or the practice of law. On the contrary, he emphasises that 'The profession of law has always been reckoned honourable in civilized countries. All the youth of distinction in Rome studied law, and the pleading of causes was a constant and well-known road to popularity and preferment.' Unlike the enlightened Romans, 'Barbarous nations have ever entertained an aversion to forms of law, and it is certainly an argument of the barbarity of these northern nations, that the profession of the law was so long regarded as a mean employment.' Indeed, of the modern European states, it is only in France that 'the ancient nobility have often put on the long robe'.[61]

This passage, from the final paragraph of lecture 48, appears as something of an afterthought, rather than a necessary conclusion to what has gone before, and may well have been added in the process of revision for the press in 1793, rather than forming part of the original lecture delivered at Warrington. If so, it would appear to reflect Priestley's most vigorous defence of the legal profession, made in the course of his *Letters to Burke*.[62] Burke, it will be recalled, had noted with disapproval the prominence of lawyers in the Assemblée Nationale, men who could not be expected to 'attend to the stability of property, whose existence had always depended upon whatever rendered property questionable, ambiguous and insecure'.[63] But if this were an accurate characterisation of the attitudes and values of the typical lawyer, Priestley asked, 'where is our policy in raising such men to the rank of judges?' (thus rather unfairly taking Burke's attack on 'the inferior, unlearned, merely instrumental members of the profession of the law, that is, such as our attornies' as a slur on the élite practitioners as well). It was hardly surprising that lawyers were prominent in French revolutionary politics, Priestley went on, since they had also taken a leading role in the first American Congress: 'lawyers, who have the talent and the habit of speaking in public, being generally conspicuous characters in all places. The study of the law, moreover, leads them to understand the constitution of the country, and their profession gives them a knowledge of mankind, and the habits of business.' He concludes with the prediction that if the French lawyers 'do as well as the lawyers of America, they will soon wipe away the reproach they may now lie under, and become the object of respect, perhaps of dread, to those who at present despise them.'[64]

---

[61] *Ibid.*, vol. II, pp. 187–8.

[62] J. Priestley, *Letters to the Right Honourable Edmund Burke Occasioned by his Reflections on the Revolution in France &c.* (Birmingham, 1791).

[63] E. Burke, *Reflections on the Revolution in France*, ed. with intro. and notes by J.G.A. Pocock (Indianapolis, 1987), pp. 37–8.   [64] Priestley, *Letters*, pp. 13–15.

CONCLUSION

Paul Lucas brought his 'Collective Biography of Students and Barristers of Lincoln's Inn, 1680–1804' (revealingly subtitled 'A Study in the "Aristocratic Resurgence" of the Eighteenth Century') to a close by suggesting that the 'comparative complacency' and 'rather unrebellious' nature of the late eighteenth-century English barrister 'may have been but another reason why England escaped a French Revolution'. The political passivity and conservatism which Lucas believes to have characterised the Bar in the 1780s and 1790s was detected by Caroline Robbins earlier in the eighteenth century; she noted that, in the reign of George II, 'Lawyers . . . were protectors of tradition and contributed little to the development of liberalism in any way.' James Bradley, who sees the law as linked with Crown and Church to form 'in some sense a unified source of oppression' during the eighteenth century, asserts that in the 1770s 'the weight of the legal profession' supported the government's coercive measures against the American colonies.[65]

At all times and in all places lawyers, like most other professional persons, are doubtless predisposed by training, corporate outlook and self-interest to support rather than undermine the prevailing order and powers that be. Yet there have been some significant individual exceptions: one thinks of John Calvin, Sir Edward Coke, John Millar, Daniel O'Connell, V.I. Lenin (and, in an Australian context, H.V. Evatt and Lionel Murphy), not to mention their numerous counterparts and fellow-travellers in the English Long Parliament, the American Constitutional Convention and the French Constituent Assembly.[66] So it is not surprising to find some strikingly heterodox figures leavening the conformist lump of the late eighteenth-century English Bar. After all Holborn, London's densely populated legal quarter, was the national centre of political and social reform movements in the 1780s and 1790s, with such groups as the London Corresponding Society and United Irishmen meeting at Furnival's Inn Cellar, just as in Queen Anne's time Dissenters organising against the Schism Act had met 'about the

[65] P. Lucas, 'A Collective Biography of Students and Barristers of Lincoln's Inn, 1680–1804: A Study in the "Aristocratic Resurgence" of the Eighteenth Century', *Journal of Modern History*, 46 (1974), 227–61 at p. 242; Robbins, *Eighteenth-Century Commonwealthman* (fn. 28), pp. 294–5; Bradley, *Religion, Revolution and English Radicalism* (fn. 10), pp. 154, 375.

[66] Prest, *Rise of the Barristers* (fn. 23), pp. 272–82; A. Cobban, *Aspects of the French Revolution* (New York, 1968), pp. 90–111, cited in L.R. Berlanstein, 'Lawyers in Pre-Revolutionary France', in W. Prest, ed., *Lawyers in Early Modern Europe and America* (London, 1981), pp. 164–80 at pp. 176–7; L.M. Friedman, *A History of American Law* (New York, 1973), p. 88.

Temple'. Even at Gray's Inn, the benchers' donation of one hundred guineas 'towards the relief of the troops at Boston employed in suppressing the American Revolution' provoked a formal resolution of protest from the barristers of the Society in 1777. This was apparently an isolated event, like the violently anti-clerical sermon purportedly preached by the radical Whig lay polemicist Thomas Gordon in the chapel of Lincoln's Inn on 30 January 1732, in conscious repudiation of the cult of King Charles the Martyr, and subsequently published in at least five editions. Unfortunately our present ignorance of the internal political and religious history of the eighteenth-century legal profession makes it very difficult to form a balanced assessment of such episodes.[67]

What seems clear is that the law and its practitioners did not invariably confront Dissent and Dissenters in attitudes of mutual antagonism. While Priestley may have been more favourably disposed towards the English legal system than most Dissenting ministers, under the regime established in 1689 by the Act of Toleration all Dissenters were obliged to come to terms with the law's definition of their rights and the necessity of using conventional legal means to protect them.[68] If this was the common condition of Protestant nonconformity in the eighteenth century, Rational Dissent and the law enjoyed a still closer relationship.

In 1769, at the urging of his Unitarian barrister friend, John Lee, Priestley issued a fierce rebuttal of what he took to be 'the most injurious reflections on that part of the community to which I belong' in the fourth volume of Blackstone's *Commentaries*, which apparently endorsed the civil disabilities of Dissent. As he later admitted, Priestley's tract was written in 'great haste', and 'not, in all respects, such as I now wish it had been'. Yet he still carefully distinguished his resentment at 'injurious representations . . . of the principles and practices of Dissenters', from his overall respect for the *Commentaries* and their author. In what Priestley himself characterised as a 'genteel and liberal answer', Blackstone acknowledged the justice of some of his principal criticisms, undertaking to amend the offending passages in future editions

---

[67] J.A. Hone, *For the Cause of Truth: Radicalism in London 1796–1821* (Oxford, 1982), pp. 8, 53–5; I. McCalman, 'Ultra-Radicalism and Convivial Debating-Clubs in London 1795–1838', *English Historical Review*, 102 (1987), 309–33; I. McCalman, *Radical Underworld: Prophets, Revolutionaries and Pornographers in London, 1795–1840* (Cambridge, 1988), pp. 74–5, 82–4; Fletcher, *Pension Book of Gray's Inn* (fn. 15), p. 326; Barlow, *Citizenship and Conscience* (fn. 10), p. 63; T. Gordon, *A Sermon Preached before the Learned Society of Lincoln's Inn on January 30, 1732* (London, 1733): I hope to discuss this tract elsewhere.

[68] Cf. R.E. Richey, 'Effects of Toleration on Eighteenth-Century Dissent', *Journal of Religious History*, 8 (1975), 350–63 at pp. 351–2.

– as indeed he did. *An Answer to Dr Blackstone's Reply* expressed Priestley's thanks for the 'generous manner' of these concessions, and reiterated his admiration for 'a work so valuable as yours': 'My pamphlet . . . was literally the creature of a day, and, figuratively speaking, its existence cannot be of much longer duration; whereas your "Commentaries on the Laws of England" will probably last as long as the laws themselves.' That a leading Rational Dissenter spokesman for religious heterodoxy and the 'Court lawyer' whose 'Tory politics' supposedly informed his 'firm defence of the Church' should have managed to resolve their differences so amicably suggests that in George III's England, ideological or theological divisions may sometimes have been more easily bridged than social distinctions.[69]

[69] Priestley, *Works* (fn. 42), vol. I, pt. I pp. 73–4, 102–3; vol. XXII, pp. 302–34. Clark, *English Society* (fn. 33), pp. 204, 207–8; rather than 'having merely altered the wording of a subsequent edition', Blackstone actually made substantial cuts in response to Priestley's criticisms. In 1775 Priestley was involved in a case tried before Blackstone: he wrote to Theophilus Lindsey that 'Judge Blackstone was exceedingly civil, and took several occasions of paying me compliments' (Priestley *Works* (fn. 42), vol. I, pt. I, p. 267).

CHAPTER 8

The nexus between theology and political doctrine in Church and Dissent

A.M.C. Waterman

It has lately been argued by Jonathan Clark that theological heterodoxy, in particular the Socinian heresy, is 'conceptually basic to radicalism in the ancien-regime sense'.

If Christ were not a person of the Trinity, the Catholic doctrine of the Atonement, held Socinians, was meaningless; if man was not in need of redemption, original sin did not descend by inheritance, and man must be assumed to be both fundamentally benevolent and capable of ordering his own affairs in all respects . . . A consequence of a denial that Christ exercised divine authority was that He could not institute a priesthood descending by apostolic succession and exercising its mediatory powers by virtue of that divine right: the Anglican clergy were thus on a par, in point of authority, with Dissenting clergy (or even with the private individual). If even the Church could not claim divine institution, the State was still more obviously secular. 'No bishop, no king' was once more a relevant challenge, if mankind was free to amend or reject its ecclesiastical and political hierarchy in the name of reason, conscience or utility.[1]

Despite certain minor infelicities – there is no one 'Catholic doctrine of the Atonement'; 'fundamentally benevolent' is not the equivalent of 'originally innocent' – this is a useful synopsis of the nexus between theology and political doctrine in both Church and Dissent. However, neither Clark nor any other author that I am aware of has provided the complete statement of which the quoted passage is a summary. It is therefore my intention in this chapter to supply such a statement with the object of throwing light upon two related questions: just what was it, exactly, that English Protestant Dissent 'dissented' from; and in what sense, if any, may we say that the Rational Dissenters were 'rational' and the orthodox Dissenters were not?

I shall argue that there existed from before 1662 until sometime after

---

[1] Jonathan C.D. Clark, *English Society, 1688–1832: Ideology, Social Structure and Political Practice during the Ancien Régime* (Cambridge, 1985), p. 281.

1800 a coherent and widely accepted body of establishment social theory rooted in Catholic ecclesiology, ultimately biblical in origin, transmitted unimpaired to the post-Reformation Church of England, and expressed most authoritatively in the *Book of Common Prayer*. Tory or High-Church ecclesiastical and civil polity was fully consistent with, if not actually entailed by, the ecclesiology of the Prayer Book. But that ecclesiology is itself a consequence of Pauline soteriology: and Pauline soteriology depended upon the central Christological conception, only defined adequately in the fifth century, of Christ as being both fully human and fully divine. The doctrine of the Holy Trinity can be regarded as a corollary of the Incarnation. Hence there is a clear conceptual nexus running from the Trinity and orthodox Christology through Pauline soteriology, Catholic ecclesiology, post-Reformation ecclesiastical and civil polity, to the political doctrines arising from and conveniently labelled by the 'grand scheme of subordination'.

Now if it could be shown convincingly both that orthodox Christology (and only orthodox Christology) implied the principle of subordination and also that the principle of subordination (and only the principle of subordination) implied orthodox Christology, we should have a convenient method of demonstrating Clark's claim that theological heterodoxy was 'conceptually basic' to 'radical' or 'democratic' political doctrines in the eighteenth century (or indeed at any other time). For if heterodoxy be defined as that which is not orthodox, and 'democratical principles' as a denial of the principle of subordination, then the logical equivalence of orthodoxy and subordination would imply the logical equivalence of heterodoxy and democratical principles.

This result would immediately suggest a criterion of 'rationality' for Dissent. Dissenters who clung to Christological orthodoxy whilst rejecting establishment polity and the principle of subordination would be clearly self-contradictory and therefore 'irrational'. Those who rejected the entire establishment package, as did many of those known to historians as Rational Dissenters, would be internally consistent and therefore 'rational'.

A case might be made that orthodox Christology and Catholic ecclesiology entail each other. There is no possibility, however, of establishing a similar relation between ecclesiology and ecclesiastical polity, hence there can be no logical equivalence of orthodoxy with the principle of subordination. Though establishment doctrine is coherent and well-formed its theological foundations do not *uniquely* determine a particular set of political principles. Hence it is and was possible in principle to deduce a different, somewhat more 'democratical' *polity* from the same *ecclesiology* and so to exonerate orthodox Dissenters from the charge of irrationality.

What this means is that some support may be found for Clark's claim that heterodoxy is 'conceptually basic' to democratical principles, but little if any for his stronger claim that such principles are, in any strictly logical sense, 'entailed by Socinianism'.[2] The most that we can say, though it is by no means negligible, is that during the period from 1662 to the repeal of the Test Act in 1828 all Dissenters confronted, and were to a significant extent excluded from participation in, an *ancien régime* based upon the unity of Church and state; that there existed a generally understood and widely accepted rationale of this régime which deduced its key political doctrine of subordination from theological first principles; and that some of the bolder spirits among that intellectual élite known as Rational Dissent took a short way with establishment by denying the entire body of establishment doctrine – a sufficient though not a *necessary* condition of their consistency in rejecting both orthodox Christology and the principle of subordination.

By *orthodox Christology* I shall mean the belief, defined in the Nicene and the Athanasian creeds, that Jesus is of 'one substance' (*homo-ousios*) with God the Father; yet also 'Substance of his Mother, born in the world; Perfect God, and Perfect Man.' The doctrine of the Holy Trinity, celebrated at length in the Athanasian creed, if not exactly a corollary, is dependent upon this definition: all varieties of Christian (not merely *Christological*) heterodoxy deny both *homo-ousios* and, therefore, the Holy Trinity in one way or another.

By *the principle of subordination* I shall mean the belief that 'Without order there is no living in public society, because the want thereof is the mother of confusion, whereupon division of necessity followeth, and out of division inevitable *destruction* . . . And if things or persons be ordered this doth imply that they are distinguished by degrees. For order is a gradual disposition.' The underlying conception of society is strictly organicist: 'the very Deity itself both keepeth, and requireth for ever this to be kept as a law, that whensoever there is a coagmentation of many, the lowest be knit to the highest by that which being interjacent may cause each to cleave unto other, and so all to continue one'.[3]

---

[2] *Ibid.*, p. 334.

[3] Richard Hooker, *Of the Laws of Ecclesiastical Polity* (1594–1662), Bk VIII, ii, 2, in *Works*, ed. J. Keble, 7th edn, rev. R.W. Church and F. Paget, 3 vols. (Oxford, 1888).

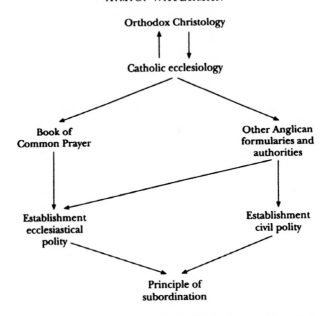

Figure 8.1: The relation between orthodox Christology and the principle of
subordination

The nexus between the two conceptions is complex and I have
attempted to illustrate it in Figure 8.1. Orthodox Christology, I maintain, is a soteriological conception which both gives rise to Catholic
ecclesiology and is implied by it. Catholic ecclesiology was transmitted
unimpaired at the Reformation to the Tudor and Jacobean Church; it
informs the *Book of Common Prayer* and other Anglican formularies and
authorities. These in turn supply the rationale of Anglican ecclesiastical polity and Restoration civil polity. The two latter are seventeenth-
century manifestations of the principle of subordination.

In constructing my argument I shall focus upon the definitive document of the post-Reformation Church of England, the *Book of
Common Prayer*. First I shall show that it transmits a Catholic ecclesiology that implies and is implied by orthodox Christology. Secondly I
shall argue that the organicism which is realised in establishment
ecclesiastical and civil polity is presupposed and articulated by the
Prayer Book and other Anglican sources *as a corollary of the Catholic ecclesiology they transmit*. In a final section I shall consider some of the
implications of these ideas for Dissenting doctrines in the eighteenth
century.

I

A dissenter is defined by that from which he dissents. The historical phenomenon known as English Protestant Dissent, or simply 'Dissent', is therefore determined, or at any rate inaugurated, by the Act of Uniformity (May, 1662). Under this Act all clerics were required to meet three tests by the Feast of St Bartholomew (17 August) following: to read publicly the daily offices of the revised *Book of Common Prayer* and make 'unfeigned assent and consent' to all that the Prayer Book contained; to renounce rebellion and the Solemn League and Covenant (1643); and to have received episcopal ordination. Though implementation of the Act was confused and uncertain,[4] some 1,700 clerics, nearly 20 per cent of the whole, either resigned their benefices or were eventually ejected under its provisions.[5] English (as distinct from Scottish and Irish) Presbyterian support for the Covenant had never been very strong[6] and rebellion was wholly discredited. Hence it was the *Book of Common Prayer*, together with the episcopacy it pre-supposed, that was the chief sticking point for those nonconforming ministers and their lay supporters who comprised the first generation of English Dissent.

The 1662 recension of the Prayer Book differed only slightly from the Jacobean and Elizabethan versions, which in turn were very conservative revisions of the second Edwardine book of 1552. Most of the significant changes in 1662, especially those made to the Ordinal, were intended to strengthen the Laudian (and indirectly pre-Reformation) interpretation of its rites which Dissenters and their Puritan forebears denied with such rancour. For, since Elizabethan times, a Protestant party in the Church of England had regarded the liturgy as 'an unperfect Boke, culled and picked out of that Popishe dunghill the Portuise and Masseboke, full of all abominations'.[7] And as late as 1773 the Earl of Chatham defended the Dissenters' zeal in a famous antithesis: 'They contend for a scriptural and spiritual worship; we have a Calvinistic Creed, a Popish liturgy and Arminian clergy.'[8]

What Chatham and the Elizabethan Puritans meant by 'popish' in

---

[4] I.M. Green, *The Re-Establishment of the Church of England, 1660–1663* (Oxford, 1978), pp. 143–54.
[5] Norman W. Sykes, *From Sheldon to Secker: Aspects of English Church History, 1660–1768* (Cambridge, 1959), p. 10.   [6] Green, *Re-Establishment*, p. 14.
[7] F. Proctor and W.H. Frere, *The Book of Common Prayer, with a Rationale of its Offices* (London, 1958), p. 114.
[8] Horton Davies, *Worship and Theology in England: From Watts and Wesley to Maurice, 1690–1850* (Princeton, NJ, 1961), p. 139.

this context is that the *Book of Common Prayer* consists almost entirely of translations – with substantial editing and modification – of pre-Reformation service books, chiefly of the Sarum use. Though the government's message to the Devon rebels of 1549 was less than perfectly ingenuous it contained a core of truth: 'It seemeth to you a new service, and indeed is none other but the old; the self-same words in English, which were in Latin, saving a few things taken out.'[9]

Whether or not Lord Chatham was correct about the 'Calvinistic Creed' and the 'Arminian clergy', it was the liturgy rather than these which determined the character and ethos of the Church of England. For creeds and their interpretation are a matter of doubtful disputation by experts. Though there were plenty of Anglican divines who interpreted the Articles and other formularies in a Catholic sense they could always be ignored or dismissed by the Dissenters as 'Romanisers' and in many cases countered by opposing passages from the writings of Low-Church (or 'Latitudinarian') divines such as Hoadley or Chillingworth. But the Prayer Book was something that every church-going English man, woman and child – that is to say, the vast majority of the population – heard continually from earliest infancy to the last hours of their lives. Common people with no education at all knew large portions of it by heart simply by hearing it so often. There is evidence to suggest that the Prayer Book was not popular before the 1640s.[10] It was probably its suppression during the Interregnum, and its replacement by the detested ranting of the Puritans, that endeared it to the general public. It was used clandestinely during the 1650s and joyfully welcomed back at the Restoration. Thereafter it became enshrined in the affections of all Churchmen and its (genuine) excellencies much exaggerated. 'Our incomparable liturgy' was regarded by ten generations of Englishmen altogether ignorant of Latin and Oriental rites as the *ne plus ultra* of Christian worship. Novelists like George Eliot and Thomas Hardy reveal its influences upon the speech, and therefore the thinking, of country folk until well into the nineteenth century. Its idiom saturated the language and remained normative for literary culture down to the Second World War.

The *Book of Common Prayer* both presupposes and inculcates what I shall call a 'Catholic' ecclesiology: by which I mean a conception of the Church not as a voluntary, human society of like-minded believers but as

---

[9] Proctor and Frere, *Book of Common Prayer*, p. 54 n.2.
[10] See, e.g., Horton Davies, *Worship and Theology in England: From Cranmer to Hooker, 1534–1603* (Princeton, NJ, 1970), pp. 213–26.

a divine society, transcending space and time, uniting the living and the dead, joined with angelic creatures in the everlasting praise of God.

> To thee all Angels cry aloud: the Heavens, and all the Powers
>   therein.
> To thee Cherubin, and Seraphin: continually do cry . . .
> The glorious company of the Apostles . . .
> The goodly fellowship of the Prophets . . .
> The noble army of Martyrs . . .
> The Holy Church throughout all the world: doth acknowledge
>   thee.[11]

The 'Holy Church throughout all the world', described in the communion office as 'Christ's Church militant here in earth' is the visible and temporal portion of a much larger society. And 'although in the visible Church the evil be ever mingled with the good,'[12] it is the means whereby the faithful in this life are united with Christ, and through him with all who now stand in the presence of God:

> Therefore with Angels and Archangels,
> and with all the company of heaven,
> we laud and magnify thy glorious Name;
> evermore praising thee . . .[13]

An individual enters the Church by faith and baptism, the latter usually in infancy. Initiation is supernatural. The celebrant prays that the child may receive 'that thing which by nature he cannot have: that he may be baptized with Water and the Holy Ghost, and received into Christ's Holy Church, and be made a lively member of the same'. Baptism is a ritual drowning after which the child is 'born again' to new life in union with Christ. The celebrant gives thanks, 'Seeing now . . . that this child is regenerated, and grafted into the body of Christ's church.'[14] The initiative comes from God, who has chosen to 'adopt' the child, who in baptism is 'made a member of Christ, the child of God, and an inheritor of the kingdom of heaven'.[15] The concluding prayer combines these themes:

We yield thee hearty thanks, most merciful Father, that it hath pleased thee to regenerate this infant with thy Holy spirit, to receive him for thine own child by adoption, and to incorporate him into thy Holy Church.[16]

The Church is variously referred to in the *Book of Common Prayer* as the 'ark' (Baptism), the 'spouse' of Christ (Matrimony, Ordering of Priests),

---

[11] *Book of Common Prayer* (hereafter *BCP*), *Morning Prayer*, Te Deum.
[12] *BCP, Articles of Religion* (1562), no. 36.   [13] *BCP, Holy Communion*, Common Preface.
[14] *BCP, Public Baptism of Infants.*   [15] *BCP, Catechism.*   [16] *BCP, Public Baptism of Infants.*

Christ's 'flock' (Baptism, Ordering of Priests, Consecration of Bishops), the 'Lord's family' (Ordering of Priests), the 'household' of God (Collects: Epiphany v, Trinity xxii), an edifice 'built upon the foundation of the Apostles and Prophets, Jesus Christ himself being the head corner-stone' (Collect: SS Simon and Jude), and 'the fellowship of Christ's Religion' (Collect: Easter iii). But by far the most frequently used image, and that which controls the meaning of all the others, is that of the Church as the 'mystical body' (or simply 'body') of Christ. God has 'knit together' his 'elect in one communion and fellowship, in the mystical body' of 'Christ our Lord' (Collect: All Saints'). In the Eucharist the worshippers know that they are 'very members incorporate in the mystical body of thy Son, which is the blessed company of all faithful people' (Communion Office). The homily provided for the marriage service contains the strongest statement of the quasi-organic unity between Christ and the faithful:

He that loveth his wife loveth himself: for no man ever yet hated his own flesh, but nourisheth and cherisheth it, even as the Lord the Church: *for we are members of his body, of his flesh, and of his bones.*[17]

It is evident that the ultimate source of these conceptions is the soteriology and related ecclesiology of St Paul (e.g. 1 Cor. 12: 12–27; Rom. 12: 4–5; Eph. 4: 4–16, etc.).

In a classic study of Pauline theology J.A.T. Robinson has shown how the concepts of *Sarx* (translated as 'flesh') and *Soma* (translated as 'body') are used by the Apostle to explain, or at any rate suggest, how the human race is 'saved' by the death and resurrection of Christ. Man is made 'the image and likeness of God' (Gen. 2: 26–7). But natural human existence is a state of radical separation from God, symbolised and explained by the Fall (Gen. 2: 17; 3: 3,4; Rom. 5: 12 –21). But the effect of the original disobedience of Adam is (potentially) reversed by the perfect obedience of Christ, the 'last Adam' (1 Cor. 15: 45), and this is made known in the resurrection:

Christ being raised from the dead dieth no more: death hath no more dominion over him.

For in that he died, he died unto sin once: but in that he liveth, he liveth unto God. (Rom. 6: 9–10; Proper Anthems for Easter Day)

It is the body of Christ *and only the body of Christ* which rises from the dead, becomes 'the first-fruits of them that slept' (1 Cor. 15 :20) and inaugurates the new life of restored unity between God and man.[18]

---

[17] *BCP, Solemnization of Matrimony*; my italics.
[18] J.A.T. Robinson, *The Body: A Study in Pauline Theology* (London, 1957), *passim*.

Now 'as in Adam all die, even so', St Paul promises (1 Cor. 15: 22), '*in Christ* shall all be made alive' (my italics). The rest of the human race participate in the victory of Christ over death and the reconciliation of God and man *precisely insofar as they may become 'members' of the body of Christ*. By faith and baptism they 'die' to the old life we inherit from Adam and rise to the new life we share with Christ.

Grant, O Lord, that as we are baptized into the death of thy blessed Son our Saviour Jesus Christ, so by continual mortifying our corrupt affections we may be buried with him: and that through the grave, and gate of death, we may pass to our joyful resurrection.[19]

It follows that the Church is the extension of the life of the Risen Christ. 'In you', St Paul reminded his Corinthian converts, 'the evidence for the truth of Christ has found confirmation' (1 Cor. 1: 6, *NEB*). His spirit will guide the Church 'into all truth' (John 16: 13); where two or three gather in his name, Christ will be in the midst (Matt. 18: 20); the Eucharist is a perpetual *anamnesis* of his death and resurrection (1 Cor. 11: 26; Matt. 26: 29) wherein the faithful are 'partakers of his most blessed Body and Blood'.[20] We may summarize the argument so far as follows: humans find 'salvation' through union with Christ; union with Christ means union with the Church, his (mystical) body; hence follows the patristic slogan, *Salus extra ecclesiam non est*.[21]

As mediator between God and man, Christ must be fully united with each. For, as St Athanasius put it in a memorable aphorism, God 'was made man, that we might be made God'.[22] A Christology that ignores or minimises the divinity of Christ (e.g. Ebionite, Arian, etc.), or that ignores or minimises his humanity (e.g. gnostic, Apollinarian, etc.), tends to undermine the Christian gospel of salvation. So does a Christology which, though recognising both the divine and the human nature of Christ, fails to maintain the unity of his person (e.g. Nestorian, Eutychian, etc.). Orthodox Christology – a Christology, that is to say, that is consistent with the evangelical understanding of salvation in Christ – requires a clear statement of union of God and man in Christ which maintains both natures in one person. This was first supplied in the creed of the Council of Nicaea (325) which repudiated the Christology of Arius and vindicated that of St Athanasius. Christ is 'of one substance with the Father' (*homo-ousios to Patri*: in the Western

---

[19] *BCP, Collects*: Holy Saturday, newly composed by John Cosin in 1662.
[20] *BCP, Holy Communion*, Prayer of Consecration.
[21] Cyprian, *Epist.* 73, 21, cited in Johannes Quasten, *Patrology*, 3 vols. (Utrecht, 1950–60), vol. II, p. 373. [22] Athanasius, *De incarn.* 54, cited in Quasten, *Patrology*, vol. III, p. 71.

Church *consubstantialem patri*), and 'was made Man' (*kai enanthropesanta*). The term *enanthropesanta*, not found in the Bible, was specially coined 'to express the *permanent* union of God with Human Nature',[23] but it proved inadequate against Apollinarian and Nestorian deviations and a more careful definition was required at the Council of Chalcedon (451). The so-called creed of St Athanasius, roughly contemporaneous with Chalcedon, greatly amplified the Christological clauses. Christ is . . .

God, of the Substance of the Father, begotten before the worlds: and Man, of the Substance of his Mother, born in the world;
. . . Who although he be God and Man: yet he is not two, but one Christ
. . . not by confusion of Substance: but by unity of Person.[24]

It is a relatively short step from a clear statement of the unity of the two natures in the person of Christ to a fully articulated doctrine of the Holy Trinity. The earliest Christian baptismal formula was Trinitarian (Matt. 28: 19) and the earliest (baptismal) creeds included the three fold affirmation of belief in Father, Son and Paraclete.[25] Once the terminology of 'person' and 'substance' had been worked out in relation to Christ it could be applied symmetrically to each member of the Trinity.

Whosoever will be saved: before all things it is necessary that he hold the Catholick Faith . . .
And the Catholick Faith is this: that we worship one God in Trinity, and Trinity in Unity;
Neither confounding the *Persons*: nor dividing the *Substance* . . .[26]

Orthodoxy means 'right (correct, etc.) *worship* (praise, etc.)'. It is impossible to regulate the way the faithful *think*. But in the tradition inherited by the Church of England it was held to be proper that the unity of the Church should find expression in a form of worship that represents as well as is humanly possible the (essentially mysterious) relation between God and man revealed in Jesus Christ.

It need hardly be said that the *Book of Common Prayer*, like all Catholic liturgy, is replete with Trinitarian references and ascriptions. The daily psalms and canticles begin and end with the antiphon *Gloria Patri*; one or more of the three creeds are recited at least twice daily; many collects and other prayers end with a Trinitarian ascription; the Litany begins with a Trinitarian invocation; the *Quicunque vult* (which Newman regarded not so much as a creed as a hymn of praise to the Holy Trinity)

---

[23] T.H. Bindley, *The Oecumenical Documents of the Faith*, 3rd edn (London, 1925), p. 39.
[24] *BCP, At Morning Prayer*, Athanasian Creed 'Quicunque vult'.
[25] Quasten, *Patrology*, vol. I, pp. 23–7.   [26] 'Quicunque vult' (fn. 24); my italics.

is appointed for Christmas, Easter, Ascension, Pentecost and other great feasts; the feast of the Holy Trinity is celebrated in its traditional place in the Western Kalender; the ancient baptismal formula is preserved; and the catechism provides an extremely simple and memorable Trinitarian doctrine for young children. Catholic ecclesiology, soteriology and orthodox Christology are interdependent. All three were handed down from patristic and mediæval times to the post-Reformation and post-Restoration Church of England in its 'popish liturgy'.

II

The *Book of Common Prayer* transmits Catholic ecclesiology. Catholic ecclesiology presents an organicist conception of the *Church* as (mystical) *body* (of Christ). Whether there be any necessary connection between the two, it was inevitable in the circumstances of seventeenth-century Britain that an organicist ecclesiology should be inextricably entangled with an organicist conception of the state. An organicist conception of ecclesiastical and civil society was then thought to imply an ecclesiastical and civil polity based upon the principle of subordination. The Dissenters' democratic principles were thus at variance with the Act of Uniformity which required 'unfeigned assent' to the Prayer Book.

The conception of civil society as a 'body', and the use of anatomical conceptions in constructing theories of social processes, was commonplace in the seventeenth and eighteenth centuries. William Petty began his *Political Anatomy of Ireland* (1691) by noting that

Sir Francis Bacon, in his *Advancement of Learning*, hath made a judicious Parallel in many particulars, between the *Body Natural*, and *Body Politick*, and between the Arts of preserving both in Health and Strength.[27]

Though there is nothing in either Petty's or Bacon's usage which particularly implies subordination, it would seem that this was understood in the earliest (Tudor) occurrences of the term.

This realm of England is an Empire . . . governed by one supreme *Head* and King . . . unto whom the *Body Politick*, compact of all Sorts and Degrees of People . . . been bounden and owen to bear a natural and humble obedience.[28]

In such cases the anatomical metaphor of society as 'body' gave expression to the belief that order must be predetermined and consciously

---

[27] William Petty, *The Economic Writings of Sir William Petty*, ed. C. Hull (repr. Fairfield, NJ, 1986), p. 129. [28] 24 Henry VIII, xii. 1532–3, cited *OED*; my italics.

maintained by the obedience of the many to the few. Archbishop Thomas Secker, an Anglican convert from Dissent, gave classic utterance to this way of thinking in an address to his ordination candidates in 1769, reprinted in 1785 for the edification of Cambridge undergraduates by the reputedly 'Latitudinarian', Whiggish Bishop, Richard Watson of Llandaff.

Without union there cannot be a sufficient degree either of strength or beauty: and *without subordination there cannot long be union*. Therefore obey, as the Apostle directs, them that have the rule over you.[29]

It is no surprise that Burke should have exploited the metaphor in his answer to Richard Price: 'He who gave our nature to be perfected by our virtue, willed also the necessary means of its perfection – He willed therefore the state – He willed its connection with the source and archetype of all perfection.' Wherefore 'our political system is placed in a just correspondence and symmetry with the order of the world, and with the mode of existence decreed to a permanent body composed of transitory parts . . . by . . . a stupendous wisdom, moulding together the great mysterious incorporation of the human race.'[30] It is this tradition of discourse, I believe, that informed establishment doctrine in the seventeenth and eighteenth centuries and that was generally supposed to authenticate patriarchy in the family, hierarchy in the Church and monarchy in the state. These putative implications of the metaphor are clearly to be seen in the *Book of Common Prayer* and other contemporaneous Anglican sources.

A single organism has only one control centre, or 'head', which must be obeyed if its life is to be sustained. For example, if man and woman become 'one flesh' in marriage, wives must obey their husbands for 'the husband is the head of the wife, even as Christ is the head of the Church'.[31] All 'members' of a body – hands, feet, ears, eyes – have interdependent functions, some 'honorable' and 'comely', others 'uncomely'. St Paul's converts 'are the body of Christ, and members in particular': hence he admonishes them to recognise and respect a differentiation of function in the Church (1 Cor. 12: 13–30). Christ is head of the body: but has 'poured down his gifts abundantly upon men, making some Apostles, some Prophets, some Evangelists, some Pastors and Doctors, to the edifying and making perfect his Church'. Bishops

---

[29] Richard Watson, *A Collection of Theological Tracts*, 6 vols. (Cambridge, 1785); my italics.
[30] Edmund Burke, *Reflections on the Revolution in France* (London, 1910), pp. 95, 31.
[31] *BCP, Solemnization of Matrimony.*

are appointed for the 'edifying and well-governing' of the Church, to 'teach and exhort', to 'banish and drive away all erroneous and strange doctrine', to 'correct and punish', and 'to be to the flock of Christ a shepherd'.[32]

The bishop has a vital part in a structure of authority. His consecration begins with a prayer which includes the people, 'that they may obediently follow the same'.[33] Priests and deacons promise at their ordination that they will 'reverently obey [their] Ordinary, and other chief minister, unto whom is committed the charge and governance over [them]'.[34] As priests are subject to bishops, so are deacons to priests. Their function is 'to assist the Priest in Divine Service'; prayer is offered that they may 'so well behave themselves in this inferior Office, that they may be found worthy to be called unto the higher Ministries in thy church'.[35] Even the bishop himself is under authority: he must 'profess and promise all due reverence and obedience to the Archbishop and to the Metropolitan Church'.[36] It is clear that the ecclesiology of the *Book of Common Prayer* is unequivocally hierarchical. The ecclesiastical polity of the Church of England, re-affirmed at the Restoration in the Caroline Act of Uniformity, is wholly consistent with Catholic ecclesiology transmitted by its 'popish liturgy'.

It is equally clear, however, that the interdependence and obedience necessary in the body of Christ are seen, in the Prayer Book, as *extending into all parts of human life, whether 'ecclesiastical' or 'civil'*. Wherefore every child must learn

To honour and obey the King, and all that are put in authority under him: To submit myself to all my governors, teachers, spiritual pastors and masters:

To order myself lowly and reverently to all my betters.[37]

Whether by accident or design, the organicism of the divine society so obviously entailed by Catholic ecclesiology has come to be applied to 'public society' as a whole. It is evident from the *Book of Common Prayer* and other sources that this extension has been achieved by subsuming the 'state' under the 'Church'.

A perfect illustration occurs in the Litany. Petition is made first 'that it may please [God] to rule and govern [his] Holy Church universal in the right way'. This is immediately followed by a series of other petitions which unpack 'Church' into the contents intended therein: 'thy Servant

---

[32] *BCP, Consecration of Bishops.*   [33] *Ibid.*, Collect.   [34] *BCP, Ordering of Priests.*
[35] *BCP, Ordering of Deacons.*   [36] *BCP, Consecration of Bishops.*   [37] *BCP, Catechism.*

CHARLES, our most gracious King and Governor'; 'all the Royal Family'; 'all Bishops Priests and Deacons'; 'the Lords of the Council and all the Nobility'; 'the Magistrates'; and finally, 'all thy people'. A similar but wider view is afforded by the prayer for the Church in the Eucharist: first 'the universal Church'; then 'all Christian Kings, Princes and Governors'; and 'specially thy servant CHARLES our King'; followed by 'his whole Council'; 'all Bishops and Curates' (an inversion of the order in the Litany, which ranks the clergy ahead of the Council); 'all thy people'; and finishing with a commemoration of (but not a petition for) 'all thy servants departed this life in thy faith and fear' (Communion Office). In a Christian country, these prayers imply, the 'Church' on earth is one and the same thing as the 'state': not because of an Erastian subordination of the former, but simply because all members of the 'public society' are united in the body of Christ.

The original version of the English litany (1544) contained a petition for deliverance 'from the tyrannye of the bishop of Rome and all his detestable enormities' but this clause was suppressed during the reign of Mary and not restored in the Elizabethan Prayer Book (1559). In principle therefore the prayers for 'all Bishops, Priests and Deacons' included the Pope. For the Church of England has always recognised the validity of Roman orders, never re-ordaining converts from that Church though insisting on the episcopal ordination of all Protestant ministers. But it is perfectly clear from the examples cited, as from many other parts of the Prayer Book, that the highest authority in Church and state is exercised not by the Bishop of Rome but by 'all Christian Kings, Princes and Governors'. The Henrician Act of Supremacy (1534) had declared the King to be 'only supreme head in earth of the Church of England'; the corresponding Elizabethan Act (1559) made the Sovereign 'the only supreme governor of this realm . . . as well in all spiritual or ecclesiastical things or causes as temporal'. The legislation claimed with some plausibility to be 'restoring to the crown the ancient jurisdiction over the state ecclesiastical and spiritual'.[38] Whatever the status of the claims and counterclaims respecting the continually shifting limits of papal and royal jurisdiction in England during the five hundred years from the Norman Conquest to the accession of Elizabeth I (1558), the relatively stable Coronation liturgy throws some light on the traditional – western – view of Christian kingship.

---

[38] Claire Cross, *The Royal Supremacy in the Elizabethan Church* (London, 1969), pp. 129, 126.

The English Coronation service descends from the *Pontifical of Egbert* (c. 750), revised for the coronation of Edgar in 973; and the twelfth-century *Pontifical of Magdalen College*. A fourteenth-century order used for Edward II (1307) draws upon each, and became the *Liber Regalis*, used at all subsequent coronations down to and including that of Charles II (1661). The service was translated into English in 1603 when the communion office from the *Book of Common Prayer* replaced the Latin mass. The most important features of *Liber Regalis* are the oath (translated in 1485) and the anointing. The King was required to swear that he will 'keepe to the people of England the Lawes and customes and Liberties graunted to the Clergie, and people by [his] Predecessors and glorious King Saynct Edward'; to 'keepe after [his] strength and power the church of God to the Clergie. And the people hoole peace and godly concord'; to make to be done 'rightfull Justice'; and to defend 'such lawes as to the worship of God shalbe chosen by your people'. At the heart of the service is the anointing, a quasi-sacramental rite of consecration: the prayers of the celebrant refer to the King's divine calling 'to rule and govern'; the choir meanwhile sings an anthem which first appears in the *Pontifical of Egbert*:

Zadok the priest and Nathan the prophet anointed Solomon king; and all the people rejoiced and said: God save the king.[39]

The annual services appointed at the Restoration to commemorate the martyrdom of Charles I (30 January) and to celebrate the end of the Great Rebellion (29 May) make frequent mention of God's 'Anointed', and on one occasion (30 January, Evening Prayer), refer to his 'sacred person'.

It would seem from this that the unity of Church and state under a Christian 'governor' is neither a Tudor nor a Protestant invention. The King of England is subject to no temporal sovereign but receives his authority from God, the 'King of kings, Lord of lords, the only Ruler of Princes' (Morning Prayer). He is bound by law, both divine and positive, the latter requiring the consent of his people. Subject only to that, he may properly be thought of as 'head' of a particular 'body': the whole people of God within his realm. There can be no denying, however, that the special circumstances of the Reformation in England gave political urgency to the doctrine, and it is no surprise to discover it stated strongly in one of the Edwardine *Homilies* (1547):

---

[39]   E.C. Ratcliff, *The English Coronation Service* (London, 1936), pp. 51, 86.

That is Gods ordinance, Gods commandement and Gods holy will, *that the whole body of every realme and all the membres and partes of the same shalbe subject to their hed, their kyng.*[40]

It is important to understand, nevertheless, that the identity of Church and state is contingent, not essential. 'A commonwealth is one way, and a church another way, defined', as Hooker acknowledged. But a 'schoolmaster' and a 'physician' are defined differently, yet 'both may be one man'. Therefore 'in such a politic society as consisteth of none but Christians . . . one and the selfsame multitude may in such sort be both': 'For if all that believe be contained in the name of the Church, how should the Church remain . . . divided from the commonwealth, when the whole commonwealth doth believe?' This is not the case 'under dominions of infidels'; nor is it 'in those commonwealths where the Bishop of Rome beareth sway'. For in the latter case 'the Bishop of Rome doth divide the body into two diverse bodies, and doth not suffer the Church to depend upon the power of any civil prince or potentate'. But 'in this realm of England . . . with us one society is both Church and commonwealth'; and 'our Church hath dependency upon the chief in our commonwealth . . . according to the pattern of God's own ancient elect people.'[41]

The argument of Section II is now complete. I have attempted to show first, that the ecclesiology of the *Book of Common Prayer*, deriving as it does from the Pauline, soteriological conception of the Church as the body of Christ, was then believed to imply an ecclesiastical polity based upon the principle of subordination. The restoration of the hierarchy in 1660 and the imposition of the Act of Uniformity two years later were more than simply political expedients: they were the logical corollary of a deeply held and coherent set of beliefs about Christ and his Church transmitted from Christian antiquity in Scripture and the liturgy. But in a Christian society the state is subsumed under the Church: 'Kings, Princes and Governors', 'Lords of the Council' and 'Magistrates' are functionally differentiated members of the Church in exactly the same way as 'Bishops, Priests and Deacons'. Only one head can rule the body, exercising supreme authority 'as well in all spiritual or ecclesiastical causes as temporal'. Civil polity therefore, like ecclesiastical polity, requires a graded distinction of ranks and function and depends upon the principle of subordination. In such a Church/commonwealth indeed,

---

[40] Ronald B. Bond, ed. *Certain Sermons or Homilies (1547) and A Homily against Disobedience and Wilful Rebellion (1570)* (Toronto, 1987), p. 169; my italics.

[41] Hooker, *Laws of Ecclesiastical Polity* (fn. 3), Bk VIII, i, 5.

ecclesiastical polity is merely a subset of civil polity and the distinction between the two is uncertain. John Jewel defended parliamentary control of the Tudor Church against papist propaganda (*Apology*, 1562) on the grounds that Parliament was 'a body of Christians, both lay and clerical, representing the whole Christian commonwealth'.[42]

Dissenters from the Restoration settlement of 1662 dissented first and foremost from episcopalian *ecclesiastical* polity and from the 'popish liturgy' which presupposed and ratified it. But in so doing they were obliged to dissent from the wider *civil* polity in which the Church establishment was embedded. Though the Presbyterians among them, at least, might have settled for the principle of subordination within a polity of their own choosing, their failure to hijack the establishment during the Great Rebellion compelled them eventually to look for an ideological alternative in democratical principles.

III

In Section I of this Chapter I have shown that the *Book of Common Prayer* transmits a Catholic ecclesiology: a biblical and patristic understanding of the Church as a divine society, appropriately represented by the metaphor of the body of Christ; in and through which – *and only in and through which* – each human individual may be reborn in the image of God and live the new life of the Risen Christ. I have also shown that because, on this view, Christ is the 'only mediator' between God and man, it is necessary that he should be both God and man. Orthodox (Nicaean and Chalcedonian) Christology implies and is implied by Catholic ecclesiology.

In Section II I have shown that Catholic ecclesiology seems to imply, and at any rate is fully congruent with, an organicist conception of the 'church militant' here on earth; and therefore with an hierarchical ecclesiastical polity dependent upon the principle of subordination. I have also shown that in a Christian society the Church subsumes the state; that kings and 'all that are put in authority' under them exercise a differentiated function within the body; and hence that ecclesiastical polity is a subset of civil polity. The principle of subordination extends to all aspects of human social life, wherein temporal society imitates the eternal. For 'God . . . appointed his angels and heavenly creatures in all obedience to serve and honour his majestie'. In the words of the Elizabethan *Homily against Disobedience and Wilful Rebellion*, ordered at the

---

[42] Cross, *Royal Supremacy*, p. 30.

Restoration to be read at the annual celebration of King Charles the Martyr: 'it is evident, that obedience is the principal vertue of all vertues, and in deede the very roote of all vertues, and the cause of all felicitie'.[43]

Enough should now have been said to make it perfectly clear just what the English Protestant Dissenters were dissenting from. It remains to consider how this may bear upon the putative nexus between the theology and the political theory of Dissent.

According to Joseph Priestley, 'as Dissenters we have no peculiar principles of civil government at all'. Both he and Richard Price were at pains to disavow republicanism or 'a pure Democracy', and affirm their attachment to limited monarchy and 'the constitution of England'.[44] The Dissenters' apprehension 'of any approach towards arbitrary power' is explained as a function of their class location in 'the middling and lower ranks of the people'. There is no connection between the Dissenters' rejection of a 'visible head in religious matters' and 'a fondness for equality, and republican maxims in the state'. Yet all Dissenters are 'friends of liberty'; and Priestley acknowledged that 'the religious system of the Dissenters is unfriendly to arbitrary government in any form, but favourable to liberty in general'.[45] This began to be politically important during the American War, when 'a consistent pro-Americanism was publicized by the Dissenting pulpit thundering forth the rhetoric of liberty', accompanied in many cases by more active opposition to the government.[46] By the end of the century a former Dissenting minister could write that

as a collective body of men (for there are some truly loyal and excellent individuals among them) the protestant dissenters have been aiming to adopt Dr Priestley's elegant term, 'to undermine and blow up the constitution'.[47]

The revolution in France was viewed by the Dissenters 'with an enthusiasm bordering upon frenzy'.[48] Despite Priestley's disclaimer therefore, it should be and actually is possible to distil out of his writings and those of

---

[43] Bond, *Certain Sermons*, p. 209.
[44] Joseph Priestley, *The Theological and Miscellaneous Works &c. of Joseph Priestley, LL.D., F.R.S., &c. with Notes by the Editor*, ed. J.T. Rutt, 25 vols. in 26 (London, 1817–32; repr. New York, 1972), vol. XXII, pp. 354, 357, 351 (hereafter cited as *Works*); Richard Price, *Two Tracts on Civil Liberty, the War with America, and the Debts and Finances of the Kingdom* . . . (London, 1778), containing I, *Observations on the Nature of Civil Liberty* . . . (1776), and II, *Additional Observations* . . . (1777), separately paginated, II, p. 42, 8, n.(a).
[45] Priestley, *Works*, vol. XXII, pp. 356–8.
[46] James E. Bradley, *Religion, Revolution and English Radicalism: Nonconformity in Eighteenth-Century Politics and Society* (Cambridge, 1990), pp. 10, 16.
[47] David Rivers, *Observations on the Political Conduct of the Protestant Dissenters* (London, 1798), cited in the *Anti-Jacobin Review* (1798), 626.   [48] *Anti-Jacobin Review* (1798), 630.

Richard Price a coherent set of political principles which stand sharply opposed to the 'principle of subordination'; and which may be regarded as characteristic of the most articulate, as well as the most extreme of the 'third and last generation' of the Dissenting 'Commonwealth men'.[49] I shall label these principles 'Dissent' to acknowledge that they may not have been held in their entirety by all, even among the tiny intellectual élite known as 'Rational Dissent'.

'Without Religious and Civil liberty', wrote Price in 1776, man is 'a poor and abject animal . . . bending his neck to the yoke of every silly creature who has the insolence to pretend to authority over him.'[50] 'Dissent' begins with a total repudiation of the doctrine that 'obedience is the principal vertue of all vertues . . . the cause of all felicitie'. Obedience of some kind there must be, of course, else society 'cannot avoid falling into a state of anarchy', as Price made clear in his famous sermon 'On the Love of our Country'. But such obedience is due, not so much to one's superiors in Church and state as to those 'regulations agreed upon by the community' without which 'the ends of government cannot be obtained'. The principle of subordination is to be abandoned and a merely instrumental obedience put in its place: 'the dominion of Kings changed for the dominion of laws, and the dominion of priests giving way to the dominion of reason and conscience'.[51]

By *civil liberty* Price generally means what Priestley more carefully defined as *political liberty*.[52] Now such 'liberty . . . is too imperfectly defined when it is said simply to be "a Government by LAWS and not by MEN"'. It is essential that 'all the members of a state' should participate in the making of such laws;[53] and also that they have the power 'of arriving at the public offices, or, at least, of having votes in the nomination of those who fill them'.[54]

Priestley had shrewdly noted that Dissenters 'agree in nothing but in dissenting from the doctrine and discipline of the Established Church': as a body they are so scissile that 'it is almost impossible for them to act in consent on anything'.[55] Price argued that 'to be free is to be governed by one's own will, and to be governed by the will of another is characteristic of *Servitude*'.[56] It is this view of the intransigent individualism of their

---

[49] Caroline Robbins, *The Eighteenth-Century Commonwealthman* (Cambridge, MA., 1961), p. 7.

[50] Price, *Two Tracts* (fn. 44), I, pp. 5–6.

[51] Ellis Sandoz, ed., *Political Sermons of the American Founding Era, 1730–1805* (Indianapolis, 1991), pp. 1016, 1027.   [52] Priestley, *Works* (fn. 44), vol. XXII, p. 11; cf. Price, *Two Tracts* (fn. 44), II, p. 13 n.(a).

[53] Price, *Two Tracts* I, pp. 7–8.   [54] Priestley, *Works*, vol. XXII, p. 11.   [55] *Ibid.*, pp. 341, 335.

[56] Price, *Two Tracts* I, p. 11.

co-religionists that informs the 'Dissenting' conception of society inspired by John Locke, as 'a number of persons united by their common interest, and by the use of the same measures to promote that interest'. The state is not a divinely ordained *remedium peccatorum*: it is a man-made instrument for achieving the – strictly limited – common goals of a number of radically isolated individuals. It follows immediately from this that '*all civil power is ultimately derived from the people*' and not '*from God*'; that 'kings, senators, or nobles . . . are the *servants of the public*'; and that 'an injured and insulted people' may 'assert their natural rights' and punish a delinquent executive. In the seventeenth century most 'friends of liberty' still believed in the '*sacredness of kingly power*'; but 'whenever that superstitious notion shall be obliterated' then even regicide 'will appear an immortal honour to this country'. What also follows is what, with the aid of hindsight, we recognise as the most literally 'radical' doctrine of 'Dissent': which is that 'the good and happiness of the members, that is *the majority of the members of any state*, is the great standard by which every thing relating to that state must finally be determined'.[57] 'It was this passage', according to one commentator, 'that inspired Jeremy Bentham'.[58]

What is the connection between these 'democratical principles' so vigorously maintained by 'Dissent', and the heterodox Christology of the '*Rational* or *Unitarian* Dissenters' who held that religion ought to be 'put upon the same footing with other branches of knowledge'?[59] It has already been noted that no *unique* link exists between Catholic ecclesiology (the Church as body of Christ) and establishment ecclesiastical polity (hierarchy). For as Hooker had conceded, plenary authority was left to 'the whole body of the Church', wherefore though bishops may 'vouch with conformity of truth that their authority is descended . . . from . . . the . . . apostles' yet they 'must acknowledge that the Church hath power . . . to take it away'.[60] It is possible in principle for a Presbyterian or Congregational polity to be determined by the authority of the whole Church. It is also possible, moreover, that such a polity might be consistent with a high degree of subordination in civil polity. During the interregnum, as Priestley observed, 'The *Presbyterians* . . . would have made a most intolerant [establishment], similar to that of the Church of England in those days'.[61]

[57] Priestley, *Works*, vol. XXII, pp. 383, 20, 18, 19, 25–6, 13; my italics.
[58] Michael P. Watts, *The Dissenters* (Oxford, 1978), p. 478.
[59] Priestley, *Works*, vol. XV, p. 45; vol. XXII, p. 131; see also vol. V, pp. 154, 264, 267, 285, 489, 493.
[60] Hooker, *Laws of Ecclesiastical Polity* (fn. 3), Bk VII, v, 8.   [61] Priestley, *Works*, vol. XXII, p. 315.

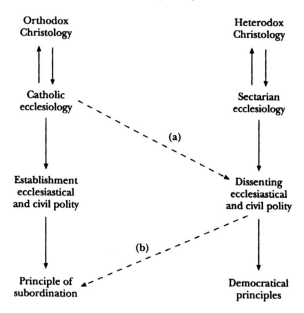

Figure 8.2: Possible connections between Christology and political principles

These possibilities are displayed in Figure 8.2, in which the dotted arrows show the trains of reasoning by which an orthodox Dissenter could adopt democratic principles on the one hand (a), and a Rational Dissenter maintain the principle of subordination on the other (b). But in fact these lines of argument seldom appear in the Dissenting literature of the period. Though Hooker had admitted – to use modern terminology – that episcopacy is of the *bene esse*, rather than the *esse* of the Church, the conditions for a change of polity ('universal consent upon urgent cause') are too stringent to have been met either then or previously. As for the second link (b), it has been strongly argued by James E. Bradley that

The distinctive contribution of nonconformity to political radicalism is found neither in its orthodoxy nor its heterodoxy, but in its interpretation of human autonomy and *ecclesiastical polity*, and the application of these doctrines in a revolutionary setting.[62]

Though many or most Dissenters, especially among the wealthy, may have insisted upon subordination in their households and businesses,[63]

---

[62] Bradley, *Religion, Revolution and English Radicalism* (fn. 46), p. 137 and *passim*; my italics.
[63] See, e.g., Priestley *Works*, vol. xxv, pp. 36–8.

their political principles are adequately described by the 'Dissent' of
Priestley and Price. Though it cannot be rigorously demonstrated,
therefore, that 'radical politics' are actually 'entailed by Socinianism',
there is much to be said for Priestley's view that 'the religious system of
the Dissenters is unfriendly to arbitrary government in any form'.
Above all this is the case with the 'religious system' of the Rational
Dissenters.

For – to paraphrase the quotation from Jonathan Clark at the beginning of this article – a Christology that denies the two natures in the one
Person of Christ (and that therefore rejects the doctrine of the Holy
Trinity) destroys the conception of Christ as a mediator between God
and man. It is not possible for humans to restore the *imago dei* defaced by
the Fall – to achieve union with God by union with Christ in his mystical
body, the Church. The Pauline conception of the church, and its patristic and mediaeval elaboration in Catholic ecclesiology, can be dispensed
with. The Church can be regarded not as a divine society outside of
which there can be no salvation, but simply as a voluntary association: an
option for 'those that dislike that mode of worship which is prescribed by
public authority'.[64] The link between ecclesiology and ecclesiastical
polity is broken; and so is that between ecclesiastical and civil polity.
Church order becomes a private matter to be decided by each association of like-minded believers choosing to describe itself as a 'Church'. As
to public order, 'liberty' can take pride of place and 'obedience' be radically deflated. A substantial portion of Priestley's published works – certainly more than 50 per cent – can be regarded as a sustained attempt to
establish these propositions.

Priestley's fundamental assumption is that Christianity is and ought to
be capable of being 'properly *understood*'. His 'great outline' takes exactly
one hundred words and contains 'nothing that any person could imagine
would lead to much subtle speculation, at least such as could excite ani-
mosity'. Any appearance of 'mystery' in Christianity is evidence of some
'corruption' of its pristine intelligibility. The use of ritual, symbol, artis-
tic or poetic imagery is always 'superstitious' and must be ruthlessly eliminated by all the 'rational'. An example of the Corpus Christi procession
in Paraguay 'fully confirms . . . the boundless exuberance of the human
imagination in things of this nature, and thereby supplies a strong argument for an early and vigorous opposition to them'. 'The friends of
genuine . . . and rational Christianity' are therefore grateful to infidels

---

[64] Price (1789) in Sandoz, *Political Sermons* (fn. 51), p. 1015.

such as Gibbon, for by their attacks 'whatever has been found to be untenable has been gradually abandoned'.[65]

Upon this basis Priestley constructed his *Institutes of Natural and Revealed Religion*, the *History of the Corruptions of Christianity, An History of Early Opinions Concerning Jesus Christ, A General History of the Christian Church, Discourses on the Evidences of Revealed Religion*, and *Notes on all the Books of Scripture*.[66] Texts of scripture which seem to support the doctrine of the Incarnation (e.g. John 1:14, 8:58, 9:38, 20:28; Matt. 28:18, etc.) are dismissed as 'figurative', or given a naturalistic explanation, or simply ignored. Passages in the gospels (e.g. John 14:6) or Epistles (e.g. 1 Cor. 15:22) which imply that Christ mediates between God and man and that the latter have access to God, 'in' 'through', 'by', or 'with' Christ are similarly treated. All evidence that Christ made 'Atonement' for the human race is merely 'figurative'. It is to the Pelagian controversy that 'we owe the doctrines of *original sin, predestination* . . . and ultimately that of *atonement*': because of St Augustine's 'superstitious and absurd opinion' that baptism is a 'washing away sin'. It 'immediately follows' from the recovery by Faustus Socinus of 'the original doctrine of the proper *humanity of Christ*' that 'his death could not in any proper sense of the word, atone for the sins of other men'.[67]

Because of Priestley's denial of, or inability to comprehend, the Pauline doctrine of the Church as the 'mystical body of Christ' there can be 'no *human authority* in matters of religion'.[68] Moreover, even were Christ incarnated in the Church, a denial of the Atonement destroys any idea of the Church as 'the ark of salvation'. There can be no reason to insist on unity, hence no meaning to be attached to Hooker's conception of the identity of Church and state in 'this realm of England'. Priestley derided Burke for his view of 'church establishment . . . as . . . an indissoluble union'; that for the English, 'church and state are ideas inseparable in their minds'.[69] His polemical strategy, repeated in many of his writings, is to ignore the theologically defensible conception of a *union* of Church and state; attribute to his opponents the entirely different, Warburtonian theory of an *alliance* between the two; and then to dispose of the latter. Now Warburton's 'alliance' is fatally vulnerable to the necessity of regarding 'Church' and 'State' as separate entities. By ignoring the conception of union and concentrating on that of alliance,

---

[65] Priestley *Works*, vol. v, pp. 10, 480, 233; vol. XXII, p. 364; vol. v, p. 493.
[66] These works, published between 1772 and 1804, may be found in Priestley *Works*, vols. II, v, vi, VIII–X, XV, and XI–XIV, respectively. [67] *Ibid.*, vol. v, pp. 105–21; vol. VIII, pp. 522–3; vol. v, p. 151.
[68] *Ibid.*, vol. v, p. 434. [69] Burke, *Reflections* (fn. 30), pp. 147–8; cited Priestley *Works*, vol. XII, p. 191.

therefore, the way was opened for Priestley's view of the state as an instrumental association of individuals, and to his claim that 'a multiplicity of sects' is 'beneficial to the state'.[70]

I hope it is clear from the foregoing that the correspondence between the Arian or Socinian Christology of the Rational Dissenters and the democratic principles of 'Dissent' is sufficiently close for the former to be justly regarded as 'conceptually basic' to the latter. Whether the orthodox Dissenters should therefore be regarded as 'irrational', and whether all the Rational Dissenters perceived the congruence between their theology and their politics as acutely as Priestley did, are matters for a larger inquiry. One thing is certain: the Rational Dissenters as a class had the intellectual ferocity to go for the jugular: the central Christian conviction that Jesus Christ is mediator between God and man. The destruction of this one proposition, as I have shown in Sections I and II, is sufficient to bring down the entire structure of establishment social theory.

Professor Horton Davies[71] has described the evolution of Unitarian worship during the eighteenth century. Beginning with proposals by heterodox Churchmen such as Clarke and Whiston for revision of the Prayer Book, and ending with William Wood's Mill Hill liturgy of 1801, there are certain common themes. In the first place a pre-composed liturgy was desired by the Rational, partly as a safeguard against enthusiasm, partly to distinguish their meetings from the uncouth spontaneity of their social inferiors, the orthodox Dissenters. Secondly, the three creeds, the *Gloria Patri* and all other references to the Holy Trinity were to be expunged. Thirdly, the traditional endings of prayers, 'through Jesus Christ . . .', all prayers addressed to Christ, all biblical material relating to the Incarnation of God in Christ (including the Virgin Birth), and any hint that baptism is incorporation into the body of Christ were gradually abandoned; for these imply or suggest in some way the fundamental doctrine to be denied: that Christ is mediator. Finally, as the inevitable (and sought for) consequence of that denial, hierarchy and the sacerdotal function of ministers were eliminated: absolutions and consecrations had to go and even blessings were suspect.

If Christ be not the mediator, the question must arise as to his function, if any, in a theology of true religion. In general, Rational Dissenters were silent on this point though Priestley at any rate believed in the Resurrection and the Second Advent.[72] Whether from habit or

[70] See, e.g., Priestley, *Works*, vol. XXII, pp. 88–99, 229, 233, etc., and *ibid.*, 373–9.
[71] Davies, *Worship and Theology* (fn. 8), ch. 4.   [72] Priestley *Works*, xv, pp. 325–48.

deference to scriptural phraseology both Price and Priestley made occasional, infrequent allusion in their sermons to Christ as 'saviour'.[73] The question then becomes, from what are humans believed to be 'saved' by Christ? Any recognition of the traditional Pauline, Augustinian doctrine of original sin and the Fall was deeply repugnant to Rational minds, partly because it mocked their religion of benevolence and enlightenment, partly because any useful theory of the Atonement seemed bound to lead back to the 'gloomy and cruel superstition' that God and man are estranged, and that Christ can reunite the two.

It was left to the last generation of Rational Dissent to accept the full implications of this difficulty; and also to push to its furthest extent the repudiation of the principle of subordination. In that he weakened somewhat in his third edition, the second edition of William Godwin's *Political Justice* (1796) represents the intellectual high-water mark of Rational Dissent. Godwin acknowledges an 'author of the universe' who allows no miracles and whose functions seem to extend no further than creation. There is no mention of Christ. It is impossible that there should be any 'innate perverseness' in humans, 'for man is thought, and, till thought began, he had no propensities either to good or evil'.[74] Hence the 'original sin of the worst men' is the perverseness of social institutions such as private property, marriage, wage labour and the like which cause men to become evil. In principle all of these can be reduced to inequality of property, hence 'salvation' is a strictly temporal objective to be achieved by the equalisation of property.[75] This is not to be performed within political society however, but rather by the dissolution of political society. For even the instrumental 'obedience' admitted by Price and Priestley is objectionable; moreover, all society requires interdependence, and it is interdependence that underlies the principle of subordination, as Jonathan Swift explained so lucidly in his sermon *On Mutual Subjection*:

God Almighty hath been pleased to put us into an imperfect state, where we have perpetual occasion of each other's assistance. There is none so low, as not to be in a capacity of assisting the highest; nor so high, as not to want the assistance of the lowest.[76]

---

[73] See, e.g., Sandoz, *Political Sermons* (fn. 51), pp. 1022, 1025, 1027; Priestley *Works*, vol. xv, pp. 356, 381, 443.

[74] William Godwin, *Enquiry Concerning Political Justice and its Influence on Morals and Happiness.* 2nd edn, 2 vols. (London, 1796), vol. II, p. 340.

[75] A.M.C. Waterman, *Revolution, Economics and Religion: Christian Political Economy, 1798–1833* (Cambridge, 1991), pp. 72–81.   [76] *On Mutual Subjection.*

Now 'where there is a mutual dependence, there must be a mutual duty, and consequently a mutual subjection'; and 'the practice of this duty . . . would make us rest contented in the several stations of life, wherein God hath thought fit to place us'.[77] Godwin faced the problem squarely and frankly. 'Everything', he declared with characteristic rigour, 'that is usually understood by the term cooperation, is in some degree, an evil.' All human society, even that of marriage and the family, must go: 'we ought to be able to do without one another'.[78] Neither 'rationality' nor 'dissent' could further go.

[77] *The English Sermon: an Anthology*, 3 vols. (Cheadle, 1976): vol. II, 1650–1750, [ed.] C.H. Sisson, pp. 309, 312.
[78] Godwin, *Enquiry Concerning Political Justice and its Influence on Morals and Happiness*. 3rd edn, 2 vols. (London, 1798), vol. II, pp. 501, 503.

CHAPTER 9

Anglican latitudinarianism, Rational Dissent and political radicalism in the late eighteenth century

John Gascoigne

Eighteenth-century religion, once consigned to the unfashionable outer suburbs of the historical polity, has become increasingly central to historians' understanding of the way in which eighteenth-century society functioned. Where once easy generalisations about the growth of secularisation in the eighteenth century prevailed, historians have become ever more attentive to the way in which contemporaries continued to draw on religious roots in justifying the varied facets of their lives from politics to family life. Such an emphasis on the role of religion forms part of a more general reassessment of the place of ideology in a century where once political behaviour was explained in Namierite fashion as being explicable in terms of such uncomplicated human motives as the quest for office. Indeed, it was often the task of the historian of eighteenth-century politics to strip away the outer ideological garments sometimes used to cloak such motives and to expose the naked ambition that such rhetoric sought to conceal. Later historians of the eighteenth century who drew on Marxist conceptions of the workings of society were also inclined to discount such ideological outpourings as a mask for a different set of more basic motivations based around class interest.

Conflicts which once might have been explained in Namierite terms as the clash of political cliques – or, in Marxist terms, as the consequences of the collision of class interests – have come increasingly to be viewed as explicable in terms of the ideological justifications advanced by contemporaries themselves – justifications that drew extensively on religious language. Both the work of Clark and Bradley, for example, place religious considerations in the foreground of their explanation of the dynamics of Hanoverian political life. In his seminal study, *English*

This essay is a partially revised version of my article 'Anglican Latitudinarianism and Political Radicalism in the Late Eighteenth Century', *History*, 70 (1971), 22–38. I am grateful to the editor of *History* for permission to reproduce it.

Society 1688–1832 (1985), Clark trenchantly argues the case for viewing eighteenth-century England as an aristocratic confessional state dominated by a traditional, land-owning class whose position was shored up by the ideological mortar provided by an Anglican political theology. It follows, then, that for Clark the political radicalism that emerged in the age of the American Revolution had religious roots drawing on the increasingly assertive stance of the Dissenters and on the religious heterodoxy, especially in Trinitarian theology, which infiltrated both Dissent and the Established Church. His recent work, *The Language of Liberty 1660–1832* (1994), represents a further extension of this thesis since he argues that the American Revolution can be viewed as in some senses a war of religion. The ideological clashes generated by the conflict between Britain and its refractory Thirteen Colonies can, he suggests, be regarded as the magnification on to a larger screen of the debates between the Established Church and Dissent which were increasingly colouring political life within Britain itself. As Clark writes, 'the American Revolution displays, on a vast canvas, all these ancient British and ecclesiastical conflicts, played out to a conclusion'.[1]

For Bradley, too, Dissent played a critical role in transforming British political life in the age of the American Revolution both in the realm of ideas, by creating new forms of political ideology that questioned the traditional ascendancy of the landed classes, and in the realm of action, by mobilising opposition to British policy towards the American colonies from within their own ranks and, more menacingly, from artisans of all religious hues. But, for Bradley, in contrast to Clark, such behaviour indicates the political and religious pluralism that the traditional constitution could accommodate. '[S]ociety', he argues, 'was not as unified politically, socially, or religiously as recent revisionists would have us believe.'[2] For, in Bradley's account, British political life was sufficiently diversified and flexible not to depend on the ideological dominance of the Established Church. Dissenter and Anglican might have different conceptions of the way in which society should be ordered but both could work within the framework of eighteenth-century political life, albeit with some inevitable conflict.

Given such a polarisation in the historiography of late eighteenth-century political radicalism between Clark's conception of an Anglican

---

[1] J.C.D. Clark, *The Language of Liberty 1660–1832. Political Discourse and Social Dynamics in the Anglo-American World* (Cambridge, 1994), p. 305.
[2] J.E. Bradley, *Religion, Revolution and English Radicalism. Nonconformity in Eighteenth-Century Politics and Society* (Cambridge, 1990), p. 421.

hegemony being undermined by the Trojan horse of Dissent and Bradley's view that Dissenting and Anglican-based political ideologies could coexist peacefully, if noisily, it is instructive to take as a case study a group of Anglican religious radicals who ultimately joined with the Rational Dissenters. In the first place the fact that such Anglican heterodox writers reached theological and political conclusions very similar to the more radical Rational Dissenters, despite their varying institutional origins, suggests that such religious and, by extension, political radicalism cannot be explained solely by the contrasting forms of Church government within the Dissenting and Anglican folds. It does, therefore, suggest some qualification to the view advanced by Bradley that 'While some so-called rational Dissenters derived their political views in part from their heterodox theology, the common heritage of a radically separated ecclesiastical polity was controlling for both the "rational" and the orthodox alike.'[3] For, as this study attempts to show, such Anglican radicals arrived at a critique of the existing constitution in Church and state which drew on theological roots that were independent of a Dissenting polity.

However, the fact that – as this study also attempts to show – such radical political and religious conclusions were reached from the Anglican theological tradition of latitudinarianism, which had long been a part of the theological landscape of the Established Church, also suggests that Clark's conception of a unified Anglican hegemony needs qualification. The range of theological positions within the late eighteenth-century Church ranging from sympathisers with the erstwhile Anglican radicals to their determined opponents reflects the wide boundaries of theological debate within the eighteenth-century Church more generally. This theological diversity was reflected in political divisions within the Church over the American War with a small group of Anglican clergy (including a few bishops) siding with the opponents of the War while the great bulk of the clergy supported the government. Nonetheless, the increasingly strident challenges to the constituted order in Church and state in the late eighteenth century meant that Anglican ultra-latitudinarians found the Church less hospitable to those sharing their heterodox beliefs. The exclusion or marginalisation of such dissidents gives credence to Bradley's contention that this period sees 'a perceived resurgence of authoritarianism in Church and State'[4] – a view

---

[3] *Ibid.*, p. 4.
[4] *Ibid.*, p. 2. See also J.E. Bradley, 'The Anglican Pulpit, the Social Order, and the Resurgence of Toryism during the American Revolution', *Albion*, 21 (1989), 361–88.

about which Clark, who views the eighteenth-century Church as being more consistently conservative, is sceptical.[5]

Nonetheless, Clark's view that religious heterodoxy was one of the viruses that destroyed the old unreformed order is borne out by the wide measure of political change that such former Anglican religious radicals came to advocate. Clark, indeed, sees such religious radicals, whether of Anglican or Dissenting provenance, as the equivalent of the *philosophes* who paved the way for the ideological overthrow of the continental old régime[6]. But the forms of thought we associate with the Enlightenment – an emphasis on the role of reason, on the possibilities of progress and human improvement – could be used by both the defenders as well as the opponents of the established order. Again the wide ideological boundaries of old-régime Britain are evident – the language of Enlightenment could be embraced by an establishment confident that it had nothing to fear from the exercise of reason and confident that its institutions were no bar to human progress even if it might recoil from the more radical conclusions that might be drawn from such premises. For though Churchman and Dissenter frequently wrote and acted as though they inhabited two different nations, both the eighteenth-century Established Church and its separated Protestant brethren responded in similar ways to the challenge of integrating Enlightenment thought and traditional Christian theology. In both communities theologians sought to illustrate how the choicest fruits of human reason – of which the ultimate exemplar was the great work of Newton – could be combined with belief in the Christian deity. Both Churchman and Dissenter also frequently laboured to show that many of the received practices and even some doctrines of the Christian Church were *adiophora* – things indifferent – which should not be permitted to stand in the way of an enlightened Christianity or a more fully comprehensive Church order.[7] The object of this essay, then, is to show how within the Anglican fold such an emphasis on rational Christianity could – as it did in the case of the

---

[5] J.C.D. Clark, 'England's Ancien Regime as a Confessional State', *Albion*, 21 (1989), 450–74.

[6] J.C.D. Clark, *English Society, 1688–1832* (Cambridge, 1985), p. 7.

[7] Among the works on late eighteenth-century Dissent and political radicalism are A. Lincoln, *Some Political and Social Ideas of English Dissent* (Cambridge, 1938); U. Henriques, *Religious Toleration in England 1787–1833* (London, 1961); R.E. Richey, 'The Origins of British Radicalism: The Changing Rationale for Dissent', *Eighteenth-Century Studies*, 7 (1973–4), 179–92; I. Kramnick, 'Religion and Radicalism: English Political Theory in the Age of Revolution', *Political Theory*, 5 (1977), 505–34; and J.E. Bradley, *Religion, Revolution and English Radicalism* (fn. 2). O.M. Griffiths, *Religion and Learning* (Cambridge, 1935), provides the fullest survey of theological developments within eighteenth-century Dissent, though it has little to say about any possible links between theology and political thought.

Dissenters – produce agitation for change which challenged the accepted order in both Church and state. Indeed, by the late eighteenth century the Established Church had produced its own Dissenting separatists in the form of a group of Cambridge Unitarians who pushed the boundaries of enlightened Christianity beyond even the elastic limits tolerated by the Church.

Like the proponents of Rational Dissent, too, the advocates of 'enlightened Christianity' within the Established Church naturally looked to the Whigs for political and ideological succour. The Whigs were the defenders of the Revolutionary Settlement and the Protestant succession in the House of Hanover and, in consequence, were associated with a style of kingship and Church order that reflected the imperatives of these constitutional upheavals: hence their emphasis on the role of Parliament and, conversely, their efforts to decrease the Established Church's liking for sermons on the 'divinity doth hedge a king'. However inappropriately, too, the Whigs claimed that their political principles – such as the theory of the social compact – were based on reason in contrast to the appeal to tradition which was the hallmark of the Tories. Whig political principles and 'enlightened Christianity' – whether in its Anglican or Dissenting dress – formed a natural partnership in the face of the continuing nostalgia for a divine-right monarchy and a confessional state which shaped the outlook of many of the lower ranks of the Anglican clergy.

The continuing allegiance of many of the lower clergy to the Tory cause did mean that the Church, during the reigns of George I and George II, harboured many a critic of the constitutional practices of the Whig oligarchs[8] – a tradition which, in turn, helps to account for the existence of a smaller but very vocal body of Whig clergy who tirelessly asserted that the activities of their Tory clerical counterparts endangered the Revolutionary Settlement in Church and state and that Whig principles and Anglican doctrine, if correctly viewed, could exist in peaceful amity. While the Whig oligarchs naturally encouraged such clerical defenders of the Hanoverian order, a number of these apologists were to become so committed to the reforming 'Commonwealth' tradition of Whig ideology – as historians of the intellectual origins of the American Revolution such as Robbins, Bailyn and Bonwick have shown[9]

---

[8] L. Colley, *In Defiance of Oligarchy: The Tory Party 1714–60* (Cambridge, 1982), pp. 104–17 and 153–7.

[9] C. Robbins, *The Eighteenth-Century Commonwealthman* (Cambridge, MA, 1959); B. Bailyn, *The Ideological Origins of the American Revolution* (Cambridge, MA, 1967); and C. Bonwick, *English Radicals and the American Revolution* (Chapel Hill, NC, 1977).

– that they developed views about the nature of Church and state that could no longer be comfortably accommodated within the confines of the unreformed constitution. While such Churchmen naturally tended to focus their criticisms of the eighteenth-century constitution on the defects of the Church, this concern for ecclesiastical reform was in turn to lead to a more critical attitude to the constitution generally – a transition from theological to political radicalism which is the theme of this chapter.

The name given to the clerical Whigs was generally 'the latitudinarians', a word that dated back to the highly-charged religious atmosphere of the late seventeenth century. Its meaning was vague – one pamphlet described a latitudinarian as 'a Gentleman of a wide swallow'[10] – but the term was meant to suggest theological breadth rather than depth and an emphasis on the few essentials that could unite English Protestants rather than the inessentials that divided them. The latitudinarians were also known for their emphasis on natural rather than revealed theology since they believed that the essentials of Christian revelation could be confirmed by the study of nature which made manifest the mind of its Creator – thus they were among the earliest of Newton's disciples and played an important part in the dissemination of his work.[11] Though the latitudinarians did not form a clearly defined party, contemporaries (and, in particular, High Church critics) used the term to designate an important, and increasingly influential, body of opinion within the Established Church.

The eighteenth-century latitudinarians' view of Church and state had been shaped in the vitriolic debates between High and Low Churchmen which came to a head in the reign of Queen Anne. While High Churchmen such as Sacheverell set out to demonstrate that the Glorious Revolution did not undermine traditional Anglican reverence for passive obedience to the Lord's Anointed, latitudinarians such as Hoadly argued that the Revolutionary Settlement demanded a different understanding of the relations between Church and state – indeed, Hoadly delighted in being called by such abusive labels as *Low Churchman or Moderate Man* since these were 'Names made use of to revile those who are the firmest Friends to the *Late Revolution*'.[12] In his pamphlet, *The*

---

[10] E. Fowler, *The Principles and Practices of Certain Moderate Divines of the Church of England* . . . (London, 1670), p. 10.
[11] M.C. Jacob, *The Newtonians and the English Revolution 1689–1720* (Hassocks, Sussex, 1976); J. Gascoigne, 'Politics, Patronage and Newtonianism: The Cambridge Example', *Historical Journal*, 27 (1984), 1–24.
[12] *The Works of Benjamin Hoadly*, ed. John Hoadly, 3 vols. (London, 1773), vol. II, p. 622. Cited in E.R. Bingham, 'The Political Apprenticeship of Benjamin Hoadly', *Church History*, 16 (1947), 162.

Happiness of the Present Establishment and The Unhappiness of Absolute Monarchy (1708), Hoadly put forward the view that the Glorious Revolution demanded that doctrines of divine right and passive obedience had to give way to some notion of a contract between the governing and the governed: 'The great *End* of *Government*', he wrote, 'is the Happiness of the *governed Society*' and 'the *Happiness* of a *governed Society* consists in the Enjoyment of *Liberty*, *Property*, and the *free Exercise of Religion*' – prerogatives that Englishmen owed 'entirely to the late *Revolution*, and those *Principles* upon which it was founded'.[13]

What was to make Hoadly 'the best-hated clergyman of the century amongst his own order' (as Leslie Stephen described him)[14] were the implications for Church government that Hoadly drew from his political principles. To Hoadly, the basis of High Church opposition to the Revolutionary Settlement lay in the claim that the Church had a right to an existence independent of the state – it was this view that had led to the schism of the Nonjurors, who claimed to be maintaining the purity of Anglican doctrine in opposition to the constituted government of the realm, and which lay behind the High Church claim that Convocation was independent of Parliament. Consequently, in his *Preservative against the Principles and Practices of the Nonjurors* (1716), Hoadly maintained a position of a thorough-going Erastianism. In the following year his sermon, 'The Nature of the Kingdom or Church of Christ' – a work which sparked off the famous Bangorian Controversy – elaborated further these principles to the point where he argued that the Church was an entirely human institution which should be organised by the state since Christ had 'left behind Him no visible, human authority . . . no judges over the consciences or religion of His people'.[15] Even Hoadly's fellow Whigs on the episcopal bench drew back from the full force of such arguments which, in Bolingbroke's words, reduced a bishop to being 'nothing but a layman with a crook in his hand';[16] but, as Hoadly's steady advance from the lowly see of Bangor to those of Hereford, Salisbury and Winchester indicates, such views were rewarded handsomely by the Whig administration. Moreover, Hoadly outlived most of his critics and

---

[13] Benjamin Hoadly, 'The Happiness of the Present Establishment, and Unhappiness of Absolute Monarcy', in *Works*, vol. II , p. III. On Hoadly's influence in New and old England see Bailyn, *Ideological Origins* (fn. 9), pp. 37–9, J. Kenyon, *Revolution Principles: The Politics of Party 1689–1720* (Cambridge, 1977), p. 116, and R. Browning, *Political and Constitutional Ideas of the Court Whigs* (Baton Rouge, Louisiana, 1982).

[14] L. Stephen, *History of English Thought in the Eighteenth Century*, 2 vols. (London, 1876, repr. 1962), vol. II, p. 129.   [15] Hoadly, *Works* (fn. 12), vol. II, p. 404. Cited in Sykes, 'Hoadly' (fn. 13), p. 143.

[16] Stephen, *History of English Thought* (fn. 14), vol. II, p. 135.

by his death in 1761 it was claimed that he had 'lived to see the Nation become his converts and sons have blushed, to think their Fathers were his foes'.[17]

Though many of the lower clergy and even a number of the bishops continued to oppose Hoadly's view, these (along with those of his ally, Samuel Clarke) took root in Cambridge, their mutual *alma mater*, where both the Dukes of Newcastle and Grafton[18] during their terms as Chancellors (1748–68 and 1768–1811 respectively) were to use their influence to advance the careers of those who shared Hoadly's Erastianism. When Hoadly's views were attacked, he was defended by an eager flock of Cambridge clients. Thomas Herne (who wrote under the pseudonym, *Phileutherus Cantabrigiensis*) set out, in his pamphlet on the Articles of Religion, to defend Hoadly's view that Church ordinances had no divine force; consequently, Herne argued, it was wrong to compel subscription to the Thirty-Nine Articles when 'CONSENT is the only FOUNDATION of *Ecclesiastical* as well as of *Civil Government*'.[19] Similarly, John Jackson, another of Hoadly's Cambridge admirers, argued that just as it was erroneous to think that there are

any *Civil* Powers . . . which are not deriv'd from the People; so it is no less an Error on the other hand to believe that there are any *Spiritual* or *Religious* Powers, the *Exercise* of which may not be deriv'd from them also.

From this it followed, Jackson maintained, that no Church had the right to impose any doctrine 'which is not *clearly* and *expressly* contain'd and *declared to be necessary* in the Gospel'[20] and, suiting the action to the word, he refused to take any further oaths of religious orthodoxy. Ironically, then, Hoadly's Erastianism helped to promote among his followers the view that some of the practices of the Established Church – particularly the imposition of the Thirty-Nine Articles – needed to be reformed, an irritant that was gradually to help produce a more general dissatisfaction with the established order in Church and state.

Nonetheless, like Hoadly himself, most of the latitudinarians continued to subscribe to the Articles, justifying any doubts about the

---

[17] J. Nichols, *Literary Anecdotes of the Eighteenth Century*, 9 vols. (London, 1812–15), vol. III, p. 141.
[18] Grafton was active in advocating ecclesiastical reform and was a warm admirer of Clarke's Arian views on the Trinity. He also defended the Feathers Tavern petitioners from the charge which had been 'industriously propagated by the court party' that the petition was 'set on foot by faction'. Duke of Grafton, *Hints Submitted to the Serious Attention of the Clergy, Nobility and Gentry* (London, 1789), pp. 30–1, 41.
[19] T. Herne, *An Essay on Imposing and Subscribing Articles of Religion* (London, 1719), p. 8.
[20] J. Jackson, *The Grounds of Civil and Ecclesiastical Government* (London, 1718), pp. 20, 38.

doctrine they embodied by arguing that such oaths meant no more than a declaration of loyalty to the Church of England as established. But though few latitudinarians refused to take such doctrinal tests before the reign of George III, some of their number continued to develop Hoadly's views about the nature of the Church. Edmund Law (who became Bishop of Carlisle in 1768 thanks to the influence of the Duke of Grafton, a former student at Peterhouse[21]) set out to demonstrate that revealed doctrine, like other areas of knowledge, was the daughter of time since 'as we continually advance in the study of God's *works*, we shall come to a proportionally better understanding of his word';[22] to insist on adherence to articles and creeds, then, was in Law's view to attempt to freeze Christianity at one point in its continuing development. Appropriately, Law was to be the only one of the bishops to vote in favour of abolishing clerical subscription to the Articles; indeed, in a pamphlet justifying this position, he urged all to assist in the work of improving Church and state 'by embracing all fair opportunities to further, and complete their reformation.'[23]

As Master of Peterhouse from 1756 to 1768, Law had a great deal of influence within Cambridge; his own college produced political and religious reformers such as Jebb, Liddell, Cavendish, Lowther, Meredith, Tierney and Lofft, and his ideas helped to shape the thinking of prominent Cambridge theologians such as William Paley, Richard Watson and John Hey. Significantly, when he became a bishop, he chose as his chaplain John Disney, a young member of Peterhouse who was to become a prominent Unitarian. While Bishop of Carlisle, Law produced an influential edition of Locke's works, the English translation of Locke's *De Toleratione* being undertaken by Miles Popple, a young fellow of Trinity who was later to publish a defence of parliamentary reform and an attack on the idea of virtual representation.[24]

Another of Law's admirers and defenders was Francis Blackburne, who, while an undergraduate at Cambridge, 'acquired a strong attachment to the principles of ecclesiastical and civil liberty' through the

---

[21] *Gentleman's Magazine*, 57 (1787), 744.

[22] E. Law, *Considerations on the State of the World with Regard to the Theory of Religion* (Cambridge, 1745; new edn London, 1820), p. 205. On Law see O. Chadwick, *From Bossuet to Newman* (Cambridge, 1957), p. 83, and R.S. Crane, 'Anglican Apologetics and the Idea of Progress, 1666–1745' in his *The Idea of the Humanities and other Essays*, 2 vols. (Chicago, 1967), vol. II, pp. 214–87.

[23] E. Law, *Considerations on the Propriety of Requiring a Subscription to Articles of Faith* (London, 1774), p. 37.

[24] M. Popple, *Considerations on Reform: With a Specific Plan for a New Representation, Addressed to Charles Grey, Esq.* (London, 1793).

study of Locke and Hoadly.[25] In 1758 Blackburne published a pamphlet[26] maintaining that the arguments employed by many Anglican clergymen to defend their subscription to the Articles were casuistical; though retaining his existing preferments, Blackburne refused any further promotions, since this would require further subscriptions. This work was, however, merely a foretaste of the full-scale attack Blackburne launched on subscription in his highly influential *The Confessional, or a Full and free Enquiry into the Right, Utility, and Success of Establishing Confessions of Faith and Doctrine in Protestant Churches* (1766). Echoing Chillingworth's famous declaration that 'the Bible is the religion of Protestants', Blackburne argued that it was sufficient for intending Anglican clergymen to profess a belief in the Scriptures as the word of God. As a result of the controversy generated by this work, a meeting was held at Feathers Tavern in London in July 1771 and a petition, drawn up by Blackburne, requesting that subscription to the Articles for clergy and graduates be abolished, was signed by some 250 people and sent to the House of Commons. Like Hoadly, Blackburne argued in the petition that the Church was not empowered to prescribe and enforce belief, this being among the 'rights and privileges which they [the petitioners] hold of God only'.[27] Though the term 'rights' is here used in a theological context, it has the overtones of a political demand[28]; it is not surprising, then, that many of the petitioners were subsequently active in political reform movements, particularly after the defeat of the petition in the Commons in February 1772 by 217 votes to 71. The petition, which was largely the work of Cambridge graduates, did, however, lead to Cambridge University abolishing in 1772 the requirement that BAs subscribe to the Articles, though they still had to declare that they were *bona fide* members of the Church of England as by law established.[29]

The case against the Feathers Tavern petition was put with greatest vehemence by Sir William Newdigate, MP for Oxford University, who successfully exploited the fears and prejudices of the Commons by emphasising the political aspects of the issue: 'if you remove this institution', he declared,

[25] F. Blackburne, *Works, Theological and Miscellaneous* . . ., 7 vols. (London, 1804), vol. I, p.iv. On Blackburne's long and close friendship with Law see *ibid.*, pp. xxii–xxiii.

[26] F. Blackburne, *Remarks on the Rev Dr Powell's Sermon in Defence of Subscriptions* (London, 1758).

[27] W. Cobbett, ed., *The Parliamentary History of England: From the Norman Conquest . . . to the Year 1803*, 36 vols. (London, 1806–20), vol. XVII, p. 251.   [28] Lincoln, *Political and Social Ideas* (fn. 7), p. 182.

[29] C.H. Cooper, *Annals of Cambridge*, 5 vols. (Cambridge, 1842–1908), vol. IV, pp. 363–6. A similar proposal was defeated at Oxford in the following year. J.R. Green and G. Robertson, *Studies in Oxford History* (Oxford, 1901), pp. 323–4.

I cannot see how the State can for a moment subsist. Civil and Religious establishments are so linked and incorporated together that, when the latter falls, the former cannot stand. They seem to me to be as inseparably connected as soul and body.[30]

Like North, Burke argued that the risks of reviving 'the dissensions and animosities, which had slept for a century' outweighed the benefits of any change in the Articles which, in any case, should 'remain fixed and permanent like our civil constitution' in order to 'preserve the body ecclesiastical from tyranny and despotism'.[31]

To its opponents, then, the Feathers Tavern petition raised the risk of the canker of change spreading from Church to state; some even regarded the campaign against subscription as the work of crypto-republicans – James Ibbetson, one of Blackburne's first critics, argued that abolition of the Articles would aid Dissenters, 'men of latitude and free thinkers' and others 'who are averse or very indifferent to the regal Government'.[32] There were indeed some grounds for their suspicions: Blackburne was the friend and biographer of the republican, Thomas Hollis, and in the preface to his *Confessional* Blackburne described himself as one of those who have been seized with that 'epidemical malady of *idle* and *visionary* men, THE PROJECTING TO REFORM THE PUBLIC [sic]', a stance that naturally followed from his view that 'The single sole purpose of instituting civil government, is to provide for the temporal security and happiness of mankind.'[33] Appropriately, Blackburne was later a supporter of Wyvill's campaign for parliamentary reform and proposed a variety of measures to limit the power of ministerial patronage including restrictions on the voting of bishops in the House of Lords.[34]

Furthermore, the supporters within the Commons of the Feathers Tavern petition were also known to be sympathetic to reform in matters political.[35] Sir William Meredith, who introduced the bill, had written pamphlets in defence of Wilkes and among its other supporters were men such as John Sawbridge (an ally of Wilkes and one of the founders of the Society for the Supporters of the Bill of Rights), John Dunning (of

---

[30] Cobbett, *Parliamentary History* (fn. 27), vol. XVII, p. 255.   [31] *Ibid.*, pp. 276, 288.

[32] J. Ibbetson, *A Plea for the Subscription of the Clergy to the Thirty-Nine Articles* (London, 1767), p. 48.

[33] Blackburne, *Works* (fn. 25), V, p. 56 and VI, p. 55.

[34] C. Wyvill, *Political Papers Chiefly Respecting the Attempt . . . to Effect a Reformation of the Parliament of Great Britain*, 6 vols. (York, 1794–1802), vol. III, pp. 134–7.

[35] Ditchfield has shown that there was indeed a strong correlation between those MPs who supported the petition and those voting for the Parliamentary Reform Bills of 1783, 1785 and 1793. G.M. Ditchfield, 'The Parliamentary Struggle over the Repeal of the Test and Corporation Acts, 1787–90', *English Historical Review*, 89 (1974), 557–8.

Dunning's motion fame) and Sir George Savile whose bill to secure the rights of voters (which was also actively supported by Sawbridge) had been defeated in the previous year. The link between political and religious reform, then, was quite apparent and does much to explain the failure of the Feathers Tavern petition – a failure which prompted some of its supporters to look even more critically at the deficiencies of the unreformed English constitution.

The most immediate effect of the petition's defeat was to prompt a small group of the signatories to leave the Established Church, the most notable of these being Blackburne's son-in-law, Theophilus Lindsey, a former fellow of St John's College, Cambridge. Blackburne himself strongly opposed Lindsey's departure from the Church of England, since he feared that the latter's open espousal of Unitarianism would undermine the anti-subscription movement as a whole. Indeed, Lindsey did pose a continuing challenge to the Established Church since, after resigning his living, he founded the first Unitarian chapel in Essex Street, London, where the liturgy was based on one that had been drawn up (but never used) by Samuel Clarke in the early eighteenth century, with modifications by 'his friends Dr Jebb, Mr Tyrwhitt, and a few other learned and liberal members of the University of Cambridge'.[36] Though anti-Trinitarianism was forbidden by law, the Essex Street Chapel was allowed to function and became a focus for many in London who held radical religious and political views; among those who attended its services were Benjamin Franklin, Sir George Savile and, in later life, the Duke of Grafton (the Chancellor of Cambridge). Later Lindsey was joined by John Disney, Edmund Law's former chaplain and another of Blackburne's sons-in-law, who, though disappointed by the failure of the Feathers Tavern petition, did not resign his living until 1782.

Disney's political principles are evident in his choice of subject for a sermon on 4 November 1792 (the anniversary of the Glorious Revolution), an address he entitled 'The Progressive Improvement of Civil Liberty'. At a time when the reaction in England against the French Revolution was gathering force, Disney exulted that 'The invasion of the liberties of France, by a leagued conspiracy of foreign force, hath, happily for the liberties of all mankind, been hitherto repelled' and went on to praise America for having 'already redeemed herself from

[36] T. Belsham, *Memoirs of the Late . . . Theophilus Lindsey . . . together with . . . a General View of the Progress of the Unitarian Doctrine . . .* (London, 1812), p. 103.

colonial oppression'. Civil institutions, he insisted, should be formed by the 'expressed agreement, or, implied consent, of their subjects'; if they were not 'there can be no better justification for throwing off the galling yoke, than the first practical opportunity that offers'. His links with the seventeenth-century commonwealthmen are apparent in his dismissive references to the notions of divine right which he associated with High Church sermons on 'the anniversaries of the pretended martyrdom of the tyrant-hypocrite [Charles I] or the restoration of his profligate son [Charles II]'. Lastly, he listed the benefits which would flow to Britain if 'her people were restored to their just and equal share in one branch of the legislature' in what virtually amounted to a description of the Unitarians' overall programme of action: disestablishment of the Church, reform of the criminal law, reduction of taxation and the powers of the state, abolition of slavery and elimination of war.[37]

Ex-Anglican Unitarians such as Lindsey and Disney were naturally drawn to those of a Dissenting background who had come to espouse similar political and religious views – thus Lindsey was a close friend of Priestley (to whom he had been introduced by Blackburne[38]). However, though men like Lindsey and Disney were naturally sympathetic to Dissenters who shared their views – particularly as it became apparent that the wholesale reformation of the Established Church along Unitarian lines, for which Lindsey hoped, was not going to eventuate – the bonds of common education and even intermarriage[39] meant that the former Anglican Unitarians remained a distinct group. The number of those following Lindsey's lead proved very small – only about ten Anglican ministers left the Church and only four became Unitarian ministers[40] – but their energetic espousal of public causes made them a significant group in late eighteenth-century English life.

Perhaps their most notable publicist was John Jebb (another of Law's protégés[41]) who left a tutorship at Peterhouse, Cambridge, in 1775, both on account of his Unitarian beliefs and because of his frustration at the thwarting, by various vested interests, of his proposals for strengthening

---

[37] J. Disney, *Sermons*, 4 vols. (London, 1793–1816), vol. I, pp. 221–9.

[38] Joseph Priestley, *Life and Correspondence of Joseph Priestley, LL.D, FRS*, ed. J. T. Rutt, 2 vols. (London, 1831), vol. I, pp. 80–1.

[39] Lindsey, Disney and Frend (another Cambridge Unitarian) were respectively husbands of Blackburne's step-daughter, daughter, and grand-daughter. The political reformer, Major Cartwright, with whom they were associated, was a cousin of Disney.

[40] E.M. Wilbur, *A History of Unitarianism*, 2 vols. (Cambridge, MA, 1945–1952), vol. II, p. 290.

[41] J. Jebb, *The Works of . . . John Jebb, with Memoirs of the Life of the Author, by J. Disney*, 3 vols. (London, 1787), vol. I, pp. 10, 20.

the University's examination system and broadening its curriculum. Though Lindsey wished Jebb to join him as a minister at the Essex Street Chapel, he turned, with considerable success, from the study of theology to medicine, while maintaining his close involvement with radical politics, which had been evident as early as 1769, when he opposed a loyal address from Cambridge University condemning the Wilkites. At the end of 1779, he put before the freeholders of Middlesex proposals which he had outlined to Sir George Savile as early as 1776: that they should establish an assembly to ensure 'the blessing of an equal, annual, and, universal representation of the commons', making the radical claim that if the Commons ignored such demands the electors could 'in solemn council, declare, that the present house of commons was dissolved'.[42] To further the cause of parliamentary reform Jebb joined with Major John Cartwright in establishing the Society for Constitutional Information in the following year, an association which also had the support of Lindsey and Disney. Cartwright also shared with Jebb – whom he described as 'the friend of my bosom, the pattern of my conduct' – an abhorrence of subscription to the Articles (which Cartwright, as a layman, was spared) and a belief in the inconsistency of 'pure Christianity' with 'the Doctrines of Toryism'.[43] Jebb would also have shared Cartwright's view that 'Religion and politics are . . . much more nearly allied than is commonly imagined, and, indeed, I cannot consider politics in any other light than as practical religion, and pre-eminently so under the Christian dispensation.'[44]

Indeed, the Society owed much of its early vitality to Jebb and his former Cambridge pupils, such as Capel Lofft and John Baynes, and with his death in 1786 its sense of purpose wavered.[45] It was Jebb who developed the view that extraparliamentary conventions had the right to suspend the powers of the Commons if it refused to enact the reforms for which the Society stood and who even suggested that taxes might be withheld to compel Parliament to reform itself. Such a stance increasingly alienated Jebb from the more constitutionally minded Christopher Wyvill, founder of the Yorkshire Association, whose preoccupation with what Jebb saw as mere palliatives, such as Burke's proposed economic

---

[42] *Ibid.*, vol. I, p. 168 and vol. II, pp. 481, 479. See also I.R. Christie, *Wilkes, Wyvill and Reform* (London, 1962), pp. 77–9.

[43] F.D. Cartwright, ed., *The Life and Correspondence of Major Cartwright*, 2 vols. (London, 1826), vol. I, pp. 165, 179; vol. II, pp. 287–8; and vol. I, p. 162.   [44] *Ibid.*, vol. II, p. 216.

[45] E.C. Black, *The Association: British Extraparliamentary Political Organization 1769–1793* (Cambridge, MA, 1963), p. 177, and Jebb, *Works* (fn. 41), vol. I, p. 155.

reforms, prompted Jebb to exclaim to him in August 1781 that 'the spirit of accommodation will ruin us all . . . Equal Representation, Sessional parliaments, and the Universal Right of Suffrage, are points alone worthy of an Englishman's regard . . .'[46]

The theological roots of Jebb's radicalism are evident in his comment that 'the evils of government and the want of felicity in the governed . . . arise from the want of a moral and religious principle, which the religion of the gospel, unveiled in its native excellence can alone afford'. In his view, then, the 'right arrangement of political power' and the 'philological knowledge of the Scriptures'[47] were 'combined causes'; thus, as well as playing a major role in establishing the Society for Constitutional Information, he was also one of the founders of the Society for Promoting the Knowledge of the Scriptures which met at Lindsey's Essex Street Chapel (an organisation which, thanks to Jebb, had the support of Bishop Law). This belief that political and religious reform were intertwined is evident in Jebb's open letters of 1772 written in support of the Feathers Tavern petition, where he described those bishops who opposed abolishing subscription as 'firm and steady supporters' not only of religious but also of civil despotism.[48]

Since Jebb was one of the Unitarians' main publicists, his reputation for being (in Priestley's words) outstanding for his 'ardent zeal for the cause of civil and religious liberty in their full extent'[49] naturally helped to strengthen further in the public mind a strong association between Unitarian theology and agitation for radical political change. But this reputation helped to make the Unitarians an obvious target in the years of reaction that followed the events of 1789 (though Jebb himself died in 1786); the depth of feeling against the Unitarians being evident in the defeat by 142 votes to 63 of Fox's attempt to remove the penal sanctions against anti-Trinitarianism in 1792. In the debate on this bill Burke maintained that the Unitarians were 'not confined to a *theological* sect, but are also a *political* faction', citing a letter of Priestley to Pitt as evidence 'that the designs against the church are concurrent with a design to subvert the state'.[50] Though no Unitarian was prosecuted on theological grounds, the risks involved in promoting the political principles with

---

[46] Wyvill, *Political Papers* (fn. 34), vol. IV, p. 505. On the split between Jebb and Wyvill over the question of an extraparliamentary convention see T.M. Parssinen, 'Association, Convention and Anti-Parliament in British Radical Politics', *English Historical Review*, 88 (1973), 509–10.

[47] Jebb, *Works* (fn. 41), vol. I, p. 189.   [48] *Ibid.*, vol. III, pp. 73–5.

[49] Priestley's warm praise of Jebb forms part of his dedication to Jebb of the *Doctrine of Philosophical Necessity* (1777). Jebb, *Works* (fn. 41) vol. I, pp. 129–30.

[50] E. Burke, *The Works of . . . Edmund Burke*, new edn, 16 vols. (London, 1815–27), vol. II, p. 476.

which this new denomination had become associated were made painfully obvious in the case of Thomas Fyshe Palmer, a former pupil of Jebb, who, after becoming a Unitarian minister at Dundee, was transported to Botany Bay in 1794 for his involvement in the reform movement. Though Palmer was not formally prosecuted for his religious views, the prosecutor warned the jury that the accused was 'a clergyman of that description whose principles are as hostile to the religion of his country, as to the established government of it'.[51]

Another, though less heavily penalised, Cambridge Unitarian who was a victim of the reaction that followed the execution of Louis XVI was William Frend, a fellow of Jesus College, Cambridge, where the latitudinarian tradition was particularly strong. Like Lindsey and Disney (to whom he was later related by marriage), Frend's religious radicalism was associated with a critical attitude to the existing political order. Indeed, it was his sympathy for the goals of the French Revolution that led to his expulsion from the University in 1793, largely at the instigation of the Vice-Chancellor, the evangelical Isaac Milner, a declared foe of 'Jacobins and infidels'. Frend's offence was compounded by the fact that, though a member of a university primarily devoted to the training of clergy for the Established Church, he criticised the constitutional position of the Church of England as well as its Trinitarian theology, arguing that 'The established church of England can be considered only as a political institution' which considerably strengthened the power of the executive in a state where the king was head of the Church.[52]

After leaving Cambridge, Frend became actively involved in London radical politics and was a member of the London Corresponding Society, the first major parliamentary reform organisation to establish links with working-class radicalism. In May 1794, the leaders of both this Society and the Society for Constitutional Information were arrested, the two bodies having co-operated in planning an English national convention along the lines originally suggested by Jebb. The man who had done most to bring the two societies together was Wilkes's former lieutenant, John Horne Tooke, a friend of Lindsey and Disney with whom he had attended the famous meeting of the [Glorious] Revolution Society on 5 November 1789, when Richard Price had delivered his

[51] T.B. and T.J. Howell, eds., *A Complete Collection of State Trials*, 34 vols. (London, 1809–26), vol. XXIII, p. 333.

[52] W. Frend, *Peace and Union Recommended to the Associated Bodies of Republicans and Anti-Republicans* (St Ives, 1793), pp. 26–7. On Frend's trial see F. Knight, *University Rebel: The Life of William Frend 1757–1841* (London, 1971).

sermon celebrating the beginning of the French Revolution,[53] an address which had prompted Burke's *Reflections*. Tooke was also closely associated with Jebb, a fellow founding member of the Society for Constitutional Information; indeed, it was largely thanks to Jebb that Tooke obtained his MA from St John's College, Cambridge, in 1771, despite opposition from Paley, who took exception to Tooke's disrespectful views about the episcopacy. Though Tooke regretted having taken orders – he apologised to Wilkes for having the 'infectious hand of a bishop . . . waved over me' – he differed from his Unitarian colleagues in remaining 'a great stickler for the church of England: not on doctrinal points, but on the surer foundation of "civil utility"'.[54]

Despite the desire of Scott, the Attorney-General, to see Tooke hanged, he and his fellow defendants were acquitted in a series of *causes célèbres*, having been ably defended by Thomas Erskine (a graduate of Trinity College, Cambridge). The finances for the defence were raised by a committee of the London Corresponding Society, which included Frend and was chaired by Thomas Clarkson, whose devotion to the anti-slavery cause had been awakened while an undergraduate at Cambridge. Though the celebrated treason trials of 1794 ended in acquittal, they nonetheless largely accomplished the government's aims, for thereafter the Society for Constitutional Information ceased to meet, while the Corresponding Society lost many of its members and was increasingly infiltrated by government informers. The harassment of the reform movement continued throughout the 1790s, coming to a head in 1798 when the fear of a French invasion reached almost panic proportions as a result of Wolfe Tone's abortive uprising in Ireland and the mutiny at Spithead in the previous year. This was the background to the prosecution of Gilbert Wakefield in 1799 for his attack on Bishop Watson's pamphlet in support of Pitt's war policy. Like Frend, Wakefield was a former fellow of Jesus College turned Unitarian, who nonetheless remained on good terms with Bishop Law.[55] While Wakefield was more extravagant in his language than Frend, the two men concurred in their criticisms of the constitution of both the Church and the state. To Wakefield the present 'Anti-christian tyranny which is now ripe for

---

[53] B.R. Schneider, *Wordsworth's Cambridge Education* (Cambridge, 1957), p. 134. Pages 112–63 of this book provide a useful survey of late eighteenth-century Cambridge radicalism.

[54] A. Stephens, *Memoirs of John Horne Tooke*, 2 vols. (London, 1813), vol. I, pp. 320–1, 76 and vol. II, p. 477.

[55] G. Wakefield, *Memoirs of the Life of Gilbert Wakefield*, new edn (by J.T. Rutt and A. Wainewright, who wrote vol. II), 2 vols. (London, 1804), vol. I, pp. 444–6.

summary vengeance' (by which he meant Pitt's Government) was
bolstered up by an Established Church which was 'a fraudulent usurpation over that liberty "with which Christ has made us free"'.[56]

Ironically, the origins of this anti-establishmentarianism lay partly
within the Established Church itself. The latitudinarian tradition's
attempt to broaden the doctrinal boundaries of the state Church led to
scepticism among some of its later products about the need for any such
boundaries. The fact that the latitudinarians regarded bishops as providing a convenient (though by no means mandatory) form of ecclesiastical organisation rather than being a divinely ordained office also helped
to create an intellectual climate that led some of the ultra-latitudinarians
of the late eighteenth century to question the traditional hierarchical
ordering in Church and state. Jebb, for example, wrote in his *Letter to the
Right Reverend the Bishop of Lincoln* (1772) that bishops were 'the firm and
steady supporters of civil and religious despotism'.[57] In taking such a view
the former Anglican Unitarians naturally found common ground with
the Dissenters for, as Bradley writes, 'Socially, nonconformity was
grounded in an anti-hierarchical sentiment that grew out of their own
ecclesiastical polity and quasi-accepted legal status.'[58]

Like the Dissenters, the latitudinarians-turned-Unitarians saw themselves as challenging the existing order both on the grounds of reason
and in accordance with God's will as revealed through a reading of
Scripture unsullied by ecclesiastical tradition. As Disney put it in his
sermon 'The Cause of Separation from any Established Church':

> The principles of a rational and protestant dissent are not only justifiable, as
> being founded in reason and revelation; but they are honourable, as they
> bespeak obedience to God, rather than to man.[59]

Some of the former Anglican Unitarians went so far as to challenge
not only the theological justification for an Established Church but also
even that for a separate clerical order. Their strong aversion to sacerdotal
pretensions and clerical power could result in an Enlightenment-
tinctured anti-clericalism of the kind evident in Frend's diatribe in 1789
against

---

[56] G. Wakefield, *A Reply to Some Parts of the Bishop of Landaff's [sic] Address to the People of Great Britain* (London, 1798), p. 39. For a recent account of Wakefield's trial see F. Prochaska, 'English State Trials in the 1790s: A Case Study', *Journal of British Studies*, 13 (1973), 63–82.
[57] Jebb, *Works* (fn. 34), vol. III, p. 75.
[58] Bradley, *Religion, Revolution and English Radicalism* (fn. 2), p. 418.
[59] Disney, *Sermons* (fn. 37), II, p. 201.

the Power of the Priesthood [which] has, in every age, and in every Part of the World, been the Cause of Error, Confusion, and Bloodshed; and as human nature is the same in all ages, we may rest assured that as long as Priesthood remains, so long will our Liberties, spiritual, and Temporal be in danger.[60]

It is a passage that gives point to Clark's remark that 'the critique which English radicals levelled at their own society had strong parallels with the anticlericalism and theological heterodoxy of the intelligentsia of the European Enlightenment'[61] – a comment that applies to the anticlerical tone evident in the work of both some of the more *avant-garde* Dissenting intellectuals (such as Priestley) and to Anglican latitudinarians-turned-Unitarians like Frend.

The inflammatory language of Frend and his fellows may partly reflect the fact that by the late eighteenth century the latitudinarian tradition was no longer viewed with the favour which, in the earlier part of the century, had enabled it to prosper and to attract talented propagandists. While Hoadly and his followers had advanced views about the nature of the Church that were not always congenial to their clerical brethren, their determination to enlist the Church's support for the post-revolutionary order had made them an influential and (before the reign of George III) generally a well-favoured grouping within the Church. But after 1760 the latitudinarians tended to find their road to high office blocked by a king who no longer mistrusted the Tories or feared the revival of clerical claims; indeed, this lack of opportunity may help to account for the frustration that prompted some talented clergy with latitudinarian leanings to turn to the cause of ecclesiastical and, subsequently, political reform. Moreover, thereafter the revival of an emphasis on revealed (as opposed to natural) religion, whether in the form of evangelicalism or, later, Tractarianism, tended to discredit the basic premise of latitudinarian theology which Tillotson (and after him men like Hoadly and Clarke) had promulgated, that 'Excepting a very few particulars, they (natural law and Christianity) enjoin the very same things'.[62] One of the early evangelicals, Rowland Hill, regarded late eighteenth-century Cambridge as being 'almost in total Darkness'.[63] While William Wilberforce set out to eradicate

---

[60] W. Frend, *Mr Coulthurst's Blunders Exposed: or, A Review of Several Texts . . . Produced as Proofs of the Established Doctrine of the Trinity* (London, 1788–9), p. 2.

[61] J.C.D. Clark, *English Society 1688–1832* (Cambridge, 1985), p. 6. For an important discussion of the linkages between political and religious radicalism in the late eighteenth century see pp. 277–348 of this work.   [62] H.R. McAdoo, *The Spirit of Anglicanism* (London, 1965), p. 175.

[63] C.H.E. Smyth, *Charles Simeon and Church Order* (Cambridge, 1940), p. 178.

the deadly leaven of Hoadly's latitudinarian views which had spread to an
alarming extent among the clergy; and whilst numbers confessedly agreed with
his Socinian tenets, few were sufficiently honest to resign with Mr Lindsey the
endowments of the church.[64]

Nonetheless, the latitudinarians' emphasis on simplicity of doctrine,
their resolute anti-sacerdotalism and their stress on the need to demonstrate the congruity between Christianity and human reason had important implications for the character of political and religious debate in the
late eighteenth century. In both ecclesiastical and civil matters they
tended to dismiss the importance of tradition and their common-sense
approach to religion left little place for the almost mystical view of kingship held by their High Church opponents; to the Nonjuror Hearne, for
example, Hoadly had appeared to be 'of vile republican principles',[65]
while even George II had accused Hoadly of being a trimmer in matters
both secular and sacred since 'he is [ready] to take favours from the
Crown, though by his republican spirit and doctrine, he would be glad to
abolish the power of it'.[66] The latitudinarians' emphasis on the need for
simplicity of doctrine (which led to the Feathers Tavern petition) was
reflected in the agitation by some of their number for a simplification of
the Church's liturgy and administration or even its disestablishment; this
critical approach to one aspect of the unreformed constitution naturally
predisposed them to favour reform more generally. It also naturally led
to some association with the Dissenters, and particularly the Rational
Dissenters, who held similar theological principles and, in many cases,
aspired to similar political goals.

The inveterate Tory, William Cole, a late eighteenth-century antiquary, asserted that there was a link between the latitudinarians and
political radicalism in a long tirade he wrote against Jebb. Jebb, he complained, was one of 'a restless generation who will never be contented till
they have overturned the Constitution in Church and State'. Cole saw
this movement as part of a plot to allow the Dissenters to undermine the
defences of the Established Church, a conspiracy which had been supported by 'Tillotson and a thousand other moderate and latitudinarian
Clergy' and was based on 'the Principles in Fashion ever since the glorious Revolution'. Within his own university of Cambridge, Cole traced

---

[64] R.I. Wilberforce and S. Wilberforce, *The Life of William Wilberforce by historians, R. J. W. and S. W.*, 5
vols. (London, 1838), vol. I, p. 129.

[65] T. Hearne, *Reliquæ Hearnianæ: The Remains of Thomas Hearne . . . Being Extracts from his MS Diaries*, collected with a few notes by P. Bliss, 2nd edn, 3 vols. (London, 1869), vol. III, p. 157.

[66] H.T. Dickinson, 'Benjamin Hoadly', *History Today*, 25 (1975), 352.

this dangerous tradition back to Hoadly who 'was made a Deity of'.[67] Though to Tories like Cole the radicalism of Jebb and his allies was a natural extension of the latitudinarian principles of Hoadly, by no means all latitudinarians were opposed to the existence of an Established Church or felt compelled to leave the Anglican fold. Among their ranks could be found figures such as Bishop Watson who, while Regius Professor of Divinity at Cambridge from 1771 to 1816, drew on both Dissenting and latitudinarian theological texts in his teaching and used methods which (as he put it) 'gained me no credit with the hierarchy' though 'it produced a liberal spirit in the University'.[68] But, even though his ardour cooled in the aftermath of the French Revolution, Watson, too, was an advocate of political and religious reform,[69] another indication of the extent to which latitudinarian theological principles tended to be associated with a more critical view of the late eighteenth-century constituted order in Church and state – even if such criticism did not always extend to the radical demands of the former Anglican Unitarians.

The tangible fruits of the latitudinarians' activities were few. The agitation against subscription failed, but it played a part in preparing the way for the greater toleration granted to the Dissenters by the Act of 1779,[70] and it may also have helped create the climate of opinion for the passage of the Catholic Relief Act of 1778; certainly, the Protestant Association (which provoked the Gordon riots) saw the 'latitudinarian Infidels' as being among those responsible for the Act.[71] The societies for political reform with which the Anglican latitudinarians and their parted Unitarian brethren were associated brought about even less change and had disappeared by the end of the century, though their example helped shape the organisation of the revived radicalism of the early nineteenth century. Thus Cartwright's Hampden Clubs were partly modelled on the Society for Constitutional Information[72] and included among their earliest supporters Capel Lofft and John Disney. More fundamental,

---

[67] British Library, Cole MSS, Add. MS 5873, pp. 48–9.

[68] R. Watson, *Anecdotes of the Life of R. Watson ... revised in 1814* (London, 1817), p. 39.

[69] J. Gascoigne, *Cambridge in the Age of the Enlightenment: Science, Religion and Politics from the Restoration to the French Revolution* (Cambridge, 1989), pp. 206–10, 215–18, 239–47.

[70] Belsham, *Memoirs of ... Theophilus Lindsey* (fn. 36), p. 67.   [71] Black, *The Association* (fn. 45), p. 155.

[72] A. Goodwin, *The Friends of Liberty: The English Democratic Movement in the Age of the French Revolution* (London, 1979), p. 494. In *The Friends of Peace: Anti-War Liberalism in England 1793–1815* (Cambridge, 1982) J.E. Cookson argues that the 'rational Christians' (among whom he includes the Unitarians and latitudinarian Anglicans like Wyvill) not only helped to shape the anti-war sentiment of the period 1793 to 1815 but also contributed to the growth of the reform movement in the post-war period.

however, was the influence of Hoadly and those who shared, and further developed, his views on Church and state, in moulding the traditions of intellectual and political radicalism that surfaced both in England and the Thirteen Colonies in the age of the American Revolution; a movement which, though its initial fruits were blighted in England by indifference and reaction, nonetheless helped foster the slow realisation that the old order was not immutable, that its provisions and practices, however hallowed by time, could be improved, and that reform did not necessarily mean revolution. It was the slow, almost glacier-like, pressure of such ideas that was finally to help move the craggy rocks of the British Constitution.

CHAPTER 10

The state as highwayman: from candour to rights

Alan Saunders

I

The history of British radicalism has usually been written by radicals, or at least by their grateful posterity. Perhaps the most important consequence of this has been the creation of radicalism itself: that great russet-coated army, Wat Tyler in the van, Lollards and Ranters behind him, shoulder to shoulder with poor stockingers, Luddite croppers, hand-loom weavers, utopian artisans and followers of Joanna Southcott, all marching towards the New Jerusalem to the beat of a miners' band. But perhaps the ranks are not as steady as they might be, and perhaps this is not surprising, because these people are most of them conscripts and not volunteers. Hindsight has put them where they are, a desire on the part of modern radicals to construct a tradition of which, once they have constructed it, they can claim to be the products.

This is where the Rational Dissenters are normally allowed to belong, but there are times when even the most determined anachronist might question their right to be here: these sober people, altogether a little too pleased with themselves, who read pamphlets on the propriety of infant baptism and own warehouses in the North of England.[1] The Rational Dissenters were part of the Enlightenment – nobody seems to have had any doubt about that – and it has been generally agreed that, since the

---

[1] Among the writers who do not merely describe Rational Dissenters as radicals but actually try to find them a place in a radical tradition are Leslie Stephen, *History of English Thought in the Eighteenth Century*, 3rd edn, 2 vols. (London, 1902; repr. New York and Burlingame, 1962), ch. 5 §5; Roy Porter, *English Society in the Eighteenth Century* (Harmondsworth, 1982), p. 197; J.C.D. Clark, *English Society, 1688–1832* (Cambridge, 1985), ch. 5; and Marilyn Butler, from whose *Romantics, Rebels and Reactionaries* (Oxford, 1981) we learn (p. 169) that 'Priestley, Paine, Godwin and Blake . . . came from the classic stock of the English left, the Dissenters.' A similar movement of thought is clearly at work in the writings of Isaac Kramnick: see his *Republicanism and Bourgeois Radicalism* (Ithaca and London, 1990), chs. 1–3. If there has been a serious overemphasis in his work on the radicalism of Dissent, he has nonetheless been careful to stress its essentially bourgeois nature. This has enabled him to locate the Dissenters in an American tradition of liberal thought.

Enlightenment was progressive and radical, then the Rational Dissenters deserve to march with the radical platoons. But it can also be argued that, however enlightened their philosophy may have been, their aspirations were too modest to win them a place in these ranks. 'Price and Priestley', wrote Harold Laski back in 1936, 'did little more than demand formal recognition for a status for the nonconformists which was already largely implicit in the practice of the English State.'[2] And if their political ambitions were too confined, so was their membership. E.P. Thompson allows them scarcely any role at all in the making of the English working class: their cold, polite religion may have appealed to a few tradesmen and shopkeepers in the great metropolises but it had little to say to the labouring poor in town or country.[3]

Nonetheless, a number of recruiting sergeants, even in recent years, have tried to argue that the radical army is indeed where the Rational Dissenters belong. In a book that boldly seeks to identify a radical tradition extending from the middle-class campaigners of 1760 to the more proletarian Chartists of 1848, Edward Royle and James Walvin argue that the links in the chain were the overlapping memberships of successive organisations and a literature that ensured the transmission and accumulation of radical ideas.[4] A few years before Royle and Walvin, Albert Goodman argued that, diverse though radical thought may have been before 1789, the debates arising from the French Revolution helped to focus the political resentments of the excluded. He points out that, though the French revolutionaries may originally have drawn some of their inspiration from the English Revolution of 1688, they soon began to export original ideas of their own.[5] Central to these ideas, of course, is an appeal to the rights of man. This is something altogether more generous than a plea for recognition of the status of Dissent and thus it is that Rational Dissenters, who gave voice to this appeal at the end of the century, can be united with the working-class radicals in whom Thompson is interested.

But perhaps Rational Dissent turned its attention to rights even earlier than the 1790s. As long ago as 1938, Anthony Lincoln argued that a move towards what he called a 'far more political and universalist language' had been a significant result of the frustration of Dissenters' hopes in

---

[2] Harold J. Laski, *The Rise of European Liberalism* (London, 1936), p. 106.
[3] E.P. Thompson, *The Making of the English Working Class*, rev. edn (Harmondsworth, 1968), p. 31.
[4] Edward Royle and James Walvin, *English Radicals and Reformers 1760–1848* (Brighton, 1982), p. 181.
[5] Albert Goodwin, *The Friends of Liberty: The English Democratic Government in the Age of the French Revolution* (Cambridge, MA, 1979), pp. 19–21.

1773.[6] These hopes had been modest: the Corporation Act of 1661 and the Test Act of 1673 denied public office to those who were unwilling to take communion according to the Anglican rite and acknowledge the supremacy of the Crown in matters ecclesiastical, but it was not from these Acts that Dissenters sought relief. Since 1689, the Toleration Act had permitted their ministers to preach on condition that they abjured the doctrine of transubstantiation and subscribed to most of the Articles of the Church of England, including the Trinitarian creeds. It was from this obligation that Dissenting ministers hoped to be discharged, some because they objected in principle to confessions of faith, others because the articles to which they were expected to subscribe were inconsistent with their Arian or Socinian views.[7] According to Lincoln (and to a later historian, Richard Burgess Barlow), their plea for relief was an appeal to the candour of those in power; it was not an appeal to universal human rights. Lincoln found the fullest expression of the appeal to candour in an essay published in 1772: Joseph Fownes's *Enquiry into the Principles of Toleration*. What Fownes demanded for his fellow Dissenters was not citizenship but toleration and legal security. He argued, in Lockean manner, that civil society had been brought into existence in order to protect its members from injury. Every injury was a violation of some right, hence it followed that men took these rights with them when they entered into society. These, then, were primary and universal rights – 'independent of all human grant, not derived from any compact' – and of these the most sacred and incontestable was the right of private conscience in matters of religion. Laws that circumscribed the exercise of conscience were thus inconsistent with the very founding principles of the state.[8]

---

[6] Anthony Lincoln, *Some Political and Social Ideas of English Dissent 1763–1800* (Cambridge, 1938; repr. New York, 1971), p. 239.

[7] For the background to the Toleration Act and the legislation from whose penalties it provided relief, see Michael R. Watts, *The Dissenters* (Oxford, 1978), pp. 259–60. For the Dissenters' application for relief from the obligation to subscribe, see John Stephens, 'The London Ministers and Subscription, 1772–1779', *Enlightenment and Dissent*, 1 (1982), 42–71.

[8] Joseph Fownes, *An Enquiry into the Principles of Toleration; the Degree, in which they are admitted by our Laws, and the Reasonableness of the Late Application made by the Dissenters to Parliament, for an Enlargement of their Religious Liberties*, 2nd edn (Shrewsbury, 1773), pp. 3, 5–7, 15. For Lincoln's account of the argument, which he tells us was 'the fullest, as it was the last, exposition in the old idiom which the ideology of the French Revolution was about to supersede; the idiom of natural jurisprudence of Grotius, Pufendorf and Barbeyrac', Lincoln, *Political and Social Ideas* (fn. 6), pp. 194–6. For arguments similar to Fownes's see Philip Furneaux, *An Essay on Toleration: with a particular View to the Late Application of the Protestant Dissenting Ministers to Parliament, for Amending, and rendering Effectual . . . the Act of Toleration* (London, 1773), pp. 1–2, 18–22, and [Robert Robinson] *Arcana: or The Principles of the Late Petitioners to Parliament for Relief in the Matter of Subscription . . .* (Cambridge, 1774), pp. 35–6.

In the early 1770s, many Dissenters, surveying the political scene, found reason to hope that the state would voluntarily remove this inconsistency. They saw, or thought they saw, what one of their number, Andrew Kippis, described as 'a generous prince of the Brunswick line: a seemingly equitable administration: moderate and wise members of both houses: candid bishops: a liberal spirit in all ranks of men and Toleration lifting her voice loudly in Europe'.[9] They were disappointed: in 1773 the bill for their relief was passed by the Commons but thrown out by the Lords.

Clearly the appeal to candour had struck no responsive chord in the establishment's heart. So it was about this time, according to Barlow and Lincoln, that the language of the universal rights of man began to seem very attractive to Rational Dissent. By employing this language of rights they would appeal not to the generosity of those in power but to their moral intelligence and their consciences. They would not be asking for something to be granted them: they would be asking for recognition that they already possessed it. These were the principles that underlay their later campaigns for repeal of the Test and Corporation Acts. 'The cry in 1790 was "give us back our rights which your government has usurped"', writes Lincoln, 'but in 1772–3 it was no more than a plea for co-operation in erecting a common monument to Justice.'[10] It was now right and not toleration that was to be sought (and sought for all, for Catholics and atheists as well as for Protestant Dissenters). In 1774, in the wake of defeat, Joshua Toulmin told his fellow Dissenters that their application, had it succeeded, would have been 'a step towards an universal toleration', granted to all not as Christians 'but upon consideration of our right to it, as Men'.[11] Toulmin represents the state as something quite other – a tyranny imposed from without upon Dissenter, Jew, deist and

---

[9] Andrew Kippis, *A Vindication of the Protestant Dissenting Ministers with Regard to their Late Application to Parliament* (London, 1772), pp. 51–2, quoted in Lincoln, *Political and Social Ideas* (fn. 6), p. 210. For descriptions of the situation that gave rise to this optimism, see *ibid.*, pp. 196–7 and Richard Burgess Barlow, *Citizenship and Conscience: A Study in the Theory and Practice of Religious Toleration in England During the Eighteenth Century* (Philadelphia, 1962), pp. 171–2.

[10] Lincoln, *Political and Social Ideas* (fn. 6), p. 211. The implicit reference here must be to Fownes, *Enquiry* (fn. 8), p. 98: 'Had the bill passed, it would have been a noble addition to the proofs, which the church of England has given of her moderation to dissenting protestants; and had the fathers of the church been zealous in promoting it, they would have erected MONUMENTUM AERE PERENNIUS to their praise.' An argument similar to Lincoln's and Barlow's – that what took place was a shift of the debate from a theological to a political plane – is put with admirable clarity and brevity by H.T. Dickinson in his *Liberty and Property: Political Ideology in Eighteenth-Century Britain* (London, 1977), pp. 202–3.

[11] Joshua Toulmin, *Two Letters on the Late Application to Parliament by the Protestant Dissenting Ministers* (London, 1774), pp. 15, 79.

Moslem – but the new spirit of opposition is perhaps best captured in a disenchanted metaphor which Joseph Priestley had first used even before the rejection of the appeal:

> A highwayman may be so whimsical, as not to let me pass without robbing or murdering me, unless I will tell him whether I have adopted the *Cartesian* or *Newtonian* philosophy. In this case I may surely tell him the truth, in order to save my life or my money, though that truth has no natural connexion with his business as a highwayman, or with the saving of life. We may argue, as it appears to me, in the same manner with respect to the civil magistrate inquiring about our religion.[12]

By likening the state to a highwayman, who has no natural call on our attention and no authority but that of his pistol, Priestley has adopted a very familiar radical stance. He has also depicted a situation in which that conversational virtue which the eighteenth century called 'candour' seems to have little relevance. Lincoln and Barlow represent the subscription controversy as the bridge that enabled the rest of Dissent to follow Priestley from the world of candour to the radical world of rights.

Like most historians who have studied the politics of Dissent, Lincoln and Barlow spend the greater part of their time at the level of ideology, which is why their attention has lighted upon that ideologically vocal minority who called themselves Rational Dissenters. But however heterodox Joseph Priestley, Richard Price and the rest may have been in their theology, their politics can indeed seem as tame as Laski took them to be. A more generous view of the radicalism of English nonconformity may perhaps be had only from a vantage point that takes in not just the garrulous metropolitan pamphleteers of Rational Dissent but also those 'many Dissenting ministers in the provinces', whose preaching James Bradley has recently invoked in an attempt to (as he puts it) relate 'social discontent to religious ideology'. A few of these preachers, Bradley tells us, even went so far as to identify themselves with the poor; many more helped to popularise political dissent by associating themselves with progressive causes and by anticipating modern values (these Whiggish formulations are Bradley's own). At the time of the American War of Independence, nearly twenty years before the debates over the French Revolution, these ministers, politically radical but theologically orthodox, began to foster political discontent among the lower

---

[12] Joseph Priestley, *A Letter of Advice to those Dissenters who Conduct the Application to Parliament for Relief from Certain Penal Laws* (London, 1773), repr. in *The Theological and Miscellaneous Works of Joseph Priestley*, ed. J.T. Rutt, 26 vols. (London, 1817–31), vol. XXII, p. 475. See also Toulmin, *Two Letters*, pp. 4–5, 9–11.

orders. Bradley uses them in a very significant attempt to forge anew the link between the radicalism of the 1790s and that of the 1770s. He argues that the Rational Dissenters were indeed both marginal in their influence and mild in their radicalism and that a concentration on them rather than their provincial brethren has encouraged historians in a view of English society in the eighteenth century as socially and economically unified.[13]

Rational Dissent is not excluded from Bradley's account but it is brushed to one side, and with it theology. A surprising footnote, the second in his book, informs us that 'Little attention will be given in this study to the distinction between Particular (Calvinistic) and General (Arminian) Baptists, or to the Presbyterian drift into Unitarianism.'[14] Nor is the subscription controversy, so important a watershed in Lincoln's and Barlow's accounts, given much attention here. Bradley's point is that, though some of the Rational Dissenters may have derived their political views from their theology, what really matters is the heritage that they shared with all Dissent: an insistence on the sovereign authority of the Bible and an ecclesiastical polity founded on egalitarianism and independence. So the very basis of their Dissent was nothing less than a challenge to an Established Church which drew its authority from tradition as well as the Bible, which was hierarchically constituted and married to the state.[15]

This is a curiously Anglican view of the Dissenters: as a swarm of hornets, all essentially similar, all equally dangerous to the established order. Nor does it do justice to the possibility that the Presbyterians were able to drift towards Unitarianism (the languid verb conveys none of the personal anguish that may have been involved) because of their particular attitudes to authority and independence. Since the seventeenth century the Congregationalists had conceived of themselves as a gathered community of the elect under the lordship of Christ; they restricted membership to those able to give an account of the work of grace in their souls. The Presbyterians, on the other hand, who did not believe that it was possible to determine with certainty who was elect and who was not, allowed into their ranks any who lived respectably and had some knowledge of the Christian faith. Unlike the Congregationalists, they were careful to exclude the unlearned from the ministry. Their ministers, well educated at the Dissenting academies of which the

---

[13] James E. Bradley, *Religion, Revolution and English Radicalism* (Cambridge, 1990), pp. 12, 14, 18, 22, 129–430.   [14] *Ibid.*, p. 1.   [15] *Ibid.*, pp. 4, 417–18.

Presbyterians were particularly enthusiastic patrons, answerable neither to bishops nor, like Congregationalist preachers, to regular church meetings, enjoyed that greater freedom of thought and speculation which led many of them towards Unitarianism.[16] So the Presbyterians and the Congregationalists drifted apart on this vital issue because they differed in their interpretation of that common inheritance which Bradley sees as a uniting factor.

As far as the letter of the law went, those Presbyterians who had embraced Unitarianism were now in a worse position than their orthodox brethren: blasphemers of the Trinity were liable to imprisonment if they preached their doctrines.[17] But though the law may not have shared Bradley's indifference to a drift towards Unitarianism, the important question as far as the present argument is concerned is whether this drift had any political consequences within Dissent. Or to put it another way, if (as Bradley allows) Rational Dissenters could derive some of their political views from their theology, did Calvinistic orthodoxy have political consequences too? Here again the crucial episode is the subscription controversy of 1773 and what makes it crucial is the fact that the one thing that had guaranteed the failure of the petitioners had been a counter-petition from provincial Dissenters – Calvinists and Trinitarians – who resented this attempt of urban Socinians to speak as though theirs was the voice of all Dissent.[18] So, in at least one instance, theological orthodoxy led to political conservatism.

This does not greatly embarrass Bradley's thesis, but it does suggest that no analysis of the radicalism of English Dissent can be made to rest on too simple an account of Dissenting religious thought. The matters on which orthodox Dissent was prepared to be radical were determined by its theology. The same was true of Rational Dissent, though I shall try to argue here that Barlow's and Lincoln's claim that this episode marked a transition in Dissenting thought is mistaken, at least in its emphasis. The Rational Dissenters do indeed begin to look radical to modern eyes when their theology is at its lightest and when their political aspirations are couched in a theory of rights, but that theory was inseparable in their thought from an attachment to the obsolescent idea of candour. The problem for Rational Dissent was that, by the end of the century, candour was almost all they believed in, so their claim to a place in the radical ranks is most convincing just when they begin to lose intellectual coherence as a group.

---

[16] See Watts, *Dissenters* (fn. 7), pp. 168–72, 291–318, 366–82, 390–1, 464–71.　　[17] *Ibid.*, p. 372.
[18] See Lincoln, *Political and Social Ideas* (fn. 6), pp. 228–35; Barlow, *Citizenship and Conscience* (fn. 9), pp. 179–89; Stephens, 'London Ministers' (fn. 7), pp. 48–55.

II

Generally, to be candid was to value others for their sincerity and personal virtues, no matter how heretical their opinions might seem to be. This use of the word – meaning, as Samuel Johnson put it, 'free from malice; not desirous to find fault' – is one of five given in the *Oxford English Dictionary*. The first of these definitions, 'white', derives directly from the Latin *candidus*, and the second is clearly a figurative use of the first: 'Splendid, illustrious; fortunate' and 'Pure, clear; stainless, innocent'. The third definition 'freedom from mental bias', dates from at least as early as 1635, and there is yet another, 'frank, open, ingenuous, straight-forward', of which the first instance given is from 1675.

It is by no means always clear which of these several meanings an eighteenth-century user of the word may intend by it. When, for example, Sir William Blackstone says that from Priestley's *History of Electricity* he 'conceived a very favourable impression of his talents as a *candid* and *ingenious* writer', is he praising Priestley for the frankness with which he writes of the errors of electrical scientists, for the amiable disposition which causes him to mention these errors only when they have contributed to the discovery of truth, or for something else?[19] It is difficult not to suspect that in cases like this, 'candour' and 'candid' function merely as buzz words: candour is a quality you unreflectingly attribute to somebody you like or wish to compliment.

Even when employed with deliberation, the word was in the eighteenth century made to do an inordinate amount of work, a fact well brought out by D.O. Thomas in his study of Priestley's friend Richard Price, Dissenting preacher and philosopher. According to Thomas, candour involves not merely integrity and 'a sweet and reasonable disposition' but also 'the claim that all beliefs should be subject to rational criticism', the assumption 'that in principle the truth can be discovered and communicated', the belief that 'the appeal to reason is the only legitimate form of persuasion', the requirement that we be dispassionate, patient and humble in our search for the truth, 'a sense of the equality of rational agents and a sense of community in the search for

---

[19] [William Blackstone], *A Reply to Dr. Priestley's remarks on the Fourth Volume of the Commentaries on the Laws of England. By the Author of the Commentaries* (London, 1769), pp. 5–6. For the candid philosophy underlying Priestley's work as an historian of science see the preface to *The History and Present State of Electricity, with Original Experiments*, 3rd edn, 2 vols. (London, 1775). There is a useful discussion of this preface in J.G. McEvoy, 'Electricity, Knowledge, and the Nature of Progress in Priestley's Scientific Thought', *British Journal for the History of Science*, 12 (1979), 1–30.

knowledge'.[20] Thomas can hardly be said to be offering us a definition. Instead he combines most of the meanings of the word and then freely extrapolates from them. But there is no confusion in what he has to say, only in what he describes, because he accurately reflects the complex concept that the word summoned up for Dissenters of Price's day and persuasion. In particular, his account reveals, as the Dictionary's does not, a change in the use of the word which had great significance for Dissenting thought: candour, which once meant being impartial as between persons, came eventually to mean being impartial as between ideas. To understand how this came about we need to look at the very origins of Rational Dissent.

What matters most about the Rational Dissenters is not, *pace* Bradley, what they have in common with the orthodox, but what they have abandoned of orthodoxy. The most important defining characteristics of their Dissent are its rejection of Calvinism and the tensions which that act of rejection set up. One of the great attractions of Calvinism is that it provides a way out of what Richard Popkin has called 'the intellectual crisis of the reformation'. By abandoning Calvinism, the English Rational Dissenters plunged back into the crisis and so needed to find a new means of resolution.

In Popkin's account, the crisis has its origins in Luther's defiance of the Holy See. To defy Rome was to challenge the criterion by which the truths of Scripture had for centuries been ascertained. But how can such a criterion, once challenged, be either defended or refuted? Where is the criterion, accepted by all the contending parties, according to which this criterion and its rivals may be judged? In the apparent absence of such a criterion, Catholic theologians would ask how the Protestant, who claims to found his faith upon Scripture, knows that he has interpreted the Scriptures correctly. How, indeed, does he know that the Bible is the word of God? How does he know which books constitute the Holy Scripture? The Catholic answer is that unaided human reason cannot help us to such knowledge: where reason fails us, we have no alternative but to turn to the authority of the Church. But the sceptical project can be carried much further before this or any other stop is put to it.

---

[20] D.O. Thomas, *The Honest Mind: The Thought and Work of Richard Price* (Oxford, 1977), pp. 99–100. For further modern discussion of the concept of candour, see William Empson, *The Structure of Complex Words* (London, 1951), ch. 15; Susie I. Tucker, *Protean Shape: A Study in Eighteenth-Century Vocabulary and Usage* (London, 1967), pp. 212–14; Donald Davie, *A Gathered Church: the Literature of the English Dissenting Interest* (London, 1978), pp. 139–41, and his *Dissentient Voice: The Ward-Phillips Lectures for 1980 with some Related Pieces* (Notre Dame, 1982), ch. 6.

Montaigne showed that it could be carried as far as the ancient sceptics had carried it, putting into question all the evidence of the senses and even the faculty of reason itself.[21]

Eventually, a solution would be found to these doubts in the form of what Popkin calls 'mitigated scepticism'. While admitting the force of the sceptical assault, mitigated scepticism allowed that though our knowledge of the world may fall short of mathematical certainty, yet it is probable enough for most of the purposes of life. The growth of mitigated scepticism in the seventeenth century coincided, of course, with the rise of empirical science; and science, like religion, was in need of standards of proof less rigid than those that the sceptics assumed. The result was the abandonment of the old scholastic dichotomy between certain knowledge, the preserve of logic and the mathematical sciences, and the merely probable knowledge that belonged to the humanities, to rhetoric and the empirical sciences. In its place was put a continuum of knowledge, stretching from fiction to the morally certain. And, though standards of proof were now less formal, the scientific enterprise imposed a new obligation to assess the value of testimony, both the testimony of one's own senses and the testimony of others.[22]

Though many Calvinists were involved with the new science, these new standards of knowledge did not touch their theology at all. For the Calvinist, God is so infinitely removed from humankind that knowledge of him is inaccessible to human reason. Certain knowledge of God's grace can be had only when God chooses to make himself known in some great revolution of the spirit. It follows, then, that to abandon Calvinism with its inner authority without either embracing the Apostolic authority of the Catholic faith or abandoning Christianity altogether is to find oneself back in the grip of the sceptical crisis of the Reformation.

Though these modifications in the standards of proof are commonly associated with the early Royal Society and the first Newtonians, it would be a mistake to suppose that matters had been resolved by the mid-eighteenth century. On the contrary, the persistence of anti-Newtonian and non-Newtonian theodicies and the controversy that surrounded the work of David Hume indicate that these were still live issues. So Protestants like Joseph Priestley, seeking some new and secure ground of belief, did so in an atmosphere of intellectual turmoil. It was

---

[21] See Richard H. Popkin, *The History of Scepticism from Erasmus to Spinoza* (Berkeley and Los Angeles, 1979), especially chs. 1, 3, 6 and 7.

[22] See Barbara J. Shapiro, *Probability and Certainty in Seventeenth-Century England* (Princeton, 1983), chs. 1 and 2.

out of this turmoil that there arose the notion of Rational Dissent. This came to mean two things: first, a determination to find objective justification for religious belief in either the books of Scripture or the book of nature; secondly, an opposition to all civil jurisdiction over religious belief and practice.[23]

The attempts of the civil power to exercise such jurisdiction remind us of the nature of the society in which the crisis of the Reformation arose. It was a society in which all thought was – or was supposed to be – so unified that religious dissent looked like political dissent. This is the world that Peter Laslett has memorably called 'the world we have lost': a world of small groups, in which the principal unit of economic organisation was the family, in which the affective relationships that govern life in the family also governed other connections, political as well as economic, so that political factions were described as the 'friends' of their leading figure. Though Dissenters could not be full members of this patriarchal system of loyalty and patronage, it would be a mistake to suppose that they stood completely outside it: their catechism reminded them that 'The fifth commandment requireth the preserving the honour and performing the duties, belonging to every one in their several places and relations, as Superiors, Inferiors or Equals.'[24] But the Rational Dissenters did devise a political philosophy that challenged the basis of the old society, and it is clear that they did so by turning on it the same radical gaze that they had brought to bear upon religious doctrine.

They laboured, though, under a serious difficulty. Reason was of the greatest importance to them, but the concept of reason had, along with the standards of proof, been modified in the seventeenth century. In the heyday of the old society, reason, like political legitimacy, had exerted its authority downwards: it was 'the candle of the Lord', a guide to wisdom. But by the eighteenth century it was a merely ratiocinative faculty, incapable of action until moved by the passions. David Hume

---

[23] For the concept of Rational Dissent see Russell E. Richey, 'The Origins of British Radicalism: The Changing Rationale for Dissent', *Eighteenth-Century Studies*, 7 (1973–4), 179–92; James E. Bradley, 'Whigs and Nonconformists: "Slumbering Radicalism" in English Politics, 1739–1789', *Eighteenth-Century Studies*, 9 (1975), 1–27; John Seed, 'Gentlemen Dissenters: The Social and Political Meanings of Rational Dissent in the 1770s and 1780s', *Historical Journal*, 28 (1985), 299–325.

[24] *The Westminster Shorter Catechism* (1647), question 69, quoted in Peter Laslett, *The World We have Lost – Further Explored*, 3rd edn, (London, 1983), p. 218. For these aspects of the old society, see *ibid.*, chs. 1, 2, 7, and Harold Perkin, *Origins of Modern English Society* (London, 1959), ch. 2. The Westminster Catechism, it is worth remarking, is the one Priestley claims to have learnt at his mother's knee: see *The Memoirs of Dr. Joseph Priestley, to the Year 1795* . . . (London, 1806), ed. Jack Lindsay as *Autobiography of Joseph Priestley* (Bath, 1970), p. 69.

acknowledged this change in his well-known declaration that 'Reason is, and ought only to be the slave of the passions, and can never pretend to any other office than to serve and obey them.'[25]

There are various ways in which one might try to find a home in a world where reason has lost much of its authority. One might urge the importance of direct divine illumination, which is what John Wesley, the founder of Methodism, did; one might argue that there is a human faculty more useful than mere ratiocination, which is what was done by the Scottish philosophers of the common-sense school; one might assume that human society is the only proper sphere of human activity and that human society is a given and unarguable fact in no need of rational justification, which is the assumption underlying republican thought. None of these solutions – all offered by men who were aware of the difficulties now surrounding the idea of reason – was acceptable to Joseph Priestley. He, of all Rational Dissenters the man most willing to grapple with such fundamental issues, saw no difficulty at all. He thought that both Wesley and the common-sense philosophers were, in their different ways, irrationalists; he thought republican political philosophy oppressive; and he saw Hume as little more than a destructive sceptic. Instead, he proposed an intellectual project in which objective certainty was to be sought in every area of knowledge. Nothing was to be taken on trust: scriptural truth was to be sought in history, truths about the natural world in the incorrigible perceptions of the mind.[26]

As Priestley saw it, his project could be carried on only by a mind cleared of prejudice and prepared to engage in unacrimonious debate.

---

[25] David Hume, *A Treatise of Human Nature*, ed. L.A. Selby-Bigge (Oxford, 1888), p. 415. On the old concept of reason see S.L. Bethell, *The Cultural Revolution of the Seventeenth Century* (London, 1951), ch. 3; Robert Hoopes, *Right Reason in the Seventeenth Century* (Cambridge, MA, 1962), especially chs. 7 and 9; Aharon Lichtenstein, *Henry More: The Rational Theology of a Cambridge Platonist* (Cambridge, MA, 1962), pp. 55–69, 133–55; Christopher Hill, *Change and Continuity in Seventeenth Century England* (London, 1974), ch. 4; Lotte Mulligan, '"Reason," "Right Reason," and " Revelation" in Mid-Seventeenth-Century England', in Brian Vickers, ed., *Occult and Scientific Mentalities in the Renaissance* (Cambridge, 1984), pp. 103–23. For the new concept of reason, regarded 'rather as an acquisition than as a heritage', see Ernst Cassirer, *The Philosophy of the Enlightenment* [*Die Philosophie der Aufklärung*, 1932], trans. Fritz C.A. Koelln and James P. Pettegrove (Princeton, 1951), pp. 12–15, and Genevieve Lloyd, *The Man of Reason: 'Male' and 'Female' in Western Philosophy* (London, 1984), ch. 3.

[26] John Wesley (not the most philosophically acute of religious thinkers) tackles the problem of reason in *An Earnest Appeal to Men of Reason and Religion* (Bristol, 1743), repr. in *The Works of John Wesley*, ed. F. Baker *et al.* (in progress), vol. 1 (Oxford, 1975), pp. 28–35. Of the Scottish philosophers, it is the embarrassingly incompetent James Oswald who is most explicit about the new status of reason: see his *An Appeal to Commonsense in Behalf of Religion*, 2 vols. (Edinburgh, 1766–77), vol. 1, pp. 24–5, 171, 233. For the thoughts on reason of a republican thinker whose writings provoked one of Priestley's most important works see [John Brown], *Thoughts on Civil Liberty, on Licentiousness, and Faction*, 2nd edn (London, 1765), pp. 39–42, 99. Priestley's most developed reply

Hence the importance to him and to his fellow Rational Dissenters of the concept of candour. But though candour was especially dear to them, they were not alone in holding it in high regard. The revolution in standards of scientific proof had given a new significance to testimony as a source of knowledge and hence to candour as a principle regulating the giving and receiving of testimony. And the appeal of candour went further even than this. In the late seventeenth and early eighteenth centuries, polite conversation – easy, familiar and free from theological and political rancour – came to be regarded as the ideal of civilised communication. Its chief advocates were Joseph Addison and Richard Steele, authors of the *Spectator* and the *Tatler*, but it found its way into Dissenting thought in the writings of Isaac Watts and Philip Doddridge. Neither of them could possibly be called a Rational Dissenter but they taught the men who were later to become Rational Dissenters.[27]

Doddridge's theological lectures at his Dissenting academy at Northampton were undogmatic – charitable to all, comprehensive in their coverage of every side in controversial issues – and in this their author appears consciously to have followed in the footsteps of his great seventeenth-century predecessor, Richard Baxter. Inspired by a great hatred of the sectarian strife of his age, ever ready to associate with good men of all parties, Baxter had prided himself on being 'a CHRISTIAN a MEER CHRISTIAN . . . of that Party which is so against Parties.'[28] His influence was profound, especially in an age whose sensibilities were turning away from the rigours of orthodox Calvinism, and Doddridge, ever careful to explain that he was not a 'High' Calvinist, was happy to place

to the Methodists is contained in the Introductory Address in *Original Letters by the Rev. John Wesley and his Friends . . . to which is prefixed an Address to the Methodists* (Birmingham, 1791). For his reply to the Scottish philosophers see the preface to the third volume of his *Institutes of Natural and Revealed Religion*, 3 vols. (London, 1772–4) and *An Examination of Dr. Reid's Inquiry into the Human Mind on the Principles of Common Sense, Dr. Beattie's Essay on the Nature and Immutability of Truth, and Dr. Oswald's Appeal to Common Sense on Behalf of Religion* (London, 1774; facs. repr., London and New York, 1978). He replies to Brown in *An Essay on the First Principles of Government, and on the Nature of Political, Civil, and Religious Liberty* (London, 1768) and to Hume in *Letters to a Philosophical Unbeliever, Part I* (London, 1787; facs. repr., New York and London, 1974).

[27] On the notion of civility in the works of Addison and Steele, see Edward A. and Lillian D. Bloom, *Joseph Addison's Sociable Animal* (Providence, RI, 1971) and Michael G. Ketcham, *Transparent Designs: Reading, Performance, and Form in the Spectator Papers* (Athens, GA, 1985). On polite conversation in the eighteenth century, see Herbert Davis, 'The Conversation of the Augustans', in Richard F. Jones et al., *The Seventeenth Century: Studies in the History of English Thought and Literature from Bacon to Pope by Richard Foster Jones and Other Writing in his Honor* (Stanford, CA., 1951), pp. 181–97; Donald Davie, 'Berkeley and the Style of Dialogue', in Hugh Sykes Davies and George Watson, eds., *The English Mind* (Cambridge, 1964), pp. 90–106.

[28] On these aspects of Baxter's thought, see N.H. Keeble, *Richard Baxter: Puritan Man of Letters* (Oxford, 1982), pp. 24–5, 30, 32, 109, 135–236, 144.

himself in the Baxterian tradition. Like Baxter he desired Christian unity – or at least Protestant unity – above all things. 'Your innate candour and benevolence,' wrote one of his many correspondents in 1745, 'your contempt of party distinction, joined to a worthy pursuit of usefulness and good fame, have induced you sometimes to attempt the reconciliation of parties to each other, and to show yourself a friend to both; but this is not an age for success in such schemes.'[29] In the interest of unity, Doddridge advised preachers to decline 'the highest points of Calvinism, even supposing them to be believed, *viz.* the imputation of Adam's sin, Reprobation, Irresistible grace, &c'.[30] In his system of divinity he concentrated on non-sectarian issues: the nature of the human mind, proofs of the existence and attributes of God, the immortality of the soul and the authenticity of Scripture.

David Bogue and James Bennet, nineteenth-century nonconformist historians, dated the decline of Protestant Dissent from the lectures of Doddridge. Reasonably enough, they pointed out that if Doddridge and his followers really believed, as they claimed to believe, that the mind began as *tabula rasa*, then it was very wrong of them to inscribe error as well as truth upon the tablet and then expect the innocent young to make up their own minds upon the subject. Nor were they impressed by the defence that candour demanded such evenhandedness:

The misapplication of the word candour was more injurious in its effects on religious sentiments, than can now be well conceived. It was supposed to possess indescribable virtues. Candour was sounded from many a pulpit; and like charity, it was supposed to hide a multitude of sins. An orthodox minister who had candour, was to believe that an arian or socinian was a very good man; and that if he was sincere in his opinions, and not rigid in condemning others, he ought not to be condemned himself. The influence of this idea was exceedingly pernicious; for it led to an indifference with respect to truth and error, which depraved both their sentiments and dispositions, which relaxed the springs of Christian integrity and conduct, and gradually brought them to call good evil and evil good, to put light for darkness and darkness for light.[31]

We can, perhaps, conjecture why things should have come to this. First we have Richard Baxter, himself firmly rooted in the intellectual and

[29] *Correspondence and Diary of Philip Doddridge*, ed. J.D. Humphreys, quoted in G.F. Nuttall, *Richard Baxter and Philip Doddridge: A Study in a Tradition* (London, 1951), p. 11.

[30] Philip Doddridge, *Lectures on Preaching*, quoted in Nuttall, *Richard Baxter and Philip Doddridge*, p. 3. See also G.F. Nuttall, *The Puritan Spirit* (London, 1967), chs. 15 and 16.

[31] David Bogue and James Bennet, *History of Dissenters, from the Revolution in 1688 to the Year 1808*, 4 vols. (London, 1808–12), vol. III, p. 384. This passage is discussed in Davie, *Gathered Church* (fn. 20), pp. 139–41.

spiritual traditions of English Calvinism, anxious to reconcile the contending parties of his time, choosing to stress in his writings that which unites 'mere Christianity', rather than that which divides. Thus Baxter can say of someone whose religious opinions were repugnant to him that, though 'an unlearned Antinomian-anabaptist . . . yet (abating his separation) I never heard that Bunnian was not an honest godly man. If then he attained the design of Christianity, was he not a Christian?'[32] In other words, he can say that Bunyan is to be accepted *in spite* of his heresies but not *regardless* of them. These heresies are put in their place but they are not ignored. After Baxter we have Doddridge, inspired by similar benevolence but coming very close to bestowing it upon doctrines as well as men.[33] Accordingly, controversial doctrines are either ignored (as Doddridge advises preachers to do) or taught with no bias to any side of the controversy (as he did at Northampton and as his followers did at Daventry Academy, where Priestley was educated). But how are students to decide between the various parties in any controversy, lacking, as they are presumed to do, any particular bias of their own? Why indeed should their tutors not do as Bogue and Bennet ironically suggest, and teach atheism and deism, as well as Christianity? The answer, of course, is that the touchstone of religious truth is still the Bible. But then arises, as we have seen, the problem of how the Bible is to be interpreted without the magisterium of the Church. This is answered by the new concept of candour to which Thomas refers: 'One of the important elements in the ideal of candour is the claim . . . that the appeal to reason is the only legitimate form of persuasion.'[34] And so candour – which once meant treating all men alike in spite of their doctrines and then came to mean treating all (or almost all) doctrines alike – now means subjecting all doctrines alike to the scrutiny of an externally obtained principle of rationality.

Candour is less a quality of feeling than a quality of the behaviour that mediates between people. It is, moreover, a quality of specifically public behaviour: its historical importance is that it modifies and refines the behaviour of people who do not yet, and may never, know each other well. It is a thing needed not in the village but in the city, not in the

---

[32] Quoted in Keeble, *Richard Baxter* (fn. 28), p. 24.

[33] See, for example, Doddridge's *Christian Candour and Unanimity Stated, Illustrated and Urged: A Sermon preached at a Meeting of Ministers at Creaton in Northamptonshire*, repr. in *The Works of the Rev. Philip Doddridge, D.D.* [ed. E. Williams and E. Parsons], 10 vols. (London, 1802–5), vol. III, especially pp. 266–7.　　[34] Thomas, *Honest Mind* (fn. 20), p. 100.

organic community but in the public square and the market place. This
surely is why it was so much favoured by those Dissenters who called
themselves rational. For one thing, they were socially unknown qualities
– to others, at least – as soon as they stepped outside the meeting-house.
Separated, as they were believed to be, from the traditional and well-
understood network of social relations, the world of patriarchal authority and religious establishment, they were strangers meeting strangers.
As such they faced the problem of establishing relationships of trust
with those who could not rely upon a common loyalty to squire or
parson. The problem was increased by the fact that many of them lived
in cities – the monstrously burgeoning London or the new industrial
centres of Birmingham and Leeds – for the city was a world of strangers, people whose material concerns were similar but who had not yet
come to recognise their community of interest. (Their interests were of
course commercial, but commercial interests did not furnish the
obvious and solid focus of attention that real estate provided.) They
were people whom one could not 'place' in the old ways: in terms of
family, property or traditional trade. Some of them, indeed, were aware
of their situation: 'This day I have very different company – at some
part, professors, at another part, profane', a Leeds Dissenter confided to
his diary in 1754. 'To carry well among all requires the wisdom from
above.'[35] Naturally, people thus situated needed forms of social intercourse that were polite but not too personal: a repertoire of conventional phrases and gestures, displayed in order not to reveal the self but
to establish connections between those who were, and might remain,
strangers to each other.

III

The political context in which such discourse arose was so different from
that in which seventeenth-century nonconformity had been so loud a
voice that a number of historians have claimed that Dissenters took no
active part in politics until the French Revolution roused them from their
quietist slumbers. It has been further suggested that this very exclusion
preserved their radicalism in all its native purity: there was nothing that
could force them to compromise and nothing to diminish the sense of

[35] John Ryder in H. McLachlan, 'Diary of a Leeds Layman', *Transactions of the Unitarian Historical
Society*, 4 (3) (1920), 263, quoted in Seed, 'Gentlemen Dissenters' (fn. 23), p. 314. On the changed
nature of public roles in the eighteenth century, see Richard Sennett, *The Fall of Public Man* (New
York, 1977), ch. 3.

grievance that exclusion inspired in them.[36] But it would be an error to suppose that their need for candid discourse never arose in a political context.

Of course, the élite of Rational Dissent were political and they were radical, and their noisy eloquence has persuaded many historians to equate religious and political dissent and to ignore those loyalist Dissenters who were enemies to insubordination at home and revolution abroad.[37] As for Joseph Priestley himself, most prominent apologist of Rational Dissent, he was so loud in his protestation that Dissenters must by their very nature be friends to civil liberty that it is easy to overlook his repeated insistence that Dissenters as such had 'no peculiar principles of government at all'.[38] The two claims are reconcilable, of course, but together they seem decidedly disingenuous. Priestley did indeed wish to father certain political principles on his fellow Dissenters but he wished also to imply that these principles, being dictated by reason, were such as no reasonable person could take exception to. The claim that Dissenters had no political principles of their own is, then, an ideological one; it is a way of excluding from the thinking world all who reject those principles that Dissenters did in fact hold; it is a way of representing the interests of Rational Dissent as the common interests of all thinking people.

In describing the political affiliations of Dissent, Priestley has in fact two claims to make, one theoretical and the other historical. The

---

[36] Bradley's 'Whigs and Nonconformists' (fn. 23) is a discussion and rebuttal of these claims. His *Religion, Revolution and English Radicalism* (fn. 13) addresses the same subject at greater length, as does Colin Bonwick's *English Radicals and the American Revolution* (Chapel Hill, NC, 1977). For some particularly vigorous assaults on the equation of political and religious dissent, see Davie, *Gathered Church* (fn. 20), pp. 130–5, and *Dissentient Voice* (fn. 20), pp. 24, 94–123. Stephens points out, *London Minister* (fn. 7), p. 71 that a reliance solely on literary evidence has led many writers – he singles out Anthony Lincoln – to overstate the radicalism of eighteenth-century Dissent.

[37] For some of them see Lincoln, *Political and Social Ideas* (fn. 6), pp. 21–2; Bradley, *Religion, Revolution and English Radicalism* (fn. 13), pp. 122–4; Donald Davie, 'Disaffection of the Dissenters under George III', in Paul O. Korshin and Robert R. Allen, eds., *Greene Centennial Studies: Essays Presented to Donald Greene in the Centennial Year of the University of Southern California* (Charlottesville, 1984), pp. 320–50.

[38] Joseph Priestley, *A View of the Principles and Conduct of the Protestant Dissenters with Respect to the Civil and Ecclesiastical Constitution of England* (London, 1769), in *Works* (fn. 12), vol. XXII, p. 354. In the same piece (p. 341), he says of his co-religionists that 'as Dissenters they agree on nothing but in dissenting from the doctrines and disciplines of the Established Church'. Similarly, in his anonymously published *A Free Address to Protestant Dissenters as Such, by a Dissenter* (London, 1769), he says (p. iv) that 'Dissenters as such have nothing in common but a dissent from the established church: and it by no means follows that they, therefore, agree in any thing else.' In another anonymous work, *An Address to Protestant Dissenters of all Denominations . . . with Respect to the State of Public Liberty in General . . .* (London, 1774) he tells his fellow Dissenters that '*Religious liberty*, indeed, is the immediate ground on which you stand, but this cannot be maintained except on the basis of *civil liberty*' (*Works* (fn. 12), vol. XXII, p. 483). See Lincoln, *Political and Social Ideas* (fn. 6), ch. 2.

theoretical claim, whose validity he often takes for granted, is that the logic of the Dissenters' situation obliged them to advocate not only the reform of the Test and Corporation Acts but also other reforms in the state. The historical claim is that Dissenters did in fact advocate such reforms.

Priestley's tale is one of suffering bravely borne, the memory of which has given the Dissenters their zeal for civil liberty. Their cause, battered by the Tudors, was nearly done to death by the Stuarts, but the Stuarts were so bold in their attempts to enslave the nation that at last it rose in its own defence. The battle lines are depicted for us in primary colours: on one side are ranked King Charles and his haughty gang of papists and High Churchmen, all bent upon absolute despotism of the French or Spanish kind; on the other side, muskets primed in defence of its 'natural and civil rights', is nothing less than 'the *nation*, not the Dissenters only.'[39]

But before long this boldly sketched account of the Great Rebellion runs into difficulties, and these difficulties arise directly from Priestley's wish to depict Dissent as both politically neutral and conducive to a love of civil liberty. The Dissenters, he says, finished the war, as they had begun it, friends to monarchy; but it is the military leaders who 'will necessarily give the law to the state in all convulsions of this nature', and the leaders of this Rebellion happened to be Independents and republicans. Few but they wanted to cut off the King's head (though he deserved nothing less than a thousand deaths for what he had done), but nobody had the power to stop them. Their action was, however, dictated solely by political principle and not by religion.[40]

Here is Priestley's dilemma. He has said that Dissenters have no political principles peculiarly their own: he has said that they are friends to the English monarchy: so clearly he cannot approve of this project to found a republic. But neither can he approve of what he calls 'the usurpation of *Cromwell*', for Cromwell was a dictator and Dissenters are friends to civil liberty. What then would he have approved of? Surely not the restoration of the dead King's son, 'an avowed papist' whose 'uniform aim was to establish Popery in this kingdom'.[41] The necessary admission – that the King was beheaded because he stood in the way of a political settlement whose architects were indeed motivated, in part at

[39] Priestley, *Remarks on Some Paragraphs in the Fourth Volume of Dr. Blackstone's Commentaries on the Laws of England Relating to Dissenters* (London, 1769), p. 29. See also *A Free Address*, p. 37.

[40] Priestley, *Remarks* (fn. 38), p. 31.

[41] Priestley, 'An Answer to Dr. Blackstone's Reply', *St. James's Chronicle* (1769), repr. in *Works* (fn. 12), vol. XXII, p. 332 (see also the editor's note to this passage) and *Remarks* (fn. 38), p. 32.

least, by theological doctrine – is never made, though Priestley does at one point confess that the trick cannot be worked, that the Puritans cannot be depicted as friends alike to monarchy and to what he calls liberty. The liberty they sought was liberty for themselves alone. Had they been able to do so, they would have established a tyranny as severe as that of their enemies.[42] Since then, however – and despite severe persecution under the restored Stuarts – the Dissenters have been the true friends, perhaps the truest friends, of their country. They have educated it in the ways of civil liberty; they have opposed the worst of its rulers and been loyal to the best.

Such expressions of loyalty are commonplace, but Priestley, pursuing his own political agenda, will not go as far as his fellow Dissenter Andrew Kippis in protesting gratitude not only to the Prince of Orange and the first two Georges but also to 'the prince who now adorns the British throne'.[43] For Priestley everything changed with the accession of a new King 'who knows not Joseph', and from whom clergymen have hidden the truth.[44] Now there can be no certainty that the loyalty of Dissent will continue to be rewarded: 'that those who actually guide the measures which are now carrying on in this country, are equally enemies to civil liberty and to you, can no more be doubted, than that William III, of glorious memory, and the two first princes of the house of Hanover, were friendly to both', wrote Priestley in 1774.[45] This was a time when his anxieties and those of his radical friends had begun to find new focus in the American colonies. But it was a more local event that, they claimed, had first alerted them to the extent of ministerial corruption. This was the unconstitutional attempt by the administration to remove one of the chiefest thorns in its side: John Wilkes, MP.

'It has been said', Priestley remarks, 'that a great part of the resentment of the court against the Dissenters has arisen from a notion that they were the chief abettors of *Mr. Wilkes*; and I believe that, in general, they were the friends of his *cause*, because it was the cause of liberty and of the constitution.'[46] He is careful to explain that the Dissenters played no greater part in Wilkes's affair than any other patriots, except in so far

---

[42] [Priestley], *A Free Address* (fn. 37), p. 23.   [43] Kippis, *Vindication* (fn. 9), p. 23.

[44] Joseph Priestley, *Familiar Letters to the Inhabitants of the Town of Birmingham*, 5 pts (Birmingham, 1790), part I, p. 15. See Ian Christie, *Stress and Stability in Late Eighteenth-Century Britain* (Oxford, 1984), ch. 2, for an account of what the author calls 'this quite baseless political myth'.

[45] [Priestley], *Address to Protestant Dissenters* (fn. 37), pp. 484–5.

[46] *Ibid.*, p. 486. 'A Dissenter and a Wilkite were synonymous terms', said the *Anti Jacobin Magazine* many years later (quoted in Lincoln, *Political and Social Ideas* (fn. 6), p. 26).

as, being so dependent on public liberty, they naturally had a greater interest than others in its defence. But he must have known full well that Dissenters were not necessarily lovers of liberty as he understood it, and besides, his kind of Dissent is radically different from the orthodox kind: neither Calvinist nor Trinitarian, it is largely negative, consisting of the rejection of corrupt doctrine, and it depends for its propagation on the clash of opinions in public and the mutual interference of associations in the mind. Priestley was not alone in these opinions – Andrew Kippis agreed with him that the basis of Dissent was no longer a set of particular objections to the doctrines and government of the Established Church but rather an opposition to any attempt to impose tests or creeds on the conscience of the believer – but his form of Dissent was nonetheless a form to which few subscribed; Presbyterianism may have been going Priestley's way, the way of Rational Dissent, but there were still orthodox Dissenters, like the Independents and the General Baptists, who remained loyal to Calvin, and orthodox Dissent had always been ready, as militant heterodoxy was not, to circumvent the Test and Corporation Acts by way of occasional conformity.[47] Priestley, however, represents the political principles of Rational Dissent as something to which all Dissenters must necessarily adhere; and, since he says that they have no political principles peculiarly their own, it is easy to depict them as people sensitive not merely to their own needs but to those of the country at large. Needing civil liberty more than others, they are its particular friends. Its friends are their friends, and so they have always been grateful adherents of the House of Hanover. The implication is clear: surely only some very singular and unprecedented

---

[47] Kippis, *Vindication* (fn. 9), pp. 23–38. On the negative nature of Rational Dissent, see Richey, 'Origins of British Radicalism' (fn. 23). On the political implications of these developments, see Clark, *English Society* (fn. 1), pp. 315–21 and Bradley, *Religion, Revolution and English Radicalism* (fn. 13), pp. 88–90. In 1786, Ralph Harrison declared that Dissenters agreed on nothing but the importance of impartiality and of being persuaded in one's own mind as to the truth of the religious doctrines to which one adhered. There were, he said, no political tenets peculiar to them. See his *A Sermon at the Dissenting Chapel in Cross-Street Manchester . . . on Occasion of the Establishment of an Academy in that Town* (Warrington, 1786), p. 27. On the distinction between orthodox and Rational Dissent, see Bogue and Bennet, *History of Dissenters* (fn. 31), vol. III, pp. 383–6, 395–401; vol. IV, pp. 370–83; and Watts, *Dissenters* (fn. 7), pp. 376–82. Watts explains (p. 376) that at the Salters' Hall controversy of 1719 – which Kippis cites (p. 28) as evidence for his view of Dissent – while 'the majority of Presbyterian and General Baptist ministers took their stand on the sufficiency of Scripture, the majority of Congregationalists and Particular Baptists insisted on subscription to a Trinitarian Creed. And within a century most Presbyterian meetings and many of the General Baptist churches connected with the General Assembly had become Unitarian, while the Congregational and Particular Baptist churches not only remained Trinitarian but continued to honour the theology of John Calvin.'

breach of the constitution could have driven such loyal subjects into opposition.[48]

At least one of the reasons for his adopting this attitude can easily be inferred: if the intellectual universe is to be in all respects – intellectual, moral and theological – a place in which there is nothing that is merely inherited, nothing that is unquestioned, nothing that is not freely chosen, then it will be better if there can be free debate and a multiplicity of sects. There can be no orthodoxy, no establishment. ('In the present state of christianity, I am for increasing the number of sects rather than diminishing them', Priestley wrote in 1770, when it was suggested that Dissenters act in concert with reforming clergy in the Church of England.[49]) Hence the need for that free market in opinions which is his idea of civil liberty. The government's ineptitude in dealing with Wilkes afforded him an opportunity of pressing even more strongly his claims for civil liberty, and he was able to magnify the threat to liberty by asserting that even the Dissenters, hitherto the House of Hanover's most loyal subjects, have been driven into opposition by the dark schemes of the young King and his ministers.

Of course, the free market in ideas which candour made possible had many friends other than the Rational Dissenters. Hume, Montesquieu and Gibbon, and after them the political economists of Scotland, agreed that the liberty and equality of classical republican society engendered a certain gracelessness and were unfriendly to the polite arts. It was proper, they declared, that the citizen take advantage of what a market economy with its division of labour had to offer, that he pay specialists to defend and to govern him, so allowing himself leisure for the polite conversation and cultivated pursuits of which antiquity knew nothing. Here the intellectuals of Edinburgh and Glasgow found a model in the image of polite society, urban and urbane, which Joseph Addison had described in London.[50] During the first two decades of the century, Addison had used the pages of the *Spectator* to describe the club of which his eponymous narrator was a

---

[48] Priestley, *View* (fn. 37), pp. 355–6. It is possible to offer a very different account of the origins of Dissenting radicalism. Clark suggests, (*English Society* (fn. 1), pp. 217, 292–3) that the loyalty of the Dissenters to the House of Hanover was merely prudential and that it was withdrawn when the Jacobite threat waned.

[49] Dr Williams's Library, Mss., 12.45, ff. 68–9: Priestley to Thomas Lindsey, 21 February 1770 (repr., with some alterations, in Priestley, *Works* (fn. 12), vol. 1, p. 112). See also Priestley, *View* (fn. 37), p. 374.

[50] See J.G.A. Pocock, '*The Machiavellian Moment* Revisited: A Study in History and Ideology', *Journal of Modern History*, 53 (1981), 49–72, and *Virtue, Commerce and History* (Cambridge, 1985), pp. 131, 235–8. On this aspect of Addison's work, see Bloom and Bloom, *Joseph Addison's Sociable Animal* (fn. 27), chs. 1–3.

member, where the country squire, the rich merchant, the soldier, the lawyer and the clergyman could all meet and talk together freely on terms of equality. It was a microcosm of a world which did not yet exist but which might come to be: an orderly, tolerant society in which man could realise himself as the sociable animal that he truly was.[51] Addison's ideal was middle-class and mercantile, but he rejected Daniel Defoe's naked, buccaneering picture of capitalism in favour of something very close to what we later find in Priestley's writings on the subject. Trade, even trade in what is merely 'convenient and ornamental', smooths down the rough edges of English provincialism, making Englishmen 'kind, benevolent, and open-hearted to their fellow-creatures'. In short, it makes them candid, in the full eighteenth-century sense of the term.[52]

What Mr Spectator and his friends achieved in their club, Priestley (who admired Addison's work) sought to achieve by correspondence. In 1769 he founded the *Theological Repository*, a journal 'Consisting of Original Essays, Hints, Queries, &c. calculated to promote Religious knowledge'. He explained in his introduction to the first number that the best way of promoting such knowledge was to promote the communication of ideas; and, in order that the range of available ideas be as wide as possible, the pages of the *Repository* would be open 'not only to all denominations of Christians, but to persons who disbelieve Christianity and revelation in general'. Christians were to be encouraged to publish objections to their own faith, for everything was to be open to examination and all arguments were to be treated with 'candour and respect'.[53] It was a bold concept, assuming as it did a national constituency of the like-minded and the candid, and Priestley celebrated it by displaying on the title page of his first number an epigraph from the *Epistles* of Horace:

> ... *si quid novisti rectius istis*
> *Candidus imperti* ...

---

[51] Addison, *Spectator*, no. 9, 10 March 1711, quoted in Bloom and Bloom, *Joseph Addison's Sociable Animal*, pp. 4–5.

[52] Addison, *Spectator*, no. 464, 22 August 1712, quoted in Bloom and Bloom, *Joseph Addison's Sociable Animal*, p. 12; Spectator, no. 69, 19 May 1711 and *Freeholder*, no. 42, 10 April 1716, quoted in Bloom and Bloom, *Joseph Addison's Sociable Animal*, pp. 64–5. On Addison's repudiation of Defoe's ideas, see Pocock, *Virtue, Commerce and History* (fn. 49), pp. 236–7. For Priestley's views on the civilising effects of commerce, see his *Miscellaneous Observations Relating to Education* (Bath, 1778), repr. in *Works* (fn. 12), vol. xxv, pp. 1–80, at pp. 17, 22–3, 60–3, and *Lectures on History and General Policy* (Dublin, 1788), pp. 313–16, 322–3, 332, 337, 354, 356, 362. On '*le doux commerce*' in the eighteenth century, see Albert O. Hirschmann, *The Passions and the Interests: Political Arguments for Capitalism before its Triumph* (Princeton, 1977).

[53] Priestley, editorial introduction to *The Theological Repository* (London, 1769), repr. in *Works* (fn. 12), vol. vii, pp. 514–20, at pp. 514, 517–18.

These lines – which a contemporary translator rendered as, 'If you know any maxims betten than these, impart them with your usual candour . . .' – seem to have meant a good deal to educated men in the earlier part of the century: Pope wrote an imitation of the epistle in which they appear, and he used the lines themselves as epigraph to his *Essay on Criticism*; Lord Chesterfield quoted them in three of his letters; Fielding quoted them in his journalism; Steele used them as epigraph to an issue of the *Tatler* and Addison as epigraph to an issue of the *Spectator*.[54] There is something poignant in this, particularly in Priestley's use of lines which Addison also had employed: even as he wrote, the candid society which Addison had evoked in the *Spectator*, and which he had tried to invoke by means of the *Repository*, was slipping irrevocably from the realm of the possible. The year 1763 may serve us symbolically as a turning-point, for it was in that year that the Reverend Charles Churchill published his *Epistle to William Hogarth*.

Churchill wrote publicly to Hogarth because the artist had published a malicious caricature of Churchill's friend John Wilkes, having sketched his eminently-caricaturable features whilst the Court of Common Pleas was restoring him to liberty. Virtues like Wilkes's, says Churchill, seldom go unpunished; but then, after fifty-two lines, the flow of his indignation is checked:

> CANDOUR, who with the charity of *Paul*,
> Still thinks the best, when'er she thinks at all,
> With the sweet milk of human kindness bless'd
> The furious ardour of my zeal repress'd.[55]

Candour, 'of all alike the puling friend', urges the poet to abandon his satire and to follow 'soul-soothing PANEGYRIC's flow'ry way'. But the poet will have none of this, because Candour, 'cold monster', though an 'equal-blooded judge', is not just. She is 'half foe, half friend', not merely to Churchill but to everyone. She gives to all more or less than their due, and so cannot be a true friend because she cannot be a true enemy.[56]

Of course, Churchill cannot have been the first person in eighteenth-century England to be possessed by an honest rage which was not to be checked by the voice of moderation. He is distinctive, however, in

---

[54] For these references, see Caroline Goad, *Horace in the English Literature of the Eighteenth Century* (n.p., 1916; repr., New York, 1967), pp. 157, 336–7, 374, 389, 484, 503, 591, 597, 600. The translation from Book I of Horace's *Epistles* is from David Watson, *The Works of Horace, Translated into English Prose*, rev. edn by W. Crakelt, 2 vols. (London, 1792; facs. repr. New York, 1976), vol. II, p. 233.

[55] Charles Churchill, *An Epistle to William Hogarth*, ll. 55–8, repr. in *The Poetical Works of Charles Churchill*, ed. Douglas Grant (Oxford, 1956), pp. 211–30.   [56] *Ibid.*, ll. 102, 165–82.

finding it necessary to clear candour from his path before giving vent to his anger. The reason for this – the reason, that is, which the poem offers us – is that he had been provoked into speech by the threat of ruin to the nation's liberties and to 'that GREAT CHARTER, which our fathers bought with their best blood . . .' So great is his antipathy to candour that even when he does take notice of his victim's good points, he describes himself as acting not candidly but justly, for it is justice who

> . . . with equal course bids Satire flow,
> And loves the Virtue of her greatest foe.[57]

Of course, justice implies more than the lazy toleration of conflicting opinions: it also implies judgement between them. And, though the *Epistle to William Hogarth* was extreme, though candour had never been what Churchill represents it as being, it is worth asking why it was that a virtue which was so eminently the virtue of polite conversation could now be made to seem so insipid.[58]

One would expect that function of candour in establishing a bridge between strangers would have recommended it to all but the most isola-tionist of Dissenters. However, its appeal to Rational Dissenters surely lay also in its impersonality, in the fact that candour and sincerity were not the same thing. The old Puritans put their trust in those who could speak sincerely of the motions of the spirit within their hearts; the new Rational Dissenters, trusting to more objective criteria of religious authenticity, had less need of sincerity and its manifestations than of forms of behaviour that would enable people to deal honestly with each other without any spiritual interrogation. To move to their world of candour from the world of sincerity is to divert one's gaze from what people are and what they feel to what they say and what they do.[59] This being so, any alteration of the rhetorical atmosphere that pushes person-ality to the fore in public events is likely to have the most damaging effect on candour. Such a change was wrought by Churchill's friend John Wilkes, and Churchill's poem is a symptom of that change. Wilkes may

---

[57] *Ibid.*, *ll.* 401–2, 539–40.

[58] David Garrick found Churchill's poem 'the most bloody performance that has been published in my time' (R.B. Peake, *Memoirs of the Garrick Family*, quoted in Churchill, *Poetical Works*, p. 519). On candour and on the difficulty of maintaining truly candid conversation see Davie, 'Berkeley' (fn. 27).

[59] Cf. Sennett, *Fall of Public Man* (fn. 34), p. 39: 'to the extent a public geography exists, social *expres-sion* will be conceived of *as presentation* to other people of feelings which signify in and of them-selves, *rather than as representation* to other people of feelings present and real to each self'. I am also indebted here to some remarks by Lionel Trilling in his *Sincerity and Authenticity* (London, 1974), pp. 21–5.

not have been the first figure in English political life to derive his power from the magnetism of his personality (according to J.H. Plumb, he was just beaten to the post by the elder Pitt), but there was something strikingly new in the breadth and nature of his appeal.[60] The common people, artisans and labourers, felt that he was their friend and equal. His cause, he told them, was their cause, and responsibility for its success lay with them, even the humblest of them. Never had an English politician appealed so personally to so many people. As John Brewer remarks, Wilkes's aspirations may not have been radical but his methods were.[61]

It was at the height of the Wilkes affair that Edmund Burke condemned as cant the popular motto of 'not men, but measures', and a couple of years later, Junius, pseudonymous writer of letters to the press and scourge of the ministry, spoke of it in very similar terms. He called it 'the common cant of affected moderation', adding that 'such gentle censure is not fitted to the present, degenerate state of society'.[62] In earlier times character had mattered only in so far as it might lead a man to support particular policies. Now, however, policy was seen to be embodied in character: Wilkes embodied liberty, his enemies embodied tyranny. 'An assassination of their character sufficed to delegitimate the measures with which their names were associated', writes the sociologist Richard Sennett. 'The very basis of a public gesture was therefore erased: public speeches of both friends and enemy did not signify of themselves; they were only guides to the character of the speaker.'[63] So Churchill readily joins the mob in coupling the names of Wilkes and liberty, and upon Wilkes's enemy Hogarth, vain lackey of the tyrant, he heaps the most personal abuse.[64]

---

[60] In his *England in the Eighteenth Century* (Harmondsworth, 1950), Plumb says (pp. 108–9) that Pitt 'could create the sense in all who listened to him that he was their mouthpiece'.

[61] John Brewer, *Party Ideology and Popular Politics at the Accession of George III* (Cambridge, 1976), p. 198. See also pp. 170–1.

[62] Footnote (1772) to a letter of 7 October 1769, *The Letters of Junius*, ed. John Cannon (Oxford, 1978), p. 230; Edmund Burke, *Thoughts on the Causes of the Present Discontents* (orig. publ. 1770), as repr. in Ian Harris, ed., *Edmund Burke: Pre-Revolutionary Writings* (Cambridge, 1993), p. 188.

[63] Sennett, *Fall of Public Man* (fn. 34), p. 104. (This is quite consistent with Clark's claim that after 1760 political commitment became depersonalised. His point (*English Society*) (fn. 1), p. 197) is that in a hierarchical society the state was personified in its ruling family, so that political attitudes were cast 'within in a personal mould, creating the possibility of expressing political choices in terms of dynastic allegiance'. After 1760, he believes, the choice lay between parties and not dynasties. But, of course, dynasties do not embody principles such as liberty, nor do they do as Pitt and Wilkes did and pose as the people's mouthpiece. Before 1760, we may say, politics were personalised, in that political principle consisted of allegiance to persons; after 1760 politics were more truly personalised, in that abstract principle was held to be personified by certain individuals who had no dynastic standing.) On Wilkes as the embodiment of liberty see, for example, Junius's letter of 8 July 1769 (in *Letters* (fn. 61), pp. 80–6). [64] See, for example, Churchill, *Epistle* (fn. 54), *ll.* 419–86.

In such a climate, it was difficult to play the Addisonian censor, sociable though high-minded, just though forbearing, but that is what Priestley wanted his fellow Dissenters to do. In a sermon preached in 1764, he had reminded them that they must live for others and not for themselves. The Creator, he told them, has appointed that all our appetites and desires should point to something beyond themselves: for by this means he has insured the 'mutual connexion, dependence and harmony' of his works. There can be no pleasure in solitude – all our passions, whether gloomy or cheerful, are contagious – and daily, as man advances 'to general happiness', the connections between men grown more numerous.[65] In a later sermon, he explains how such obligations are to be discharged: Christians owe to all their sympathy and charity, but they must also, 'according to their several stations in life', labour to suppress vice and to advance virtue and religion. From this duty to advise and to set a good example, in the hostile world as well as in the meeting-house, not even 'the most ignorant, poor and necessitous' are exempt.[66]

It was a heavy duty to lay upon a set of religious outcasts. Years before, Addison, by placing his own surrogate, Mr Spectator, at the centre of a group of individuals who, though very disparate, were all members of the same club, had been able to give an earnest account both of his forbearance and of theirs. But now it was becoming increasingly difficult to hate the sin while loving the sinner – in politics at least, sin and sinner were close to being one – and amidst such difficulties the spirit of candour began to grow faint.

But as we have seen, it was the language of candour, rather than the language of rights, that metropolitan Rational Dissenters spoke when, in 1772, they sought repeal of the Trinitarian articles of the Toleration Act. Their failure was doubly disillusioning: in the first place, it appeared to show that candour was not to be looked for in bishops or ministers of state; in the second place, and perhaps more importantly, it showed them that even their fellow Dissenters were not to be trusted.[67]

---

[65] Priestley, 'The Duty of Not Living to Ourselves', a sermon 'preached . . . at Manchester, May 16th, 1764', repr. in *Works* (fn. 12), vol. xv, pp. 1–190, at pp. 125–9.

[66] Priestley, 'Christians the salt of the earth', p. 10, and the second of two untitled sermons on Matthew xxiv, 12, 13, p. 17 (MS. sermons, Manchester College, Oxford). See also pp. 6–7 of the latter sermon.

[67] Andrew Kippis's *Vindication* (fn. 9) is, as its title implies, something of an expression of this disillusionment. Kippis is anxious to establish (pp. 66–7) that the debate is about toleration and not about particular doctrines, whether Arian or Socinian. He is concerned also (pp. 78–81) to acquit the London ministers of the charge that they have ignored the opinions of the country clergy and to warn 'the very small number of Ministers who were unfriendly to their brethren in the late

Even before the failure of 1773, Priestley was telling his fellow Dissenters that where they had hitherto appealed as Christians, they should 'stand forth now in the character of *men*'; they should 'ask for the common rights of humanity'.[68] With the rejection of the appeal, he abandoned his willingness to compromise: if nothing could be won by an appeal to candour, then why not go all the way and demand toleration as of right? In 1773 he had been prepared to admit that there was at least no harm in the state's demanding a religious declaration of the citizen; by the following year, however, after the defeat of the appeal, he would no longer countenance such accommodations. They had been made, he said, in the belief (engendered 'by the artifices of courtiers') that they would further the Dissenting cause. Now they should be abandoned, having been shown up as futile.[69] But Priestley could never abandon the appeal to candour: it was as essential to his thought as the rights of man, if only because he believed that rights were most clearly apparent to a candid gaze. Some such idea as this seems implicit in much of the propaganda of Rational Dissent. Philip Furneaux, for example, argues that Locke's 'doctrine of Toleration' must seem both reasonable and agreeable now that it has been 'freed from the mist of prejudice, and set in a just light', and the same thinking is apparent even in the *Appeal* with which the London ministers sought the repeal of the Test and Corporation Acts.[70] The authors of this pamphlet, published in 1787, put little trust in the good nature of bishops and ministers of state. It is true that they set out their case in *An Appeal to the Candor, Magnanimity, and Justice of those in Power*, but this trio of moral substantives – each of them the sort of thing it was usually thought one ought to appeal to – may have been chosen in haste or without much thought. The same commodious title goes on to mention *Severe and Opprobrious Severities and Penalties*, and anyone who begs to be relieved of severe severities is either in a great hurry or deaf to the niceties of language. In fact the *Appeal* is very clear that toleration is not what is looked for here: the word implies

---

affair' that they may suffer as a result of their co-operation with the establishment: 'The time is probably fast approaching when the Thirty-nine Articles will be revised and altered . . . and . . . there can be little doubt but that strict Calvinism will be excluded, and an Arminian turn be given to the established doctrines.'

[68] Priestley, *Letter of Advice* (fn. 12), pp. 442–3, 450. Both Barlow, *Citizenship and Conscience* (fn. 9), pp. 195–8, and Lincoln, *Political and Social Ideas* (fn. 6), pp. 218–35, cite this work in illustration of their argument about candour, though, of course, having been written before the rejection of the appeal, it cannot be taken as one of its effects.

[69] [Priestley], *Address to Protestant Dissenters* (fn. 37), p. 485.

[70] Furneaux, *Essays on Toleration* (fn. 8), p. 2. On the *Appeal* and the committee responsible for it, see Barlow, *Citizenship and Conscience* (fn. 9), pp. 223–30.

sufferance or forbearance and 'ought not to be used in a free state'.
Nonetheless the authors clearly hope that the spread of 'knowledge and
truth' throughout the world, especially in a country so 'free and illu-
mined' as England, will help to ensure their success.[71] The same idea is
displayed even more clearly in the words with which, as late as 1790,
Priestley's friend Anna Laetitia Barbauld addressed the defenders of the
Test and Corporation Acts:

> We know you will refuse us while you are narrow minded, but you will not
> always be narrow minded. You have too much light and candour not to have
> more ... We appeal to the certain, sure operation of increasing light and knowl-
> edge.'[72]

It is important to be clear as to what is going on in such appeals as
these. Sometimes they can seem merely ingenuous, as when
Furneaux, in calling for a renewed appeal to the candour of
Parliament, says that he cannot believe that 'any Christian Bishops'
would really be capable of thinking as these bishops are said to think.[73]
Is this what it seems to be, a very naive view of episcopal psychology?
Or is it an attempt at irony, couched in the only language available to
Furneaux as a Rational Dissenter? Most probably it is neither:
Furneaux does not quite mean what he says – he knows exactly what
to believe of these Christian bishops – but he is not just being ironic.
Rather, he is giving them the benefit of the doubt, which is what
candour, considered as a methodological principle, requires him to do.
On the other hand, what he has to say is certainly not without irony.
Candour is an essential part of rationality and the imperative to be
candid is therefore a universal one, applying equally to Dissenters and
to bishops. To say that you are sure that bishops must be candid –
when you know and your readers know that they are not – is simply to
underline their lack of candour. Furneaux and others are able to make
this sort of point because the appeal to candour is necessarily something more than the appeal to the good nature of those in power that
Barlow and Lincoln take it to be.

I would suggest, then, contrary to what Lincoln and Barlow seem to
imply, that the language of candour as employed by the Rational
Dissenters was no less universal in its application than the language of
rights. After 1773 they might speak more of rights than hitherto, but they

[71] *An Appeal to the Candor, Magnanimity, and Justice of those in Power to Relieve from Severe and Opprobrious Severities and Penalties, a Great Number of their Fellow Subjects* ... (London, 1787), p. 8.
[72] [Barbauld, Anna Laetitia], *An Address to the Opposers of the Repeal of the Test and Corporation Acts* (London, 1790), p. 30.   [73] Furneaux, *Essays on Toleration* (fn. 8), pp. x–xi.

could not speak less of candour, though candour, as we have seen, was now a much more suspect thing than it had been in Addison's day.

The Rational Dissenters had played their own part in emptying the word of meaning. They could certainly be accused of having behaved uncandidly in 1772 by claiming to speak for Dissent as a whole when they very obviously did not. And their new tactic is similarly suspect. They now asked for the recognition of their rights, and of course that recognition need not be swayed by numbers, so no amount of counter-petitions by provincial Dissenters would (according to the presuppositions of this doctrine) affect the justice of their case. They could now appeal over the heads of Calvinist Dissent.

IV

In 1777, the Reverend David Williams urged that 'dissent, which used to be an opinion of superior orthodoxy and superior purity of faith,' should now abandon this rationale 'for another which is the only rational and justifiable reason of dissent – the inalienable and universal right of private judgement, and the necessity of an unrestrained enquiry and freedom of debate and discussion on all subjects of knowledge, morality, and religion'.[74] Now, it is probably important not to follow Barlow in taking Williams as representative of Dissent, even of Rational Dissent at its most radical. He was an improbable figure with a taste for the theatre and for self-dramatisation. 'My haunts are among the mountains, and I love the terrific and sublime among the works of God', he once said. 'In moral as well as natural scenes, my delight has ever been in climbing rocks and tempting dangers.'[75] By 1777, he had left the orthodox Dissenting ministry – or, according to his account, had been forced to leave 'by the intrigues of a lady' – and had set up his own chapel, using a liturgy of his own composition which won the praise of Voltaire and of Frederick the Great. *The Letter to the Body of Protestant Dissenters*, from which Barlow quotes, is, as the Dissenting historian Alexander Gordon puts it, 'a plea for such breadth of toleration as would legally cover such services as his'.[76] Even before then, his *Essays on Public Worship, Patriotism, and Projects of Reformation* had sounded a clearly heretical note, advocating a liturgy so trimmed of theological doctrine 'as to please a conscientious

---

[74] David Williams, *A Letter to the Body of Protestant Dissenters* . . . quoted in Barlow, *Citizenship and Conscience* (fn. 9), p. 194.
[75] [David Williams], *Essays on Public Worship, Patriotism, and Projects of Reformation*, 2nd edn (London, 1774), Appendix, p. 2.　　[76] Alexander Gordon, 'David Williams', in *DNB*.

Deist'.[77] Here his object, he says, is to enable honest men of all religions to put aside rancour and come together in public worship. To this end, faith must be replaced by honesty, and religion founded solely on principles of piety and morality: 'We might in this manner give a specimen of that worship which should employ all creatures of God; and of that candor and charity which are the great honor and happiness of human nature.'[78]

Williams is eccentric only in his extremism. He carries as far as it will go a tendency common to all Rational Dissent. Priestley stops a little short of Williams, but in both of them the theological basis for Dissent had been replaced by a methodological principle. Indeed, Priestley was even to go so far as to suggest that candour might be more valuable than the 'right decision in any controversy': a candid controversy was one in which all the evidence was properly exhibited and both sides displayed a 'truly christian temper' and 'the love of truth'.[79]

This is how the Rational Dissenters earn their place in the ranks of radicalism: their methodological principle seems to have a gratifyingly modern air and can be seen as a plea for free speech, free inquiry and toleration. It also happens that this principle, conflicting as it did with the basis upon which the British state was founded, forced the Rational Dissenters into opposition and eventually helped to win for some of them the status of martyrs when their meeting-places and houses, Priestley's among them, were destroyed by an angry mob.

Unfortunately, these Dissenting principles are largely without positive content, and they reach their fullest expression just when some very positive principles are being packed up and crated on the Paris wharves ready for export to the United Kingdom. Once these Jacobin principles had arrived they were able comparatively easily to fill the vacuum in Rational Dissenting thought. Thus we find Priestley, ever in the vanguard, seizing with enthusiasm on Joel Barlow's *Address to the Privileged Orders*, and the second and more radical part of Tom Paine's *Rights of Man*.[80] The principle of candour now seems thoroughly compromised.

---

[77] [Williams], *Essays* (fn. 74), p. 65. For his own deistic sentiments, presented in a sympathetic account of the religion of Thomas More's Utopians, see pp. 17–20.

[78] *Ibid.*, p. 65. See also pp. 20–1, 34, 60.

[79] Priestley, *A Third Letter to Dr. Newcome, Bishop of Waterford, on the Duration of our Saviour's Ministry*, quoted in Martin Fitzpatrick, 'Toleration and Dissent', *Enlightenment and Dissent*, 1 (1982), 3–31 at p. 27.

[80] 'Such boldness', wrote Priestley, '...was never seen before in this or any other country.' (British Library, Add. MSS. 44, 992, ff 48–9v: Priestley to William Russell, Clapton, 15 February 1792.

George Canning's poem 'New Morality', first published in the *Anti-Jacobin Review* in 1798, represents it as a refusal to judge when judgement is most urgently demanded. This is what Churchill had done more than thirty years before, but Canning's attack on the word is more ideological than Churchill's. It is a call for a revival of satire in a society pervaded by a 'deep infection' that has transformed its moral virtues into political vices. For Canning, the candid are people who distract your attention with polite conversation while somebody else is trying to pick your pocket. They plead for open-mindedness, for a willingness to see the good in everybody, but the time for fairness and open-mindedness is past because there are now forces on the march in whom no just eye could possibly see any good: the vengeful, murderous forces of Jacobinism before whom the candid seem either deluded or deluding.[81]

[81] George Canning, 'New Morality', repr. in *The Poetical Works of George Canning* . . . (London, 1823; facs. repr. New York and London, 1973).

CHAPTER 11

Priestley on politics, progress and moral theology

Alan Tapper

My aim in this chapter is to set Priestley's political theory in its theological context. The whole subject is larger than I can manage here, so a few restrictions are required. Priestley interests us partly because we want to understand how intelligent thinkers can have been so naively optimistic about the French Revolution. My discussion is designed to lead up to that question, to supply some of the background to it; but I will not otherwise be concerned with his practical politics. Priestley, though not a political actor, was a frequent commentator on the events of his day, but his views on practical politics are rather complexly related to his general political theory. My purpose will be only to make sense of the general theory.

On the theological side I will not attempt to discuss Priestley's millenarianism, which is itself closely interconnected with his general theological thought. In the late 1790s his millenarianism, his political utopianism, his more general progressivism and his personal disappointments all interact in a way which is fascinating, confusing and unsettling. My central subject is not the deeply troubled Priestley of these last years, but the serene, active and boundlessly optimistic younger man at the height of his powers – 'the Voltaire of Unitarianism', as Hazlitt described him – just before the intellectual world he so much symbolised, the confident world of Rational Dissent, began to disintegrate under pressure from events in the political arena.

Some of my subject is familiar, perhaps over-familiar. Is there anything still to be explained about Priestley's political theory? I will not attempt to answer that question directly here, but that there is something to be explained may be suggested by beginning from what he did not hold to. Priestley was not a natural-rights theorist, at least not a defender of natural rights. He was not a democrat who tied political status to (male) personhood. He was not a radical individualist or anarchist in the manner of Godwin. Nor was he a primitivist radical looking back to an idealised pre-Norman past. He was not a revolutionary, though he supported both the American and French Revolutions. His radicalism, if he was a radical, has none of the agrarian utopianism or artisan populism to be found in some of his contemporaries. Nor, I believe, was he in any obvious sense a republican: he was not much bothered by mobile property, standing armies, division of labour, or indirect political representation; he did not see personal virtue as fulfilled in political action, nor did he believe that the well-being of the state rests heavily on the virtue of its citizens.

Yet if all this is true – and I shall provide at least some argument for some of these claims – in what sense did he belong to the eighteenth-century tradition of liberal radicalism? Is he a quite new departure within that somewhat complex collection of ideals and ideas? Do we need a new category here? Geoff Gallop has suggested the concept of 'commercial radicalism'.[1] This seems about right to me, but it leaves out the moral and religious background which makes Priestley both commercial and radical. The problem of evil, I shall suggest, is for Priestley in part a political problem and the problems of politics are aspects of the problem of evil. My purpose will be to show how his moral theology ties together his commercialism and his radicalism. The ironic, or tragic, twist at the end of this story is that it was at least in part his moral theology that desensitised him to the actual evils brought about by the radical cause that he supported in France.

Priestley's political views are of course religious in a quite obvious sense. As a primitivist Protestant (primitivist at least in his view of Revelation, not in his philosophical theology) he believes that worldly power is both unnecessary and positively harmful to the cause of true religion, and that the New Testament directly opposes state involvement in matters of religion. As a Dissenter he is committed to the full toleration of Dissenters and to their right *qua* citizens to participate fully in all civil offices. As a Rational Dissenter he is committed to the full toleration of all religious or non-religious minorities, if they abide peacefully by the laws of the state. As a believer in the rationality of true religion he regards political support for religion as heterogeneous and distracting. On religious grounds, then, he wishes to see a complete separation between Church and state, entailing the disestablishment of the Church of England. Most of Priestley's efforts in practical politics are directed to

---

[1] Geoff Gallop, 'Politics, Property and Progress: British Radical Thought, 1760–1815' (D. Phil. Thesis, University of Oxford, 1983), pp. 208–24.

this end, nor can we imagine him holding any political philosophy that conflicted with that cause. However, it does not follow that his political philosophy is simply Dissenter politics writ large. Rather, he regarded the cause of the Dissenters as fitting easily into a larger development, the growth of liberalism.

There is another sense in which his moral theology feeds into his political theory. Before he was a political theorist Priestley was a philosophical theologian. In his first published work, the three-volume *Institutes of Natural and Revealed Religion* (1772–4), and pervasively in much else that he wrote, in ways which seem peculiar to us, Priestley turned and returned to the problem of evil. Taking his writings as a whole he presents five distinct 'answers' to the problem: that good can only be appreciated fully if evil exists as a contrast to it; that any finite creation must be imperfect; that the evils attendant upon a system-like natural order are less than those that are produced when every natural occurrence is a particular act of God; that human virtues can only be acquired in a struggle against adversity; and that history shows divine providence steadily bringing good out of evil, which affords a presumption that this process of amelioration will continue, even beyond death. The one defence not employed by him, the appeal to free-will, is of course precluded by his determinism.

John Hick's distinction between 'Augustinian' and 'Irenaean' theodicies is useful here, though it is striking that Priestley sees no difficulty in being *both* Augustinian and Irenaean.[2] His first three defences, resting on the notions of contrast, finitude and system, are plainly Augustinian but the dominant 'character-formation' theodicy, involving moral progress through the discipline of suffering, is unmistakably Irenaean.

The relation between virtue and suffering is a central theme in all Priestley's moral, political and historical thought. When he has to summarise his theodicy as briefly as possible it is to the character-formation defence that he turns.

This world, we see, is an admirable nursery for great minds. Difficulties, opposition, persecution, and evils of every other form, are the necessary instruments by which they are made.[3]

---

[2] John Hick, *Evil and the God of Love* (London, 1966), ch. 12. Hick makes no mention of Priestley, and presents Schleiermacher as the first modern 'Irenaean'.

[3] The Dedication to *The Doctrine of Philosophical Necessity Illustrated*, 2nd edn (1782), in *The Theological and Miscellaneous Works of Joseph Priestley*, ed. J.T. Rutt, 25 vols. in 26 (London, 1817–31; repr. New York, 1972), vol. III, p. 450 (hereafter cited as *Works*).

Further, his historical progressivism contains a kind of gradualist conservatism: change is justifiable only if it preserves the accumulated achievements of past generations. Lasting human happiness can only be won in a lengthy struggle:

> all great improvements in the state of society ever have been, and ever must be the growth of time, the result of the most peaceable but assiduous endeavours in pursuing the slowest of all processes – that of enlightening the minds of men.[4]

This slowest of all processes cannot be hastened without losing the object to be obtained, and is thus the fastest route to its destination.

The connection in Priestley's thought between theology and politics is not simply through the theory of historical progress, for that theory itself involves a relation to progress in science which requires more discussion. Social progress is in part modelled on scientific progress. Scientific knowledge flourishes best where there is free exchange of ideas, and so too does social improvement.

The acquisition of scientific knowledge depends vitally on the free exchange of ideas, for this stimulates the imagination and thus promotes the production of hypotheses. Without imagination to suggest hypotheses science could not begin. Hypotheses in turn suggest experiments. In the practical arts and in social affairs the same holds good: according to the *Essay on Government*, 'of all arts, those stand the fairest chance of being brought to perfection, in which there is opportunity of making the most experiments and trials, and in which there are the greatest number and variety of persons employed in making them'.[5] And the greatest barrier to social progress is state-imposed uniformity, whether that uniformity be religious, intellectual or economic.

The acquisition of scientific and social knowledge through the free exchange of ideas is part of the story of progress but for the progressivist it is equally important to explain how such knowledge might accumulate. This part of the process of progress contains a difficulty. With progress in science and society, the *Essay on Government* tells us,

> nature, including both its materials and its laws, will be more at our command; men will make their situation in this world abundantly more easy and comfortable; they will probably prolong their existence in it, and will grow daily more

---

[4] *The Proper Objects of Education in the Present State of the World* (1791), in Priestley, *Works*, vol. xv, pp. 438–9.
[5] *An Essay on the First Principles of Government and on the Nature of Political, Civil and Religious Liberty*, 2nd edn (1771), Section iv (hereafter cited as *Essay on Government*), in Priestley, *Works*, vol. xxii, p. 44.

happy, each in himself, and more able (and, I believe, more disposed) to communicate happiness to others.[6]

'More able', yes, but 'more disposed'? Priestley's hesitation here has an explanation. He is not certain that achievements in morality can be accumulated in quite the same way as can achievements in science and society.

Accumulation involves transmission, for if each, or any, generation fails to pass on what it has learnt, no level of achievement, no matter how great, can amount to real progress. Conversely, the smallest achievements, if passed on incrementally, may eventually constitute some large improvement in the human lot. While the painfully acquired habits of virtue may make the practice of virtue easier within one person's life, there is no obvious sense in which such habits can be collective achievements. They are not readily or reliably transmissible from person to person or from generation to generation.

This is not, from Priestley's perspective, merely an unfortunate obstacle to moral improvement. His whole account of character-formation entails that moral achievements can not be passed on directly, for the simple reason that the struggle and suffering that produced them cannot be shared. The attempt to pass on even ordinary goods, to be enjoyed without effort, is likely to misfire:

when a provident, but unwise parent, submits to toil and hardship, in order to leave an estate to his son, he only provides him something to waste and dissipate, but not to enjoy. The prodigal youth is even generally much less happy in spending the estate than the father in getting it; though the object of his toil has been to make his son more happy in being exempt from it.

This comes from the *Observations on Education* of 1778, which itself arose partly from the difficulties he experienced in designing a 'liberal and virtuous' course of education for sons of the aristocracy, when he supervised the studies of Lord Shelburne's sons.[7] Such considerations were still in his mind thirteen years later in his *Political Dialogue*:

The man who makes a sensible use of riches which he has not acquired must be something almost above humanity; and therefore it is not to be expected in the ordinary course of things; and when hereditary titles, and other distinctions, are added to hereditary wealth, the danger must be greatly increased.[8]

Here the individualism of Priestley's morality has come into conflict with the collectivism of his theory of (moral) progress, and it is the

---

[6] *Ibid.*, XXII, p. 9.
[7] J. Priestley, *Miscellaneous Observations relating to Education*, in *Works*, vol. XXV, p. 61.
[8] J. Priestley, *A Political Dialogue on the General Principles of Government* (1791), in *Works*, vol. XXV, p. 93.

progressivism that has to give way. If morality cannot progress of and by itself, what is needed is some other account of how progress in general can lead to progress in morals. Somehow progress that is morally neutral must lead to morally desirable results.

However, there is in Priestley's thought another variation on the relation between scientific and moral matters. As he maintains in the preface to his *History of Electricity*, science has a moralising influence because it reinforces the credibility of theism.

The more we see of the wonderful structure of the world, and of the laws of nature, the more clearly do we comprehend their admirable uses to make all the percipient creation happy, a sentiment which cannot but fill the heart with unbounded love, gratitude, and joy. Even every thing painful and disagreeable in the world appears to a [natural] philosopher, upon a more attentive examination, to be excellently provided, as a remedy of some greater inconvenience, or a necessary means of a much greater happiness . . . Hence he is able to venerate and rejoice in God, not only in the bright sunshine, but also in the darkest shades of nature, whereas vulgar minds are apt to be disconcerted with the appearance of evil.[9]

Suffering ennobles, but its influence is restricted to the improvement of individuals. But science also edifies, theologically, and progress in science, by strengthening theism, thereby promotes progress in morality.

Even so, moral character depends more on the experience of adversity than on the inspiration available from the contemplation of design, though both contribute to moral ends. The two are complementary: scientific progress reinforces theism, which in turn motivates a movement towards the mastering of adversity and evil, out of which may arise a deeper understanding of the purposes of Providence.

Priestley's world, in which science, religion and morality enjoy such harmony, may strike us as remote. Yet Burke, for instance, was a progressivist of a kind, and it is interesting to compare his view of the place of religion and science in progress with Priestley's. When Burke attacks the abstract reasoning of the radicals he does so in the name of the accumulated wisdom of past ages; he assumes that history is, on the whole, a process of gathering and preserving such wisdom. Yet his theory of progress is mechanically quite opposite to Priestley's. Instead of science supporting religion and morality through the idea

---

[9] J. Priestley, *The History and Present State of Electricity, with Original Experiments* (1767), Preface, in *Works*, vol. xxv, p. 351.

of design, for Burke it is religion and morality that made science possible. Only when once-mediæval Christianity and chivalry had tamed and civilised men was it possible for the great co-operative ventures of modern science, technology, commerce and industry to flourish.

From these opposite starting-points Burke and Priestley draw opposing political conclusions. In Priestley's view progress rests on a broad social base – the 'industrious classes', of which the scientist, the industrialist and the merchant represent only the tip. For Burke the heart of all progress remains with the guardians of good manners, the nobility and the clergy. For Burke progress can never be more than extremely fragile, for everything depends on the ability of the clergy and nobility to preserve and propagate the special and difficult ethos of civilised restraint, and the clergy at least must be always vulnerable to materially powerful predators. For Priestley, by contrast, the civilising agencies are also the creators of a new kind of material power and prosperity. Progress is intrinsically robust; it is not always, as Burke thought it was, in danger of sinking into barbarism.

Various eighteenth-century thinkers, of whom Rousseau is only the best known, had come to the conclusion that progress, Priestley's kind of progress, is a self-defeating process: the more the arts and sciences contribute to human well-being, the more they sap men's capacity for genuine virtue. Progress, by making life easier, makes character-formation more difficult. For Priestley character-formation requires adversity, and we might expect this side of his theodicy to lend itself to a Spartan conception of private and civic life. However, in political matters this Spartanism is one of the things he seeks to combat. The dominant theme of his politics is a defence of liberalism based on his progressive interpretation of history. The interesting theological issue is whether this defence requires him to sacrifice the emphasis on adversity and difficulty so prominent in his purely theological writings.

After the American Revolution Priestley shared with the radicals the belief that (in England at least) liberty had begun to decline, but he rejected their diagnosis of the causes of the decline. He sought to draw a sharp distinction between 'luxury', which was on the whole a good, and 'idleness', which he saw as the chief cause of his age's ills. Luxury is evil only in so far as it is associated with idleness; in every other way it is to be approved of. This distinction, as I shall try to show, is the key to his politics.

'Idleness', Priestley tells us, is 'the great inlet to the most destructive vices'.[10] By 'idleness' he means, of course, not rest after labour but life without labour. We are constitutionally unfitted for a life of ease, and without 'the constant, but moderate, exertion of our faculties' we cannot be happy, his *Observations on Education* argue.[11] Material progress ('luxury') is morally beneficial so long as its connection with effort is not broken; when, however, we seek enjoyment without effort ('idleness') the result is morally detrimental. The theological aspect of his view of labour and leisure is obvious: idleness is simply the avoidance of the kind of difficulty prescribed by the character-formation regimen, while luxury is the morally harmless end-product of the long historical struggle against adversity.

Priestley's belief in the corrupting effects of idleness underlies his disagreement with Burke in the 1790s. Less obviously, his defence of luxury marks him off from many of his fellow radicals, who attacked aristocratic predominance in government (and Burke as its apologist) for its propensity towards a corrupting surrender to luxury.

To summarize it very diagrammatically, the debate over the French Revolution was triangular, though not in the sense of a disagreement about three possible rates to a single process of change; rather, three positions were taken about two possible kinds of change. One axis of the argument concerned political participation, with opposing views about the virtues and vices of aristocracies and democracies. The other axis was economic, about the virtues and vices of economic progress. The radicals tended to regard economic progress as detrimental to political liberty. Burke defended aristocratic leadership, but in a manner that included a commitment to the generally beneficial effects of material and scientific progress. Priestley's position cut across these two, to form the third corner of the triangle. He belonged with the radicals in rejecting aristocracy, which Burke saw as essential to political order. But he also rejected the economic assumptions of the radicals, and thus sided with Burke in defending the main trend of progress. He was both politically radical and economically progressive, and at bottom this combination rested on theological premises.

By 1789 Priestley had concluded that the governments of both Britain and France were on the brink of financial bankruptcy and that the cause of this imminent catastrophe was to be found in the moral bankruptcy of their aristocracies. Burke shared Priestley's sense of financial crisis, the

---

[10] J. Priestley, *Lectures on History and General Policy* (1788), Lecture I, in *Works*, vol. xxiv, p. 340.
[11] Priestley, *Works*, vol. xxv, p. 60.

belief that 'Nations are wading deeper and deeper into an ocean of boundless debt', which 'threatens a general earthquake in the political world'; but, against that, he contended that the French nation was generally prosperous, and that the crisis gave no warrant to those who would exploit the situation for the purpose of political change.[12]

Priestley, by contrast, thought radical reform the only remedy. In *A Political Dialogue on the General Principles of Government* the French national debt is central to his discussion; however, his objection is not to public credit itself, but to the misuse of public credit in the hands of the aristocracy. Government expenditure is out of control because fiscal decisions are in the hands of an hereditary class which bears no commensurate responsibility for the raising of revenue. Enjoying unearned honours, offices and authority, this class has occupied its idleness with grand schemes of empire and conquest, paying little regard to their cost to the public. The aristocratic system is not just inefficient, it is corrupting, and not least to those who appear to profit from it. It is the fate of men of rank to suffer 'debasement of their characters, with the deprivation of all real enjoyment'. The system is bound to fail, for it destroys the connection between difficulty, effort and virtue. It separates leisure from labour and thus causes luxury to degenerate into idleness. Public finances can only be restored when those who produce public monies, the 'industrious classes', have the greatest say in how they are spent. Then only will government work for the public good. The hereditary system must eventually bow before 'that prevailing spirit of industry and commerce to which it was ever hostile, and before that diffusion of knowledge on the subject of government . . . which has burst out in the last half century'.[13]

Priestley's views on aristocracy are best brought out by a contrast with those of Burke. Burke's defence of the French aristocracy is couched partly in terms of the utility and innocence of 'idleness'. A leisured class is essential to ensure the political wisdom that can come from education and financial independence, and hereditary privileges are the best security for such a class. Hereditary wealth and distinctions are, at their best, the privilege of men of virtue and ability, or of the patrons of such men; 'at the very worst, [they are] the ballast in the vessel of the commonwealth', a counterbalance to the disturbing effect of men with ability but no property. This stabilising influence is all the more necessary because it

---

[12] Edmund Burke, *Reflections on the Revolution in France*, ed. Conor Cruise O'Brien (Harmondsworth, 1969), pp. 263–5, 231–8, 127.   [13] J. Priestley, *A Political Dialogue*, in *Works*, vol. xxv, p. 92.

is likely to be always under threat from the rest of the populace. However responsible the French aristocracy may be for the national debt (Burke thinks that France's fiscal difficulties result from mismanagement, not anything fundamental), any revolutionary régime that seeks to take the place of the aristocracy is certain to act with a 'contempt of justice'. Greed and envy will cause it to expropriate all that it can, even to the extent of debasing the currency in its own interests. In short, nothing good can be expected from the self-appointed representatives of the people, whatever motives they may profess, and the people themselves, lacking sufficient moral self-restraint, must be taught to hold their institutions in 'social awe'.[14]

Burke's argument is two-pronged: the aristocracy is on the whole protected from moral degeneration by the privilege of 'idleness', whereas when 'the people' try to overhaul society they are always in moral danger from the temptations of greed and envy. Priestley takes the opposite stance: idleness is the chief source of moral danger, and in civilised societies it is popular opinion that has come to embody 'a sense of justice and honour' in acting as a check upon encroachments by the state on civil liberties.[15] Yet while holding antithetical views on idleness, Burke and Priestley are in agreement about luxury, which they both see as socially beneficial. As Burke puts it, 'the love of lucre, though sometimes carried to a ridiculous, sometimes to a vicious excess, is the grand cause of prosperity to all states'.[16] In this respect they are both allies and heirs of Adam Smith.

Furthermore, Burke endorses Priestley's insistence on a theological dimension to the notion of difficulty. 'Difficulty is a severe instructor, set over us by the supreme ordinance of a parental guardian and legislator, who knows us better than we know ourselves, as he loves us better too.'[17] The words are Burke's, but could be Priestley's. Curiously, Burke's portrait or caricature of the radical, carried away by his 'idle' speculation and theoretical dreams, has features in common with Priestley's portrait or caricature of the 'idle' aristocrat. Burke's radical 'delights in the most sublime speculations; for, never intending to go beyond speculation, it costs nothing to have it magnificent'.[18] Priestley's aristocrat also favours the grandiose gesture, for it costs *him* nothing to have it magnificent, though it may bankrupt the state. The theological element in Priestley's

[14] Burke, *Reflections* (fn. 12), pp. 139–41, 236–7.
[15] J. Priestley, *Essay on Government*, section III ('Of Civil Liberty'), in *Works*, vol. XXII, p. 34.
[16] Discussed in Michael Freeman, *Edmund Burke and the Critique of Political Radicalism* (Oxford, 1980), p. 52.   [17] Burke, *Reflections* (fn. 12), p. 278.   [18] *Ibid.*, p. 155.

later politics can be further highlighted by contrasting his road to reform
with that taken by many of his fellow radicals. There are two essential
contrasts here, one concerning natural political rights, the other concerning luxury. Out of these differences arise different pictures of the
historical process.

Unlike Paine or Cartwright, and contrary to what is frequently
implied by Burke, Priestley makes little of the notion of natural political
rights. In limiting natural rights to civil rights Priestley and Burke are at
this point in close agreement. Epistemologically, this is the view we might
expect Priestley to hold – in politics, much as in moral theology, everything depends on 'historical facts', and observation and experiment are
'the only safe guides'. His 1767 *Essay on Government* follows Pope's maxim
concerning forms of government: 'Whatever is best administered, is
best.'[19] This pragmatic attitude to political systems prevents Priestley
from embracing complete democracy even when he has become hostile
to aristocracy. The point requires emphasis because, from Burke
onwards, the radicals have been regarded as if they were all natural-
rights democrats in the manner of Paine. According to Burke the radicals 'are always at issue with government, not on a question of abuse, but
a question of competency, and a question of title'.[20] This seems inaccu-
rate in Priestley's case: his formal argument reasons from questions of
abuse (the national debt) to questions of competence (the nature of aristocracy) and only then to questions of title (political rights).

Priestley differs from his fellow radicals in other ways. He is quite
immune to the 'primitivism' of radical Whig mythology. Many of his
fellow radicals looked back to pre-Norman England for their standard of
virtue. Priestley could admire that era only relative to its position in the
scheme of progress. He had no wish to return to a pre-commercial existence, with the urban poor resettled on the land. Economic redistribu-
tion, sometimes pursued as a means of abolishing luxury, was also no
part of his programme. Fundamentally, he thought that if wealth had
been honestly earned it could be safely enjoyed. Along with this went a
defence of the means of modern wealth, commerce, credit and manu-
facturing. The defence rests on the assumption that wealth is the result of
effort and industry, and thus has a theological sanction.

If the economic foundations of modern society are morally sound,
then it can present no great danger at the political level. On the whole
the effects of luxury will be favourable to liberty. 'When men, by the

---

[19] J. Priestley, *Essay on Government* in *Works*, XXII, p. 30.   [20] Burke, *Reflections* (fn. 12), p. 149.

practice of the arts [of luxury], acquire property, they covet equal laws to secure that property.'[21] Nor does luxury endanger liberty by opening the commonwealth to the threat of external aggressors. It does not make men effeminate and cowardly: 'surely more spirit and courage may be expected from a man who has had good nourishment, and who has something to defend, than from one who is almost starved, and who has little or nothing to fight for'.[22] Besides, Priestley adds, modern knowledge is itself a source of power for the defence of the state. The real danger to modern society has come from the enforced idleness of Europe's aristocracies, leading as it does to fiscal disaster and, subsequently, to revolutions.

Priestley's radicalism, then, rests on a different moral basis from that of the opponents of luxury. It derives from his theodicy which links difficulty, effort and character, while rejecting the Spartanism of some of the other radicals. This theodicy denies that material progress must produce its own moral nemesis and thus perpetuate a sequence of historical cycles. It contends for the opposite conclusion, that material progress brings both moral and political benefits. It is Priestley's emphasis on the political benefits of progress that distinguishes him most sharply from both Burke and many of his fellow radicals. In his writings we can see how heavily early liberalism depended on the assumption of moral progress.

All their differences notwithstanding, the British 'balanced constitution', and the American and French Revolutions are, Priestley believes, the fruit of a long process of political maturation. In modern societies such as Britain, France and America, civil and political liberty is no longer constantly endangered by evil and corruption; in these societies liberty can indeed be safely expanded. The assumption of moral progress, as Margaret Canovan has observed, meant for Priestley that

There was no longer any need for the state to watch jealously over the morals and manners of the citizens, and to fight constantly against human nature. Opinions and private habits were no longer politically important, and could become a part of civil liberty precisely because they had become politically indifferent, things that could neither make nor mar the state.[23]

Because he thought men had become more self-disciplined and governable, Priestley came to see the art of government as being less

---

[21] J. Priestley, *Lectures on History*, Lecture 51, in *Works*, vol. XXIV, p. 310.

[22] *Ibid.*, Lecture 55, in *Works*, vol. XXIV, p. 339.

[23] Margaret Canovan, 'Two Concepts of Liberty – Eighteenth Century Style', *The Price–Priestley Newsletter* 2 (1978), 38.

intrinsically difficult than it had been represented by earlier thinkers. Not so for Burke: for him the difficulty of rational government and the scarcity of political wisdom are leading considerations. In his view, only a wealthy, leisured and educated class can adequately master the required skills. He accuses the leaders of the French National Assembly of wanting to 'evade and slip aside from difficulty', preferring 'tricking short-cuts, and little fallacious facilities' to the hard business of reconciliation and compromise, so that in the end, by 'a slow but well-sustained progress', one advantage 'is as little as possible sacrificed to another'.[24] When it comes to matters of politics it is Burke who emphasises and praises difficulty, not Priestley.

For Priestley's *Political Dialogue* 'the business of states is not so difficult, but that persons who give proper attention to it may easily prepare themselves for the conduct of it'.[25] It is beyond the competence only of the uneducated and those morally disabled by habitual idleness. The skills required are relatively abundant simply because they are not particularly complex or special. Because of this there is nothing to be feared from an extension of the franchise. Priestley is voicing a commonplace when he observes that 'Virtue and public spirit are the necessary supports of all republican governments.'[26] What is novel in his outlook is the conviction that such virtue and public spirit are readily available to create a new kind of society.

Burke, arguing in the 1790s, will allow the people to dissolve a bad government only when they have been driven by it to sheer desperation. Any such dissolution would be a 'resort to anarchy', dissolving not just a government but the society itself. Popular revolution of any less desperate kind would be not just inept, but catastrophic. Yet elsewhere he wants to defend the common sense of the common man, as in his remark that 'The species is wise, and, when time is given, as a species it almost always acts right.'[27] Here, however, the qualification 'when time is given' is crucial, for, when time is not given, the popular mind will leap to disastrous conclusions. Much depends on whether their intellectual leaders allow the people to develop at their own pace or seek to hurry them along.

---

[24] Burke, *Reflections* (fn. 12), p. 279.   [25] Priestley, *Works*, vol. xxv, p. 91.
[26] J. Priestley, *Lectures on History*, Lecture 41, in *Works*, vol. xxiv, p. 239.
[27] Quoted by J.G.A. Pocock, 'Burke and the Ancient Constitution', in his *Politics, Language and Time: Essays on Political Thought and Ideology* (London, 1971), pp. 226–7, from Burke's never-delivered speech 'On a Motion Made in the House of Commons . . . for a Committee to Enquire into the State of the Representation of the Commons in Parliament'.

In general – we need to except the utopian phase aroused by the beginnings of the French Revolution – Priestley shares the gradualism Burke is here espousing. Even the Political Dialogue, his most radical tract, declares that 'Things once established should be respected by speculative politicians, because they will be respected by the people at large; but every thing should be put into the way of as much reformation as it is capable of.'[28] But he never concedes that the people are as easily inflamed by the rhetoric of agitators as Burke would have it. If such rhetoric succeeds there must be some substantial reason for the discontent it arouses. 'A whole people is not apt to revolt, till oppression has become extreme, and been long continued, so that they despair of any other remedy than a desperate one.'[29]

These differences about the moral and political competence of 'the people' is another version of the conflict between robust and fragile accounts of progress, and in turn this conflict rests on whether moral progress tends to follow material progress, as Priestley contends, or material follows moral, as Burke would have it. Burke's emphasis on fragility is remarkable: 'Rage and phrenzy will pull down more in half an hour than prudence, deliberation, and foresight can build up in a hundred years.'[30] Priestley will not allow that progress can so easily disintegrate, partly because for progress to occur at all it must become part of the ingrained character of a people, a second nature built up by innumerable habits or 'associations'. Curiously, Burke's conservatism employs a similar psychology. He defends 'prejudice' partly on the grounds that it embodies hard-won habits and national characters, the destruction or attempted destruction of which will be disastrous.

Liberty, both civil and political, according to Priestley's early *Essay on Government*, gives a man 'a constant feeling of his own power and importance, and is the foundation of his indulging a free, bold and manly turn of thinking.'[31] But this is an isolated remark: Priestley's commitment to political liberty has more to do with freedom of thought than with the feeling of power and importance. Political activity, important as it is, is not an essential part of a fully virtuous life. To hand over some responsibility to a parliamentary representative is, he contends against Rousseau, no great loss of liberty or virtue, for politics is only one among many possible spheres for progressive endeavour.[32] He considers civil affairs – commerce, industry, agriculture, science, philosophy and

[28] Priestley, *Works*, vol. XXV, p. 107.   [29] J. Priestley, *Letters to Burke*, Letter 1, in *Works*, vol. XXII, p. 155.
[30] Burke, *Reflections* (fn. 12), pp. 279–80.   [31] Priestley *Works*, vol. XXII, p. 37.
[32] *Ibid.*, vol. XXII, p. 10.

religion – the main arena for the pursuit of virtue, and these matters are for him all areas in which the state can make little useful contribution. In this respect it is Burke, not Priestley, who upholds the 'republican' tradition, usually associated with radicalism, according to which political wisdom and action is at the heart of manliness and self-mastery. By restricting the scope of government Priestley diminished the status of the political virtues. Priestley wants to replace an 'idle' political class unwilling to submit to moral discipline – the aristocracy – with a class which has learned self-discipline in the civil sphere; yet he employs the idea of moral progress to emphasise that the art of government is by no means as difficult as it has been traditionally thought to be.

The rediscovery of republicanism since the 1960s has greatly deepened our appreciation of the moral dimension of that one stream of political thought and action. Modern liberalism, when it is not utilitarian, tends to be morally agnostic. Priestley's radical liberalism, or liberal radicalism, I suggest, is marked by its own particular moral ethos, an ethos that is in the first place theological. Its paradigm is not civic virtue, but commercial virtue; and its demands are perhaps no less strenuous than those of republicanism. It was a paradigm that did survive into the nineteenth century, but it had been wounded and weakened by its encounter with the (mainly republican) revolution in France. So severe was the blow that few afterwards were able to take seriously Priestley's benign deity who makes his purposes known through science and social improvement. Personal piety could continue to see itself as guided by a severe instructor, and moral life be viewed as a struggle with adversity; but what was lost was the argumentative self-confidence that permitted Priestley to seek to unify all knowledge and social life as forms of rational piety.

CHAPTER 12

Rational piety

R.K. Webb

To many, the title of this chapter must seem an oxymoron, in the ordinary, non-rhetorical sense of the word: an improper linking of two incompatible qualities of mind or personality. There are good grounds, both historical and psychological, to reject that contention, but establishing the legitimacy of rational piety is no easy task.

Indeed, the very notion of piety is shrouded in obscurity. The relevant entry in the *Oxford English Dictionary* (under the question-begging head of 'the quality or character of being pious') points to three categories – 'habitual reverence and obedience to God (or the gods); devotion to religious duties and observances; godliness, devoutness, religiousness' – each of which will find a place in this chapter.[1] Now, the earliest citations in the *OED* date from the beginning of the seventeenth century, but it seems possible that piety came into its own only later in that century, with 'godliness' the earlier preference.[2] The word was a commonplace to Tillotson, however, and in the eighteenth and nineteenth centuries it was omnipresent in sermons and devotional literature and appears on thousands of tombstones and memorial tablets. To those who put it there, the word had to be more than merely gestural, yet when we search the interpretive scholarship for a fuller understanding of its function and significance, we are baffled. The concept makes no explicit appearance in Basil Willey's *The Eighteenth Century Background*, in Gordon Rupp's *Religion in England*,

I would like to thank Dr Michael Hooker, formerly president, and Mr Adam Yarmolinsky, formerly provost, of the University of Maryland, Baltimore County, for the opportunity offered by a research professorship to pursue the reading on which this chapter is based. In addition, I owe a great debt to Professor John Passmore for a careful reading and criticism of an earlier version.

[1] Johnson's *Dictionary* gives two trenchant meanings: (1) discharge of duty to God, (2) duty to parents and those in superior relation.
[2] To one Rational Dissenter in the eighteenth century, indeed, 'piety' and 'godliness' were interchangeable. See Nathaniel Lardner, Posthumous Sermons III and IV on 'The Promise Annexed to Godliness', in *The Works of Nathaniel Lardner*, 5 vols. (London, 1815), vol. v., esp. p. 203.

1688–1791, or in Owen Chadwick's *The Victorian Church*. It is not to be found in that remarkable compendium of nineteenth-century attitudes, Walter E. Houghton's *The Victorian Frame of Mind*, though it is no doubt partly, but only partly, encompassed in the chapters on 'Earnestness' and 'Enthusiasm'. The admirable *New Catholic Encyclopedia* has a long entry on 'familial piety' – on the respective duties of husbands and wives and of parents and children – but any more general sense must be abstracted from a brief, mildly tautological entry in technical theology on 'gift of piety', which does not seem to square very effectively with the implicit sense of usual English usage.[3] The more recent, vast *Encyclopedia of Religion*, published in 1986 under the editorship of Mircea Eliade, says nothing at all under that head, nor does the older *Hastings Encyclopædia of Religion and Ethics*.

The *New Catholic* has a suggestive and helpful entry on the associated term, 'devotion'. The article on that subject in the *Encyclopedia of Religion*, while touching on all the conventional ingredients, is spread thin by the mission of the publication to comprehend the world's main religions, but its bibliographical note alerts us to the absence, even at this late date, of works on devotion as a religious phenomenon: the only books listed deal with discrete aspects of it – asceticism and monasticism, mysticism, prayer and hymns. But, despite some crossing over – the *OED* refrains from using piety as even a loose equivalent of devotion, but does allow for the adjectives 'devout' and 'pious' to be incidentally interchangeable – the modern understanding of devotion remains generally limited to cult, and leaves us adrift with regard to devotion as an aspect of piety in general.

A more helpful tack may be to inquire into the usage and significance of a family of terms much used in the eighteenth century – *practical* piety, or religion, or theology or Christianity – some of which are still with us. Again the *Encyclopedia of Religion* is silent on the subject, but *Hastings* addresses the question in its classification of the theological sciences. There, grouped under the normative or constructive aspect of theology, as opposed to the historical or phenomenological perspective, practical theology is subdivided into six headings – homiletic, liturgical, catechetical and pastoral theology, along with ecclesiastical polity and evangelistic theology or theory of missions – a classification that foreshadows the emphasis of twentieth-century writers on the subject on ecclesiastical

---

[3] Piety is 'the gift of the Holy Spirit that perfects the acts of the infused virtues of religion and piety. ... [It] moves the soul to venerate God as the Father of mankind', elevating the soul 'to approach God more perfectly than religion does'. Its consequences are meekness, justice and mercy.

and pastoral concerns.[4] This professional and institutional emphasis runs counter to both the historical and commonsense association of the term, in the Protestant context, with the conduct, public and private, of individual Christians.[5]

At the end of the eighteenth century, some Rational Dissenters rediscovered dogmatic or systematic theology and, for a generation or so, committed (usually younger) ministers made older congregations uncomfortable by preaching Unitarian theology and by working to spread its principles through the land. But for most of the eighteenth century, one of the highest compliments that could be paid to a minister was to say that he was a practical preacher, that is, that his sermons led his hearers to a wide range of reflections on living a Christian life. The compliments did not extend to the preaching of strictly political sermons – apart from exhortations to patriotic or dynastic loyalty in times of crisis – or to pointed injunctions about the daily conduct of business or the relations of one social group to another. But if the index of complacency seems high about matters that came to preoccupy increasing numbers of liberal Victorian ministers, Georgian congregations were encouraged to serious mental and emotional effort in contemplating the ways of God to man and how men and women might walk daily in the footsteps of their Lord.[6]

---

[4] A sampling of works explicitly devoted to practical theology in the Library of Congress – where the catalogue under that head is structured more or less in accordance with early twentieth-century American understandings – displays some suggestive national characteristics. German writers tend to the elaborately analytical within a churchly framework, e.g., Johannes Steinbeck, *System der praktischen Theologie* (Leipzig, 1928); Günter Biemer and Pius Siller, *Grundfragen der praktischen Theologie* (Mainz, 1971); Norbert Mette, *Theorie der Praxis: Wissenschaftsgeschichtliche und methodologische Untersuchungen zur Theorie-Praxis-Problematik innerhalb der praktischen Theologie* (Düsseldorf, 1978). The bias of the American agenda toward the minister's business is set out in the introduction to Ferdinand S. Schenck (of the Reformed Church), *Modern Practical Theology* (New York, 1903), pp. vii–viii; Paul W. Howell, *How to Make Your Church Hum* (Nashville, 1977). Although the author recognises the impulse of the Holy Spirit, it is the minister's business and public-relations skills that count. There is an extensive Dutch literature, but the English seem to be quite unrepresented.

[5] A brief sketch of the history of the term from a Catholic (and post-Vatican II) perspective is René Marlé, *Le Projet de théologie pratique* (Paris, 1979). Thomas A. Langford, *Practical Divinity* (Nashville, 1977) does not go beyond its subtitle, *Theology in the Wesleyan Tradition*, and considers theology in the broadest sense. Note can also be taken of a much more restricted view of practical theology so far as it concerns the conduct of life, i.e., casuistry broadly defined. See [Robert Clarkson], *The Practical Divinity of the Papists Discovered to be Destructive of Christianity and Men's Souls* (London, 1676), and the Scots minister, John Brown, *Practical Piety Exemplified in the Lives of Thirteen Christians . . . and Illustrated in Casuistical Hints, or, Cases of Conscience, concerning Satan's Temptation–Indwelling Sin–Spiritual Experience–Godly Conversation–and Scandalous Offences* (Pittsburgh, 1818).

[6] By the early nineteenth century, the distinction between practical and doctrinal or evangelistic preaching had come to be taken as a rough indicator of the fault line between Arian and Unitarian. But some evolution was taking place in a problem at once theological and generational. Cf. R.K. Webb, 'John Hamilton Thom: Intellect and Conscience in Liverpool', in P.T. Phillips, ed., *The View from the Pulpit: Victorian Ministers and Society* (Toronto, 1978), pp. 211–43 at pp. 223–4.

This broad, generalized and demotic sense of practical religion and the congruent conception of piety are set out as the eighteenth century understood them in a source that must seem unimpeachable to those who might question the possibility of rational piety. In 1811, Hannah More published *Practical Piety; or, The Influence of the Religion of the Heart on the Conduct of Life*, a two-volume work that went through an extraordinary number of editions in succeeding decades.[7] Her concerns are not so much with prescriptions for Christian conduct in the encounters of daily life as with ensuring that the individual Christian will internalise divine expectations so thoroughly that every hour will be lived in entire submission to God, in public and private worship, in prayer, in self-examination and in continual awareness and joyful acceptance of the divine superintendence of all things, including adversity and death. Divine in origin, foretold in prophecies and confirmed by miracles, warranted by the sacrifice on the Cross, the 'pure, sublime, consistent' doctrines of Christianity are no mere code of laws that might have served man in a state of innocence; they are, rather, a means of salvation. Christianity is not a religion of 'forms, and modes, and decencies' but a call to a complete transformation of the heart, 'an inward devotedness . . . in his service'.[8]

This 'religion of the heart', Hannah More points out, has been 'perverted both by the cloistered and the un-cloistered mystic', whose 'pious error . . . has furnished to the enemies of internal religion arguments . . . against the sound and sober exercises of genuine piety'. Nor can the religious formalist understand: because he has probably never sought and obtained God's spiritual mercies, he dismisses internal religion, a dismissal with no more justification than a conclusion by inhabitants of 'the frozen zone' that there are no 'cheering beams of a genial climate'.[9] It is suggestive that More's stern criticism is limited to mystics and formalists – the non-juring and the civil traditions within the Church of England – and that religious rationalists are not included in her strictures.

But mere feelings are not enough to assure the religion of the heart; rather, the happy Christian – 'though with much alloy of infirmity . . . [and] an experimental persuasion that his chief remaining sorrow is, that he does not surrender himself with so complete an acquiescence as

---

[7] *The Works of Hannah More*, new edn, 11 vols. (London, 1830), vol. VIII. *Practical Piety* and its successor, *Christian Morals*, receive only brief, and not entirely accurate, mention from her modern biographer, who points out that the former was a huge success with all but the High Calvinists. M.G. Jones, *Hannah More* (Cambridge, 1952), pp. 199–200. The *DNB* cites a nineteenth edition in 1850.
[8] More, *Works*, vol. VIII, pp. 1–4   [9] *Ibid.*, pp. 8–9, 11

he ought' – is aware, realistically and so without the danger of spiritual pride, of 'a perceptible change in . . . desires, tastes, and pleasures', of 'a sense of progress, however small, in holiness of heart and life'. Theory carries no man to heaven, nor is the way shown by those 'few sublime spirits, not "touch'd but rap't", who soar above the world'. God made religion for the world at large, for 'active, busy, restless' beings; through them, the governing principle of the love of God actuates, as a powerful spring, 'all the movements of the rational machine'. The essence of religion, then, lies less in actions than in affections, in rooted habits that lead to the implementation of Christian principles through practical Christianity. 'A Christian cannot tell in the morning what opportunities he may have of doing good during the day; but, if he be a real Christian, he can tell that he will try to keep his heart open, his mind prepared, his affections alive, to do whatever may occur in the way of duty. He will, as it were, stand in the way to receive the orders of Providence, doing good in his vocation.'[10] Hannah More does not say it in so many words, but the true Christian is a serf of God. To the inculcation of that prepared spirit through devotion and holiness her injunctions are directed. Piety is the sum of that spirit realised and of its consequences in individual demeanour and action, towards God and towards men.[11]

Before turning to adherents of rational religion, a certain amount of ground-clearing is required. 'It has been said', James Martineau wrote in 1861,

in benevolent apology for Mr. Spurgeon's pulpit style, 'True, it has its taint of vulgarity; but vulgar people exist, and must have their religion.' It seems to be forgotten at the other end that men of letters and science exist, that hosts of academic and professional youth exist, and, being human, must have their religion. The culture of the age preoccupies their minds with habits of thought variously traversing the 'message' of the Church, and with many distinct objections to parts of the Bible and the creed. Is no notice to be taken of this state of mind? Do you expect that, on hearing the message, it will die out of itself? Will you treat it as a delirium, – as a mere fretful illusion, – to be coaxed into cure by

---

[10] *Ibid.*, pp. 17–38, *passim.*
[11] When Hannah More published her *Christian Morals* two years later, she was not notably more situational, but wrote extensively on adapting to providence, on the formation of habits, on prejudices the Christian might encounter, and on the place of evangelicalism in the Established Church. It is worth noting that, in the chapter on habits, she quotes William Paley, whom she describes as 'one of the most sagacious observers of man'; she is, however, very severe on Richard Porson and Horne Tooke, whose learning and genius she recognises but who stand condemned, one for 'gross sensuality and corrupt principles', the other for 'infidelity and profligate political principles'. Cf. More, *Works*, vol. IX, pp. 323, 122–3.

changing the subject and speaking home to another part of the nature? Or is all sympathy to be withheld from the mental strife of the intellectual classes? and are they to limp on as they can in the rear of a faith, that will not turn its face to answer them a word?[12]

The savagery of Martineau's questions speaks to an inbuilt prejudice, understandable enough given the weight of numbers and the force of theological difference, on the part of nineteenth-century religious leaders. It seems to have followed, as it were by extension, that historians or other scholars, looking back at religion in the period since the mid-seventeenth century, must be concerned with the bigger battalions, that our main effort (since it is an effort) must go towards understanding the cast of mind most alien to ours.[13] We must work at grasping the unarticulated faith of the simple believer, beset by terrible miseries and uncertainties and equipped only with a rudimentary weaponry that mingled rough understanding of the Bible, a chiliastic sense of the future and a certain admixture of superstition. When we confront the relatively advantaged, in status and intellect, we must give pride of place to those for whom religion is literally agonistic – a sense of fierce struggle, marked by a profound sense of sin and loss and a corresponding triumph when a sense of salvation is attained.

Many of the great religious writers of the past three centuries speak to that awesome and moving circumstance, Søren Kierkegaard above all. But even a great, distanced observer made the same point. The fierce depression from which William James escaped with his life helped him to sense the despair felt by the sick soul and underlay his wonderful empathy with the twice-born. But, in encouraging his Edinburgh audience and his twentieth-century readers to take serious religion seriously, he tipped the balance against the healthy-minded, to use his own term for a class to which, in any total evaluation, he himself belonged. No one could maintain that the work he did in his Gifford Lectures was unnecessary; indeed, it was as salutary as

---

[12] James Martineau, 'Tracts for Priests and People', *National Review*, 1861, reprinted in his *Essays, Reviews, and Addresses*, sel. and rev., ... 4 vols. (London, 1890–1), vol. II, p. 433. Compare the leading article, 'The Connexion between Mental Culture and Devotion', *Unitarian Herald*, 20 January 1871: 'In proportion as our intelligence becomes characterised by power, refinement, and spirituality, does it fit us for holding communion with God. It is not the ignorant, uninstructed mind that can form any idea of Infinite perfection; it is not the grovelling, sensualised intellect that can worship the Eternal and Invisible. For this there needs to be an enlightened and refined intelligence ...' Cf. More, *Works*, vol. IX, pp. 178–86.

[13] Or in the case of some historians, that cast of mind most familiar, through inheritance and training, even though they may have emancipated themselves from it.

any work of interpretation could be. But, in the larger historical perspective, James may have done his work too well.[14]

This chapter is in part an attempt at redress. But, in offering a sympathetic response to Martineau's grievance, my principal purpose is to arrive at a more just estimate of a major, if minority, religious tradition. In doing so, I shall take my departure from a few well-known figures in the religious history of the late seventeenth and eighteenth centuries, though much of my evidence will be drawn (as with Hannah More) from the early nineteenth century. Nineteenth-century responses to still-present eighteenth-century texts and examples not only help to illuminate their meaning and relevance but reinforce the contention, put forward earlier in this volume, that rational religion existed in a continuum lasting over two centuries or more, and in a symbiotic relationship with the orthodoxy from which it was separated by now greater, now lesser degrees.[15]

Early in this century, a young American theologian, Gerald Birney Smith, called attention to the divorce that had taken place in Protestantism between 'the scientific and practical ends of theological study'. Calling Thomas Aquinas as his witness, he insisted that the separation was unknown in Roman Catholicism; there, the four modes of exegesis – historical, allegorical, moral and analogical – were all means of turning knowledge to the end of man's eternal blessedness. Accordingly, Catholic schools of theology knew no science for its own sake, but only study to promote the faith and life of the Church. In nineteenth-century Protestantism, however, the enormous strides made by historical theology had turned ministers into scholars, and, as nothing could be read into a passage in the Bible that was not scientifically ascertained to be part of its meaning, broadly considered, the kinds of interpretation known in past ages had been invalidated. With the scholarly and practical sides of religion split apart, it fell to departments of practical religion to try to bridge the gap.[16]

Smith insisted that this separation was not the result of the Reformation but of the importation of scientific and historical method into theological scholarship in the nineteenth century, and he cited the spiritual inspiration on every page of Luther's exegesis to make his point.

[14] William James, *The Varieties of Religious Experience: A Study in Human Nature*, Gifford Lectures (London, 1902), lectures 4–8.
[15] See Webb, 'The Emergence of Rational Dissent', Chapter 2 of this volume.
[16] Gerald Birney Smith, 'Practical Theology: A Neglected Field in Theological Education', in *Decennial Publications of the University of Chicago* (1903), first ser., vol. III, pp. 69–87.

That same unity is to be found in the sermons of English preachers in the seventeenth and eighteenth centuries, even among the rationally inclined, though what is said by many historians would lead one to think otherwise. To Horton Davies, the example of Tillotson and his imitators was decisive: Anglican and Dissenting ministers alike preached sermons that were learned lectures or were 'more like discourses or essays than prophetic proclamations'; like the essays of Addison and Steele, they developed a central theme as clearly as possible to appeal to 'the enlightened common sense and politeness' of readers and hearers. Indeed, so lost was Anglican pulpit discourse in moral platitudes, that 'if you were a rationalist you would find much more enthralling rationalism in the Unitarian congregations of Lindsey and Priestley, where scientific enterprise, philosophical daring, and advanced political views' were to be found.[17] To this indictment can be added the easy dismissal of the 'Arian blight', in which many have seen the principal cause of Dissenting decline prior to the recovery of the evangelical revival.[18]

A magnificent corrective has been applied by Gordon Rupp in a few trenchant pages on Anglican preaching. He points out that Tillotson was borrowed from again and again for appreciative audiences, and that Archbishop Secker, despite his lack of style and sparkle and his tendency to expound the obvious, retailed Tillotsonian moralism to large and welcoming congregations wherever he went. 'One would say that nobody would give the latitudinarian sermons to a man whose sins had found him out, save that this is exactly the place where Samuel Clarke spoke to the condition of an anguished Samuel Johnson.'[19] To which we may add that while Priestley was certainly daring, both scientifically and philosophically, his sermons were largely devoted to quite other ends; Unitarian preachers kept their advanced political views for those occasions, like government-appointed days of humiliation, when theological candour required that the true sources of humiliation be addressed or that congregations be reminded of the futility of seeking special interventions by providence.[20]

---

[17] Horton Davies, *Worship and Theology in England*, 5 vols. (Princeton, NJ, 1961–75), vol. III: *From Watts and Wesley to Maurice 1690–1850*, pp. 67, 74.

[18] This despite the fact that F.J. Powicke offered a very powerful refutation almost eighty years ago in 'An Apology for the Arians of the 18th Century', *Transactions of the Congregational Historical Society* 7 (1916–18), 110–24.

[19] E. Gordon Rupp, *Religion in England, 1688–1791* (Oxford, 1986), pp. 513–16.

[20] In 1817 and 1818, the *Monthly Repository* published a fascinating correspondence on Priestley's preaching, specifically his candidly acknowledged borrowing of sermons from William Enfield and others. In the preface to *Notes on all the Books of Scripture for the Use of Pulpit and Private Families* (1803), in *The Theological and Miscellaneous Works of Joseph Priestley . . .*, ed. J.T. Rutt, 25 vols. in 26

Still, Davies may seem to have a point, as Tillotson's sermons, and great numbers that followed them, emerge from the printed page; they have indeed many characteristics of lectures. A topic is announced and an expository strategy, set out in numbered headings and subheadings, is followed, with an abundance of scriptural citation, to an inexorably logical conclusion. But if one conjures up the sonorities and the stately periods unfolding at a hieratic pace, and if, above all, one can see them unrefracted through the distorting lens of later fashion, there is in that deliberate, lapidary form something of the conclusiveness and sense of awe that one finds in a complex mathematical demonstration, in the working out of an involuted exercise in counterpoint – or even in a masterly lecture.[21] To be sure, there were deadly preachers in the eighteenth century, as there are in every age, and even the best of them (as is also true in all times and places) may well have been most fully appreciated by a relative few. But the widening circles of that appreciation cannot simply be waved away.

We must go further to address the implications of the term 'moral', so often and so deprecatingly applied to eighteenth-century sermons. The term carried the broadest possible implications. Again Tillotson:

Two things make up religion, the knowledge and the practice of it; and the first is wholly in order to the second; and God hath not revealed to us the knowledge of himself and his will, merely for the improvement of our understanding, but for the bettering of our hearts and lives: not to entertain our minds with the speculations of religion and virtue, but to form and govern our actions.[22]

A century later, John Jebb, still within the Anglican fold, echoed Tillotson: 'Know then all thou canst, but forget not to practice according as thou knowest; for, in proportion to the improvement of thy powers and capacities of action, shall be the future mercies of thy omniscient judge.' In an expansion of that view he wrote: 'By a principle in morals,

---

(London, 1817–31), vol. xi, pp. 5–7), Priestley himself explained that, while he regularly expounded the Scriptures from the pulpit, he did not in that exercise 'make many observations of a practical nature. To enforce the practice of moral duties, I considered as the more particular province of *preaching*.' For examples of political preaching commanded by the occasion, see also Newcome Cappe, *A sermon preached on the thirteenth of December the late day of National Humiliation . . .* (York, 1776) and *A sermon preached on Wednesday, the 21st of February, MDCCLXXXI the late day of National Humiliation . . .* (York, 1781).

[21] I know of no better illustration than the manuscript sermons of James Scott, minister at the Unitarian chapels at Cradley and Stourbridge in the latter years of the eighteenth and early years of the nineteenth centuries, held by the solicitor to the congregation. It was in reading them that I first sensed what power the form could convey. Scott's published sermons illustrate the case, but the reiteration of the form in the manuscripts is singularly impressive.

[22] See Sermon CXII, 'Knowledge and Practice Necessary in Religion' (on John 13: 17), in *The Works of Dr. John Tillotson*, 10 vols. (London, 1820), vol. v, p. 472.

we must be understood to mean the prevailing disposition of the mind, or its approbation of any particular course of action evidenced in our conduct.' Thus, a man constantly attentive to his own advantage is said to be governed by 'a selfish principle'; while a man who, in the ordinary course of life, sacrifices generosity, justice, candour and sincerity to some advantage in the political world is said to be motivated by the principle of party. When, however,

we observe a person, throughout the whole of his demeanour, conducting himself with a submissive attention to the will of that almighty being, from whom he received the powers of thought, and capacity of action; when we behold him, regulating every part of his conduct, in conformity to the dictates of sound reason and his conscience; and, emulative of the joy of God, when he beholds an happy world, dispensing the means of happiness to all around him; in life, the friend of man; in death, with holy trust, confiding in his God; we pronounce him to be actuated by a 'principle of piety and benevolence', or, in other words, we attribute to him justly, whatever be his mode of faith, or outward worship, the honourable appellation of the 'religious man'.[23]

Jebb returned to the point again and again. From those religious truths that we learn from the exercise of our natural powers 'arise those pious affections of gratitude and love, and that upright conduct which our reason informs us, must necessarily be the duty of man; this is true religion, the religion of the heart'.[24] In his invocation of the religion of the heart, Jebb is at one with Hannah More.

Moralism, even in this very broad sense, did not exhaust the eighteenth-century sermon. Another major component, either as a subject in itself or entwined with moral concerns, was devotion. Here we might note with advantage a warning offered by James Martineau in his brilliant essay on Joseph Priestley, that 'with the utmost fervent confidence in the moral power of truth, it may yet be doubted whether the largest portion of Unitarian piety has not been imported from orthodoxy'. Many Unitarians were Unitarian, as the Quakers say of themselves, 'by convincement', and brought with them habits established in the dispensation they had left behind. This must have been the case with the ship's captain who was a member of Edward Higginson's congregation at Hull in the mid-nineteenth century. Enlarging, as Higginson recalled, with

[23] See *The Works, Theological, Medical, Political and Miscellaneous of ... John Jebb ...* with memoirs of the life of the author by John Disney, 3 vols. (London, 1787), vol. II, p. 99, and vol. III, pp. 196–8. I am grateful to Dr Martin Fitzpatrick for calling my attention to Jebb as an exemplar of rational piety.
[24] Sermon II (on Prov. 3: 17), *ibid.*, vol. II, pp. 34–5.

delight on 'what he had seen of the works of the Lord & his wonders in the deep', the old man would cite Psalm 107 and describe how stormy winds rose and fell, imitating the waves and the calm with his hands, 'and his voice shook with pious emotion as he concluded his recitation: "Oh that man would praise the Lord for his goodness, and for his wonderful works to the children of men."'[25]

Yet another caution is suggested by a report in *Fraser's Magazine* in 1865 that a young Unitarian minister trying to evangelise the lower reaches of the Potomac in the United States was told by a physician that he would make no converts there: 'Everybody almost in this northern neck of Virginia has more or less the liver disease; they are sure to be Calvinists. You'll do more near the mountains. You'll never get the belief in everlasting hell out of this neighbourhood except by better drainage, with less bilious fever.' David Hume would have understood: '. . . Men are much oftener thrown on their knees by the melancholy than by the agreeable passions . . . Every disastrous accident alarms us, and sets us on enquiries concerning the principles whence it arose . . . [and] the mind, sunk into diffidence, terror, and melancholy, has recourse to every method of appeasing those secret intelligent powers, on whom our fortune is supposed entirely to depend.'[26] But to suggest generational or pathological origins of religious attitudes does not rule out the possibility of rational piety; rather, they enrich and integrate it.

Tillotson preached on the efficacy of prayer and on the means and advantages of encouraging early piety. Almost a century later, John Jebb urged attendance on public religious services but warned against undue reliance on them.

The true, the conscientious Christian . . . will consider them as helps to virtue, and not as constituting the real essence of devotion: he knows that, as he is sent into this world by the God of reason and of nature to fulfil his pleasure, his real service must consist in the imitation of his creator's bounty, and the intire resignation of his will to the will of the supreme: he is sensible how much mankind are influenced by what strikes the imagination and the senses; and will therefore cultivate in himself, and endeavour to promote in others, a manly piety, an unbounded benevolence . . . and will be careful to distinguish between

---

[25] J. Martineau, 'The Life and Works of Dr. Priestley', originally published anonymously in the *Monthly Repository* in 1833, reprinted with changes in *Essays* (fn. 12), 1, p. 8. Edward Higginson, MS memoir, Dr Williams's Library, MS 38.64. See also Catharine Cappe's description of the piety of Theophilus Lindsey while still vicar of Catterick, whose example she followed at her home at Bedale: *Memoirs of the Life of the Late Mrs. Catharine Cappe . . .* (Boston, 1824), pp. 97–107.

[26] *Fraser's Magazine*, quoted in *Inquirer*, 4 March 1865. David Hume, *The Natural History of Religion*, ed. with intro. by H.E. Root (London, 1956), p. 31.

the outward profession, and the real practice of religion . . . While perpetual fears shall haunt the guilty breast; while innumerable scoffers shall affright the superstitious worshipper; inbred peace, the fruit of virtuous conduct, shall surround thy dwelling; and calm devotion, spread sweet tranquillity over every scene of life.[27]

Let us pursue these concerns through that consummate impersonation of eighteenth-century rationality, Joseph Priestley. James Martineau argued that there was little distance between Priestley's intellectual and moral character. For him, duty followed ineluctably from truth, a matter of conviction rather than affection: 'show him on evidence the reasonableness of any habit or train of feeling, and he would set himself to its cultivation without further demur; he would no more have thought of not doing what was right, than of not believing what was true.'[28] Of course, Priestley repudiated the instinctive moral sense of the Scottish philosophers. The moral sense philosophy, Martineau said, was the natural resort of those whose intellects are slow and whose moral judgement is faster than the mental eye can trace. Priestley was the reverse: emotions never interfered with his capacity to observe; his intellect kept up with and directed them; moral judgements were so like assent and Dissent that both shared an origin in the association of ideas.[29] How, then, can piety help us to understand this cool, rational, logical, utilitarian man, or such a man help in understanding piety?

It might be granted that, in so far as piety implies obligation and duty, Priestley had it in full measure, even if powered more by conviction than emotion. As scientist and as theologian, he was filled with reverence for God and felt himself entirely subject to divine command, a faith not in the least qualified by his certainty that many of God's ways were not beyond discovery. But with respect to devotion – in the sense of forms of worship and of prayer – or to general Christian demeanour, Priestley might seem ill-suited for the characterisation of pious – too knowing, too hurried, too little racked by the doubt that surfaces in humility or despair and that seeks reassurance through ritual and petition. Such a conclusion would be erroneous.

---

[27] Tillotson, *Works* (fn. 22) vol. x, pp. 99–132.: Sermons CCLI and CCLII, 'The Efficacy of Prayer for Obtaining the Holy Spirit'; see also Sermon LIV, 'Of the Advantages of an Early Piety', *ibid.*, vol. III, pp. 552–76. Cf. Jebb, *Works*, (fn. 23), vol. II, pp. 69–85: Sermon IV. The insistence on manly piety is to be found throughout. Elsewhere (e.g. in Disney's memoir, vol. I, pp. 124–5, 136, and in the 'Theological Propositions', vol. II, pp. 172–4) it is made plain how much Jebb's notions of piety owed to the *Observations on Man* of his father's friend, David Hartley.

[28] Martineau, *Essays* (fn. 12), p. 29.

[29] For this and what follows, see Martineau, *Essays*, (fn. 12), vol. I, pp. 29–32.

A now mostly forgotten figure who loomed large in Priestley's time and in the affectionate recollection of many in the next generation was the poet and essayist Anna Laetitia Barbauld. In 1775, Mrs Barbauld published *Devotional Pieces compiled from the Psalms of David, with Thoughts on the Devotional Taste and on Sects and Establishments*. She was persuaded, as she wrote the next year to Nicholas Clayton, that the large views of nature and nature's laws arising from the 'current philosophy' made possible 'a more magnificent idea of the Deity'. But this very magnificence, she feared, might seem to put God at a distance and so to be

attended with such an annihilation of ourselves as is nearly painful . . . Yet I do not mean that such philosophical views should not be indulged, for they enlarge the mind, give some high pleasures & set religion upon a broad & firm basis. All I would say is, that we must correct what unfavorable tendency they may have, by often suffering our minds to dwell on those more affecting circumstances which arise in what we may call the more personal intercourse of a devout heart with its maker. The former is the *sublime*, the latter the *pathetic* of Religion.[30]

In a memoir of her aunt, Lucy Aikin said delicately that the selection met with no great success, 'nor did the essay escape without some animadversion'.[31] Animadversion, indeed! Consistent with the new meaning of candour that was coming into use in these years – not openness and receptiveness but an obligatory statement of views, however hurtful – Priestley responded to Mrs Barbauld's request for his judgement of the book by telling her 'freely' what he thought of it and of their differences.[32]

He sternly disapproved of the very idea of 'devotional taste', as if devotion were an elegant enjoyment of life that might be done without; moreover the phrase seemed likely to offend by debasing the subject with the language of sentiment. To her suggestion that philosophy is unfavourable to piety, he answered that, if she meant false philosophy, she should have said so, while true philosophy, 'founded on the most just and exalted conceptions of the Divine Being and his providence that we can attain to', by raising our conceptions of God, deepens the sense of

---

[30] Mrs Barbauld to Nicholas Clayton, 21 February [1776], Nicholson Collection, Liverpool Public Library.

[31] *The Works of Anna Laetitia Barbauld, with a Memoir by Lucy Aikin*, 3 vols. (Boston, 1826). The essay appears in vol. II, pp. 146–66, and Lucy Aikin's comment appears in vol. I, p. xix.

[32] Priestley to Mrs Barbauld, 20 December 1775, in Priestley's *Works* (fn. 20), vol. I pt I, pp. 278–86. On candour, Martin Fitzpatrick, 'Varieties of Candour: English and Scottish Style', *Enlightenment and Dissent*, 7 (1988), 35–56, and my own similar interpretation, put forward in 1987 in 'A Christian Necessity: The Context and Consequences of Joseph Priestley', in Gordon Schochet, ed., *Empire and Revolutions* (Washington, DC, 1993), p. 58, and briefly summarised in 'From Toleration to Religious Liberty', in J.R. Jones, ed., *Liberty Secured? Britain before and after 1688* (Stanford, CA, 1992), pp. 185–6.

humility and reverence, strengthens confidence in divine care and goodness, and makes more profound our resignation to His will.

Mrs Barbauld had defended establishments on the ground that they
prevent worship from sinking into contempt: 'An establishment affects
the mind by splendid buildings, music, the mysterious pomp of ancient
ceremonies; by the sacredness of peculiar orders, habits, and titles; by its
secular importance; and by connecting with religion, ideas of order,
dignity, and antiquity.'[33] Priestley would have none of it. On the
Continent but also in the Church of England, he said, devotion, which
should be 'a security for the practice of virtue, . . . too often [becomes]
the substitute for the most substantial part of virtue'. Moreover, because
they have little connection with the duties of social life, 'the feelings that
are inspired by solemn processions, pictures, images, music, &c., are very
improperly called devotion'. Against her contention that devoutness and
religious dispute are incompatible, he insisted that 'no person can have
practical religion much at heart, who has not a value for religious truth',
which must be striven for, as did Jesus, St Paul, the great reformers and
the Puritans; and he remarks wryly that those with the greatest reputation for piety and devotion, the orthodox Dissenters, are also those commonly taken as the most disputatious.

But he seemed most shocked by her effort to bring sentiment to bear.
'Let us not be superstitiously afraid of superstition', she argued. Though it
might be abused, superstition is still human, the product of association of
ideas. Many rational Christians, she pointed out, would enthusiastically
visit Stratford or celebrate the birthday of a patriot or hero, but scorn the
poor Christian who might feel similarly about the events of the life of Jesus
or about places hallowed to the service of religion.[34] Indeed, she thought,
devotional writers have been unjustly reproached for using the language of
love, while in fact love and devotion have much in common: prone to
superstition and excess, nourished by poetry and music, and felt with
greater fervour in warmer climates, they 'carry the mind out of itself, and
powerfully refine the affections from every thing gross, low, and selfish'.
Priestley simply denied the appropriateness of the language of human love
to the relation of man to God and upbraided his friend for resorting to the
sentimental and the pathetic, which, as we saw, was exactly her intention.

---

[33] Barbauld, *Works* (fn. 31), vol. II, pp. 160–1. Actually, her discussion of how sects tend to establishment and of the accompanying psychological impulses is suggestive and sophisticated.
[34] It may be pointed out that Victorian Unitarians were second to none in their quest for the historical Jesus or their enthusiasm for visiting the Holy Land. On the general phenomenon, see John
Pemble, *The Mediterranean Passion: Victorians and Edwardians in the South* (Oxford, 1987), pp. 182–96.

James Martineau made much of this exchange and characterised it admirably: in it a passion for the sublime and the beautiful confronted a passion for the truth; an attitude that saw some elements of adoration in all creeds came up against one that saw creeds as mostly error; the language of art was incompatible with a worship that would transcend the physical to attain 'the simplicity of a spirit in space'. 'Perhaps each was right, except in condemning the notions of the other', for religion appeals to the whole soul and draws every faculty into worship. We can agree, no doubt, that there is no need to limit 'the modes of devotional conception' or to warn off any emotion or thought. But Mrs Barbauld's position has had the better press, and it is important to redress the balance to appreciate, as Martineau did, that the rational, Priestleyan approach carried an equal validity and may, indeed, have come closer to the orthodox view of piety than even Martineau thought. A few years earlier, Priestley had pleaded with orthodox believers to consider the religious principles to which he had come from an orthodox background. The truths he contended for, he said, were no mere abstract propositions but 'nearly affect the sentiments of our hearts, and our conduct in life'. The God of Calvinist theologians may be the object of dread and terror but scarcely of love or reverence. 'And what is obedience without love? It cannot be that of the heart, which, however, is the only thing that is of any real value in religion.' Like Tillotson, like Jebb, Priestley saw true religion as seated in the heart and as involving a fundamental transformation of a person's entire being. We come once again to Hannah More.[35]

Unitarian devotion moved in two directions. Its public course lay in the development of a Unitarian liturgical tradition, surfacing first in the short-lived Octagon Chapel in Liverpool in the 1760s and 1770s and then carrying over directly from the Church in the form of worship devised by Theophilus Lindsey for Essex Street.[36] But the use of set forms of service or of written as against extempore prayer produced repeated

[35] *An Appeal to the Serious and Candid Professors of Christianity* (1770), in Priestley's *Works* (fn. 20), vol. ii, p. 402. Note should be taken of one effort to explore the connection between Priestley's theology and his views on worship: Russell E. Richey, 'Joseph Priestley: Worship and Theology', *Transactions of the Unitarian Historical Society*, 15 (1972–3), 41–53, 98–104. But the articles are diffuse, and the discussion of worship and the Lord's Supper is brief and superficial.

[36] See the brief, perceptive account of Unitarian liturgical efforts in A. Elliott Peaston, *The Prayer Book Reform Movement in the XVIIIth Century* (Oxford, 1940), pp. 9–24. Peaston deals only in passing with nineteenth-century Unitarian liturgies, and Unitarians appear in his *The Prayer Book Tradition in the Free Churches* (London, 1964) only as they are involved in the Free Catholic movement early in this century. But see his listing of Unitarian liturgies in 'The Unitarian Liturgical Tradition', *Transactions of the Unitarian Historical Society*, 16 (1976), 63–81.

disagreements throughout the nineteenth century and even after, at the congregational level and in debates in the Unitarian press. And for decades ministers (including Priestley) and concerned laymen among the Unitarians had to devote special effort to securing attendance at communion, which encountered residual Dissenting reluctance and the lingering sense that participation presupposed an unusual degree of religious commitment. As the editor of the *Inquirer* wrote in 1854:

> The true charm of the Anglican Church, which endears her to the rustic and the feminine heart, so that neither class trouble themselves much with her credentials, is the deep, simple, and domestic piety of her devotional forms, which early fascinate the imagination, and wind themselves closer and closer round the spirit, with every grief, with every joy, with every self-sacrifice – almost with every sin. At once simple and elastic, her liturgy fits the spirit of the child, and stretches out to the full dimensions of the man . . . And why – because there are here and there some things easily omissible in that service which jar our sense of truth and simplicity – need we cut ourselves off from the many rich spiritual advantages which the use of the greater part of it would afford us?[37]

The argument was not one that could be stipulated. One correspondent waxed ironic: here was indeed a solution for the shortage of ministers, for, given a fixed form of prayer, why should not laymen step in? 'Our forefathers left us endowments, we would bequeath a liturgy . . . their endowments send us to sleep, and our liturgy may lull our descendants.' The real question was the zeal of the congregation, and what in that regard would be the gain in merely adopting a liturgy, even assuming agreement could be reached?

Free prayer, wrote another reader, is the guarantee of religious meditation in a minister: 'there is something in the spontaneous outpouring of the heart that cannot be had in any set form of prayer – an essence too subtle to be fixed, and which escapes the attempt to preserve and hand it down for the constant reproduction at will of emotions which can only spring from the living contact of fervent souls'. And did not liturgy, in perpetuating itself, risk transforming a passing belief into a quasi-creed, in a denomination that prided itself on its capacity to evolve?[38] But however sharp these disagreements about liturgy, they were couched in language that bespoke an intense concern for devotion and piety.

---

[37] *Inquirer*, 14 October 1854, p. 1.
[38] *Inquirer*, 21 and 28 October 1854. See also the correspondence on attendance at London churches, which was essentially a debate about liturgy, *Inquirer*, 30 January, 6 and 27 February 1904. On communion, e.g., leaders and correspondence in the *Inquirer*, 30 October to 27 November 1874.

Again, Horton Davies has provocative things to say. He admires the Puritans but generally comes down against their devotional style, no doubt useful, as he sees it, in times of crisis and upheaval but not nearly so effective in settled situations and among large groups. But not even the persistence of the Anglican liturgy can save the eighteenth century from his dismissal: the age was 'not conducive to worship in general', being concerned with moral duties and with the individual, while resisting tradition and mystery. The decorum of the Anglicans was akin to the whitewash that covered dark corners of Gothic churches, while 'perhaps later Latitudinarian whitewash is appropriate for the embellishment of what looked uncommonly like a sepulchre'. Unitarian liturgies were a sort of liturgical gnosticism, 'preparing a formulary suitable only for the intelligent few, for the initiates of rationalism', justifiable only in so far as they stimulated the genius of James Martineau.[39] Some criticism of Unitarian liturgical efforts is certainly just, though scarcely warranting that degree of dismissal. But Davies entirely overlooks a second course, private devotions.

Much as Tillotson had done, Priestley sought to encourage the practice in his sermon on habitual devotion.[40] It was important, he insisted, that the mind not be too much preoccupied with worldly cares, that a day be set aside for '*calling off our eyes from beholding vanity, and . . . quickening us in the ways of God*', advice aimed particularly at those employed in the arts and manufactures, who were more likely to be fully absorbed in their work than the husbandman whose situation is peculiarly favourable for the contemplation of God's works. Priestley insisted on the importance of regular worship of God: 'the intercourse we keep up with God by prayer . . . promotes a spirit of devotion', and makes it easier for the ideas of the Divine Being and his providence to occur to the mind on other occasions, when we are not formally praying to him. On such occasions prayers, whether public or private, should be kept short, to avoid diluting the fervour, and devotional exercises should allow for 'intervals of meditation, calculated to impress our minds more deeply with the

---

[39] Davies, *Worship and Theology* (fn. 17), vol. II: *From Andrewes to Baxter and Fox, 1603–1690*, pp. 522–35; vol. III, pp. 52–5, 74–5, 76–93 at pp. 52, 75, 90.

[40] 'A Discourse on Habitual Devotion' (1780), in Priestley's *Works* vol. 15, pp. 104–21. Priestley devoted much attention to public worship and to liturgical forms, but much of what he wrote, like his extensive exegesis of the Bible, was intended for private use or for small groups who had withdrawn from unacceptable orthodox worship to meet together 'without a learned Ministry'. See *A Free Address to Protestant Dissenters on the Subject of the Lord's Supper*, with subsequent discussion, *Works*, vol. XXI, pp. 249–373; *A Free Address . . . on the Subject of Church Discipline, ibid.*, pp. 374–448; *Forms of Prayer and other Offices for the Use of Unitarian Societies, ibid.*, pp. 474–572.

sentiments we express'. Used with no strict regard for 'particular times, places, or posture of body', these exercises should 'consist chiefly of meditation upon God and his providence', offering an advantage over direct address to God, which can lead to the confusion of means and ends and to spiritual pride. Again, the constant awareness of and humility towards God's governance is as nearly identical as may be to the prescriptions of Hannah More.

Throughout most of the nineteenth century, this concern for private devotion called forth a steady stream of Unitarian publications, which found their uses in individual meditation, in small groups cut off from any organised congregation, and in family prayers, which were conducted in Unitarian households, such as that of the manufacturer Samuel Greg.[41] One such manual was *Devotional Exercises for the Use of Young Persons*, published in 1801 by Charles Wellbeloved, Unitarian minister at York. 'The design of it is to lead your thoughts frequently to God ... to teach you to pray; to furnish you with subjects of serious reflection suitable to your age', and, in time, using his reflections as a model, to 'gradually habituate yourselves to the giving of your own thoughts utterance', making piety not only 'a crown of glory to the hoary head [but] an ornament of peculiar beauty upon that which has not seen many years'. In form, which Wellbeloved's biographer believed was original with him, the little book is a succession of reflections and prayers for morning and evening of each day of the week, inculcating gratitude and praise, humility and service, and constant awareness of the grandeur and continual presence of God.

Wellbeloved was Anglican by upbringing, with Wesleyan overtones, and had been expelled from Homerton Academy for heterodoxy. Despite this background, there was, said John Kenrick, nothing ascetic in his rule of life, 'nothing romantic in his philanthropy, nothing morbid in his conscientiousness, so there was nothing mystical or overstrained in his devotion. His prayers were the expression, from the Christian point of view, of the feelings, the wants, and the convictions which the condition of human nature, the experience of life, and the suggestions of conscience, make common to all mankind in whom any sense of religion

---

[41] Cf. the memoir in Samuel Greg, *A Layman's Legacy in Prose and Verse: Selections from the papers* ... With a prefatory letter by A.P. Stanley ... and a brief memoir (London 1877). See also John Relly Beard, ed., *Sabbath Leisure: or Religious Recreations in Prose and Verse* (London, 1857) and *Sermons designed to be used in Families: Accompanied by Suitable Prayers*, 2 vols. (Manchester, 1829), and John Page Hopps, *Prayers for Private Meditation and the Home*, 2nd ed (London, 1866) and *Readings for Public Worship and the Home* (London, 1884).

exists.' In 1832, Wellbeloved supplied the second week of addresses and prayers promised in the first edition, the long delay sufficiently accounted for by the demands of his principalship of Manchester College, York, which had begun in 1803.[42]

A younger and eventually more famous Unitarian author was Harriet Martineau. In 1823, at the age of twenty-one, she had ventured anonymously to fill the still-existing gap in Wellbeloved's work, under an almost identical title and in the same format.[43] Her Norwich publisher endeavoured to find out through Wellbeloved's publisher in London if the little book would be a duplication, and, no reply having been received, publication went forward. Then apparently there was 'a time race between Harriet's book of Devotions and a second part of Mr. Wellby's ([of]which Harriet had never heard).' But it was a false alarm: Wellbeloved's new volume did not appear, and he welcomed her book 'in terms most generous, which has deeply gratified her'. It must have been even more gratifying when some Quaker friends in Norwich found the book 'surprisingly different from their supposition of Unitarian opinions', so she used the occasion to convince them that there was a far wider ground of religious sympathies than they had supposed possible.[44] In 1832, the same year as Wellbeloved's expanded eighth edition, Harriet Martineau's little book reached its third edition, with the authorship avowed to a Unitarian public which already knew her well.

Martineau's book was part of a decade-long preoccupation with the practice and the theory of devotion. The consolation that Harriet Martineau had found in religion during an unhappy childhood extended well into her maturity; her early letters to her brother James contain occasional religious musings that break through in a way that shows them as anything but exceptional. Thus, on a birthday:

How can anyone on such days as these refuse to rejoice in the presence (almost the manifest presence) of the Parent of all. May it ever be my delight, as it is at this moment, to ascribe every blessing which has made my life as cheerful and peaceful as a summer's morning, to His bounty, Who has strewed my path with

---

[42] John Kenrick, *A Biographical Memoir of the late Revd Charles Wellbeloved* (London, 1860), pp. 77–9, 242–3.

[43] H. Martineau, *Devotional Exercises: consisting of Reflections and Prayers, for the Use of Young Persons* . . . To the first edition (London, 1823) was appended a defence of holy communion (*A Treatise on the Lord's Supper*), but that was supplanted in the third edition of 1832 by *A Guide to the Study of the Scriptures*.

[44] James Martineau's shorthand abstracts, made in the 1840s, of letters from Harriet, 30 October 1823, 12 November 1824, and 28 April 1826. The abstracts and a transcription by William S. Coloe are in Manchester College, Oxford. 'Wellby' was the nickname by which the York students referred to their Principal.

flowers. May they not fade and die, but may their beauty continue so apparent that I may ever be thankful to understand that He has ordered the giving thereof.[45]

It is significant that this preoccupation ran in tandem with her systematic study of Locke, Hume, Priestley, Southwood Smith and Hartley, which made her the most complete and dogmatic of adherents of necessarian-ism, a deterministic philosophy she held to the very end and long after she had abandoned the Unitarian connection and had rejected religion for free thought.

Indeed, her first published work, in the *Monthly Repository* in 1822, was a pair of articles on 'Female Writers of Practical Divinity', chiefly Mrs Barbauld and Hannah More, with More's *Practical Piety* serving as the centrepiece of her account.[46] Although she claimed to differ from Hannah More on certain doctrines as much as one Protestant could differ from another, these differences were as nothing to the areas of agreement – More's defence of religious conversation, her injunction to prayer, her summons to a true religious life: the way might be hard, but 'who would not resign the world and its fleeting pleasures, for an immor-tal inheritance, and for such a transition to it as is here described?'

But while she devoted more space to Hannah More, it was Mrs Barbauld who drew her greatest encomiums. With More, she says,

we listen to her warnings with an awe which would make us believe that we are on no equality with her. We stand reproved under her solemn exhortations. But with Mrs Barbauld it is different. She meets our ideas, and seems to express what had passed through our own minds, much more forcibly than we ourselves could have done. We have a fellow-feeling with her . . . and . . . thus . . . are tempted to overlook all errors, and all that borders on extravagance, in consideration of the justice with which she paints our passions and emotions, and touches every chord of feeling in our bosoms.[47]

Almost a decade later, she expressed very similar views about Philip Doddridge, in reviewing successive volumes of his correspondence and diary. Her admiration for him as a devotional writer and as a religious inspiration was immense, and the correspondence proved him 'as

---

[45] Letter of 12 June, 1825, Manchester College, Oxford. On her religious musings as a child, see *Harriet Martineau's Autobiography* . . ., 2 vols. (Boston, 1877), vol. I, pp. 1–17. It is curious to note how largely flowers figure in her childhood recollections, and it is also significant that she says virtually nothing about her early literary efforts.

[46] *Monthly Repository*, 17 (1822), 593–6, 746–50. She used the pen-name Discipulus, not, as recalled in her autobiography, the initial V.

[47] Harriet Martineau approved of Mrs Barbauld's essay on devotional taste, which had brought down Priestley's wrath.

devotional as his works shew him to be. He was a fit example for us in the fervour of his piety, the unremitting influence of his principles, and the gentle virtues of an affectionate and ingenuous spirit.'[48]

In the same year as Martineau published her *Devotional Exercises*, another Unitarian, who became as celebrated, and often as reviled, as she, entered the field. John Bowring, ten years older than Harriet Martineau and from a very similar Unitarian and commercial background, had already established himself in London, as an intimate of Jeremy Bentham and also a leading figure in the tight, radical community of London Unitarianism. As MP for two periods in the 1830s and 1840s and as the holder of a number of government appointments, Bowring made free trade his particular cause; eventually, he became Consul in Canton and then Governor of Hong Kong. It is hard to decide whether his chief posthumous fame (or notoriety) arose from his part as Bentham's friend and editor or from his role in the incident that began the second Chinese war in 1856.[49] What is important here is that, a lifelong Unitarian, he was also a prolific writer of religious verse, the best known being the hymn, 'In the Cross of Christ I glory'.

Bowring's *Matins and Vespers, with Hymns and Occasional Devotional Pieces* was modelled on a work with which he had become acquainted around 1820, *Morgen- und Abendopfer in Gesängen*, by Dr J. H. W. Witschel, and which, he claimed, had had considerable success in Germany. Like the Wellbeloved and Martineau volumes, there are reflections, in verse, for the week, but quadrupled for the four seasons. The first edition was dedicated to Lant Carpenter, the Unitarian minister of Lewin's Mead Chapel in Bristol, a leading Unitarian theologian and the teacher, at different times, of Bowring and both James and Harriet Martineau. In the second edition, which quickly followed, the dedication was to Mrs Barbauld; the reason for the change, as Bowring confessed with embarrassment to Carpenter, was that a review had singled out the dedication to so notorious a Unitarian as proof of the heretical tendency of the volume, whereas Mrs Barbauld, who could claim wide appreciation, was far less controversial.[50]

It is curious to reflect on the wry contrast between Bowring's Christian week and the contemporaneous publishing phenomenon of John Keble's *The Christian Year*. Suffice it to say that Bowring's verse is less obscure and scans better than Keble's,[51] and that Keble's poems,

[48] *Monthly Repository*, n.s., 4 (1830), 15–26, 385–9, and 5 (1831), 59, 321–5.
[49] R.K. Webb, 'Sir John Bowring and Unitarianism', *Utilitas*, 4 (1992), 43–79.
[50] Bowring to Carpenter, 23 and 31 December 1823, Manchester College, Oxford.
[51] *DNB*, *s.v.* Keble.

published in 1827, went through ninety-five editions before his death in 1866. The vast disparity of the two audiences is probably explanation enough, but it seems worth mentioning that, while the Unitarian verses display a strenuous devotion, Keble's book avowed as its chief purpose the exhibition of 'that *soothing* tendency in the Prayer Book'.

Unitarian works of devotion are suffused with the immensity of God's work in creation, with the glory of his sovereignty and the duty to which he calls men and women in this world. But Harriet Martineau thought devotion only one, inferior, aspect of piety. In an ingenious pair of essays published in 1829, which show the deep impress of Hartleian psychology, she suggested that religious feeling, like any feeling, is valid only in so far as it leads to the formation of habits of benevolence.[52] Here she was at one with Priestley and with Hannah More in believing that the prepared heart, the first and central matter, would issue not in indiscriminate action but in action owing everything to the dictate of God's will mediated through the affections. But if Hannah More's Christian was a serf awaiting in ignorance the call to do good, Priestley's and Martineau's Christian was an agent carrying out a course ultimately dictated by God but rationally discoverable by human intelligence. The origins in God's will and the results in man's actions were the same; what differed was the link between the two. But for both the evangelical and the rationalist, piety was a compound of attitude and action, of reconstruction of the heart which underlay both private and public behaviour. Piety was the means, differing in accidents but not in essences, through which God's work was done in this world. So far as that equivalence is accepted, the possibility of rational piety must be accepted.

---

[52] H. Martineau, 'On the Agency of Feelings in the Formation of Habits; and on the Agency of Habits in the Regeneration of Feelings', *Monthly Repository*, n.s., 3 (1829), 102–6, 159–62. She also responded enthusiastically to an invitation from the editor, W.J. Fox, to write a tale illustrative of devotion, an opportunity, she thought, to treat the subject in a truly masculine way, in contrast to the feminine quality of what most men had written on the subject; she thought, too, that it might serve for her generation as Sir Thomas Browne's *Religio Medici* had served almost two centuries earlier (Harriet Martineau to Fox, 4 December 1829, R.S. Speck Collection, Bancroft Library, University of California, Berkeley). It is probable that 'True Worshippers', which appeared in *Monthly Repository*, 4 (1830), 307–15, is the result of that exchange. The tale, in which no evidence of Sir Thomas Browne is apparent, is a portrait of an untutored lay preacher of great power, an argument for suiting the Christian message to the educational levels of different audiences, and a defence of public worship, exemplified in the little band of worshippers that formed around the primitive preacher. It is tempting to speculate that her vision of this little gathered church may have been influenced by Priestley's *Forms of Prayer and other Offices*, in *Works* (fn. 40) vol. xxi. That volume of Priestley's *Works* was published in 1822, and Harriet Martineau was given 'Rutt's Priestley' in 1825. James's abstracts are not entirely clear, but the mention of paying thirteen guineas would suggest that it was the complete set (1 and 12 October 1825, Manchester College, Oxford).

Harriet Martineau then offers a quite original perception of a possible consequence of this right ordering of personal commitment. The rationalist who, like Priestley and Martineau, also underwent a species of second birth, might end in a not entirely admirable state. Having done the work for which they were given us, Harriet Martineau argued, the feelings might then decline into apparent coldness and indifference, but the formation of habits of piety, on a higher level than the devotion that gave rise to them, would at last regenerate the feelings on a new plane of maturity and permanence. This regenerative process was far preferable to a constant, disordered state of religious passion. In her review of Doddridge, she maintained that, had he always been such a saint as he had been made out to be by his admirers, had his harp of a thousand strings remained ever at a stretch, the strings would have snapped, 'as we cannot but know from our experience of the mournful effects of religious excitement'. It was a relief to learn from his letters that, though he was 'a saint in the closet, he was a man among men', charming, witty and utterly entrancing. When she came to consider the diaries, however, she found a man who suffered in his closet, suffering which she laid entirely at the door of his theology. At last he could be seen not as he had been painted by misrepresenting admirers but as something more. His hold on the admiration and affection of those who came after was, and deserved to be, as strong as ever, but, as a sufferer, he had 'an irresistible claim to our compassion and respectful sympathy'.

Geoffrey Nuttall has argued that 'the tradition of Baxter and Doddridge is to be distinguished . . . from the tradition which led on into Unitarianism, and which also looked back to Baxter for inspiration'.[53] That Harriet Martineau, at the very peak of her Priestleyan enthusiasm, should rank Doddridge so highly in her pantheon – as, of course, did Priestley himself – suggests that there may be more of an obligation than Nuttall was willing to allow. Contradictions remain, but Doddridge entered into the amalgam of rational religion and enriched it with a depth of devotion and piety that few later commentators have been prepared to concede.

But what Mrs Barbauld or even Hannah More might have been willing to allow, not all evangelicals were willing to grant. In the brace of reviews that so alarmed Bowring's publisher and so embarrassed him, we can estimate the wide differences that separated rationalist from

---

[53] G.F. Nuttall, *Richard Baxter and Philip Doddridge: A Study in a Tradition*, Friends of Dr Williams's Library, 5th Lecture (London, 1951), n.71.

evangelical. The Carpenter identification was raised by the reviewer in the *Christian Observer*, who Bowring had heard was William Wilberforce, but who was also somewhat more complimentary about the qualities of the verse than was the writer in the *Eclectic Review*.[54] Both, however, agreed that Bowring's approach to the Almighty was over-familiar, even blasphemous, and that the great want was recognition of the divinity and sacrifice of Christ. To the reviewer in the *Christian Observer*, the 'melancholy and painful spectacle' of this lapse explained 'a deficiency, a dampness, a chillness'. The *Eclectic* reviewer was far more severe. This 'anomalous product and rare specimen of Unitarian devotion' might have been thought by a stranger coming to it to be a translation of some Greek or Latin odes, 'the very rant of pantheism'. 'Such is Unitarian piety! . . . a piety that knows of no repentance towards God, no faith in the Mediator; a piety without humility, without contrition, without love . . .'

To the *Eclectic*, Unitarian devotion was a rarity and, when accomplished, empty. The review in the *Christian Observer* thought that even the devout Christian could find much edification and pleasure in Bowring's pages; proceeding from the bedrock of certainty, the orthodox Christian could thrill to the delightful language 'of hope, of joy, of love, of gratitude, of filial confidence, of beatific anticipation'. But when the poet insists that death has no terrors,

to whom does the declaration apply? Does the Scripture intimate any thing like *universality* in its application, to the sinner and the saint, the righteous and the wicked, those that fear God and those that fear him not? . . . Once teach men that heaven is the destined residence of God's universal creation . . . and where is the sanction for rectitude of conduct, at least among the great majority of mankind, who are governed more by hope and fear than by nice considerations of the rectitude and beauty of virtue?

Debates are won by those who control the definitions, and the evangelicals were generally determined to deny the warrant of devotion or piety to those who differed from them on specific, certainly important theological points. But it is worth once more recalling William James, to whom saintliness was a matter of excess. For all his rollicking good fun in showing the saints of Christian history for the human horrors so many of them were, James still considered them central actors in the human drama, deserving of every honour save that of unreserved imitation: 'Is it necessary', he asked, 'to be quite as fantastically good as that? We who

---

[54] *Christian Observer*, 23 (1823), 697–708; *Eclectic Review*, n.s., 20 (1823), 162–71.

have no vocation for the extremer ranges of sanctity will surely be let off at the last day, if our humility, asceticism, and devoutness prove of a less convulsive sort . . . Religious phenomena, like all other human phenomena, are subject to the law of the golden mean.' In the many mansions of our Father's house, each must discover for himself 'the kind of religion and the amount of saintship' that goes with his mission and vocation, with no guarantees of success and no set orders.[55]

In that humane perspective, the deeply felt reverence for creation and for law, the love descending from and rising towards the Father, the stern sense of duty commanded by divine decree must be allowed to qualify serious Unitarians – of which their numbers yielded no small proportion – for more than honorific ascription of devotion and piety. Whatever theological issues divided the orthodox from Unitarians in the early nineteenth century, and from the dwindling band of rational Christians in other denominations, it is a serious historical error to overlook or deny the possibility of rational piety, as in its main outlines the eighteenth century would have understood the term.

In the long run, of course, we are all dead, and by the middle of the nineteenth century the whole question of piety was, as we have seen, becoming a matter for scholarly reflection or forgetfulness. The subduing of refractory human nature by the transformation of the affections to a greater usefulness in this world was being transformed into a new quest – for the best means of forming and establishing character. In that high-Victorian concern, institutions and collaborative effort played a far greater role than the reading and private meditation on which serious religion had relied for at least two centuries to accomplish the same end.[56]

---

[55] James, *Varieties of Religious Experience* (fn. 14), Lectures 14 and 15.

[56] Casting his view across Europe and America in the Victorian age, Peter Gay finds that 'Character, that magical word, intoned daily, encompassed all these cherished bourgeois ideals and anxieties. It meant realism, self-control, temperance, thrift, hard work, purposeful energy, and the rest – in short, aggression disciplined and sublimated.' *The Bourgeois Experience: Victoria to Freud*, vol. III: *The Cultivation of Hatred* (New York, 1993), p. 502. See also Reba N. Soffer, *Discipline and Power: The University, History, and the Making of an English Elite, 1870–1930* (Stanford, CA, 1994).

CHAPTER 13

New Jerusalems: prophecy, Dissent and radical culture in England, 1786–1830

Iain McCalman

On 16 February 1790 a London engraver, James Sayers, produced a caricature entitled 'The Repeal of the Test Act. A Vision'. The first English print to register hostility to the French Revolution, it also satirised nonconformist advocacy of civil and religious emancipation by depicting Priestley, Price and Lindsey as fanatical enthusiasts of seventeenth-century stamp. Whilst Price prays for the patriot members of the French National Assembly, Priestley appears to vomit airy flames of Atheism, deism, Socinianism and Arianism, blasting a passing angel in the process. Below cavort a hideous cast of ratbags and revolutionaries – demons carrying American and Cromwellian favours, the English Jacobins Fox and Paine, the failed regicide enthusiast Margaret Nicholson and, significantly, a Cromwellian soldier watching a bearded Jew despoil the sacred symbols of the Established Church.[1] Within the year Edmund Burke – in the midst of his celebrated attack on Price – gave a gloating warning of the fate that awaited such lunatic Dissenters and Judaists:

> We have Lord George Gordon fast in Newgate; and neither his being a public proselyte to Judaism, nor his having in his zeal against Catholic priests and all sorts of ecclesiastics, raised a mob . . . which pulled down all our prisons, has preserved to him a liberty of which he did not render himself worthy . . . We have rebuilt Newgate, and tenanted the mansion. We have prisons almost as strong as the Bastile, for those who dare libel the Queen of France. In this spiritual retreat, let the noble libeller remain. Let him there meditate on his Thalmud, until he learns a conduct more becoming of his birth and parts and not so disgraceful to the ancient religion to which he has become a proselyte.[2]

[1] Published by Thomas Cornell, 16 February 1790, 'Personal and Political Satires', M. Dorothy George Collection, British Museum [BM] Department of Maps and Drawings, no. 7628. See also Martin Fitzpatrick's fascinating study of this print and others, 'Priestley Caricatured', in A. Truman Schwartz and J.G. McEvoy, eds., *Motion Towards Perfection: The Achievements of Joseph Priestley* (Boston, 1990), pp. 161–218.

[2] Edmund Burke, *Reflections on the Revolution in France* . . . (London, 1790), pp. 124–5.

Figure 13.1: BMC 7628 16 February 1790, James Sayers. This is a satire on the efforts of radicals and Foxite Whigs to repeal the Test and Corporation Acts in 1790. Richard Price, Joseph Priestley and Theophilus Lindsey, who are all Dissenters, are in a pulpit. Price, in particular, is attacking the Church and the constitution and supporting the revolution in France. Fox, Stanhope, Thomas Paine and Andrew Kippis are in the congregation. Price's famous sermon to the Revolution Society, 'A Discourse on the Love of Our Country', led to his being attacked in Burke's *Reflections*.

Five years later Sayers's chief engraver rival, James Gillray, produced
a series of three prints which again linked a similar cast of revolutionaries and ideas: 'Jacobin prophecies', Judaism, irreligion and pro-French
revolutionaries rub shoulders with religious Dissent, inspired on this
occasion by the apocalyptic prophecies of ex-naval lieutenant Richard
Brothers, known to his followers as 'Prince of the Hebrews and Nephew
of the Almighty'.[3]

All this has the ring of typical 1790s loyalist propaganda in which
liberal causes are promiscuously coupled, particularly given the apparent distance between the worlds of scholarly Dissenting rationalists like
Priestley and unlettered, supposedly deranged, enthusiasts like Gordon
and Brothers. Moreover, Gillray was at this time already taking government commissions, Sayers was a salaried ministerial scribbler and Burke
was being assiduously wooed by Pitt.[4] Even so, these propagandists knew
their enemy. Sayers showed an informed and consistent antipathy to
Dissent throughout his career as an engraver. Gillray had been reared a
Moravian and the Brothers prints reveal an accurate knowledge of, as
well as some sneaking sympathy for, the prophet's antiestablishment
mission. Burke, of course, had been connecting Dissenting politics with
subversion long before the Price sermon; fears for his house and family
during the Gordon riots probably account for much of his later anti-
Dissenting rabidity.[5] By linking enthusiastic prophecy with Judaism, all
three men were also satirising a familiar Puritan prophetic tradition,
sometimes known as radical restorationism or Dissenting philosemitism
– a tradition which resurfaced strongly during the 1780s and 1790s
amongst London's numerous artisan and 'middling sort' literati, artists,
virtuosi and 'seekers after truth'.

I propose, in this chapter, first to sketch the broad intellectual contours
of this restorationist revival, suggesting in the process some surprising
affinities and connections between the ideas of Joseph Priestley and
those of Gordon, Brothers and their radical 'seeker' followers; second, to
argue that this brand of radical prophecy took on a new shape and significance during the Napoleonic Wars, to become a key ideological
element in the struggle between oppositionists and loyalists; and, finally,

[3] James Gillray, 'Prophet of the Hebrews', 5 March 1795; 'Light expelling Darkness', 30 April 1795;
'Presages of the Millennium', 4 June 1795; George Coll., nos. 8627, 8644.
[4] Lucyle Werkmeister, *The London Daily Press, 1772–92* (Lincoln, 1963), p. 264; A. Aspinall, *Politics and
the Press, 1780–1850* (London, 1949), p. 165.
[5] On Sayers, see Fitzpatrick, 'Priestley Caricatured' (fn. 1), p. 213; On Burke, see Ian Hampsher-
Monk, Book Review, *History of Political Thought*, 12 (1991), 179–83.

to suggest some ways in which 'restorationist' ideas and images became incorporated into the resurgent popular radical and romantic culture of the 1820s and 1830s.

I

By publishing a series of *Letters to the Jews* between 1786 and 1794 Joseph Priestley gave new shape and life to a body of ideas already long familiar to Dissenting scholars. Restorationism can be defined, crudely, as the eschatological claims in the Books of Daniel and Revelations that the millennium would be immediately preceded by the conversion and restoration of the Jews to their former homeland and glory. During the seventeenth century these ideas had been eagerly taken up and elaborated by a succession of Puritan scholars and preachers who found a compelling analogue, or literal source of identification, in the epic sufferings and promised redemption of the people of Israel. Priestley could draw on the legendary seventeenth-century scholarship of Joseph Mede and Thomas Brightman, the Unitarian restorationism of Francis Kett, and a series of more recent works, ranging from Thomas Newton to Hartley. Like his Puritan predecessors, he was also moved to advance his restorationist manifesto by the urgency of contemporary events which seemed to portend the onset of the last days. Following the promise of the American Revolution, he combed the newspapers throughout the 1780s for news of developments in places with key providential implications, such as the papal territories, infidel Turkey, Palestine, and throughout the regions of the Jewish diaspora. At the same time he possessed an intense and informed sympathy for God's peculiar people whose plight seemed to resemble that of Dissenters oppressed by a corrupt and discriminatory religious and civil establishment.

Despite debts to David Hartley, in particular, Priestley's restorationist ideas are distinctive in their vehement hostility to the Established Church, their explicit, if limited, republicanism, their intense commitment to religious and political toleration and, above all, their liberal theological attitudes to Judaism. He aimed less to convert the Jews than to eliminate needless obstacles preventing a genuine convergence between purified Christianity and enlightened Judaism. As an anti-Trinitarian he shared the Jewish belief in the fundamental unity of God. He also rejected the pre-existent divinity of Jesus Christ, another Jewish objection to Christianity. Further, and crucially, he sought to reconcile Christian and Jewish eschatology. He regarded Christ's mission as perfectly compatible with Jewish belief in a future Prince of David who would restore his people to their lost greatness in the latter days. Adoption of true Christian principles would not mean the abandonment of Jewish law and ceremony. After the millennium, enlightened Jew would coexist with purified Christian in peace and harmony, ruling with Christ from the new Jerusalem and having natural pre-eminence as 'the older branch of the family'. He promised that an imminent general declaration in favour of Unitarianism would end the appalling 'idolatrous worship of Jesus Christ' and that those who had persecuted God's special people would be made to pay.[6]

Priestley was thus both affronted and hurt when an unlettered Jewish hatdresser, David Levi, wrote a series of replies which bluntly rejected these overtures, suggesting that the Unitarian divine had no right even to call himself a Christian, let alone to convert Jews. True, as Priestley worked to allay sources of misunderstanding and Levi later elaborated his defence of Judaism in a more scholarly series of *Dissertations on the Prophecies* (1793–1800), their differences narrowed and a mutual respect developed. Amongst the numbers of pamphlets engendered by the controversy, those of Dissenters such as Priestley, the radical Baptist James Bicheno and the physician Richard Worthington came closest to what Levi called 'the true spirit of candour and liberality'.[7] Levi and Priestley continued to disagree, however, on the precise prophetic status of Jesus Christ, on the appropriate criteria for establishing authenticity of miracles and, most fundamentally, on whether the restorationist promise should be interpreted literally or allegorically. Levi rejected Priestley's belief that the Jews would be gathered and restored literally to their homeland in Palestine, positing instead a spiritual restoration that would take place globally within the existing lands of the diaspora.[8]

[6] Joseph Priestley, *Letters to the Jews: Inviting them to an Amicable Discussion on the Evidences of Christianity* (Birmingham, 1786), esp. pp. 2–6, 9–10, 38–53. For secondary accounts, see J. Fruchtman, *The Apocalyptic Politics of Richard Price and Joseph Priestley: A Study in Late Eighteenth-Century Republican Millenarianism* (Philadelphia, 1928); J. Van den Berg, 'Priestley, the Jews and the Millennium', in David Skatz and Jonathan I. Israel, eds., *Sceptics, Millenarians, Jews* (Leiden, 1990), pp. 257–74.

[7] David Levi, *Letter to Mr. Bicheno, occasioned by his Friendly Address to the Jews* (London, 1787), p. 128; see also Richard Worthington, *A Letter to the Jews* (London, 1787); Joseph Priestley, *Letters to the Jews, Part II* (Birmingham, 1787).

[8] David Levi, *Letters to Doctor Priestley in answer to his Letters to the Jews, Part II . . . also letters to Dr. Cooper, Mr. Bicheno, Dr. Krauter, Mr. Swain and . . . Anselm Bailey* (London, 1789), esp. pp. 40–2, 109.

II

This dialogue between Priestley and Levi is instructive because historians are inclined to draw a sharp distinction between the polite and respectable millennialist scholarship of figures like Priestley and the unlettered enthusiasm of those with their roots in popular culture. Autodidactic intellectuals, virtuosi and seekers recognised no such distinction, tending to see Priestley in a different light from that of much modern scholarship. To them he was 'gunpowder Priestley', who had threatened to blow the Established Church to smithereens, had publicly welcomed the French Revolution, glossed over the September massacres, corresponded with the Jacobinical John Hurford Stone, had been elected, with Tom Paine, to the French National Assembly and subsequently burned in effigy by loyalists.[9] A proto-type 'Modern Masters' pamphlet on Priestley issued from Newgate by the Painite publisher, H.D. Symonds, in 1794 summed him up as 'an enemy to all political restraint . . . the advocate of every reform, and every revolution that seems . . . to promise the least encrease [*sic*] to civil liberty'.[10] This was the man whose fast day speeches of 1793 and 1794 communicated an adventist urgency of a kind that had rarely been aired from pulpits since the days of Cromwell.

At the same time Priestley's emphasis on a millennium of reason fostered through free inquiry, intellectual debate and an enlightened quest for liberty appealed strongly to those marginal artists and writers who felt themselves to be outside the formal knowledge or patronage system. Levi, a self-proclaimed 'inquirer after truth', was briefed for the contest with Priestley by a poor hack and nostrum-monger called Henry Lemoine, who introduced the ragged Jewish scholar into a circle of plebeian freethinkers and mystics gathering at the Chiswell premises of bookseller James Lackington.[11] Lemoine's acquaintance with the restorationist tradition probably derived from Huguenot parents and an education at the French Calvinist free school in Spitalfields. He believed that 'to all the people of the earth [the Jews] were formerly and are still to all civilized nations, a beacon set upon a hill . . . to light them to the

[9] Clarke Garrett, *Respectable Folly: Millenarians and the French Revolution in France and England* (Baltimore, 1975), pp. 141–3, 165.

[10] *The Character of Dr. Priestley, Considered as a Philosopher, Politician and Divine* . . . (London, 1795), p. 5.

[11] On Levi, Lemoine and this circle, see *Gentleman's Magazine* 82 (1812), 673–4; *Memoirs of the First Forty-five Years of the Life of James Lackington* . . . *Written by himself* (London, 1791); *The Confessions of James Lackington, late Bookseller at the Temple of the Muses* . . . (London, 1804); *DNB, s.v.* Lackington; Lemoine; Levi.

sanctuary of a God, holy, just and good'.[12] Seekers of his kind were also drawn to Judaism for its hermetic and freethinking possibilities. A contemporary satire sneered at the shabby hatdresser Rabbi Levi as 'a kind of conjuror, an adept in the abstruse science of physiognomy . . . a profound critic, and a rigid reviewer of *whims, dreams, riddles, romances, enigmas, tales of ghosts, hobgoblins and so forth*'.[13] This was certainly an apt description of his friend, Lemoine, producer of a series of fugitive periodicals like the *Wonderful Magazine*, a precursor of Robert L. Ripley's *Believe it or not!*, which attempted to publicise the wonders of both occult and rational-empirical science. Extracts from Hunter's lectures on the natural healing of fractures and James Ferguson's philosophy were placed side by side with speeches of the Cromwellian enthusiast Hugh Peters, or with accounts of occult possession, the dissolution of bones, astrological portents, divine miracles and the differences between 'natural and diabolical magic'.[14]

This was also the world of popular Kabbalism and of the legend of the Wandering Jew, a hermetic symbol of the quest for eternal life because of his inability to die until the end of the world. At the same time Jewish critics of Christianity forged sympathetic alliances with seeker sceptics. Oilman John Denis, Lackington's sometime bookseller partner, was steeped in the mystic writings of Jane Lead and the French prophets, yet prided himself on 'pulling systems to pieces . . . he had no faith in the Gospel, disbelieving in the divinity of Christ and the doctrine of atonement'.[15] It was he who temporarily shook the faith of the Methodist Lackington by debating with him at the Horse and Groom and introducing him to Amory's *Memoirs of John Buncle*.

One of the personal testimonies of ghost experiences contained in Lemoine's quasi-scientific anthology, *Visits from the World of the Spirits*, came from the pen of another plebeian seeker and sceptic named William Hamilton Reid.[16] An orphaned son of domestic servants, who

---

[12] [Henry Lemoine], *Lackington's Confessions Rendered into Narrative . . .*, by Alan Macleod [pseud.] (London, 1804), p. 42.

[13] [Thomas Hastings] *The Regal Rambler; or, Eccentrical Adventures of the Devil in London . . .* trans. from the Syriack MS of Rabbi Solomon (London, 1793), pp. 3–6.

[14] *The Wonderful Magazine and Marvellous Chronicle . . . A Work recording authentic accounts of the most extraordinary productions, events and occurrences, in providence, nature and art*, 5 vols. (London, 1793–8), esp. vol. I, pp. 83–6, 136–8, 191; vol. II, pp. 295–302, 377–82; vol. III, pp. 391–2; vol. IV, pp. 96–9, 357–8, 451–9; vol. V, pp. 142–7.

[15] Lemoine, *Lackington's Confessions* (fn. 12), p. 4. See also *Wonderful Magazine*, vol. III (1795), 'Anecdotes of Lackington', p. 13.

[16] H. Lemoine, comp., *Visits from the World of the Spirits, or Interesting Anecdotes of the Dead . . .* (London, 1791), vol. II, pp. 259–60.

had been a Soho silver-buckle maker in the late 1770s, then perforce a struggling poet, translator and journalist, Reid testified at length to the detonating impact of Priestley's ideas and prophecies on Jacobin alehouse debaters and conspirators during the 1790s. Many had believed 'they were the very persons designated by Doctor Priestley, but a few years before, for the important and momentous task of setting fire to the train so long accumulating under the Established Church'. As aspiring philosophers, as well as critics of clerical corruption and vice, Reid and fellow alehouse infidels associated Priestley's rationalist and libertarian sermons with those preached by the deistical 'Priest of Nature', Dr David Williams, at Margaret Street in 1775–6. Not surprisingly, they were also touched by Priestley's millennialist ardour; Reid ascribed to him the widespread expectation amongst alehouse Jacobins that an apocalyptic explosion would purge Christendom of slavery and superstition around the middle of the 1790s. A ragged old clothes seller of Duke Street had even fancied that he was personally called to deliver the Jews.[17]

At least one aspirant to this last role could boast more aristocratic lineage though he drew many of his followers from Duke Street. Lord George Gordon's conversion to Judaism in the mid-1780s has been interpreted by most historians as a final plunge from instability to insanity – a view shared by many of his respectable contemporaries. Yet the trajectory so deplored by Burke, from instigator of the Gordon riots to Jewish prophet, seemed logical enough to those who sympathised with the ideas of radical restorationism. Thomas Spence's commemorative tokens of Gordon depicted him wearing Jewish garb as leader of the riots in 1780.[18] Though technically incorrect, this was not so far off the mark. Gordon's conversion to militant Scottish Presbyterianism at the end of the 1770s connected him with a powerful apocalyptic idiom which – like its Huguenot counterpart – set the suffering and restoration of Israel against the conspiracies and oppressions of the papal antichrist.[19] Gordon took up the Protestant Association cause with the fervour and style of a seventeenth-century sectarian. To Holcroft he had 'the air of a Puritan, a figure tall and meagre, hair straight and dress plain'.[20] His

[17] William Hamilton Reid, *The Rise and Dissolution of the Infidel Societies in this Metropolis* . . . (London, 1800), pp. 23–4, 90. For further details on Reid and his milieu, see my chapter 'The Infidel as Prophet: William Reid and Blakean Radicalism', in S. Clark and D. Worrall, eds., *Historicizing Blake* (London, 1994), pp. 24–42.

[18] Israel Solomons, *Lord George Gordon's Conversion to Judaism* (Edinburgh, 1914), an advance fascicle of *Transactions of the Jewish Historical Society of England*, 7 (1915), 222–71.

[19] See esp. Lord George Gordon, *Innocence Vindicated . . . and the Intrigues of Popery* . . ., 2nd edn, 2 pts. (London, 1783), part I, pp. 3–4, 8, 15.   [20] Solomons, *Lord George* (fn. 18), p. 228.

disciple and biographer, the Scottish doctor Robert Watson, described Gordon as 'well versed in the history of the protectorship; his language, his manners, and customs were strongly tainted with the characteristics of that age. He always talked respectfully of the Commonwealth, regretted the Restoration, and seemed to have our republican ancestors constantly in his view.'[21]

Gordon's extremism frightened off many of the earlier leaders of the Scottish Protestant Association; they had not bargained for violent denunciations of George III, or talk of setting up a 'Political Presbytery', arming for a new civil war and linking up with the political reform movement.[22] Shortly before the riots Gordon was also visited by some Edinburgh gentlemen who had allegedly scribbled down the raving prophecy of a Sussex spinner, Martha Fry: 'the May bush of four score, shall set open the prison door – a young man of noble blood shall come out of the North, and he shall ride by spirit on the winds, and set on the waves, and he shall trouble the money changers and he shall fall by the hands of the Queen'.[23] No wonder the Protestant Association prints of this time are saturated with prophetic images of the beast and whore from Revelation 17, the wickedness of Manasseh's reign from 2 Kings 21 and the lurid violence of Nebuchadnezzar's dream from Daniel 4: all of them intensely reminiscent of Blake.[24] They were also much more reminiscent of Priestley than we might expect. His *Free Address* to Gordon and his supporters, published immediately after the riots, extolled a religious zeal 'unawed by civil power and regardless of all political parties' and sympathised with their fears of Rome as 'a bloody persecuting religion'. Though he urged toleration, Priestley's aims were ultimately as antipapist as Gordon's. He merely disputed 'the means used to secure your great object'.[25] Prominent pro-Dissenting members of the SCI, including Samuel Whitbread, Alderman Frederick Bull, Brass Crosbie and

[21] Robert Watson, *The Life of Lord George Gordon, with a Philosophical Review of his Political Conduct* (London, 1795), p. 76; anon, *The History of Lord George Gordon* (Edinburgh, 1780); for a similar, though more hostile, linking of Gordon with commonwealth republicanism, see Hastings, *Regal Rambler* (fn. 13), pp. 96–9.

[22] Public Record Office [PRO], Treasury Solicitors Files [TS], 11/338/1212, Summary of the correspondence between Lord George Gordon, Ralph Bowie and Revd David Grant, 1779–80, fos. 5–24; Privy Council Papers [PC] 1/3127, Examinations of Ralph Bowie and Revd David Grant, 6 and 11 October 1780. See also Eugene Charlton Black, *The Association: British Extraparliamentary Political Organization 1769–1793* (Cambridge, MA, 1963), pp. 149–53.

[23] *Wonderful Prophecies, being a Dissertation on the Existence, Nature and Extent of the Prophetic Powers in the Human Mind*... (London, 1795), p. 63.

[24] BM, Dorothy George Coll. (fn. 1), esp. nos. 5534, 5643, 5671.

[25] Joseph Priestley, *A Free Address to Those who have Petitioned for the Repeal of the late Act of Parliament in favour of Roman Catholics* (Birmingham, 1780), pp. 3, 6, 11, 21.

William Vaughan, also signed the Protestant Association petition.[26] Another Vaughan – Benjamin – a Unitarian doctor, former pupil and close friend of Priestley was soon to exile himself in France and then America in support of 'restorationist' and revolutionary doctrines. His treatise from Paris, showing that the Revolution entailed a fulfilment of the Book of Daniel, proved so extreme that he was persuaded to withdraw it from publication.[27]

By the early 1790s Gordon, too, had become an ardent supporter of the French Revolution: he is depicted in prints of the day as a titular prophet of the Revolution presiding in Newgate, where he had long been incarcerated for libelling Marie Antoinette. With his penchant for extremism, Gordon had also become Israel ben Abraham, Jewish convert. Circumcised and admitted to a Birmingham synagogue, he continued in Newgate to be instructed in lore, ritual and Hebrew by David Levi and a young scholar, Meyer Joseph, who recalled him looking like a patriarch with his long flowing beard, phylacteries and bag of the Tallith.[28] He regularly conducted services for poor Polish and Turkish Jews who believed he would lead them 'back . . . to their *fathers land*'.[29] To fellow Newgate inmates – the Jacobin activists Gerrald and Frost, Painite propagandists Eaton, Symonds, Ridgway and Pigott, and international revolutionaries Williams, Adrain and Lloyd – Gordon was also a model of austere Jacobin probity, who rejected Christianity, sympathised with 'the religion of nature' and had 'opened a correspondence with societies and individuals entertaining the same views in the surrounding nations; a mutual exchange of freethoughts and essays upon civil and religious settlements . . . general candour and inquiry after truth'[30]

As an enquirer after truth Gordon seems also to have connected with the fugitive mystical strains of Judaism that we noted earlier. It was his outspoken support for 'Count Cagliostro', when that notorious mountebank and magician fled to Britain in the wake of the Diamond Necklace affair, that led to Gordon's initial imprisonment in Newgate. Cagliostro,

[26] Black, *Association* (fn. 22), p. 157; John Sainsbury, *Disaffected Patriots: London Supporters of Revolutionary America 1769–1782* (Montreal, 1987), pp. 156–7.

[27] John G. Alger, *Englishmen in the French Revolution* (London, 1889), pp. 96–7; see also, John H. Sheppard, *Reminiscences of the Vaughan Family, and more particularly Benjamin Vaughan* . . . (Boston, 1865), pp. 8–9.

[28] Moses Margoliouth, *A History of the Jews in Great Britain*, 3 vols. (London, 1851), vol. I, p. 122.

[29] Watson, *Life of Lord George Gordon* (fn. 21), pp. 79–80, 89.

[30] *Ibid.*, pp. 88, 91; see also Werkmeister, *London Daily Press* (fn. 4), p. 439; Charles Pigott, *Persecution: The Case of Charles Pigott, contained in the Defence he had Prepared* . . . (London, 1793), p. 41; BM, Dorothy George Coll. (fn. 1), no. 8342, 'Promenade in the State Side of Newgate', pub. William Holland, 5 October 1793.

a professed mesmerist, alchemist, hermeticist and Kabbalist, had long profited from the rumour that he was 'the man of 1400 years, the Wandering Jew'.[31] Like Gordon, he also professed to love the Jews and venerate the patriarch Moses. His costly prescription for rejuvenation and eternal life combined a panacea of salts with a regime of diet, exercise and fasting modelled on the Jewish prophets and practised by Gordon. This was evidently a further source of attraction for one of Gordon's most devoted gaol visitors, Martin Van Butchell, a physician who had trained with the Hunters, but whose fame derived from self-publicised achievements as a dentist, 'sympathiser', healer of fistulas and inventor of fashion accessories. Van Butchell shared Gordon's revolutionary politics, commitment to beards, natural healing and vegetarian diet, associating all these both with Judaism and with primitive Christianity.[32] He also published long extracts from Giovanni Marana's *Turkish Spy*, originally written in Paris in the 1670s, in which the Wandering Jew was made to relay the Joachimite prediction that there 'shall arrive a certain man in England from his obscure center; a Person filled with all manner of Divine Knowledge and Wisdom, endowed with the *Spirit of Prophecy* . . . his words shall be like the sparks of an eternal fire . . . A Prodigious Army shall be gathered together out of all the Christian Nation, to conduct him to *the Holy Land*, and to crown him in *Jerusalem*.'[33]

By the time Van Butchell published this prophecy in 1795 he had in mind, not Gordon who had been dead two years of gaol fever, but his logical successor Richard Brothers, self-styled 'Prince of the Hebrews'. Radical seekers were clearly primed for Brothers's political and prophetic advent in 1794–5; their works feature prominently amongst the eighty or so publications that his apocalyptic prophecies generated. Recent scholarship suggests that Blake may have been partly influenced by Brothers's predictions of French victories and of Babylonian London's imminent engulfment,[34] as well as the prophet's promise to gather both visible and 'invisible' English Jews and lead them to a restored New Jerusalem. Blake's engraver associate, William Sharp,

[31] [Giuseppe Balsamo], *Memorial, or Brief, for the Comte de Cagliostro . . . From the French original by Parkyns Macmahon* (London, 1786), p. 60.

[32] [Giuseppe Balsamo], *The Life of Joseph Balsamo, commonly called Count Cagliostro . . .*, trans. from the original . . . publ. at Rome . . . (Dublin, 1792), pp. 142–5.

[33] Martin Van Butchell, *Causes of Crim. Con.; also Barrenness – and the King's Evil . . . His Address to Nathaniel Brassey Halhed on Richard Brothers . . .* (London, 1795), pp. 14–15. For biographical details, see *British Biographical Archive*, pp. 360–7; J. Menzies Campbell, 'Martin Van Butchell, 1735–1814', offprint, *Dental Magazine and Oral Topics*, 1952, pp. 3–15.

[34] See esp. article by Jon Mee in Clark and Worrall, *Historicizing Blake* (fn. 17), and his *Dangerous Enthusiasm: William Blake and the Culture of Radicalism in the 1790s* (Oxford, 1992).

needed no persuading; his portrait of the prophet published on 16 April 1795 carried the caption: 'Fully believing this to be the Man Whom God has appointed:- I engrave his likeness.' In the tense atmosphere engendered by legal repression, soaring bread prices and wholesale impressment, a millenarian reversal of fortune must have seemed understandably attractive to many of London's struggling artisans and middling sorts. Of course, not all were persuaded; David Levi entered the lists against Brothers and his Jewish disciple, Moses Pereira, who had published a *Jew's Appeal on the Divine Mission of Richard Brothers . . . to Restore Israel, and Rebuild Jerusalem*. Levi objected, largely on the grounds that Brothers had failed to show good faith by undergoing full conversion: '[Jews] . . . will sooner remain in bondage for ever, than consent to be led home by an uncircumcised Philistine.'[35] Other seekers, including Sharp's friends William Bryan, a sometime printer, bookseller, druggist and healer, and John Wright, a carpenter and healer, enrolled themselves as disciples only after close and critical investigation.

In many respects Brothers echoed a more literalist and activist strand of Jewish restorationism than did Priestley, a tradition that had inspired the Ranter farmer John Robins to declare himself 'King of Israel' in 1650, and Thomas Venner to stage a Fifth Monarchist uprising against Cromwell seven years later. Yet the 1790s saw the rise of a new printed genre which worked to bridge the gap between the writings of scholarly eighteenth-century contemporary Dissenters like Priestley and so-called Ranter enthusiasm – to dissolve any distinction, indeed, between word and spirit, ancient and modern, literal and allegorical prophecies. Numerous cheap anthologies with Bunyanesque titles like *Wonderful Prophecies* or *God's Awful Warning to a Giddy, Careless, Sinful World* carried a bewildering array of prophetic extracts, dreams, visions and personal testimonies. With scant respect for conventional intellectual categories, scholars like Mede, Fleming, Jurieu, Bicheno and Priestley were cemented together with Camisards and Civil War illuminists. The Presbyterian martyr, Christopher Love, proved a notably popular inclusion, especially in several anthologies produced by Brothers's publisher-disciple, George Riebau.[36] Love had allegedly calculated that the popish antichrist would fall in 1790 to be succeeded by a great prophet and

---

[35] David Levi, *Letters to Nathaniel Brassey Halhed, MP . . .* (London, 1795), p. 47; Moses Pereira, *A Jew's Appeal on the Divine Mission of Richard Brothers . . . to Restore Israel, and Rebuild Jerusalem . . .* (London, 1795). It is unclear whether or not this is a pseudonymous work.

[36] See, for example, Christopher Love, *Extracts from the Prophecies given to Christopher Love* (London, 1794).

deliverer in the year 1795. The anthology *Wonderful Prophecies* tacked together portions of Priestley's 'Fast Sermon' of 1794, extracts from Brothers's *Revealed Knowledge* and several prophetic anecdotes of Lord George Gordon. For good measure it also threw in prophecies from Nostradamus, Lilley, Love, Trapnel, Jurieu, Fleming, Lacey, Swedenborg, the contemporary astrologer and philanderer Sibley and a physician of the Royal College, Dr Gideon Hervey.[37] *Extracts from Mercurius Teutonicus* produced a condensed version of 'the mystical writings of Jacob Behmen' alongside the preachings of Ranter prophets.[38] A few years earlier, the compiler of a similar anthology – an engraver and bookseller named Garnet Terry – had also produced cheap reprints of two long-buried works of Ranter and Antinomian complexion, John Saltmarsh's *Free Grace* and Samuel 'Cobbler' How's *Sufficiency of the Spirit's Teaching*.[39]

If, like William Blake's *Marriage of Heaven and Hell*, such seeker anthologies were deliberately structured so as to disrupt orthodox exegesis, they tended nevertheless to stress certain themes common to Radical Dissent. Extracts from Priestley and Bicheno, when severed from their respectable scholarly context, could be made to align remarkably with key prophecies in Brothers's widely selling work, *Revealed Knowledge*. They agreed on the imminence of the millennium and its link with the regicidal French Revolution, interpreted as part of God's providential plan. Deists and infidels on the French National Convention were seen to be accomplishing divine work by their attack on the religious establishments of the antichrist. Even so, the millennium would not arrive without great cataclysms and violence. England, having elected to pursue Babylonian policies of corruption, slavery, greed, repression and bellicosity, risked incurring God's wrath. Only God's peculiar people, the literal and/or spiritual Jews who had chosen the path of liberty, would be exempt. They would be gathered and literally or symbolically restored to reign with Christ in a New Jerusalem of peace, toleration and enlightenment.[40]

It is not hard to see why English loyalists and government officials should, in the troubled climate of 1795, have seen Brothers as a political enthusiast in the seventeenth-century mould,[41] dangerous enough to

[37] *Wonderful Prophecies* (fn. 23), pp. 17–18, 46–8, 60–3.
[38] Jacob Boehme, *Extracts from Mercurius Teutonicus . . . Being divers Prophetical Passages . . . gathered out of the mystical writings of Jacob Behmen* (London, 1795).
[39] Mee, in Clark and Worrall, *Historicizing Blake* (fn. 17).
[40] R. Brothers, *A Revealed Knowledge of the Prophecies and Times* (London, 1794), esp. pp. 15, 39–58. Cf. Joseph Priestley, *Comparison of the Institutions of Moses with those of the Hindoos and other Ancient Nations . . . and an Address to the Jews . . .* (Northumberland, PA, 1799), esp. pp. 393–429.
[41] See esp. Joseph Moser, *Anecdotes of Richard Brothers . . .* (London, 1795), pp. 8–12.

need locking away. The Painite publishers, J.S. Jordan and H.D. Symonds, both issued pro-Brothers pamphlets, as did Painite sympathisers Garnet Terry, George Riebau and Martin Van Butchell. Many of the numerous anonymous tracts were equally subversive. Some ardent disciples were also enrolled members of Jacobin clubs. John Binns, a United Irish plumber and member of the London Corresponding Society, testified in his memoirs to the prophet's pervasive appeal. Binns's political associate William Reid recalled how prophetic, deist and republican currents had converged in the heady atmosphere of artisan alehouses like the Green Dragon in Clerkenwell. Engraver William Sharp had also been a sufficiently active member of the SCI to be swept up in the government dragnet of 1794 and questioned closely.

Interrogations revealed a familiar seeker profile. It typically included an early reading of mystics like Jacob Boehme, William Law and Jane Lead; a flirtation with illuminist sects, quickly souring into disillusion with their formal laws and ceremonies; some dabbling in alternative sciences and a gravitation towards restoration prophets and prophetesses. Before enrolling with Brothers, the Leeds carpenter, John Wright, and Bristol printer William Bryan tested out London Swedenborgianism, then took the advice of a Jew to seek the New Jerusalem amongst a circle of aristocratic mystics in Avignon.[42] Such self-made intellectuals tended to be deeply sceptical of established knowledge, believing that Brothers had aroused the persecuting jealousy of the gown and cassock.[43] Reid had learned from Cobbler How's pamphlet, as well as from a Muggletonian field preacher, that 'the whole Godhead is circumscribed in the person of Jesus Christ, still retaining the human form in heaven', and from Swedenborg that the day of resurrection was 'more a figure than a fact'.[44] Blake in his poetry and Lemoine in his popular astrological and magical journals scathingly rejected Lockean reason and Newtonian science, Blake offering 'fourfold vision' in its place, Lemoine 'true Christian theosophy'. Even Scripture was not exempt: Brothers typically amended 'errors' in the canon and supplemented it with the apocryphal text of Esdras, as well as his personal dreams and vision. On occasion he even practised direct healing amongst his followers.[45] His disciple, William Bryan, explained in turn how work as a druggist,

---

[42] William Bryan, *A Testimony of the Spirit of Truth Concerning Richard Brothers* . . . (London, 1795), pp. 17–29. See discussion in Garrett, *Respectable Folly* (fn. 9), pp. 160–1.
[43] See, for example, Samuel Whitchurch, *Another Witness! or, Further Testimony in Favour of Richard Brothers* . . . (London, 1795), p. 20.   [44] Reid, *Rise and Dissolution* (fn. 17), pp. 19, 52–3.
[45] Moser, *Anecdotes of Richard Brothers* (fn. 41), p. 32.

botanist and healer connected with the quest for mystical understanding: 'the system of physic, like all other systems, being built on a
foundation of self-love, instead of love to our God and neighbour, must
be false, but the love of God . . . opens in the mind the right science'. He
could feel the symptoms of a patient's disease vibrating through his own
body, accompanied by a message from God of how to heal them.[46]

As in Lemoine's circle during the late 1780s, some of Brothers's disciples revived a 'Real Whig' practice of using Jewish prophecy to embarrass Christian opponents. Just as the deist, John Toland, had translated
and published a French philosemitic tract in 1705, ninety years later a
prophecy from Humphrey Tindal, predicting that all established priests,
clerks and Churches would vanish under reason's onslaught, appeared in
an anthology which also claimed Brothers as 'the Elijah of the present
day'.[47] Brothers's most famous disciple, the MP and Oriental scholar
Nathaniel Brassey Halhed, argued in the manner of the sceptical
philosophers Volney and Depuis that Hindu gods were mere person-
ifications of natural forces, though this did not in any way shake his
conviction that Brothers was literally a Prince of David, sent to restore
the Jews and trigger the millennium.[48]

The presence of a sprinkling of 'respectable' scholars and scientists
within such a milieu would have created no surprise amongst seekers
and virtuosi. This had characterised the culture of the famous French
Prophets in London at the beginning of the eighteenth century[49] and
John Harrison has noted its continuation well into the nineteenth. The
author of *Wonderful Prophecies* explained in 1795 that whereas the
unlearned, children, and even idiots, were often in some mysterious way
conduits of God's spirit, their messages usually emerged in coded and
enigmatic fashion as befitted 'the natural or inherent free agency of the
human mind'. It required scholars possessed of practised skills and
judgement to interpret these 'allegoric hints and equivocal figures'.
Moreover, the possession of great learning, experience and wisdom
could also engender a type of scientific prophecy based on 'knowledge of
the necessary relation between cause and effect'.[50] The opening number
of the Swedenborgian *New Jerusalem Magazine* reflected the same outlook

---

[46] Bryan, *Testimony of the Spirit of Truth* (fn. 42), pp. 29–30.
[47] Humphrey Tindal, *The Prophecy of Humphrey Tindal . . . shewing . . . the Woefull Condition of this Kingdom* (London, 1795; orig. publ. 1642), p. 7.
[48] Nathaniel Brassey Halhed, *Testimony of the Authenticity of the Prophecies of Richard Brothers . . .* (London, 1795), p. 10.
[49] Hillel Schwartz, *The French Prophets: The History of a Millenarian Group in Eighteenth-Century England* (Berkeley, 1980), pp. 223–50.   [50] *Wonderful Prophecies* (fn. 23), pp. 12–14.

in December 1789 when it advertised an essay on 'the science of corre-spondences'.[51] Halhed too stressed that 'deciphering mysterious and allegorical codes of composition' required discipline and varied method-ologies. Prophecies that were 'compact and close' needed intense and precise elucidation, longer prophecies gave greater latitude yet might often contain phrases calculated to mislead.[52] Scientific methods and a mystical mission merged equally in the work of Brothers's disciple, Peter Woulfe. An eminent chemist, prize-winning Fellow of the Royal Society and friend of Priestley, cited in the *Experiment* [on] *Natural Philosophy* (1786), Woulfe attributed the failure of his life-long quest to find the elixir of life to 'want of due preparation by pious and charitable acts'.[53]

It is not only with the odd phrase that such seekers seem to anticipate modern deconstructionist approaches; they also shared a kindred dis-trust of rigid intellectual typologies, categories and boundaries. Just as seekers and virtuosi were happy to mingle freethinking rationalism with mystical prophecy, so too they combined emerging divergences of method and conception within the history of science. Traces of pre-Newtonian hermeticism, of moral-driven natural philosophy based on spectacular wonders, and of dogged experimental empiricism can all be found within individual writings and practices. And though it would be absurd to equate Priestley with such seeker enthusiasts, there were suffi-cient resemblances of outlook and approach to explain his appeal and affinity. John Money's fascinating recent analysis of Priestley's thought and practice within the context of late eighteenth-century popular science, belief and politics provides us with some pointers, and is worth quoting at length.

The foundations of his [Priestley's] thought and teaching were ... a benevolent God, whose works were not yet completed, and who therefore manifested himself constantly in a continuous act of infinite creation; ... an absolute denial of any difference between matter and spirit; and ... an equally absolute episte-mological egalitarianism derived from that denial and from the associationist psychology of David Hartley. From these necessarian principles, it not only fol-lowed that all men could know all things equally; it also followed, since the moral perfection of Man was to be achieved through an ever increasing knowl-edge of nature, that all men should know all things equally. For Priestley, all knowledge was one; that unity was the ground of all action and the way to it lay, not through theory, but through the candid presentation of experiential facts to the opened minds of all, not in order to exploit their reflex superstitions, but to

[51] *New Jerusalem Magazine, or, A Treasury of Celestial, Spiritual and Natural Knowledge*, prospectus, 1 December 1789, p. 2.   [52] Halhed, *Testimony of the Authenticity* (fn. 48), pp. 9–10.
[53] *DNB*, *s.v.* Woulfe.

lead them progressively to a full understanding of the truth. In such a Baconian instauration, public performance was not a mere adjunct of natural philosophy, useful if properly controlled, but its very essence . . . [The] Priestleyan avatar expected the distinction between expert and layman to vanish once mankind knew its proper place in creation. In that day, there would no longer be any division between the reasoning few and the labouring many.[54]

To artisan seekers and virtuosi Priestley thus seemed not only an experimental but also a moral and mystical scientist, who shared many of their preoccupations including a serious interest in Swedenborg's ideas and the works of Brothers and Halhed. His *Comparison of the Institutions of Moses with those of the Hindoos and other Ancient Nations* of 1799 quoted from Halhed's *Gentoo Laws*[55] and similarly probed the existence of universal underlying principles of spirituality within pagan anthropologies. In the appended *Address to the Jews*, Priestley also marshalled all his formidable forensic and deductive powers to calculate the complex scriptural chronologies and historical equations hidden in the book of Daniel, concluding that the Turkish Empire had begun to collapse and the Jewish restoration would soon commence.[56] 'The cause of science, of general liberty, of civilization, as well as that of religion call for it', he asserted.[57]

Fascination with mythology and antiquarianism of all kinds seems also to have been a common trait of radical seekers. As apprentices in the late 1770s Blake and Reid combined researches into old churches and graveyards with the writing of emotion-charged poems expressive of melancholic or ecstatic states.[58] Lemoine and Lackington saturated their writings with quotations from Young's 'Night Thoughts' and Blair's 'The Grave'. Predictably, such proto-romantic sensibilities also tended to favour allegorical, spiritual or literary interpretations of the New Jerusalem. Here too there were seventeenth-century precedents; the Fifth Monarchist, Robert Maton, had represented the Jewish restoration as purely spiritual in a work of 1646 entitled *Israel's Redemption Redeemed*.[59] The first literary representation of the New Jerusalem as an enlightened

[54] John Money, 'Joseph Priestley in Cultural Context: Philosophic Spectacle, Popular Belief and Popular Politics in Eighteenth-Century Birmingham', 2 pts, *Enlightenment and Dissent*, 7 (1988), 57–81 and esp. 8 (1989), 69–89 at pp. 69–70. These articles build on two brilliant pieces by Simon Schaffer, 'Natural Philosophy and Public Spectacle in the Eighteenth Century', *History of Science*, 21 (1983), 1–43, and 'Priestley's Questions: An Historiographic Survey', *History of Science*, 22 (1984), 151–88.   [55] Priestley, *Comparison* (fn. 40), p. 68.   [56] *Ibid.*, pp. 393–409.
[57] *Ibid.*, p. 410.   [58] McCalman, 'Infidel as Prophet' (fn. 17), pp. 5–6.
[59] Cecil Roth, *Magna Bibliotheca Anglo-Judaica: A Bibliographical Guide to Anglo-Jewish History*. new edn (of J. Jacobs and L. Wolf, *Bibliotheca Anglo-Judaica*, 1888) . . . (London, 1937), B.16, no. 3, p. 372.

republican utopia had come from the pen of Milton's contemporary, Samuel Gott, in 1613, an idea echoed by William Blake in his Hebraist-humanistic 'prophecies' of the 1790s, 'America' and 'The French Revolution'.

III

Not altogether surprisingly, both government and loyalists took Jewish restorationism very seriously. They had begun promoting anti-French prophecies in subsidised newspapers as early as 1792.[60] Many radical seekers were also caught in the rising wave of political repression after the mid-1790s. The covert financier of Jacobin revolution and philose-mitic prophecy, Jonathan 'Jew' King, was successfully compromised in 1793 and forced temporarily to disavow his Painite views. William Sharp, who was to borrow money from King for the prophetess Joanna Southcott, was seized and interrogated the following year, repudiating his Painite sympathies soon after. William Reid temporarily joined the ranks of anti-Jacobinical journalism after being netted in a raid on a notorious freethinking and Jacobin alehouse club in 1798.[61] Even the solitary and solipsistic William Blake was prosecuted in 1803 for seditious words uttered in his garden within the quiet rural village of Felpham. But if the government hoped that subversive prophecies would cease with the incarceration and ridicule of Brothers and his supporters, they had not counted on the advent of a far mightier claimant to the restora-tionist crown.

Whether sincerely or opportunistically, Napoleon Bonaparte began to play providential politics in 1798. After a daringly successful campaign in Egypt, he issued a proclamation from the foot of the pyramids 'To the Rightful heirs of Palestine', inviting the Jews of Asia and Africa to join him in emancipating and restoring their nation. English loyalists watched with fascinated horror as he proceeded to move against popish Rome and infidel Turkey and then, in October 1806, to summon repre-sentatives of European Jewry to a Grand Sanhedrin in Paris for the purpose of rebuilding an emancipated New Jerusalem.[62] An English translation of the Sanhedrin proceedings, coupled with a militant polit-ical manifesto from an Italian Jew, rapidly appeared in pamphlet form

[60] W.H. Oliver, *Prophets and Millennialists: The Uses of Biblical Prophecy in England from the 1790s to the 1840s* (Auckland, 1978), pp. 42–3; see also Garrett, *Respectable Folly* (fn. 9), p. 167.
[61] McCalman, 'Infidel as Prophet' (fn. 17), pp. 3–4.
[62] Simon Schwarzfuchs, *Napoleon, the Jews and the Sanhedrin* (London, 1979), esp. pp. 24–7, 64–5.

and in a variety of newspapers, including the semi-official *St James's Chronicle*. These reports – widely reviewed in the evangelical press – compounded Conservative fears by suggesting that Jewish literati at the Sanhedrin were tainted with deism and enthusiasm and were hailing Bonaparte as the long-prophesied messiah.[63] No wonder Mrs Piozzi gravely noted in her diary that providential portents seemed to be swinging against the English.[64]

Loyalists responded to the crisis with a sustained burst of prophetic publication. Led by the scholarly Oxford divines, Geoffrey Faber and Henry Kett, ably assisted by Bishop Horsley, they relocated the antichrist from popish Rome to Napoleonic France – a transfer which rapidly became a commonplace in English political prints as well. Kett also advanced an ingenious and influential historical-scriptural thesis to accommodate the real possibility that infidel France might accomplish a literal restoration of the Jews to Palestine. By distinguishing sharply between worldly restoration and spiritual conversion, he allowed for the possibility that the favoured maritime power of England could lead the way in the race to the millennium.[65] This in turn carried important implications for evangelical missionary work. Leaders of the London Missionary Society debated whether, in the face of the Napoleonic threat, priority should be given to the conversion of English Jews as against heathens in Africa and Catholics in Ireland. A breakaway group, the London Society for the Promotion of Christianity amongst the Jews, formed in 1809 under the leadership of an ardent Jewish convert Joseph Frey, managed to attract support from such eminent evangelicals as Wilberforce and Simeon. Frey and his associates wielded both stick and carrot in their zeal to convert. Denigrations of the morality, piety and learning of local Jewry were accompanied by financial incentives to marry Christians and enrol in evangelical educational and charitable institutions.[66]

If Napoleon struck fear in conservative English Churchmen, he gave heart to their Dissenting radical opponents. Radical restorationists met the challenge of conservative prophecy by developing scriptural support for Bonaparte's restorationist policies and by vigorous counter-propaganda against the London Jewish Conversion Society. In Pennsylvania,

[63] Diogène Tama, *Transactions of the Parisian Sanhedrin . . . 1806*, trans. with a preface and notes by F.D. Kirwan (London, 1807), esp. pp. vi–ix. For responses from the evangelical and conservative press, see extracts quoted in the prospectus of the publisher, Charles Taylor of Hatton St, London.

[64] Garrett, *Respectable Folly* (fn. 9), p. 211.

[65] Henry Kett, *History the Interpreter of Prophecy; or, A View of Scriptural Prophecies and their Accomplishment . . .*, 3 vols. (Oxford, 1799). For other conservative responses, see Oliver, *Prophets and Millenialists* (fn. 60), pp. 45–56.   [66] Margoliouth, *History of the Jews* (fn. 28), vol. II, pp. 149–51, 155–6.

Priestley excitedly read news of Napoleon's successes, an open copy of Daniel on the table beside him. He wrote to friends in 1798 of his utter conviction that the great work of restoring the Jews was 'in agitation'. At the end of the *Comparison of the Institutions of Moses with those of the Hindoos*, published the following year, he implied that Napoleon was the long-expected Jewish leader,[67] an idea developed still more explicitly, though with a trace of anxiety, in the radical Baptist James Bicheno's widely selling prophetic-historical works.[68] Plebeian radicals and seekers, however, seemed wholly elated at the prospect. The revival of the restorationist promise in such circles during the latter part of the Napoleonic Wars constitutes one of several sources of popular opposi-tionist consolation and resurgence that historians have failed to notice. Despite the debacle of 1798, surviving United Irish activists long contin-ued to pin hopes on a French landing. One such, Thomas Corbet, who had served in the French army, wrote to Paul Barras in Paris in 1799, sug-gesting the construction of a formal alliance between those two most persecuted peoples, the Irish and the 'dispersed people of the Jews', to supplement the fighting forces of France[69] – he was not to know that Harrington had long before actually suggested Ireland as a homeland for displaced Jewry.

William Reid was so inspired by Napoleon's actions that he horrified conservative patrons in 1806 by abandoning his editorship of an Anglican periodical to join Thomas Belsham's Unitarian congregation at Hackney, thus returning – like Blake in the same period – to his radical Christian origins. In years to come Reid was also to reject Unitarianism as excessively rigid and to publish sympathetic biographies of Horne Tooke and Napoleon, as well as an affirmative history of the French Revolution. More importantly for our purposes, he produced *The New Sanhedrin*, in 1807, a lengthy defence of English and European Jewry and of Napoleon's philosemitism.[70] Here, and in a series of articles published over the next four years, he sought to refute the conservative exegesis of Bishop Horsley and others, claiming that they had based their inter-pretations on popish prophecies. Against these he set the canon of Mede, Burnet and Jurieu, the lesser-known seventeenth-century works

---

[67] Priestley, *Comparison* (fn. 40), pp. 403–9.
[68] Franz Kobler, *The Vision Was There: A History of the British Movement for the Restoration of the Jews to Palestine* (London, 1956), pp. 46–7; Oliver, *Prophets and Millenialists* (fn. 60), p. 49.
[69] Schwarzfuchs, *Napoleon* (fn. 62), p. 24; Kobler, *Vision Was There* (fn. 68), p. 45.
[70] [William H. Reid, attrib.] *The New Sanhedrin* [in Hebrew] *and Causes and Consequences of the French Emperor's Conduct towards the Jews . . .*, by an Advocate of the House of Israel (London, 1807).

of Thomas Beverley and Isaac de la Peyrère, as well as the writings of the
early eighteenth-century mystic and Kabbalist, Francis Lee, who had,
like Brothers, lent heavily on the apocryphal book of Esdras. This last
had suggestively prophesied the emergence in France of a second deliverer or Prince, Cyrus, who was 'in the mystical and moral sense, Enoch'
and who would, after success in arms, bring about universal peace.

Reid also reiterated the core radical restorationist belief that the
French Revolution had unleashed 'beneficial changes' which marked the
commencement of the millennium. Drawing on the work of David Levi,
Abarbanel (Isaac Abravanel) and other 'Israelish Literati', he argued
that the Restoration should be seen as purely figurative. Jews would be
delivered 'from captivity, from oppression, and from the condition of
aliens in every country where they have been scattered', yet at the same
time be 'restored in the countries where they dwell.' Bonaparte's actions,
coupled with the abolition of the slave trade in 1808, filled Reid with
expectation that a new age of universal freedom and toleration was
beginning to dawn, overthrowing the corrupt Babylon of 'old ecclesiastical and political establishments', 'narrow minded politics' and 'persecuting priests'. In its place a spiritual city would arise whose
'splendour' would shine like 'crystal', a New Jerusalem 'belonging to this
life and not another beyond the grave'. It would be 'a city of peace,
because its conquests are to make war to cease upon the earth' and its
gates would be thrown open permanently, signifying a new universal
catholicity, the end of 'exclusive confessions and contradictory creeds'.[71]
Blake seems also to have felt this breath of hope that the freedom of
blacks and Jews prophesied in his 'Song of Liberty' might at last be
coming to pass and it was against this background that he wrote his last
great prophetic poem, 'Jerusalem'. Had he been alive, Priestley would
surely have shared such Dissenting radical exhilaration, for he too had
dreamed no less ardently of the advent of a rational and tolerant New
Jerusalem.

The Jewish Conversion Society, however, was less impressed. Its
members published scathing attacks on Dissenting restorationists like
Reid, Thomas Witherby, Bicheno and Henry Lemoine. Reid was represented as 'a modern infidel, an advocate for Bonaparte, a Jacobin', as
well as 'a famished Devotee' and hack who had hired himself out to
Jewish interests.[72] This was not entirely false. Like many marginal writers

---

[71] *Ibid.*, pp. 421–2, 430–1, 472; also articles by Reid in *Gentleman's Magazine*, 80 (1810), 12–14, 108–9; 81
(1811), 627–32.
[72] *Gentleman's Magazine*, 81 (1811), 529–35.

and artists, Reid had been forced to struggle especially severely in the hostile cultural climate of the early 1800s. He admitted to living off Literary Fund handouts and to receiving help from 'a few enlightened Jews in this metropolis'.[73] Lemoine, in even graver poverty, wrote hagiographical works for wealthy Jews like Goldsmith. The revolutionary banker and swindler, 'Jew' King, probably provided some of this patronage; from around 1806 he began to re-assert his Jewish faith, taking up cudgels against the Jewish Conversion Society and editing a new edition of David Levi's *Dissertation on the Prophecies*, in which he congratulated Unitarians and freethinkers for assisting in the destruction of Christian bigotry and persecution.[74]

Between 1810 and 1815 radical restorationists and their Jewish allies gave the Jewish Conversion Society as good as they got. Reid, Lemoine, Witherby, Tobias Goodman, Moses Samuels, Solomon Bennett, Solomon Zailick and Jacob Nickelsburger contributed a flurry of articles and pamphlets which castigated evangelical conversionists for their bigotry and intolerance and exposed some of the dubious methods employed to convert Jewish children and paupers. Pseudonymous pamphlets, some no doubt furnished by the veteran smutpedlar, King, offered more scurrilous suggestions. Joseph Frey was accused of conducting a torrid sexual affair with a reformed whore who was also the wife of one of his seedy converts. The criminal records of some of Frey's other converts were also held up to public scrutiny: they included convictions for theft, forgery, brothel-keeping and fraud. True or otherwise, the accusations were sufficiently telling to ensure Frey's hasty transfer to the United States, and an equally swift abandonment of his unsavoury conversion methods.[75]

IV

This religio-political scholarship and polemic helped to carry restorationist ideas and aspirations to new generations of radicals, rationalists and romantics who came into prominence during the popular political agitations of the 1820s and 1830s. Restorationist visions were

---

[73] *Annual Register*, 68 (1826), 253–4; *Gentleman's Magazine*, 81 (1811), 232.
[74] See McCalman, '*Infidel as Prophet*' (fn. 17), p. 18.
[75] See esp. M. Sailman, *The Mystery Unfolded, or An Exposition of the . . . Means employed to obtain converts . . . among the Jews . . .* (London, 1817), pp. 26–72; Solomon Bennett, *The Constancy of Israel . . .* (London, 1809); Tobias Goodman, *An Address to the . . . London Society for Promoting Christianity among the Jews . . .* (London, 1809), pp. 6–27; Todd M. Endelman, *The Jews of Georgian England, 1714–1830: Tradition and Change in a Liberal Society* (Philadelphia, 1979), pp. 65–78.

incorporated into the complex repertoires of Romanticism. Seekers of antiquarian and gothic manifestations found the legend of the Wandering Jew particularly compelling. Chapbook and ballad tales of the Jew cursed to live until Doomsday for abusing Jesus Christ circulated in England during the seventeenth and early eighteenth centuries, eventually being canonised in Thomas Percy's *Reliques of Ancient English Poetry*, published in 1765. At much the same time Goethe was toying with the idea of writing an epic poem on the subject, though it was Christian Schubart who published the version that reached England in translation in 1801. Young Shelley was one of its ardent readers: both his 'Wandering Jew's Soliloquy' and 'Queen Mab' offer a radical interpretation of the legend. Shelley was fascinated by the implications of human immortality as a curse and also by the idea of the Wandering Jew as a victim of persecution. Ahasuerus was also given a favourable cameo role in Lewis's *The Monk* and helped inspire a procession of doomed and cursed wanderers from Melmoth to the subversive and infidel Cain, much pirated by popular radicals.[76] To Blake, Jerusalem had been a tocsin:

> England! awake! awake! awake!
> Jerusalem thy sister calls!
> Why wilt thou sleep the sleep of death,
> And close her from thy ancient walls?[77]

But fashionable Lord Byron, whose *Hebrew Melodies* were set to music by the Jewish composer, Isaac Nathan, in 1815, incorporated the suffering people of Israel into his characteristic cast of doomed and homeless wanderers and his friend, Thomas Moore, responded the following year, in his *Advent of the Millennium*, with a version of the restoration as an analogue of Irish national liberation and renewal:

> Then Judah, thou no more shalt mourn
> Beneath the Heathen's chain,
> Thy days of splendour shall return,
> And all be new again.[78]

The ardent minor Romantic and man of letters, Lewis Way, in his epic poem of 1824 evoked the great restorationist visionaries of the past, Milton, Burnet and Newton:

---

[76] Brian Stableford, ed., *Tales of the Wandering Jew* (Sawtry, Cambs., 1991), esp. pp. 6–12, 31. A further indication of the strong contemporary literary interest in the legend can be seen in Maria Edgeworth, *Harrington. A Tale, and Ormond. A Tale* 3 vols. (London, 1817), pp. 66–7, 192, 325, 376–415. Amongst other sources, she cites the *Turkish Spy*, Percy's *Reliques*, and Priestley's *Letters to the Jews*.

[77] Kobler, *Vision Was There* (fn. 68), p. 52, quoting from William Blake, *Jerusalem* (1815).

[78] *Ibid.*, p. 53.

Where others walk in darkness – they are set
As midnight watchers waiting on the wall of their beloved
Jerusalem.

But Way, who attempted in 1818 to put restoration on the agenda at
Aix-la-Chapelle and who founded the Marboeuf Chapel in Paris in
1821, brings us closer to the emerging world of British Israelism.[79] A
different line of descent from the radical restorationism of Priestley,
Brothers and Blake can be traced amongst popular radical pressmen
and publishers of the 1820s and 1830s. Radical Dissenters, like the
satirist-publisher William Hone and unstamped pressman William
Carpenter, hated clerical establishments, campaigned for freedom of
belief and speech, and yearned for the promised radical Christian millennium. In the mid-1820s Hone published a popular edition of the
Apocrypha which included the favourite radical restorationist text of
Esdras; two years later Carpenter published a seventy-five page restorationist almanac entitled *Calendarium Palestinae*.[80] Radical freethinkers
from the same milieu continued to ally themselves with Jews to promote
toleration and to deploy Jewish prophecy to embarrass Christian opponents. In 1823 the pressman-publisher, Richard Carlile, whilst imprisoned in Dorchester gaol for blasphemy, produced popular editions of
both the scurrilous *Toldoth Jesu* and *Israel Avenged*, a polemical restorationist work written by a Portuguese Jew in 1770. During the early 1830s
Carlile also opened his notorious 'infidel theatre' and debating forum,
the Blackfriars Rotunda, to a Jewish controversialist named Solomon
Lyons and to the neo-restorationist radical prophets, John 'Zion' Ward
and James 'Shepherd' Smith. The last, a former Scots Presbyterian and
Christian Israelite, preached to packed crowds in the mid-1830s at a time
when Dissenters no longer laboured under civil and religious disabilities.
Yet it was a measure of the power and tenacity of the radical restorationist vision that he was able to transfer its millenarian promise to new
generations of Owenite socialists and feminists.[81]

[79] John Wilson, 'British Israelism: The Ideological Restraints on Sect Organisation', in Bryan R.
Wilson, ed., *Patterns of Sectarianism: Organisation and Ideology in Social and Religious Movements* (London,
1967), pp. 345–76.
[80] Roth, *Magna Bibliotheca* (fn. 59), B.21, no. 8, p. 427.
[81] I.D. McCalman, 'Popular Irreligion in early Victorian England: Infidel Preachers and Radical
Theatricality in 1830s London', in R.W. Davis and R.J. Helmstadter, eds., *Religion and Irreligion in
Victorian Society: Essays in Honor of R.K. Webb* (London, 1992), pp. 51–67 at pp. 63–4.

Index of names

IDEAS IN CONTEXT

Edited by QUENTIN SKINNER (*General Editor*)
LORRAINE DASTON, WOLF LEPENIES and J.B. SCHNEEWIND

Titles marked with an asterisk are also available in paperback